PINSTRIPE NATION

Pinstripe Nation

THE NEW YORK YANKEES IN AMERICAN CULTURE

WILL BISHOP

Sport and Popular Culture
Brian M. Ingrassia, Series Editor

THE UNIVERSITY OF TENNESSEE PRESS
Knoxville

The Sport and Popular Culture series is designed to promote critical, innovative research in the history of sport through a wide spectrum of works—monographs, edited volumes, biographies, and reprints of classics.

 Copyright © 2018 by The University of Tennessee Press / Knoxville.
All Rights Reserved. Manufactured in the United States of America.
First Edition.

LIBRARY OF CONGRESS CATALOGING-IN-PUBLICATION DATA

Names: Bishop, Will, (William Carlson)
Title: Pinstripe nation: the New York Yankees in American culture / Will Bishop.
Description: First edition. | Knoxville: The University of Tennessee Press, [2018] |
Series: Sport and popular culture | Includes bibliographical references and index. |
Identifiers: LCCN 2017029460 (print) | LCCN 2017036545 (ebook) | ISBN 9781621904021 (Kindle) | ISBN 9781621904038 (pdf) | ISBN 9781621904014 (hardcover)
Subjects: LCSH: New York Yankees (Baseball team) | Baseball—Social aspects—United States.
Classification: LCC GV875.N4 (ebook) | LCC GV875.N4 B57 2018 (print) |
DDC 796.357/64097471—dc23
LC record available at https://lccn.loc.gov/2017029460

CONTENTS

Foreword   ix
Brian M. Ingrassia

Acknowledgments   xiii

Introduction   1

1   "To Be Young and a Yankee":
Babe Ruth and the First Era of Yankee Success   11

2   "Let Me Tell You about Heroes":
The Pride of the Yankees and the Crystallization
of a Cultural Icon   35

3   "Think of the Great DiMaggio":
Joe DiMaggio and the Mythic Dimension
of Yankee Success in the Postwar Era   67

4   "Wall Street Brokers and Haughty Businessmen":
The Yankees and Brooklyn Dodger Fan Identity   101

5   "Those Damn Yankees!"
The Popularization of Yankee Hating in the 1950s   137

6   "Where Have You Gone, Joe DiMaggio?"
Decline, Cultural Change, and the 1960s   163

7 "You'd Never Guess This Was . . . the Yankees":
The "Me" Decade and "The Best Team Money
Could Buy"   193

8 "All That Once Was Good and Could Be Again":
Baseball Nostalgia in the 1980s and '90s
and the Return of the Yankees   231

Epilogue: Toward a New Millennium   269

Notes   273

Works Cited   293

Index   305

ILLUSTRATIONS

Fig. 1. Dodgers 1952 "This Is Next Year" — 118
Fig. 2. Cover of the 1951 Schedule of Home Games — 121
Fig. 3. Cover of the 1953 Schedule of Home Games — 122
Fig. 4. George Steinbrenner's Ego Cartoon — 209
Fig. 5. George Steinbrenner and Billy Martin Cartoon — 215

FOREWORD

The 2017 New York Yankees were quickly tagged with the memorable moniker "Baby Bombers." At the heart of this youthful, yet powerful, team was rookie right fielder Aaron Judge, who finished the regular season with an impressive 52 home runs, breaking the rookie record that had stood for thirty years. Not surprisingly, Judge quickly became the toast of the town. As early as May he was touted by ESPN as a potential dual Rookie of the Year and Most Valuable Player (MVP) awardee, a tiny club that includes only Fred Lynn (1975) and Ichiro Suzuki (2001).[1] Judge was featured on a humorous Tonight Show sketch that same month and even landed on the cover of *Sports Illustrated*. In that piece, titled "All Rise," writer Stephanie Apstein documented Judge's gargantuan frame (6'7", 282 pounds) and his equally gargantuan home runs, which sportscasters had dubbed "Ruthian." But Apstein was also careful to note how Judge happily met with fans between games, a practice reminiscent of Joe DiMaggio's statement, "There is always some kid who may be seeing me for the first or last time. I owe him my best." Judge's demeanor was partly the result of his years at Fresno State University, where ballplayers were fined whenever they boasted about their own achievements instead of crediting teammates. Such self-awareness may have been cultivated in California's Central Valley, but it served Judge well in the "fishbowl" of Manhattan. After all, Yankee luminary Derek Jeter once observed that the Big Apple can "humble" any ego that does not already possess a healthy sense of perspective.[2]

In *Pinstripe Nation*, scholar Will Bishop provides us with a clever and eye-opening framework for interpreting media accounts that portray contemporary Yankee greats as part of a longer tradition. After all, as Bishop eloquently argues, the Yankees are not just a Major League Baseball (MLB) franchise founded in 1901 and located in one of the world's most economically and culturally significant metropolises; rather, the Yankees exist as a cultural signifier, a semiotic marker that serves as a lens into the American psyche. Taking his cues from Ferdinand de Saussure and Roland Barthes, Bishop analyzes the cultural texts that have swirled around MLB's most successful team from the era of Ruth to the era of Jeter: *The Pride of the Yankees*, *Damn Yankees*, *The Bronx Zoo*, and *Seinfeld*, just to name a few. The New York Yankees are a cultural symbol that proves just how important sports are for understanding American culture. Bishop skillfully shows how the discourses surrounding the Yankees have transformed the men who wear the pinstripes and interlocking NY logo into baseball's veritable long gray line—a seemingly unbroken phalanx of heroes and antiheroes who articulate our nation's greatest characteristics alongside its most critical flaws.

The Yankees, we see in Bishop's deft portrayal, are a franchise of paradoxes. The ball club has been lauded for its teamwork yet shaped by its superstars and their sometimes-oversized personalities. Its narrative is one of populism but also of elitism. It is a team where assimilated ethnics like center fielder Joe DiMaggio could find a home far away from the Italian-American community of San Francisco's Fisherman's Wharf, but it is also a team that seemed to hold out against integration as long as possible—after all, catcher Elston Howard, hailing from segregated St. Louis, did not join the team until 1955, eight years after Jackie Robinson made his debut with the Dodgers and nearly a decade after Yankees management passed on the chance to add Larry Doby to their famed roster.[3] In celebrating the Yankees, Americans have frequently prized what Bishop calls "heroic masculinity"—in a time and place where masculinity was too often more hegemonic than it was heroic. The Yankees represent the American Dream, but it is a dream that sometimes startles us awake.

The story of the Yankees is a story of a team and a place and a mentality, but it is also a story of a time: the twentieth century, so often referred to as "America's Century." Babe Ruth ushered in the Roaring Twenties, Lou Gehrig helped us work our way through the Great Depression, and Joe DiMaggio recovered alongside America to enjoy the post–World War II boom. Then Mickey Mantle and Jim Bouton exposed the contradictions of America's turbulent sixties, while in the seventies, the heavy-handed, multi-millionaire owner George Steinbrenner enabled free agents like Reggie Jackson and Rich "Goose" Gossage to become signifiers for the cultures of narcissism that characterized the so-called "Me" Decade. After the Yankees' inter-strike (1981–1994) period of malaise, Derek Jeter helped return the Yankees to glory just in time for America's baseball nostalgia boom in the last years of the millennium.

This is a book about the Yankees, but it is not just for Yankees fans. In fact, Bishop recounts his own history as a Los Angeles Dodgers fan and sometime Yankee detractor, showing how the Yankees embody America's story—America's *meanings*—more than they represent America's *team*. Throughout this book are woven the teams that have served as the Yankees' foils: the Boston Red Sox, of course, and the Dodgers (especially the Brooklyn variety), but also, occasionally, the St. Louis Cardinals, Cleveland Indians, and Chicago Cubs. The pinstripes are just one uniform, just one mentality, that the nation chooses to wear come April or October.

Bishop joins a fine tradition of historians, cultural theorists, literary scholars, and political commentators who have made baseball a site for excavating America's deepest hopes, fears, yearnings, disgusts, and desires. But Bishop takes this idea one step further—perhaps to its logical conclusion—by exploring one team as a cultural icon. It is a fine model of scholarship that surpasses sports-fan chauvinism, local boosterism, regional antiquarianism, or parochial obsession with stars, stadiums, and statistics.

Once we understand the iconic status of the New York Yankees, it should come as no surprise that the franchise's most recent star is described in terms that recall past Yankee greats: Ruth, DiMaggio, Jeter. Aaron Judge's "Baby Bombers" echo the Bronx Bombers of old. As Monument Park in center field of Yankee Stadium—which itself is a twenty-first-century signifier of an iconic twentieth-century sports venue—shows us, the history of the Yankees is a timeline of greats who became heroes to New York and, in some cases, for America. But the silences, or omissions, in the story of recent Yankee greats may be just as telling. Judge has the power of a Mickey Mantle, and some have even compared his blasts to those of the Oklahoma-born switch hitter now enshrined in Cooperstown.[4] Yet such comparisons go only so far, since in many diamond minds Mantle lives on as the hard-drinking carouser immortalized in Jim Bouton's iconoclastic, tell-all 1970 memoir *Ball Four*. Certainly, Yankees partisans must hope that Judge's long ball prowess will be on display in many Octobers to come; but if that is the case, will Judge be remembered as another "Mr. October," another Reggie Jackson? Considering the controversial popularity of the 1970s free agent star who seemed never to stop boasting of his own achievements—and even successfully lobbied for his own chocolate bar—one thinks such comparisons may be limited. Depending on Judge's length of tenure in the Bronx and his consistency, comparisons with the home-grown Jeter may turn out to be more likely.

Regardless of what happens in October, we can be nearly certain that the story of the Yankees as an American icon will march onward into next spring and summer, and throughout the spring and summer and fall after that. It will likely be a story of heroes and antiheroes, a cultural tour guide for the perennial tensions of American culture. And Will Bishop has ably demonstrated how we can use sport to parse our understandings of such traditions and contradictions.

BRIAN M. INGRASSIA
West Texas A&M University

Notes

1. Andrew Marchand, "Forget Rookie of the Year, Judge is an MVP Candidate," ESPN.com, May 4, 2017.
2. Stephanie Apstein, "All Rise," *Sports Illustrated*, May 15–22, 2017, 76–80.
3. On Doby, see Adrian Burgos Jr., *Playing America's Game: Baseball, Latinos, and the Color Line* (Berkeley: University of California Press, 2007), 190; Jules Tygiel, *Baseball's Great Experiment: Jackie Robinson and His Legacy* (New York: Vintage, 1983), 213.
4. Steven Marcus, "Aaron Judge HRs are Reminiscent of Mickey Mantle," *Newsday*, June 17, 2017: http://www.newsday.com (accessed October 6, 2017).

ACKNOWLEDGMENTS

It would be both delusional and ungracious to not recognize the many who have helped me prepare this book. Deserving of particular mention is Jim Carothers, who oversaw and contributed much to the contents of these pages in their earlier incarnation as my doctoral dissertation. I am also much indebted to the staff of the University of Tennessee Press and particularly Series Editor Brian Ingrassia, who first recognized the potential of this project, and Thomas Wells, who shepherded it through several phases of revision and refinement.

On a more personal note, I am also very grateful for the friendship of all the wonderful people I have known in Boise, ID, Provo, UT, and Lawrence, KS, and for the unflagging support of my siblings, their growing families, and particularly my parents. Thanks, Mom and Dad.

INTRODUCTION

I can still recall my earliest memory of the New York Yankees. The most successful, most loved, and most hated baseball team in the country—nay, the world—entered my little existence when I was three or four years old through the shoebox diorama my older brother was constructing for the annual "Celebrate a Book" art competition held by the Boise, Idaho, school district for elementary school students. The book my brother had chosen to "celebrate" and immortalize through the media of shoebox, cardstock, pipe cleaner, and colored pencil was John Callahan's *The Wonderful World Series*, a bargain kids' paperback chronicling the outcomes of Major League Baseball's annual championship contests from 1903 through 1979. It was surely not the example of literature—even by children's books' standards—for which the contest organizers were hoping.

As he re-created a shoebox glimpse into one of many contests between those New York Yankees and their National League rivals, the Brooklyn-turned–Los Angeles Dodgers, my brother, five years my senior, calmly explained to me—at least this is how I remember it—that the Dodgers were *the good guys*. They wore bright royal blue, and we (my brother, my dad, and anyone else who wanted to be considered "family") supported them, while the other team, the Yankees, donning caps a much darker shade of blue and curious striped uniforms that looked strangely sinister to me, were *the bad guys*. To my three-year-old mind, this notion of the Yankees as the baseball equivalent of Darth Vader was supported by the way that name sounded—Yankees. It felt like the word "yuck" in my mouth.

Grateful to my brother for explaining to me, once again, the way the world worked (it wouldn't be the last time), I carried on for those next few innocent years of childhood, hardly ever giving the game of baseball a second thought other than feeling secure in knowing that I was a Dodger man and the Yankees were essentially the embodiment of pure evil.

But as I grew up, I would become gradually more and more engaged with this world of baseball. Obliviously bookish and just a little uncoordinated, this primarily took place through reading material. First, it was daily box scores of the 1991 season in the *Idaho Statesman*. And then another contribution to my education came from my older brother: the deluxe, special-edition gem of a magazine that he had collected Kellogg's cereal box tops to send away for, *Baseball's 20 Greatest Teams of All Time* by the editors of *Sports Illustrated*.

Even at eleven years of age, I was most captivated by the *history* of the game, and in that regard this tome was foundational. It was there that I first immersed myself in baseball history and really became acquainted with what the Yankees were. Chagrined that *four* of the "twenty greatest teams of all time" were Yankee clubs (the 1927, '36, '53, and '61 teams), compared to only a single Dodger entry (1955), I read every page of that early-1990s collaboration between *Sport Illustrated* and a breakfast cereal company through my Dodger-blue lens and concluded that my brother had been absolutely right: the Yankees *were* evil! Focusing, naturally, on the profile of the 1955 Dodger team, I learned of the legendary one-sided rivalry between the Brooklyn "Bums" and their intercity rivals, the Yankees. Through World Series meetings (1941, '47, '49, '52, '53) the hopeful Dodgers were routinely handed their hats by the ever-successful team in the Bronx. It was in 1955 that, at long last, the good guys—the chosen team of my family and the team to beat baseball racism, those plucky upstarts the Dodgers—finally got their miracle and prevailed over the Yankee bullies. I was now not only a Dodgers fan by birthright but by conscious choice. As far as I could tell, it was simply *the right thing to do.*

The Yankees at this point in the early '90s, of course, were pretty awful—a heartening fact that I took as a sign that perhaps justice really did prevail in this world—but they quickly improved. And even as I rejoiced when the geographically proximate and infinitely likeable 1995 Seattle Mariners prevented the Yankees' first playoff berth in a decade and a half from continuing past the first round, I began noticing that there were a lot of people who rooted for the Yankees, people who loved them as much as I loved the Dodgers, if not more. And these were not morally bankrupt, sadistic individuals who would have rooted for the Nazis in *Raiders of the Lost Ark* either. Many of these Yankee fans were people I liked and respected, people like Paul Simon, that sensitive soul engraved in the grooves of my parents' old records, or the kid in my chemistry class who was fast becoming my favorite person among Borah High School's entire sophomore roster. When I came to school one day in late October 1996 to find him exulting in the Yankees' return as World Series champions, it was as if a bucket of cold water had been thrown on our budding friendship. However, I also found plenty of people who seemed to hate the team just as much as I did, people who wrinkled their noses every time they were mentioned, as my parents did. (As a side note, I should mention here that my father, a Dodger fan from his youth, happened to matriculate at a college in the Boston area just in time for the Red Sox's 1967 "Impossible Dream" season and embraced them as his "number two team.") The Yankees, I concluded, must be the most polarizing entity in American sports.

But there was something else. Something that was a little hard to put my finger on exactly, but it had to do with the way individuals striving to be as nonpartisan as possible—people like broadcasters Bob Costas or Tim McCarver, or the writers of *Baseball's 20 Greatest Teams*—would talk about the Yankees as one might talk about Abraham Lincoln, Yellowstone National Park, or the 1957 Chevy Bel Air. When they won the 1996 World Series, many celebrated and many pouted as I did, but I was curious to find that the mainstream consensus seemed to be that, at the top of the Major Leagues once again, the Yankees were back where they belonged. Granted, after four-to-five more years of this, the consensus was likely a bit different; but in that moment the nation seemed pleased, and I realized what many already knew or at least intuitively understood: love them or loathe them, Americans tend to see the New York Yankees as a national symbol.

|||

Modern sport has played a significant role in American society since the mid-nineteenth-century beginnings of its rise to mass popularity. Inextricably intertwined with the broader culture, sports both shape and are shaped by history. But because our games operate on an elaborate set of invented rules, they also create scenarios that often seem like their own little worlds set apart from the rest of our daily existence. These little worlds walled off from the rest of society are, like my brother's shoebox diorama, hardly uncoupled from the rest of American culture, however. Far from it. In fact, what plays out in our little cocoons of sport is so often a close parallel of what is going on outside of them, only dramatized in a way that frequently makes it clearer. For example, Jackie Robinson's struggle in 1947 to succeed as the lone black man in the National League enacted the story of a nation wrestling with its long-held practice of racial segregation. In 1973 the gathering steam of the feminist movement was symbolized in the "Battle of the Sexes" tennis match between Billie Jean King and Bobby Riggs.

Because they are simultaneously part of culture but also walled off from it through their own rule structure, sports can often act as something of a microcosm, re-creating the broad strokes of our culture in miniature. Like a pantomime or a shadow play of the culture in general, the narratives that play out in the world of sport often are somehow able to help us better see and understand who we are as a society, what we value, and how we are changing. The Yankees have merely done this on a grander scale than Jackie Robinson or Billie Jean King.[1]

Not only are the Yankees the most successful club in a sport that from its very beginnings has enrobed itself in a rhetoric of nationalism, but they also emerged triumphant as the best in baseball in the same historic moment the

United States of America was establishing itself on the world stage. With the 1920 acquisition of Babe Ruth, the Yankees rose to prominence at precisely the same time the nation as a whole did in the wake of World War I, and the club stayed at the top of their game through the crisis of the Depression and the return to even greater heights of national triumph in the Second World War and postwar prosperity. Thus, the Yankees' story of success parallels and is interwoven with the narrative of American success in the twentieth century. All the restless energy, the ballyhoo, the thirst for the new of the Roaring Twenties, was mirrored in the colossal figure of Ruth. The perpetual striving and the courage in the face of peril of the country during the dire straits of the Depression and war years was matched in the pinstriped profiles of Gehrig and DiMaggio. And when the United States emerged from that crucible, the age of confidence and prosperity was almost perfectly embodied in the postwar swagger of Mickey Mantle. Then in the late '60s, as young Americans began challenging the assumptions and values of their parents' generation, the Yankees rapidly declined on the field as well. In other words, the Yankees and America peaked at the same time.

As the biggest winners in a nation that was winning, the Yankees and the country as a whole were in sync through these years in the middle of the twentieth century. As such, they were then and are now perceived in a way that links them with an interconnected web of some of the most prevalent values of that era—most specifically, the American dream of upward mobility, heroic masculinity, and a narrative of national triumph. More briefly, the Yankees became icons of mid-twentieth-century America. This means that, both then and now, when people talk about or reference the team or any of their own symbols—the distinctive interlocking NY emblem, the fittingly nationalist Uncle-Sam-hat-on-a-baseball-bat logo, the image of Yankee Stadium, or, of course, the famous pinstripes—this communication carries unspoken connotations of the triumphant nation in the middle decades of the twentieth century and the cultural values most affiliated with that era.

The Yankee franchise's cultural connotations are perhaps best understood through the framework proposed by French cultural theorist Roland Barthes. Building on Ferdinand de Saussure's concept of language as a symbolic system of "signs" linking vocalized sound or its printed representation—the "signifier"—with the concept or thing it represents—the "signified" (Saussure

646–47)—Barthes applied this framework to unspoken communication through cultural symbols. For Barthes, this structure includes communication beyond the strictly linguistic and literal, also taking in the culturally accumulated connotations of words, symbols, or visual cues "chosen by history" as well as their literal, denotative meanings (110).

Thus, the literal meaning of the word "Yankees" in a baseball context (or, for that matter, any of their symbols) is the professional American League ball club based in the Bronx, New York City. But that is not the only meaning the Yankees and their linguistic or visual symbols contain. Because of the history of the Yankees and the resulting associations that have been made between the successful club and certain values and ideas over time, they have also amassed a significant connotative (or as Barthes termed it, "second order") meaning within American culture as well (114). This, in the case of the New York Yankees, is that particular vision of the American nation itself noted above—one built on a certain standard of male heroism, the American dream of upward mobility, and a triumphal concept of America tied to its midcentury economic and military success.

For Barthes, cultural icons[2] such as the Yankees become a particularly potent tool for strengthening the power of cultural narratives or ideologies. Not only can they represent particular ideas a culture has about itself or stories and versions of history it tells about itself, but such cultural icons also provide "natural and eternal justification" for these ideologies or narratives (143). Along these lines, it could be said that for many the existence and prominent cultural presence of the Yankees at midcentury seemed to "prove" the truthfulness and correctness of what the team connotatively represented, the version of America emphasizing heroic masculinity, the American dream, and the national success story, making these ideologies seem, to use Barthes's expression, like a "natural" part of American life.

However, as I so astutely discovered as a teenager, the New York Yankees are a fairly divisive issue. And fittingly, the period of American history in which they came to prominence is far from a national fairy tale and is not without its own share of controversies: Wall Street corruption, demagoguery, the atomic bomb, and McCarthyism, to say nothing of the institutionalized racism that persisted through these years of American "greatness." Since this period of the United States' rise to prominence and power has both what might be called its *light* and its *dark* sides, it should come as no surprise that the Yankees have been used as emblems of this nation in both a positive and a negative sense: as icons of why America is great and succeeds and as the embodiment of everything that is wrong with the country.

This use of the Yankees as icons of what could be termed the *counter*-perspective on the state of the nation or the *counter*-narrative of mid-twentieth-century American history has existed as long as the Yankees have been winning. In particular, by the late 1960s, when the "Baby Boomer" children of the generation that grew up during the Depression and sacrificed during the Second World War were questioning or outright rejecting the values their parents espoused, it is no coincidence that the use of the Yankees as a negative national symbol overtook positive uses in many national conversations.

This is not to say that Yankee supporters and Yankee haters break down cleanly into people who look at twentieth-century American history optimistically and those who see it negatively or, even less so, "conservatives" and "liberals." Quite the contrary. By and large, our sports allegiances are the result of geography or, as in my case, familial precedent. Nevertheless, while those who adore the Yankees may not necessarily be the same people with an optimistic take on America (and anti-Yankee sentiment wouldn't necessarily predict dissent), the Yankees' polarizing tendency does parallel the tension between seeing the glorious triumph of the American experiment and seeing the dark underbelly of the country: our complicated relationship with and perspectives on success, wealth, power, and tradition. Collectively, we love and hate the Yankees because we both love and hate our nation and its history.

What follows here is an attempt to chronicle and analyze the ways in which the New York Yankees have been used as an American cultural icon from their rise to national prominence in the 1920s through the end of the twentieth century. In so doing, like baseball scholars Daniel Nathan and David McGimpsey, I will not just devote attention to the meaning attached to or implied in the Yankees in the rhetoric of sports reporting but will also draw on what could be termed more *peripheral* cultural artifacts, or "texts," as they deal with or utilize the Yankees as a cultural icon. These texts beyond the immediate consumption and reporting of a given sports competition would certainly include the more long-form, analytical, and introspective sports journalism that has proliferated since the 1960s but also includes the places where the Yankees have been portrayed or referenced in popular culture more broadly: in novels, movies, comics, television shows, and pop music.[3]

In fact, I would argue that it is often in these texts most peripheral to the actual baseball games themselves that the Yankees' cultural meaning is clearest. Not only does an appearance of the Yankees in a Hollywood film serve as an indication of the scope of their impact—that they have transcended the subculture of baseball itself and are known more broadly even by those who may not be baseball fans—but such peripheral texts from the general popular culture are also typically less focused on the mechanics of winning and losing and devote more attention to their broader significance: why the Yankees matter and how we might perceive them. Indeed, texts that reference the Yankees in a way peripheral even to their own narrative, such as references in Ernest Hemingway's novella *The Old Man and the Sea* (1952), or Simon and Garfunkel's hit song "Mrs. Robinson" (1968), are perhaps most illustrative of the Yankees' iconic nature, as analyzing them reveals how the Bronx club has essentially been used as a sort of cultural shorthand for certain ideas or values that all Americans would understand.

While there are certainly texts that portray, utilize, or reference the Yankees that I may have missed or chosen to leave out because of my limited space, I have identified and focused on those that I see as most important and representative of the way Americans have perceived the Yankees as icons of our nation and its recent history. This book proceeds chronologically, beginning with Babe Ruth and the Yankee teams in the 1920s, whose first successes were seen by some as a parallel of the emerging new age of excitement, innovation, and spectacle. Once still in Ruth's shadow, as their success continued after his departure in the late 1930s and early '40s, the Yankees emerged as a cultural icon in their own right with the help of Lou Gehrig and the emotional film biography based on his dramatic life, *The Pride of the Yankees*. Then, during World War II and the early '50s, the public adoration for Joe DiMaggio added a distinctly mythic dimension to the populist values the team had embodied with Gehrig.

Yet, this period was not without its Yankee detractors, as Brooklyn Dodger fans in the '40s and '50s cultivated a working-class underdog identity as a counterpoint to the perceived elitism and tyranny in their crosstown rivals. As the Bronx club's dominance continued in the 1950s, this critical attitude towards the Yankees proliferated into the American mainstream through cultural texts that saw similar flaws in the nation as a whole. By the late 1960s, this oppositional perspective on the Yankee cultural icon had largely eclipsed the original celebratory view as a much-diminished version of the team became a symbol of the "out-of-touch" values of the previous generation. Then, as the upheaval of the 1960s turned into an era of prolonged national uncertainty in the following decade, a very different team of high-salaried, squabbling Yankees only served as evidence that the values the old, heroic Yankees embodied were part of a naïve, irretrievable past. However, by the '80s and '90s an attitude of greater national optimism was reflected in the nostalgic desire to see a return of the great Yankee legacy as a token of reconciliation with the pre-1960s past.

As I seek in this book to analyze and understand the way the New York Yankees baseball club has been used as a national emblem—helping us understand who we are, who we have been, what we value, and where we want to go—I hope that implied in these arguments is a subtext asserting the significant position of sports in general, and baseball in particular, in the cultural fabric of the United States of America. Too long neglected by academics, the growing attention to sports as a site of cultural meaning is a real and important conversation this study is designed to join. If cultural theorist Raymond Williams's suggestion that "culture is ordinary" (6) has any validity, the ever-popular and ubiquitous world of sports is fundamental to any understanding of American culture in the twentieth century and the present day. As the personal preamble to this introduction suggests, the people, institutions, and traditions of American sporting culture have had a substantial influence on my own understanding of myself and the world. And I know I'm not the only one.

Chapter One
"TO BE YOUNG AND A YANKEE"
Babe Ruth and the First Era of Yankee Success

Babe Ruth is easily the most famous baseball player in the history of the United States. Even though he retired over eighty years ago and many contemporary Americans may know relatively little about the details of his life, he remains a potent cultural icon. He is also probably the most famous New York Yankee, eclipsing other legends such as Lou Gehrig, Joe DiMaggio, Yogi Berra, and Mickey Mantle, any one of whom would likely be the face of the franchise for most other baseball clubs. When contemporaries and future generations discussed the careers of those players, they were and are assessed *as Yankees*—how well did they uphold the Yankee legacy? But Ruth had no tradition to uphold. Ruth *made* the Yankees.

Because of this, even today, Ruth is the one hero from the Yankee pantheon that could be said to transcend his "Yankeeness." That was even truer during his career with the club. As teammate and pitcher Sam Jones put it, "People often forget that the Yankees of the twenties ... [were] a well-balanced club in every way. Everybody played in the shadow of George Herman Ruth" (qtd. in Ritter 245). Even the legendary Lou Gehrig, who began to gain more public attention when he challenged Ruth for the season's home-run title in 1927, was largely eclipsed by the Babe. As sportswriter Rud Rennie reported in the *New York Herald Tribune* after an afternoon's contest one day in May, "There was just as much noise when Ruth struck out in the fifth as there was when Gehrig hit his home run with the bases full in the ninth. They don't pay to see Gehrig hit 'em" (qtd. in Frommer, *Five O'Clock Lightning* 85). And so it was with the Yankees of that era. Without Ruth, they would have been considered by most Americans to be just another baseball club.

However, despite all this, the mighty Ruth only played a largely *preliminary* role in the shaping of the Yankees as a cultural icon. Indeed, during his career with the club (1920–34), the Yankees were a very good baseball team, arguably the best in either league in that period, but they had not yet achieved the iconic status within the American popular consciousness that they would possess less than ten years later after the arrival of Joe DiMaggio, the string of four straight World Series championships (1936–39), the tragic and emotional retirement and death of Lou Gehrig, and the release of the hit film based on his life, *The Pride of the Yankees*. It took success *without* Ruth for the Yankees as a team to achieve prominence in the American popular mind. Until then, to the average American, the New York Yankees were, by and large, an extension of or accessory to Babe Ruth. Only after Ruth's retirement could the Yankees as a team come out of the shadow of their most famous player and become a cultural icon in and of themselves.

Ruth's eclipse of the Yankees during his career was perhaps less complete among sportswriters and the devout and longtime baseball fans who made up their audience, however. To this subculture, the transformation of the 1920s Yankees, once an American League also-ran, into a new powerhouse of the diamond with the acquisition of Ruth and, perhaps less famously, bolstered by the management of Miller Huggins, the ownership of the deep-pocketed Colonel Jacob Ruppert, and the guidance of business manager Ed Barrow, was certainly something worth noting. The rise of the Yankees was particularly interesting when the club was compared, as they often were, to their cross-city rivals in the National League, the storied and popular New York Giants. As such, for sportswriters of the 1920s and early '30s, particularly when contrasted with the Giants, the Yankees were largely seen and written about as the embodiment of *the new:* the new contenders for, and eventual new possessors of, the throne of New York City sporting culture, the exemplars of the new "lively ball" style of baseball, the sports equivalent of "new money," and baseball's representation of the new paradigms of American culture in that decade of great change, the Roaring Twenties.

Such a characterization of the Yankees as "the new" did not necessarily trickle down to the slightly less informed, however. While Ruth was practically everywhere in the mass-media-catalyzed popular culture that was booming in the '20s and early '30s, his team the Yankees were primarily portrayed as a mere detail in his legend in such cultural artifacts, if they were portrayed at all. In popular texts outside of the sports page, the Yankees were included as the team Ruth played for but were not distinguished in any other significant way, including the "new" persona the club often took on in sports journalism and other cultural connotations. Nevertheless, this period in the New York Yankees' history remains important as it established the foundation upon which the Yankees' cultural icon was built. The hallmarks of this period—Babe Ruth and the club's first real success—were the first iteration of trends that would largely be perceived as a pattern by the end of the 1930s: the Yankee traditions of grand, heroic figures and of a nearly unbroken legacy of on-field success, upon which the Yankees' iconic personification of a triumphal perspective on midcentury America rested heavily. But before these facets of the New York ball club could become *traditions,* they had to have their first occurrence.

THE YANKEES' EARLY HISTORY

Since the persona the Yankees acquired among sportswriters and devout fans during Ruth's career is mostly derived from the events that transpired on and off the field in the first three and a half decades of the twentieth century, a brief overview of the Yankees' early history is perhaps the best place to start. In their early years, the Yankees (called the Highlanders or Hilltoppers until 1913, after their first ballpark on a hill in northern Manhattan) were an unremarkable baseball club, particularly when compared to New York City's more established and successful National League franchise, the Giants, who were led by their colorful and intense manager John McGraw. This relationship between the two teams was symbolized during much of this era by the fact that between 1913 and 1922 the Yankees were tenants of the Giants, renting their ballpark, the Polo Grounds, when the Giants were playing out of town.

But the Yankees' fortunes slowly began to change in 1915 when the club was purchased by a grandson of German immigrants and heir to a brewery fortune, Colonel Jacob Ruppert.[1] Ruppert's wealth most dramatically shaped the Yankees with the December 1919 purchase of the heavy-hitting pitcher-turned-outfielder George "Babe" Ruth from the Boston Red Sox.[2] Also the grandson of German immigrants, Ruth nevertheless had a very different upbringing from that of the Colonel, as he was largely raised in St. Mary's Industrial School for Boys, a Baltimore institution dedicated to the molding of young orphans and troubled youths. Ruth was the latter. But at St. Mary's Ruth found he could play baseball fairly well, and it soon not only became his career but eventually made him the most famous man in America. Ruth, who earned additional nicknames such as the "Great Bambino" and the "Sultan of Swat" from the colorful sportswriters of the era, was truly a Herculean figure both on and off the baseball field, and though newspapers often did their best to suppress unseemly news items concerning "the Babe," he became almost as well known for his substantial appetites of every sort as he did for the new power-hitting, home-run-focused style of play he brought to the game.

The arrival of Ruth and a host of other Ruppert acquisitions significantly improved the Yankees' on-field success, helping them win the 1921 and '22 American League championships, or pennants, pitting them against their crosstown rivals and landlords, the Giants, in both years. The histories of the two clubs and their style of play colored the way those World Series were viewed, with the storied Giants touting their traditional style of play focused on speed and strategy and the Yankees, featuring Ruth and the new power-hitting style, playing the role of the brash, iconoclastic up-and-comers. While by this time Ruth had helped the Yankees outdraw the Giants in terms of fan attendance, the Giants put these upstarts in their place by defeating them in both the 1921 and '22 World Series. And to add insult to injury, the Yankees' lease on the Polo Grounds, which the Giants had made clear they would not be renewing, ran out at the end of the 1922 season.

Ruppert and the Yankees responded by building their own ballpark, the bigger and more luxurious Yankee Stadium just across the Harlem River in the Bronx in time for the 1923 season, which ended in another rematch of the Giants-Yankees rivalry. But this time the upstarts emerged victorious. The Yankees continued to enjoy success throughout the decade, and with the addition of great hitters like Earle Combs, Tony Lazzeri, and particularly Lou Gehrig, the dominant Yankees team of 1927 earned the nickname "Murderers' Row," a hyperbolic moniker befitting the brute force of the power-hitting Yankees and their charismatic leader, Ruth. After their championship triumph in '27, they added World Series victories in 1928 and 1932. Then the aging Ruth left the Yankees after the 1934 season, upset at the front office's denial of his desire to manage the team. The Babe played for about two months of the following season for the National League's Boston Braves before retiring at the end of May 1935.

THE NEW BASEBALL KINGS OF NEW YORK

One of the key narrative threads in this story of the Yankees' rise from mediocrity to one of the very best of the Major League clubs, as told by sportswriters and consumed by devoted baseball aficionados, was the team's usurpation of the Giants' claim to the throne of New York City's sporting culture. It is hard to overestimate the hold John McGraw and his Giants had on the collective affection of the city's sports fans. Part of the National League since 1883, the Giants found great success and emerged as the city's dominant team in the late 1880s, but really established themselves as the league's crown jewel with the 1902 hiring of manager-infielder John J. McGraw, the working-class son of a troubled and tragedy-scarred family of Irish immigrants, from the American League's Baltimore Orioles (who ironically moved to New York City the following year and eventually became the Yankees).

McGraw was well known to possess a great baseball mind, both in terms of scientific and psychological strategy, and led the Giants to National League pennants ten times (1904, '05, '11, '12, '13, '17, '21, '22, '23, '24). In three of those years he also defeated the American League's champions to win the World Series.[3] Enjoying popularity among the city's Broadway and sportswriter crowds, as well as Tammany Hall connections (Weintraub, *House That Ruth Built* 49, 124–26), the Giants became ingrained in the culture of the city at a time when New York was emerging as the clear cultural center of the United States and an influential world city. As baseball historians Steve Steinberg and Lyle Spatz comment, the Giants were "a fixture in the city since the 'Rosie O'Grady' [an 1896 waltz-song fad] days of the Gay Nineties" (*Colonel and Hug* 174). Furthermore, this early-twentieth-century period when the Giants were the toast of the town was concurrent with the establishment of a synergy of professional baseball and newspapers that helped make the National and American Leagues the topic of a truly national conversation. In fact, according to Robert Weintraub, four legendary sportswriters of this Golden Age of sports journalism—Grantland Rice, Damon Runyon, Fred Lieb, and Heywood Broun—all met as new reporters assigned to baseball at the Polo Grounds on opening day of the 1911 Giants season (*House that Ruth Built* 305). Thus, claim to the throne of the first baseball kings of New York City, which the Giants certainly held, was quite an enviable possession. For many New Yorkers, including the hundreds of thousands of immigrants who arrived in New York City in the decades surrounding the turn of the century and their children, for whom baseball became an Americanizing cultural touchstone, there was nothing before the Giants.[4]

With this in mind, one sees that the challenge the newly moneyed Yankees posed to the Giants' baseball dominance in the nation's largest city once Ruth arrived would have felt like even more of a coup. Since the borough of Brooklyn was not incorporated into New York City until 1898, the occasionally successful Brooklyn-based Bridegrooms-turned-Superbas-turned-Trolley Dodgers-turned-Dodgers (winning National League pennants in 1890, 1899, 1900, 1916, and 1920) were not considered a territorial threat at this point: Brooklyn's fan base tended not to extend much beyond the boundaries of the borough in those days (Steinberg and Spatz, *1921* 5–6). And until the arrival of Ruth, the other team bearing the city's name as part of its official moniker had never risen above mediocrity. But suddenly, with Ruppert's money and Ruth's might, among other things, all that changed. The Yankees' challenge to the Giants' New York baseball hegemony coincided with a period when

McGraw and the Giants were once again at the top of their game, setting up dramatic head-to-head contests between the teams in three World Series in a row, 1921, '22, and '23. As the *Philadelphia Inquirer* summed it up before the 1921 series: "It is more than possible that the victor in this combat will plunge ahead as the chosen team of the city, and if the American Leaguers bring home the bacon it will mean much, very much to them. . . . McGraw has never lost his hold on the popular imagination of New York, and the legend that he is the greatest still exists and is still potent" (qtd. in Steinberg and Spatz, 1921 9).

The outcome of those World Series could not have played out better in terms of the narrative of succession that sportswriters adopted. The Giants' initial triumphs over their American League counterparts were spun in the press as a tale of a promising, if immature, contender being not quite yet fit for the mantle, or of an old king not yet ready to surrender his crown. For instance, after the Giants took a two-games-to-one lead in the '23 series and looked poised to win their third World Series in a row, the *New York Herald*'s Percy Hammond summed it up: "Mentally, McGraw's boys are to Col. Ruppert's as post-graduates are to freshmen. . . . 'Get away from here,' Mr. McGraw seemed to say, 'this is no place for a Yankee'" (qtd. in Weintraub, *House that Ruth Built* 324).

And when the Yankees with their impressive new stadium finally vanquished the Giants on their third try in 1923, it was described by some as a long-awaited changing of the guard in Gotham. For example, the *New York Times* reported, "Ruth showed that the Giant supremacy could be broken down. Leading the way himself, he showed that the Giants were not invincible" (qtd. in Weintraub, *House the Ruth Built* 365). And since this clash over New York supremacy took place in professional baseball's highest competition, the Yankees' role as the new kings of New York was disseminated among American baseball devotees on a national level.[5] Also, considering New York's recent dominance of professional baseball and the city's central role in the nation's culture—which only increased over the course of the 1920s and early '30s with the rise in Wall Street's importance in national life and the establishment of the nationwide radio broadcasting industry in New York—the New York Yankees, in wresting the title of the Big Apple's best from the Giants, essentially became the preeminent ball club in the country.

The Yankees' role as New York's and baseball's new champions only solidified in the late '20s, when the Yankees strung together three consecutive pennants (1926, '27, and '28) and two World Series titles in a row ('27 and '28). The 1927 season in particular helped in this regard, as the Yankees set a new American League record with 110 wins. Ruth, meanwhile, bettered his own single-season home-run record by hitting sixty and was challenged by his own Yankee teammate, the taciturn Lou Gehrig (who faded late in the season and ended up with forty-seven), in the chase for that record. The 1927 Yankees, triumphant in a four-game sweep of the Pittsburgh Pirates in the World Series, were hailed by some as the greatest baseball team ever. The Yankees' dominance was eventually usurped by owner and manager Connie Mack's Philadelphia Athletics, who beat the Bronx-based club to three straight American League pennants in 1929, '30, and '31. (They also won the World Series in '29 and '30.) The Yanks also had competition from the National League's improving St. Louis Cardinals organization, which beat them in the 1926 World Series and also won it in 1931 and '34. But the Yankees bounced back and won the championship again in 1932 in a memorable World Series against the Chicago Cubs that included the aging Babe Ruth's legendary "called shot," a dramatic home run that some accounts claimed the slugger had predicted with a gesture towards centerfield (Creamer, *Babe* 360–68).

In the second half of the 1920s and the early 1930s, the Yankees would certainly have been one of the small handful of teams considered the cream of baseball, a fact given added meaning by the Giants' relative futility in the same period. While the Yankees' stocks soared after they finally beat their crosstown rivals and former landlords in 1923, the Giants' fortunes went in the opposite direction. Though McGraw's team captured the pennant the next season, 1924, they dropped the World Series to the hitherto hapless Washington Senators. Then, from 1925 through 1932, the Giants were unable to muster anything better than second place, a record pennant drought for McGraw, who retired as manager after the '32 season. The following year the Giants made a surprise comeback. Led by new player-manager Bill Terry and helped by slugger Mel Ott and pitcher Carl Hubbell, the Giants won the 1933 World Series, their first in eleven years; but even after the surprise triumph, the club was still playing second fiddle within the city to the Yankees, a harsh reality that would be solidified by the Bronx team's success in the late 1930s, as well as the '40s and '50s, during which they would capture seventeen pennants and fourteen World Series victories. In the same period the Giants mustered only one World Series championship, beating the Cleveland Indians in 1954, and three additional World Series berths in 1937, '38, and '51, all of which they lost to the Yankees.[6] By that time, the Yanks were the established and unrivaled kings of baseball, but in the 1920s and early '30s, like their Herculean star who overshadowed them, they were, to longtime baseball aficionados, still a relative novelty: new claimants to the title of baseball's best, usurpers of their once-mighty crosstown rivals the New York Giants.

THE YANKEES AND THE NEW POWER-HITTING GAME

Still, for many sportswriters and devoted baseball fans, Ruth and the Yankees represented much more than a new baseball power in New York City. They represented a significant change in the game itself, a new style of play that for the most part still largely dominates its every level in the United States today. Prior to the 1920s, Major League baseball was characterized by a style of play heavily dependent on strategy, pitching, speed, and skill on the base paths. Hitters choked up on the bat and sacrificed leverage and the power that comes with it for more control, in an effort to "hit 'em [pitched balls] where they [the opposing team's defensive players] ain't," in the immortal words of McGraw's old Baltimore teammate, 1890s batting champion "Wee" Willie Keeler. Around 1920, however, there was a sudden increase in the number of extra-base hits, particularly home runs. This style of play focused on hitting for power and capitalized on scoring many runs at the same time or in the same inning, a contrast to the old style of scratching out a single run here and there. While there are many explanations and debates regarding the cause for this rapid change, what is clear is that Babe Ruth was the face of this new power-hitting game.[7] Ruth moved from pitcher (playing every three or four games) to outfielder (playing nearly every game) with the Boston Red Sox and hit an unprecedented Major League record of twenty-nine home runs in 1919. After his sale to the Yankees, the Sultan of Swat nearly doubled that total with an astonishing fifty-four home runs the very next year and then bettered his record once again with fifty-nine in 1921. Ruth would hit over forty home runs in a season nine more times before retiring, including the 1927 total of sixty, his personal best and a record many thought would stand forever. For both longtime baseball fans and Americans who knew or cared relatively little about the game, Babe Ruth became synonymous with the home run.

The home-run boom, or so-called "lively-ball" era in Major League Baseball, like Ruth's sale to the nation's media capital, could not have had better timing, arriving as it did in a period when tremendous growth in both technology and the nation's economy, as well as a popular desire to shake off the malaise of the Great War, contributed to a culture that prioritized entertainment. If the so-called Roaring Twenties were all about having fun, then the power-hitting style of baseball—arguably more immediate, visceral, flamboyant, and easier to follow than the "inside game"—was indeed a development in tune with the zeitgeist. And it certainly did not hurt to have a charismatic figure like Ruth at the fore of this baseball revolution. As the club's identity was so intertwined with their superstar Ruth during his career, the Yankees essentially became the team that represented this new style of play for sportswriters.

But Ruth was not the only power-hitter playing for the Yankees during this period. Bob Meusel, who also began his career with the Yankees in 1920, hit the second-most home runs (twenty-four) in 1921, the year Ruth hit fifty-nine, and a league-leading thirty-three in 1925 (a sickly Ruth missed much of the season that year and hit only twenty-five). Lou Gehrig famously challenged Ruth for the home-run crown for much of the legendary 1927 season (finishing with forty-seven to Ruth's sixty) and consistently finished near the top in extra-base-hit totals throughout the late 1920s and early '30s. The combined efforts of Ruth and Gehrig in those late '20s teams, plus the contributions of Meusel, as well as other Yankee hitters like Tony Lazzeri and Earle Combs, helped the club earn the "Murderers' Row" nickname, which conveys the force and visceral impact of this new style of play relative to the strategic "inside" game favored in previous decades. But the Yankees had something of a reputation as a power-hitting club even before the arrival of Ruth among baseball writers. In fact, in 1918, two years before the arrival of "The Great Bambino" in Gotham, sportswriters Sid Mercer and Fred Lieb both used the term "Murderers' Row" to describe the Yankees batting order, which consisted of Roger Pekinpaugh, Frank "Home Run" Baker, Del Pratt,

Wally Pip, and Ping Bodie—all relative sluggers before the power-hitting style of play really caught on (Steinberg and Spatz, The Colonel and Hug 372).[8]

With the club's reputation for power hitting mounting before the close of the "dead-ball" era and the addition of Meusel, Gehrig, and especially Ruth, it is understandable why sportswriters and baseball devotees would have strongly linked the Yankees as a team with this new style of play, but this tendency became especially clear and prominent when the Yankees faced the Giants in three consecutive World Series in the early 1920s. Since John McGraw had a reputation as the consummate baseball strategist who made the most out of the "inside baseball" style of play, the ballyhoo surrounding the 1921, '22, and '23 World Series was often presented as a narrative of McGraw versus Ruth, emphasizing their contrasting approaches to the game. McGraw made it clear that he did not like the new power-hitting style exemplified by the Yankees; in his autobiography, first published in 1923, he bluntly stated, "I do not like the lively ball. I think the game far more interesting when the art of making scores lies in scientific work on the bases" (207). This fact only added intensity to these public contests between teams and styles. For instance, in an article in the *New York Evening Journal* assessing the pending World Series of 1921, Sid Mercer wrote, "This is a National League town. John J. McGraw put his label on it years ago, and the Giants are firmly established. Up to a couple of years ago, the Yanks were just the 'other New York team.' But the immense personal popularity of Babe Ruth and the dynamite in the rest of that Yankee batting order have made the Yanks popular with the element that loves the spectacular" ("Whole City Busy"). In Mercer's comments not only is power hitting identified as the distinguishing characteristic of the Yankees and contrasted with the inside style practiced by the old-guard McGraw and his Giants, but a certain skepticism is also apparent towards the power-hitting style of play and those who enjoy it.

For writers and long-term fans like Mercer, the home-run style was a threat to the game they treasured, played in the way they linked with a certain degree of subtlety and sophistication. For example, in October 1921, Harry A. Williams of the *Los Angeles Times* echoed his colleague's skepticism toward the power-hitting style before the World Series when he bemoaned, "Baseball has switched from a science to a wild scramble" (qtd. in Steinberg and Spatz, 1921 320). The inside game required a fairly comprehensive mastery of the rules of baseball, and for New York City's many sportswriters, no one did it better than McGraw. The power game, meanwhile, had a much more immediate, mass appeal that required little previous knowledge of the game. Anyone could understand and enjoy the sight of Babe Ruth hitting a baseball out of a ballpark. Thus, for many longtime baseball aficionados, the power game was something of a threat, and pitted against the Giants, Ruth and the Yankees were this new style's *enfants terribles*.

McGraw and the Giants' defeat of the Yankees in both the 1921 and '22 World Series felt like vindication for many of the old-guard devotees—particularly since Ruth and the home-run ball played such a relatively small role in the outcome. For these traditionalists, here was proof that the inside game embodied in McGraw's Giants was the right way to play baseball. This theme colored the comments of baseball writers after the 1921 World Series, such as Fred Lieb of the *New York Evening Telegram*, who asked rhetorically and mockingly, "What became of the lively ball during the series?" (Steinberg and Spatz, *1921* 387). After the Yankees and Ruth fared even worse against the Giants in the 1922 series, Joe Vila went even further in the *Sporting News*, pronouncing the Babe "the biggest kind of bust.... The Exploded Phenomenon didn't surprise the smart fans, who long ago realized that he couldn't hit brainy pitching" (qtd. in Steinberg and Spatz, 1921 397). But with their mass appeal and their new gargantuan ballpark, which featured a close right-field fence tailor-made for Ruth's home runs, the Yankees triumphed in 1923's rematch and the revolution was all but complete. Sportswriter Grantland Rice colorfully summed up the victory for the Yankees and the power-hitting style with his comments after the fifth game: "When intellect collides with ash manipulated by thick and freckled wrists ... [the Yankees'] reply to the Mental Urge was a salvo of 14 hits ... leaving Mental flat on its writhing back" (qtd. in Weintraub, *House That Ruth Built* 346).

THE YANKEES AS "NEW MONEY"

The Yankees' power-hitting style was not the only thing about the team at which the old guard looked down their noses. While the team was well funded by owner and well-heeled brewery heir Jacob Ruppert, the Yankees were generally perceived as "new money" by journalists, spending freely in an ostentatious manner in their pursuit of the on-field success that had eluded them in the past.

Ruppert certainly came from a well-to-do family. As owner of the largest brewery in the state of New York, a business started by his German-immigrant grandfather, Ruppert was accustomed to traveling in the most elite of New York City circles. Adolescent Yankee fan and Ruth biographer Robert W. Creamer remembers Ruppert as always appearing "urbane, sophisticated, impeccably dressed . . . whenever you saw a photograph of him on the sports pages he *looked* rich" (*Baseball in '41* 62).

But prior to his purchase, the club did not have the same pedigree. Before Ruppert's acquisition, the Yankees were in a different class compared with professional baseball's most successful clubs, including the Boston Red Sox, the Chicago Cubs and White Sox, the Philadelphia Athletics, and, of course, the New York Giants. When the Yankees began spending Ruppert's conspicuous wealth to acquire players to bolster their meager roster, the baseball press was both skeptical and critical of their efforts at "buying success." John Sheridan of the *Sporting News* typified this tendency with his comments in 1920, before the Yankees had found much on-field success, teasing that they "seem to be thoroughly imbued with the New York idea that money can buy anything."

Even after their most notorious acquisition, Ruth himself, helped bring the club closer to the success Ruppert dreamed of, the Yankees were still seen as outsiders because of their controversial power-hitting style and their lack of prior success. In short, the Yankees represented the antithesis of tradition, and thus their newfound success was suspect, not unlike a freshly minted, self-made millionaire at a turn-of-the-century Newport dinner party. Sid Mercer's comment about "the element that loves the spectacular" exemplified this snobbish attitude. Though the Yankees may have been outdrawing their landlords in the Polo Grounds' ticket office, that certainly didn't make this "new money" club the Giants' equals for many longtime baseball fans. The Yanks' "new money" persona was only strengthened by their star, Ruth, who was quite literally "new money" and certainly acted like it, conspicuously displaying his working-class habits in public with frequency (Creamer, *Babe* 185–86). Ruth's less-than-refined behavior was paralleled by that of many teammates, and the club as whole had something of a rowdy, carousing reputation. Sam Murphy of the *New York Evening Mail* suggested as much in September 1920, when he wrote that if the Yankees had been as worried about "their mode of life as they [were] of getting the last dollar for their services," they would have won the pennant that year (qtd. in Steinberg and Spatz, *The Colonel and Hug* 160). This reputation for carousing was further confirmed when the team's off-field behavior on a 1922 Boston road trip drew a reprimand from Baseball Commissioner Kennesaw Mountain Landis, along with coverage in both the *Boston Globe* and the *New York Globe and Commercial Advertiser*.

And just as Colonel Ruppert's free spending to bolster his roster was perceived as gauche by many baseball traditionalists, so also was the colossal Yankee Stadium. The *New York Evening World* quipped that the stadium had "the austere dignity of a bank. Money speaks there in the low, modulated voice that is more eloquent than the shouts of a mob storming the Bastille" (qtd. in Weintraub, *House That Ruth Built* 93). In a similar vein, a critic in *American Architect* dismissed the stadium's decorative copper frieze, intended to convey class and refinement, as being "rather idiotic," too desperate in its aristocratic reach (qtd. in Weintraub, *House the Ruth Built* 46).

While their methods were and are certainly up for debate, no one can question the results of these figurative gatecrashers of baseball's elite circle, as they vanquished the Giants and the rest of both leagues to become one of the very best, if not the best, professional ball club in the period spanning the 1920s and early '30s. As such, the Yankees were, once again, quite in keeping with the spirit of the age as the stock market and real estate speculation created more than its fair share of Jay Gatsby–style *nouveau riche* and even more aspirants whose number was never called.

More broadly, the Yankees' new-money persona harkens to a narrative deep in the American vein, particularly in the way the nation saw itself in relation to Europe and its established aristocracies. In a sense, with many of the traditional powers of Western Europe in a shambles after the Great War and with the United States riding high coming off its delayed but instrumental role in tipping the scales of that conflict and enjoying the new 1920s economic prosperity, Americans were essentially new money as a nation in the realm of world affairs in this era. While these parallels between the Yankees as a ball club and the American nation as a whole largely went unobserved at the time, they nevertheless may have helped pave the way for the nationalization of the Yankees as a cultural icon that emerged in the wartime era of the 1940s.

THE YANKEES AS THE NEW AMERICAN CULTURE

As part of the sportswriters' personification of the Yankees as the *new* style of play, *new* money, and the *new* sporting kings of New York City, the team's identity also became quite intertwined with the *new* American culture of the 1920s. Much of this, of course, came through the dominant presence of Ruth, whom many have written about as the very essence of that "roaring" epoch. For example, in 1963 Oliver Pilat described Ruth as "an unequaled exhibition whose strength and accuracy with baseball were of a pace with the madness for crazy pleasure, unheard of speed, and aimless bigness convulsing through the nation" (qtd. in Sobol 125). Even some contemporaries sensed Ruth's connection to the spirit of the age. *Sporting News* writer John B. Sheridan compared Ruth's home runs with a flapper's "thrills over her cigarette and still shorter skirt" (qtd. in Crepeau 104).

From a more academic perspective, cultural historian Warren Susman describes Ruth as virtually tailor-made for his time. Arguing that the decade of the 1920s was a crucial historical moment when the old "often loosely labeled Puritan-republican, producer-capitalist culture" competed with "a newly emerging culture of abundance" (xx), Susman identifies Ruth's public persona as ideal for bridging the gap between the competing cultures in this time of transition, as he stood as "a heroic producer in the mechanized world of play" as well as "an ideal hero for the world of consumption" (146). Americans marveled at the Babe's achievements, but they also "enjoyed [his] excess" and "took comfort in the life of apparently enormous pleasure that [he] enjoyed" (146). Charles J. Shindo similarly argues that Ruth's traditional rags-to-riches backstory combined with the more excessive and viscerally titillating elements of his celebrity to make him an especially useful embodiment of the emerging new morality: the combination of traditional *and* new in the figure of Ruth made the cultural transition more palatable and negotiable to an ambivalent American public (133).

As Ruth's team, largely rising and falling with his successes and missteps over the course of the decade, the Yankees as a whole shared in these connotations, even if the way the club as a whole tapped into the cultural zeitgeist was not necessarily articulated consciously then. Nevertheless, even if the complete picture was never quite assembled at the time, the Yankees were linked by sportswriters with many of the new paradigms that made up the cultural revolution of the 1920s. For one thing, Ruth's and the Yankees' reputation as carousers fit right in with the colorful atmosphere of speakeasy culture of the "Jazz Age." As pitcher Waite Hoyt reported in 1965, the successful Yankees clubs were very much a part of that scene in the '20s, with Ruth's celebrity opening up any and every door to them: "It was a birth of something new, and everybody from the Astors [a prominent wealthy New York family] to gangsters wanted to meet baseball players. It was fashionable to say, 'I met so and so last night at such and such night club.' Another thing that is forgotten: Then we played strictly day baseball and we had ample time at night to go here and there" (qtd. in Enright).

With Ruth as lightening rod, the Yankees' extracurricular activities did not go unnoticed by the press. This was particularly true during spring training of 1922, when the Yankees lived it up in the nightclubs of New Orleans and one sportswriter filed a report with the headline "Yanks Training on Scotch" (Graham 74). While reported with a tone implying that such practices did not befit serious athletes, this lifestyle was certainly in keeping with the much-discussed nightclub scene with its bootlegged liquor, chaotic jazz music, and iconic flapper.

The Yankees likewise tapped into the emerging entertainment, media, and celebrity culture in a way no other baseball club had. Again, this was largely due to Ruth, his gargantuan home-run blasts, and easygoing persona, which the American public craved insatiably. The era would give them myriad new ways of feeding that hunger. The decade of the '20s brought new precedents in terms of media and communication technology. Not only did radio broadcasting become commonplace and the relatively young motion-picture industry continue to flourish, but the Roaring Twenties also saw either the invention of or dramatic expansion of the tabloid newspaper, the photo-centric popular magazine, film newsreels, and the modern newspaper sports section.[9] The modern advertising business has its roots in the same period, as ad executives seized on these new communication media to broadcast their products.

Ruth was a frequent presence in each of these new media, not only in radio broadcasts, newsreels, and multiple varieties of journalism related to his on-field performance but in more peripheral artifacts of popular culture as well, including two silent feature films, *Headin' Home* (1920) and *Babe Comes Home* (1927), and the endorsement of products ranging from cigarettes to milk, from underwear to Cadillacs (Tygiel, *Past Time* 84). In Susman's words, Ruth "made himself into a marketable product" (146). All this exposure placed Ruth among the small number of individuals in that decade to first receive the type of public exposure we expect of famous persons today. According to baseball historian Jules Tygiel, "In an age in which the modern ideal of celebrity was virtually invented, Ruth, along with a handful of Hollywood stars, personified that concept" (*Past Time* 77). In the increasingly mass-media-catalyzed 1920s, Ruth was nearly omnipresent. And through him so were the Yankees. While the club's pinstripe uniforms (not yet the icon they would later become) and the interlocking "NY"-logoed cap were not *always* part of Ruth's image—and the Bambino was certainly recognizable without that garb—he was, as often as not, pictured in the mass media wearing the uniform of the Yanks.

For most Americans, the Yankees' team uniform was merely one of Ruth's accessories, and the baseball club itself was notable primarily for his presence on it. Even after contributions of teammates like Lou Gehrig became more prominent in the popular consciousness, the Yankees as a team were still eclipsed by Ruth to the American masses. But for the dedicated, longtime baseball fan, one for whom the individualized logos and uniforms of different clubs carried some meaning related to those teams' players and histories, the Yankees' prominent presence through Ruth in these multiple emerging media would have been significant. It is likely that the Yanks' lack of history would have made them seem even more closely tied with the technological-cultural revolution of this decade. For the longtime baseball fan used to following the Giants, Athletics, Cubs, and Red Sox in the 1890s, 1900s, and 1910s by actually attending games or by reading the growing but comparatively meager sports coverage in newspapers, the flood of increasingly visual baseball media would have coincided with the sudden increased profile and status of the once-lowly Yankees. The overall effect of this synchronicity was to cement an association between the Bronx-based club and these new developments in mass-media sports reporting that would become staples of the twentieth century. By extension, the Yankees became associated with the dramatic cultural changes of the decade in general.

The Yankees also embodied some of the spirit of innovation and achievement that captured American imaginations during the cultural era of the 1920s. In addition to the advancement and proliferation in the field of media technology during the decade, the concept of new achievement, of humans breaking records, of doing things thought unachievable or things never even conceived of previously, particularly fascinated Americans in the Jazz Age. Charles Lindberg's solo flight across the Atlantic is perhaps the quintessential instance of this tendency, but examples would also include Gertrude Ederle's swim across the English Channel in 1926 or even the crazes of flagpole sitting and dance marathons. Ruth's home-run hitting fit right in with this "gee-whiz" facet of the spirit of the times. To again quote Susman, the Babe satisfied the appetites of Americans "wanting only something more, something bigger than life" in that roaring decade (148).

Americans in the '20s were particularly obsessed with record breaking. In the setting of new records, the people's thirst for the new converged with what Susman describes as "particular middle-class delight in what could be measured and counted," which derived from "the mechanization of life generally" and "the mounting effort to rationalize all aspects of man's activities" (141). This thirst for both the new and the measurable seemed tailor-made for Ruth, who set a new home-run record four times in the post–World War I period (twenty-nine in 1919, fifty-four in 1920, fifty-nine in 1921, and sixty in 1927). The near-superhuman aura that surrounded these feats—the fact that he set a new Major League record one year and then nearly doubled his own record total the very next year remains mindboggling—is very much in keeping with the theme of human beings achieving what was previously considered to be unachievable that was a key aspect of the 1920s zeitgeist. The same could be said for the distances that the balls Ruth hit traveled.

This association with new achievement that Ruth had in the popular mind was shared by the Yankees as a team and not only because of the presence of the Great Bambino. The 1927 team, in particular, set a new standard for wins in the American League with 110 victories, a mark not beaten until 1954; they also scored more runs and racked up more home runs and runs batted-in (RBI's) than any Major League team before them (Frommer, *Five O'Clock Lightning* 150). This '27 club was hailed by many as the greatest in Major League history at the time, an opinion still commonly held today. Richards Vidmer's comments in the *New York Times* of July 16, 1927, for instance, are particularly consistent with the broader cultural notion that the contemporary times were surpassing what had come before in many ways: "You may sing of the ancient Orioles. You may chant of the glory that was the Cubs a score of years ago. You may harken back to the Athletics before the wreckage. But before anyone starts making any broad statements concerning those teams of a past baseball era, let him consider the frolicking, rollicking, walloping Yanks of the present."

Likewise, when Yankee Stadium opened, it was not only the largest ballpark in existence, with its unprecedented triple-tiered grandstand and the highest seating capacity in baseball—58,000, although they somehow managed to squeeze in an extra 2,000 for its grand opening (Frommer, *Remembering Yankee Stadium* 34)—but it also set new precedents for opulence and refinement. (Later on, in the late 1930s and '40s seating capacity would reach 70–80,000 [55].) On the day of its grand opening, ushers in tuxedos and bow ties stood guard (Weintraub, *House That Ruth Built* 18). The aura of luxury was further conveyed through details like dugouts that were "the most comfortable in the sport," with a cushioned bench and a wooden floor, the presence of two in-crowd announcers with megaphones instead of just the typical one, and the grass that covered not only the outfield and infield but the area surrounding home plate and the on-deck circle as well, uncommon at the time (24, 18–19). But perhaps nothing bespoke opulence as much as the decorative copper frieze that hung from the roof covering the grandstand and has become the iconic, distinguishing feature of the park. As the *New York Times* summed up the new ballpark's state-of-the-art aura, "In short, the Yankees' Stadium is just about the last word in baseball plants" ("Size of Stadium Impresses Crowd"). Its grand opening was something of a gala affair as well, with the *Times* reporting, "Governors, general colonels, politicians and baseball officials gathered solemnly yesterday to dedicate the biggest stadium in baseball" (qtd. in Frommer, *Remembering Yankee Stadium* 34).

Since the feat of Yankee Stadium's architectural achievement came in the context of the Yankees' eviction from the Polo Grounds and following two consecutive World Series losses to their former landlords and crosstown rivals, the stadium was often seen in contrast to the Giants' home park, particularly for the way it seemed designed to trump the storied Polo Grounds in nearly every way.[10] As the focal point of New York City baseball and with one of the highest seating capacities in the Major Leagues, the Polo Grounds could be considered the country's premier baseball venue prior to Yankee Stadium, a fact not lost on Giants' owner Charles Stoneham, who immediately made plans to expand his ballpark once he learned what the Yankee organization was going to build just across the Harlem River in the Bronx (Weintraub, *House That Ruth Built* 140). But even an expanded Polo Grounds could not quite compete with Yankee Stadium. This theme of out-granding the grand resonates generally with the record-breaking spirit of the time and more specifically parallels the skyscraper-height wars of the 1920s, particularly the public rivalry between New York City's Chrysler Building and the Bank of Manhattan Trust Building. In fact, the *New York Times* even referred to the stadium as "a skyscraper among ballparks" during its construction (qtd. in Weintraub, *House That Ruth Built* 92). The Yankees' capture of their first World Series title in the season it opened put an exclamation point on Yankee Stadium. With Ruth and their enormous, state-of-the-art new home, the Yanks made it clear that they were not content to play the game of baseball the way it had been played in the past. Like the "roaring" decade itself, the Yankees seemed to be all about defying convention and expectations and enjoying every minute of it.

THE YANKEES IN THE SHADOW OF RUTH

While all these connotations of newness surrounding the Yankees were observed with regularity by the most dedicated baseball fans and sportswriters, by and large the team did not become, and was not used as, a cultural symbol for those facets of American culture they embodied so well during Babe Ruth's tenure as Yankee standout. As already suggested, this is largely because that job was given to Babe Ruth himself. Since the broader public had little knowledge of "the other" New York ball club prior to Ruth's arrival, the Yankees were largely perceived as an extension of the Great Bambino himself.

This notion is borne out in the way Ruth and the Yankees were portrayed in popular texts outside of sportswriting.

In the ever-expanding mass-media culture, Ruth was nearly omnipresent, including his presence in advertising and the aforementioned movie roles. In addition to his starring roles in *Headin' Home* and *The Babe Comes Home,* both critical and box-office flops, Ruth also made a significant cameo appearance in silent comedian Harold Lloyd's much more successful 1928 feature *Speedy.* In 1923 Ruth's persona was even utilized as a key character in an ambitious novel, *The Sun Field* by Heywood Broun, a New York sportswriter-turned-cultural-critic and member of the famed Algonquin Round Table. And in 1934, in the twilight of his career, Ruth lent his name to further fictionalization with the development of the Quaker Oats–sponsored radio show *The Adventures of Babe Ruth,* a serial aimed at adolescent boys that chronicled not the Babe's actual achievements on the diamond but wild, occasionally comedic, invented stories that bear the influence of pulp fiction, adventure comic strips, and other radio serials as diverse as *Little Orphan Annie* and *The Shadow.*

In each of these texts the Yankees as a team have a presence, with occasional references to other Yankees, including manager Miller Huggins (*The Sun Field, The Adventures of Babe Ruth*); successful pitchers Carl Mays (*The Sun Field*), Waite Hoyt (*The Sun Field*), and Herb Pennock (*The Adventures of Babe Ruth*); and well-known position players Lou Gehrig, Tony Lazzeri, Joe Dugan, Mark Koenig, and Bill Dickey (*The Adventures of Babe Ruth*). But generally each of these are mentions only, utilized largely for the purposes of baseball realism, names worth mentioning mostly because they are associated with Ruth.

In *The Adventures of Babe Ruth* radio show, Miller Huggins occasionally had lines and in general was portrayed as the knowledgeable, worrywart manager he was in real life. Like appearances in the show of the stern commissioner of baseball, Kennesaw Mountain Landis, and Ruth's childhood mentor, the fatherly Brother Matthias, Huggins is mostly there to act as foil to the worry-free, occasionally mischievous Ruth. Huggins's slightly sketched-out character does nothing to make the Yankees as a whole anything but a typical team that was successful largely because Ruth made them that way.

This is in stark contrast to later representations of the Yankees in texts like the film *The Pride of the Yankees* (1942), Hemingway's *The Old Man and the Sea* (1952), and Broadway's *Damn Yankees* (1955), each of which would locate the Yankees' success in an ethereal quality of the club itself that transcends any one player.

Ruth's cameo in the silent comedy *Speedy* fleshes out the Yankee organization a bit through the inclusion of a mention and the image of Yankee Stadium, as the star-struck Harold Lloyd is charged with driving the Babe there in time for the day's game. While the enormity of the stadium is difficult to downplay, *Speedy* does not linger on its image for long, and it is partially obscured by steel bridge girders that pass by the moving camera depicting the pathway of Lloyd's taxicab. Like Manger Huggins in the boys' radio serials, the stadium and the Yankees as a team are largely an appendage of Ruth in this film cameo, part of his legend. Maybe this should not come as such as a surprise considering that the stadium was popularly known as "The House That Ruth Built" from the very first year it opened.[11]

Perhaps the closest these cultural texts come to portraying the Yankees with any kind of persona during Ruth's tenure would be in Heywood Broun's 1923 novel *The Sun Field*. Here Ruth is given an intentionally thin disguise as the Yankee outfielder and home-run king "Tiny Tyler," a character the author uses to embody unfettered and unanalyzed lived experience, meant as a contrast to the cerebral existence of the book's other characters, writers and journalists who spend their lives analyzing the actions and creations of others. Broun gave Ruth a pseudonym, not to protect his identity or under any pretense of hiding his source material from readers—it seems quite evident that Broun wants us to see Tiny Tyler as a stand-in for the Bambino—but so that he could take the Ruth persona in new, hypothetical directions: in this case it is a marriage to an intellectual socialite. The Yankees are nearly an afterthought in most respects, there to ensure that readers understand he was writing about Ruth or at least the idea of Ruth. But the narrative slips in a tangential aside, a remark on a Yankees road trip from Tyler's fictional teammate "young Grasty, the little righthander from the coast," to Tyler's new wife Judith that "it's great to be young and a Yankee" (97). This line is quickly followed by unrelated information about Grasty's performance against the Detroit Tigers, and the narrative continues without returning to the ideas evoked by "young Grasty" again. But the comment that "it's great to be young and a Yankee"—an amendment to or parody of an earlier pronouncement supposedly made by New York Giant Larry Doyle to sportswriter Grantland Rice in the 1910s that "it's great to be young and a [New York] Giant"—certainly seems loaded with implications relevant to the cultural meaning or persona the Yankees might have had in that era. By linking the Yankees with youth, potential, and the future, especially in contrast to an earlier such statement about the Giants, the novel evokes an image of a team associated with the new, with the future of baseball and America, just as sportswriters at the time did, but more explicitly so. It is fitting and telling that this statement, written by a man who logged many years as a baseball writer himself, has no further elaboration, as these connotations associated with the Yankees would largely remain the knowledge of baseball aficionados, while American culture at large would, like Broun's novel, continue to focus on the Herculean personality that eclipsed his own team, Babe Ruth.

Ruth's tenure with the Yankees, particularly in the decade of the 1920s, was a cultural period where America's new vision of itself and its role in world affairs first blossomed. In many ways, the way the United States is seen by the world—or certainly, the way it was seen during the twentieth century—first came into focus in the '20s, in the wake of America's decisive involvement in World War I and during a period of unprecedented national economic development and cultural confidence. The Yankees, riding the wave of new achievement, money, and technology to success and fame, effectively embodied this new America: no longer a frontier colony or an also-ran ball club, but rich, powerful, bursting with energy and flouting convention and tradition. With the Babe and through the Babe, the Yankees played the same role in baseball and American sporting culture in general that the United States began to play in world affairs.

Having the advantage of historical distance, we can look back and see how the Yankees were the epitome of Roaring Twenties America. Some baseball writers seemed to catch on to this during Ruth's tenure as a Yankee, characterizing the team as the embodiment of "the new." But by and large, to the general public populace the Yankees were not yet the cultural icon they would later become. Independent of Ruth, who eclipsed them in nearly every way, the New York Yankees signified relatively little to most Americans.

In fact, it was probably difficult for them to imagine the Yankees without Ruth. Ironically, only after the departure and retirement of the Babe, when the team was able to find success without him, would the New York Yankees be transformed into the national icon of success and all-American heroism they are today. Nevertheless, just as the triumphant America of World War II and postwar prosperity would be rooted in the America that was in the 1920s, so also would the Yankees' iconic cultural meaning that emerged in the late '30s and early '40s and proliferated in the following decades be built on the foundation laid by the team during the wild years of the Great Bambino.

For the Yankees, as a baseball club and cultural icon, Ruth was like a legendary, semi-mystical figure at their foundation. Ruth was their creation myth, their King Arthur, or their First Thanksgiving. As part of their past, he made the Yankees special, unique among other baseball teams. While the team's continued success in the late '30s and onward would constitute the nuts and bolts and scaffolding of their legacy and cultural meaning, the ghost of the larger-than-life Ruth—even before his early death to throat cancer in 1948—would provide the kernel of mystery, the whisper of transcendence that would render the exploits of those who followed him as significant and meaningful to Americans and would help give cultural potency to the icon that the Yankees franchise, built on his legacy, would later become.

Chapter Two
"LET ME TELL YOU ABOUT HEROES"
The Pride of the Yankees and the Crystallization of a Cultural Icon

After finding success for the first time in the 1920s with Ruth and other players purchased through Jacob Ruppert's substantial monetary investment in the club, the Yankees entered a period in the late 1930s that could be described as sustained dominance. Beginning two years after Ruth's retirement, from 1936 through 1939, the Yankees won what was then a record four World Series titles in a row led by Lou Gehrig and Joe DiMaggio. Early in this period, Gehrig was the more established presence on the team, having been a valuable and successful member of the Yankees during the years of Ruth's dominance. In fact, Gehrig even won the league's MVP award the year of Ruth's famous single-season home run record in 1927. But just as the shy, reclusive Gehrig was significantly overshadowed by Ruth's larger-than-life persona in the 1920s, during the Yankees' triumphs in the later '30s, the dependable and soft-spoken slugger was largely eclipsed by the new rookie sensation Joe DiMaggio, who joined the team in 1936.

Somewhat ironically, however, Gehrig's status as overlooked and underappreciated changed dramatically in 1939 when the first baseman's dependable play rapidly and mysteriously deteriorated. In May of that year, Gehrig took himself out of the lineup, ending his streak of 2,130 consecutive games played. That summer he was diagnosed with amyotrophic lateral sclerosis (ALS), a rare degenerative neuromuscular disease that meant not only that he would never play baseball again but that he did not have long to live. The Yankee organization and community of baseball fans responded by arranging a "Lou Gehrig Appreciation Day" on the Fourth of July at Yankee Stadium, the first of its kind for the Yankees (but certainly not their last), complete with a ceremony between the games of the day's doubleheader. The emotional moment struck a chord with the fans in Yankee Stadium, who gave a two-minute standing ovation for Gehrig, and with America at large. Within two years, Gehrig was dead, but he would never be overlooked as a ballplayer or a Yankee again.

Gehrig's standing in America's collective cultural memory achieved iconic status with the release of the Sam Goldwyn–produced film based on his biography, which was penned by sports journalist Paul Gallico. Unlike many previous baseball-related movies, the Gehrig biopic, *The Pride of the Yankees,* was a rousing critical and financial success, profiting $3 million, more than any of Goldwyn's previous movies (Erickson 374). The movie shattered baseball-film precedent, perhaps bolstered by the American public's sentimental feelings towards Gehrig, who had been dead a little over a year when the movie was released in July 1942. As baseball-film critic Wes D. Gehring notes, *The Pride of the Yankees* was the first sound-era baseball biography that "broke the movie norm of associating baseball with comedy," and more important, it "helped put to rest the mistaken belief that baseball movies could not score at the box office" (49). Today, *The Pride of the Yankees* stands as an important touchstone in baseball-film history, with baseball filmographer Hal Erickson stating that it was "the most financially successful film of its kind made up to 1942" and remains "the mold from which virtually all future baseball biopics would be shaped" (368). *The Pride of the Yankees* is likewise an important text in the formation of the New York Yankees' cultural meaning, fusing the team's on-field success with Gehrig's populist heroism and a celebration of the American dream to render the Yankees a true American cultural icon of the mid-twentieth century.

The Pride of the Yankees dramatically boosted Gehrig and the Yankees' profile in the broader world of popular culture beyond the sports page. Many film historians have noted how executive Sam Goldwyn and director Sam Wood intentionally sought a broad audience, including women, for a baseball film, which stereotypically had limited appeal. The prominent role given to Lou's wife, Eleanor Gehrig (née Twitchell, played by Teresa Wright, who earned a "best actress" Academy Award nomination for her portrayal), and their courtship, as well as the relatively lengthy performances of the Irving Berlin love song "Always" and a tango by dance team Veloz and Yolanda, reveal the film's efforts to court a female audience.[1]

Unlike most of the baseball films that preceded and immediately followed it, Goldwyn's attempts to cast a wide net with *The Pride of the Yankees* were at least somewhat successful. The film set a new precedent for box-office returns among baseball films and was nominated for eleven academy awards, including best picture and best editing, the latter of which it won.[2] While Oscar nominations are only one measure of cultural impact, it could still be said that *The Pride of the Yankees* is one of a select few baseball films to gain significant mainstream success and cultural influence. As such, it plays a key role in establishing the Yankee cultural icon in the American mainstream beyond the subculture of long-term baseball aficionados and shaping the meaning of that icon.

THE SIGNIFICANCE OF "YANKEES" IN THE FILM TITLE

Many have commented on the reputation baseball films have had as "box-office poison," with Erickson even documenting a handful of instances over the years in which movie studios attempted to sell their baseball films in a way that hid the fact that they were about baseball (18–19, 202–3). Erickson's point notwithstanding, it remains true that throughout the twentieth century many baseball films have actually sought to use their baseball content as a selling point. Within the genre of baseball cinema, it is common for production companies to include verbal cues to communicate to potential ticket buyers the movie's baseball content. Terms like "ball," "league," "game," "diamond," "rookie," and "home" have frequently been included in baseball movie titles for this reason. While many of the baseball films made before *The Pride of the Yankees* have been lost to the cultural consciousness of most Americans, films like *The Busher* (1919), the Babe Ruth vehicle *Headin' Home* (1920), *Casey at the Bat* (1927), *Slide, Kelly, Slide!* (1927), and *Death on the Diamond* (1934) illustrate that filmmakers' tendency to include baseball signifiers in movie titles was firmly in place at the time the film was made, perhaps even more so than it is now. Significantly, *The Pride of the Yankees* not only used baseball terminology to announce its content, but it was the first major film to refer to a specific team of the professional Major Leagues, rather than a more general signifier of baseball.

Even in recent years, most films focused on existing or historical Major League Baseball teams refrain from specifically referencing the team in the film's title. A good example of this is 1989's *Major League*, which, while not historical, is especially dependent on the struggles of the real Cleveland Indians and the downtrodden state of the city of Cleveland during much of the 1970s and '80s, but it still uses a more generic baseball signifier in its title. *The Pride of St. Louis* (1952), about the life of St. Louis Cardinals pitcher and broadcaster Jerome "Dizzy" Dean, is similarly titled to Goldwyn's 1942 Gehrig biopic, likely an intentional parallel for marketing purposes. But notice that in this case, the studio avoided using "Cardinals" in the film's title, instead depending on the greater cultural clout of the city of St. Louis, perhaps hoping to build off of the positive cultural associations with Charles Lindberg's famous plane, the *Spirit of St. Louis,* and the more recent movie-musical hit *Meet Me in St. Louis* (1944).[3]

This prominent use of the name "Yankees" indicates how high the team's cultural profile was among the general populace by the late 1930s and early '40s. The word "Yankee" has had a long and interesting history of usage since the eighteenth century, when it was used most specifically to refer, often pejoratively, to New Englanders, particularly those of English, puritan ancestry. This meaning persisted well into the late nineteenth century, as evidenced by Mark Twain's novel *A Connecticut Yankee in King Arthur's Court* (1889) and continues to some degree today, as in *Yankee* magazine (founded 1935, Dublin, New Hampshire), a regional lifestyle and culture magazine focused on New England.[4] In the American South, particularly during the Civil War and Reconstruction, "Yankee" could mean a member of the Union army or a northerner in general. In Britain and other English-speaking former British colonies, meanwhile, it has been used since the eighteenth century to mean any American (*Oxford English Dictionary*). The regional mutability of the term is illustrated by a humorous aphorism widely attributed to E. B. White:

> To foreigners, a Yankee is an American.
> To Americans, a Yankee is a Northerner.
> To Northerners, a Yankee is an Easterner.
> To Easterners, a Yankee is a New Englander.
> To New Englanders, a Yankee is a Vermonter.
> And in Vermont, a Yankee is somebody who eats pie for breakfast.
> (qtd. in "Yankee," *National Geographic*)

With the advent of American involvement in European wars in the twentieth century, however, the association of the term "Yankee" with the entire nation of America would have become increasingly common around the time *The Pride of the Yankees* was released and in the years following. In fact, it is through this meaning of "Yankee" that the team likely acquired the name itself. In the early days of the twentieth century, newspapers in cities with a team in both the National and the American League, would often refer to these franchises as the "Nationals" and the "Americans." Possibly as an extension of this practice, New York sportswriters would occasionally substitute "Yankees" for "Americans," both in the pursuit of variation in diction and because "Yanks" could be used to make shorter headlines. Eventually the name stuck (Steinberg and Spatz, *The Colonel and Hug* 362, 286, Appel 18-19, Creamer "Babe Ruth and Lou Gehrig" 20).

This European-derived, nationalistic meaning of "Yankee" correlates with some nationalistic themes of the film that portray Gehrig as the essence of American values. To movie studio executives in 1942, however, a Yankee was clearly a baseball player, and they correctly counted on this newest of meanings for the term to eclipse two hundred years of regional definitions for the general American public. The title *The Pride of the Yankees,* presumes audiences to expect a baseball film rather than a Civil War film or a film about Vermont, for that matter. This presumption of marketers that for the average American, including the female viewers they hoped to court, "Yankees" meant baseball indicates the substantial cultural profile the team had acquired by 1942 through its on-field success and heroes Ruth, Gehrig, and DiMaggio.

But the title *The Pride of the Yankees* and a simple superficial knowledge of the film's subject matter—information one could get from a movie poster or "trailer" advertisement—also imply that the Yankees are more than just a baseball team. The title implies that the Yankees are an entity that stands for something, that can take "pride" in one individual from among its midst that could somehow represent its greater whole. For those familiar with baseball, the phrase "pride of the Yankees" might conjure up ideas about a standard of on-field excellence, as well as images of the heroes Ruth, DiMaggio, and, of course, Gehrig. For those less familiar, the sight of movie cowboy Gary Cooper on advertisements might suggest steady, dependable manliness. But it would be safe to say that all viewers would go to the film with an unspoken expectation to be instructed, or perhaps further instructed, on what it was the Yankee organization stood for and why Gehrig was qualified to represent it. In this regard, *The Pride of the Yankees* did not disappoint.

THE YANKEE PRESENCE ON SCREEN

The film itself provides ample opportunity for viewers to connect the New York Yankees with cultural ideals, particularly the desire for success and excellence. While the film's real subject is the "pride of the Yankees"—Lou Gehrig, rather than the entire team—the prominent place the team name gets in the title and the attention devoted to the team's championship legacy in the film constitute a significant motif as well. In the film's latter half, this emphasis on the Yankee legacy is clear in a time-passage montage mediated through newspaper clippings that Gehrig's wife, Eleanor, puts in her husband's scrapbook. In addition to personal achievements related to Gehrig's career communicated by fabricated (though factual) headlines such as "Lou Gehrig Named Captain of Yanks," viewers also see a review of the team's history in the 1920s and '30s, including headlines such as "Joe McCarthy Signs to Manage Yankees" and "Babe Ruth Leaving Yankees." The inclusion of the headlines about other Yankee players and managers is perhaps a bit curious, as the information seems somewhat tangential to the film's central plot. While coaching changes and the legacy of teammates are certainly somewhat relevant to Gehrig's biography, the motivation behind evoking these now legendary baseball names in a somewhat celebratory tone seems to be an attempt to present Gehrig as an integral and longstanding part of a legendary organization that excelled at what they did. For the baseball fan, the names and of Babe Ruth, Miller Huggins, Joe McCarthy, and the history of those Yankee teams additionally serve as reminders of just how successful they were.

The idea of the Yankees as the epitome of success and excellence achieves its full expression in the movie's conclusion, however. The film reaches its dramatic climax with a re-creation of Gehrig's now legendary speech at a special ceremony at Yankee Stadium wherein the hero describes his tragic diagnosis as "a bad break" yet still calls himself "the luckiest man on the face of the earth" for the opportunity he had to play with his Yankee teammates and coaches and for the support he received from fans, his parents, and his wife. Film critics, historians, and amateur movie buffs alike often cite this emotional scene for its impact on viewers and its tear-jerking potential, as evidenced by the American Film Institute's inclusion of *Pride of the Yankees* as number twenty-two on its list of "America's Most Inspiring Movies" and Cooper's "luckiest man" speech as number thirty-eight on its list of most quotable movie lines.[5] Yet this hagiographic scene, designed to lionize Gehrig, noticeably takes time to celebrate the Yankees as a team as well. As in real life, Gehrig's 1939 Yankee teammates in the film are joined by the members of the 1927 "Murderers' Row" team that was already legendary among baseball fans. The scene visually compares the Yankees of the recent past (or "Murderer's Row, our championship team of 1927," in the words of Cooper's cinematic Gehrig) with Gehrig's then-current teammates ("the Bronx Bombers, the Yankees of today") by lining them up symmetrically, flanking the centrally positioned Cooper on his left and right. The praise Gehrig gives both groups of men, calling it a "great honor" to play with the 1920s Yankees and a "further honor" to play with the then-current team, suggests to viewers that the two versions of the Yankees are roughly equal in excellence. These visuals and the verbal praise of the two generations of Yankee teams suggest the idea of the New York ball club as a proud legacy of success, a tradition of institutional excellence, with Gehrig, the "pride of the Yankees" himself, as a crucial link between the two generations of champions.

The conspicuous presence of many individuals and icons of the real-life New York Yankees furthers the heroic presentation of the Yankees in the Sam Wood–directed film. First and foremost, the film features the American living legend, Babe Ruth, who played himself in a small but much-advertised role, as indicated by the Babe's third-place billing status after Cooper and Teresa Wright. While not a skilled actor (despite his own experience as a star in his own cinematic vehicles in 1920 and '27), Ruth took his role quite seriously and managed, with his natural charisma, to steal many of the scenes in which he appeared. Ruth's large presence was supplemented by cameos from Bob Meusel and Mark Koenig, two more members of the dominant Yankees teams of the late 1920s. Bill Dickey, who in 1942 was winding down his career as an all-star Yankees catcher, also played a small but significant role as Gehrig's loyal teammate in the post-Ruth era. These famous Yankees and the numerous shots of the actual Yankee Stadium, particularly in the film's emotional closing scene, increase the team's presence in the film's narrative, linking Gehrig's eventual success and heroism with the team's legacy of success.

The presence of real-life stars Meusel, Koenig, and especially Ruth early in the film impress to viewers, particularly knowledgeable fans, the high standard of baseball excellence the protagonist Gehrig must live up to in order to join their storied ranks. Wood emphasizes this in a scene depicting the rookie Gehrig's arrival with the team with a panning shot of the empty Yankee clubhouse, allowing viewers to read the names printed on the lockers: Babe Ruth, Mark Koenig, Bob Meusel, and Tony Lazzeri.[6] A wide-eyed Cooper examines each one before finding his locker, indicated by a less official and less permanent hand-scrawled name card, signaling the need to prove himself among these established titans of Yankee baseball.

The later presence of the then-still-active Dickey, meanwhile, implies that Gehrig's success lies not only in filling the shoes of the great Yankees who came before him but also in passing that legacy down to the next generation of Yankee excellence. The fact that these men played themselves in the film makes an especially strong connection between the heroic drama of the film and the real-life American League team, conveying the idea of the team as baseball's celebrated elite to the uninitiated (and perhaps christening a few new Yankee supporters from among their numbers) and fleshing out, humanizing, and ultimately ennobling the Yankees' known success for those who were already baseball fans.

Tellingly, the Yankee organization itself actually receives a film credit for their "cooperation" in the filming. This participation by the baseball club in Goldwyn and Wood's tribute to Gehrig, including current and past players and Yankee Stadium, conveys an image of an elite organization giving special honor to one from among its storied ranks. This seems to be the attitude and tone the organization has sought in its many celebrations of itself over the years, including the special "days" given to the legends who would follow, notably Joe DiMaggio and Mickey Mantle. With the close involvement of the Yankee organization in the making of *The Pride of the Yankees*, the film became an important part of this tradition and, in effect, essentially became the cultural property of the organization, a notion that many current baseball fans and the organization itself still embrace when they view the movie.[7]

GEHRIG CONTRASTED WITH RUTH

While the presence of Babe Ruth in *The Pride of the Yankees* emphasizes continuity and the tradition of Yankee excellence of which Gehrig was the latest iteration, in another sense Ruth is used in the film to provide a significant contrast that draws attention to certain traits Gehrig possessed. Generally, Ruth's colorful, larger-than-life persona is contrasted with the portrayal of Gehrig as a consistent, hard-working everyman. The distinction eventually becomes more than just about individuals, however, as the progression of the film shows once Ruth retires and Gehrig becomes the team leader and dominant presence. *The Pride of the Yankees* depicts a narrative of the brash, colorful Yankees of the Ruth-dominated "Roaring Twenties" transforming into a more disciplined, hard-working group of ballplayers in the 1930s under Gehrig's influence. In an interesting move, considering the fact that Ruth enthusiastically agreed to play himself in the film and received third billing in advertising, the film seems to imply that Gehrig's presence was more important than that of the Babe himself in bringing the Yankees into their "true" form as the paragon of baseball excellence and an American symbol.

A few scenes in *The Pride of the Yankees* seem particularly designed to show the contrast between Ruth's and Gehrig's demeanors. The most obvious of these occurs as a competition of sorts between the two Yankee legends and is based on a semi-mythic tale about Ruth promising a home run to a sick boy during the 1926 World Series and ostensibly "curing" him, as he made good on the promise and the boy's health dramatically improved. While this tale was wildly exaggerated in newspapers at the time and has only grown more elaborate in retellings like the one featured in *The Babe Ruth Story* (1949), none of these mythic interpretations have ever included Gehrig in the action. And yet, in *The Pride of the Yankees*, Gehrig is given a role.

The scene opens with Ruth, something of a strutting peacock, posing with the sickly young Billy before an entourage of teammates, sportswriters, and photographers.[8] Grinning widely and constantly checking back on the photographers and reporters to ensure they are listening, he offers an autograph and a home run in that day's game. Obviously more interested in making a show for his hangers-on than making an impression on the boy, the Babe then further hams it up by asking which field Johnny would prefer his home run to end up in: right, center, or left. Without even pausing for a response, Ruth pretends the boy gives an answer and reports for his crowd, "What's that? Center it is!" He then saunters off with his company, presumably off to his next adventure.

After the crowd clears out, Gehrig approaches the young man and, unlike Ruth, engages in a conversation with the sick boy, offering some folksy words of encouragement. "You'll play [baseball] again," he assures him. "Billy, you know, there isn't anything you can't do if you try hard enough." Billy then turns this platitude back on Gehrig and asks him to hit not one but *two* home runs for him in the coming game.

Given this exchange, viewers are prompted to see Gehrig's agreement to fulfill the boy's request—a promise he makes good on the next day, of course—as coming from an unselfish desire to model the value of earnest effort and optimism for the downhearted child, a sharp contrast from the seemingly egotistical and indifferent Ruth. Apparently, it was not enough for Gehrig to appear as morally superior to Ruth, but it was also necessary for him to better Ruth on the baseball diamond as well, hitting two home runs for Billy over the Babe's measly one. The motivation for this sequence seems to be an effort on the part of filmmakers to show that while Ruth certainly was more famous and celebrated in American culture, in many ways Gehrig was a truer "hero," a cause in which they ironically involve the real Babe Ruth.[9]

Gehrig compares favorably to Ruth in *The Pride of the Yankees* in another, somewhat comical scene in which Eleanor Gehrig falsely insinuates to his sportswriter friend Sam Blake (Walter Brennan) that Lou has been cheating on her. The gag is played out at some length with Eleanor continually expressing how tired she is of her husband not coming home after games at Yankee Stadium. She says she has "caught him" and is going to confront him, while Blake, unbelieving, swears to her that Gehrig is "true blue." The sequence climaxes, however, with the reassuring revelation that it was all a prank and that Gehrig has only been "cheating" on his wife with the local sandlot boys, whose ballgames he jubilantly umpires. In a film that struggles to find drama in the interim between Gehrig's courtship of Eleanor and his fatal diagnosis, this sequence is effective as filler. It temporarily grabs the viewers' attention and causes them, like Sam Blake—who grumbles that he is on the verge of losing "faith in human nature"—to hope the story is not true before restoring the faith of the audience by revealing just that.

But there are other things going on here as well. Director Sam Wood seemed especially interested in threatening his viewers with the idea of infidelity on the part of the idealized baseball heroes in his film narratives; he used a very similar episode in 1949's *The Stratton Story*, an inspired-by-real-events film with James Stewart.[10] Thus, it would seem that, for Wood at least, there was a perceived public understanding that ballplayers often cheated on their wives, an "ugly truth" the director wanted to explicitly point out did not apply to *real* baseball heroes like the ones in his films. Yet, in *The Pride of the Yankees*, with the presence of Ruth playing himself, it is hard not to compare the "true blue" Gehrig with his fellow Yankee, the Babe, a notorious philanderer, during this comedic but moralizing sequence. Again, the filmmakers invite comparison between Gehrig and Ruth, leading viewers to see Gehrig as morally superior and thus more representative of "American" values.

This favorable comparison of Gehrig to Ruth carries over into the way the Yankee teams they led are portrayed in the film. Ruth's intimidating Murderers' Row Yankees of the "Jazz Age" 1920s stand in stark contrast to the post-Ruth Yankees that Gehrig captained to four straight World Series wins in the late

1930s. When Gehrig first joins the Yankees, his shyness makes him appear a bit out of place among the players, who, with the screen presence of real retired Major Leaguers Ruth, Koenig, and Meusel, not only exude real baseball credibility for audiences but also possess a brash but jubilant confidence exhibited through their locker-room joking and needling of each other. These Yankees seem to have an excess of energy and spend plenty of it off the field with elaborate practical jokes and card playing, most prominently in a scene in which some of the Yankees steal Babe Ruth's new straw hat and each takes a bite out of it.[11] Gehrig, then a shy rookie, is encouraged to take *two* bites—"if you're one of us, you'll take a bite"—and is reluctantly holding the hat when Ruth catches on. This scene establishes the brash, swashbuckling character of the team and emphasizes that the humble and sensitive Gehrig does not fit in.

Later on, after a passage of time marked in terms of Yankee history by Eleanor's scrapbook montage, the Yankees at the end of Gehrig's career are portrayed quite differently, with the staid Bill Dickey replacing Ruth, Koenig, and Meusel as the screen icon of baseball authenticity. These Yankees, under Gehrig's leadership as captain since Ruth's departure, are portrayed as more grounded and committed to success than the free-swinging Yankees of Gehrig's rookie year in 1923. A revealing scene depicts the Yankees in the locker room after a tough loss in which Gehrig, by this time unwittingly losing coordination and strength to ALS, played poorly. While most of the Yankees wear the faces of solemn disappointment, one begins complaining loudly about Gehrig's lackluster play as the reason for the loss. Upon hearing this, Bill Dickey delivers a single punch to the complainer's mouth. The player falls to the ground, but no further scuffle ensues. Soon Gehrig enters the locker room, visibly distraught over his poor performance, but summons the composure to play the role of captain and remind his teammates to "save the fight for the field, boys" in an authoritative baritone.

In this brief scene we learn all we need to about these Gehrig-led Yankees. They embody what could be described as the popular ideals of twentieth-century athletics: a commitment to maximum effort and winning, loyalty among teammates, and sportsmanship. When the one vocal player violates this ethic, Dickey swiftly acts as enforcer, with his relatively levelheaded aggression apparently coming more from loyalty to the Yankee captain, Gehrig, than from anger towards the offending teammate.[12]

The prevailing narratives of baseball history suggest that this change depicted in the film is not just a fabrication of Hollywood. For one thing, Gehrig's style of play, independent of the film, likewise builds on an image of work ethic, consistency, and honor in the pursuit of victory when compared to Ruth's style. Ruth was best known for his Herculean home runs (as well as his frequent Herculean whiffs) that were scarcely thought possible before and dramatically changed the game of baseball forever. Meanwhile, Gehrig's defining career achievement was for playing in 2,130 consecutive games, a feat of humble, workaday consistency. This image of greatness built on consistency that the Yankees of the later 1930s took on represents a significant change from the freewheeling teams from Ruth's era, but it is this more buttoned-down image that would be the one to persist in the popular memory.

The arrival of the dependable Joe DiMaggio, who is noticeably missing from the film, but in real life seemed to embody "calm, cool, and collected," reasserted and extended this tendency into the postwar era.[13] DiMaggio biographer Richard Ben Cramer endorses this view, writing of the Jazz Age Yankees, "Ruth's Yankees were all about high-hat and high times, three-run homers and 12–5 wins. . . . Of course, they swaggered: those Yankees were playing (they had invented) a different game than any other team could play" (92). Though Cramer credits the managing style of Yankee skipper Joe McCarthy as the key to the shift in character and tone in the 1930s Yankees—not Gehrig, as *The Pride of the Yankees* leaves us to surmise—the DiMaggio biographer corroborates the film's portrayal of the 1939 Yankee locker room. The late 1930s and '40s Yankees, he asserts, "were a cooler edition of the Pinstripes. When hard times hit in the 1930s and the Bambino's Bombers had played out their string, the ethic of the day became 'Buckle Down.' . . . Swagger [was something that McCarthy] simply wouldn't permit. He wanted players who did all the little things right, who took every advantage, who stuck to business at all times" (92). Two such players who did "the little things right" and "stuck to business" were Lou Gehrig and Joe DiMaggio.

Baseball-film historian Gary E. Dickerson agrees that this shift in the persona of the Yankees was part of a broader cultural shift in the first half of the twentieth century, arguing that Ruth's "flash, flair, and energy" fit the Jazz Age 1920s. In contrast, "Gehrig is [both] the blue-collar worker of the Depression ... [and] the man in the trenches in the front lines during World War II" (54), an ideal combination for the hero of a film released in 1942, as the Depression was just being eclipsed by the war effort but lingered in public memory. This cultural timing may have played into the public's embrace of the film and of Gehrig as a hero and exemplar of what were deemed to be "American values." These broader cultural shifts may have also played into the fact that the flashy and new image of Ruth's Yankees was largely eclipsed by the Gehrig era's "success through honor and work-ethic" tradition that continued into the 1940s. This later image by and large became the dominant one for the Yankees as a cultural icon throughout the twentieth century.

GEHRIG AND THE AMERICAN DREAM: ETHNIC ASSIMILATION

The significant presence of Ruth as a contrast is just one part of the film's overall heroic portrayal of Gehrig. As suggested by its title, the film presents Gehrig as the best the Yankee organization has to offer—the essence, if you will, of "Yankeeness." Through the film portrayal of Gehrig's life, this essence includes a realization of the American dream, specifically the social and economic upward mobility of white ethnics. Added to this up-by-the-bootstraps narrative is a strain of folksy populism, a celebration of the common man through Gehrig's consistent humility and work ethic. Finally, Gehrig also embodies many of the core traits of the mainstream ideals of masculinity. With this powerful combination of traits, the Gehrig of *The Pride of the Yankees* defines what it means to be a Yankee hero.

The American dream is a concept that has received much attention over the history of the United States, often making appearances in the rhetoric of politicians, a tendency that has not waned even as the twentieth century became the twenty-first. Despite this fact, or perhaps because of it, the term is actually quite slippery, supporting a range of meanings. Cultural historian Jim Cullen has suggested a number of variations of the American dream but has posited a vital link that unites them: "an abstract belief in possibility" (7). One particular and prominent incarnation that this "possibility" has taken on is what Cullen and others call "the dream of upward mobility" (59). Essentially, this phrase refers to the idea that individuals can improve themselves and their social and economic position through persistence, patience, and a healthy dose of the Protestant work ethic. With puritan and colonial roots, the dream of upward mobility was further popularized in the writings and lives of early American heroes such as Benjamin Franklin, Andrew Jackson, Henry Clay, Abraham Lincoln, and Andrew Carnegie (60–81).

Carnegie is perhaps noteworthy to call out here because he was an immigrant, albeit of British ethnic stock, and this dream of upward mobility had particular allure to immigrants throughout the nineteenth century, some of whom came to the United States with little else but a hope for a better life and excitement over the rumored promises of land and jobs. Once in the United States, however, many immigrants found their cultural, linguistic, religious, and physical differences from native-born Americans rendered them second-class citizens. Thus, their dream for "upward mobility" often included not only economic improvement, but improvement in social status as well.

Many scholars have written about the role baseball, with its rhetorical cloak of "Americanness," played in this assimilation. In Lawrence Baldassario's words:

> There is no question that baseball, more than any other sport and more than most American social institutions, has mirrored the gradual and often difficult process of assimilation experienced by a succession of ethnic and racial groups over the course of the twentieth century. For much of the first half of the century, baseball provided a window on the American Dream, creating in second-generation youth, especially those of European heritage, an awareness of those ideals that the arbiters identified as "American" and serving as a bridge between the customs of their immigrant parents and the world they found outside the home. (*American Game* 4)

Scholars also offer a similar assessment regarding baseball's role in assimilation for individual Euro-ethnic groups, in particular, including Jews (Levine 9), Italians (Baldassaro, "Before Joe D" 93), and Slavs (Pease 144–47).

Particularly relevant to Gehrig and *The Pride of the Yankees*, Larry R. Gerlach has written that "participation in the uniquely American sport was an easy means of assimilation" for German-Americans (28).

For some, baseball not only contributed social uplift but economic uplift as well, as many of the heroes of professional baseball's first several decades were second- or third-generation European immigrants, including Mike "King" Kelley, John McGraw, Honus Wagner, Hank Greenberg, and Stan Musial, as well as Yankee heroes Ruth, Gehrig, DiMaggio, Tony Lazzeri, Yogi Berra, and Phil Rizzuto. Arguably, baseball was one realm where the American dream of upward mobility was fulfilled, albeit for a "talented few" (Gerlach 28). Thus, the presence of this dream in a baseball film is something of a natural fit. Specifically, in *The Pride of the Yankees*, it provides a framework for Gehrig's personal biography and through him becomes a central tenet of the Yankees' iconic cultural meaning.

The national narrative of upward mobility shapes *The Pride of the Yankees* starting in its earliest scenes. Director Wood begins his film with a brief but memorable glimpse of Gehrig's childhood in working-class New York City. Almost immediately, the strong ethnic flavor of this neighborhood impresses itself upon viewers. While the young, undersized Gehrig struggles to gain the respect of the local boys at a pickup baseball game, a mother shouts a message to her son from a nearby tenement balcony in a pronounced Euro-ethnic accent. The precocious Gehrig surprises his peers by hitting the ball so well he breaks a shop window, and the subsequent meeting between Gehrig's parents, a police officer, and the shopkeeper solidifies this European-immigrant motif. Not only do Mr. and Mrs. Gehrig (Ludwig Stössel and Elsa Janssen), who remain important side characters throughout the film, speak in the strong German accents that one might expect from the first-generation immigrants they were ("I can't do anyfing vifout my vife," Mr. Gehrig intones), but the shop owner speaks in an excessively musical Italian accent ("I'm a-sorry"), while the policeman, stereotypically, has a prominent Irish brogue. Furthermore, this scene introduces the idea of the Gehrig family as poor, with Mrs. Gehrig asking the shopkeeper for leniency and patience in paying for the damage.

Overall, the filmmaker's intended effect seems quite clear: Gehrig comes from a working-class, German-immigrant family living in a mixed Euro-ethnic neighborhood. The use of familiar, clichéd cues to indicate its mixed ethnic flavor (the Irish cop, the hammy Italian accent, the laundry on clotheslines between apartment buildings) remind us that this type of social landscape already existed in the popular American mind.

Such a concept of the scruffy, urban, white-ethnic neighborhood was most clearly and consistently pushed to the American cultural consciousness in comedy texts and performances. This is perhaps most notable in the late-nineteenth and early-twentieth-century vaudeville-comedy theater circuit, where broad ethnic humor was the order of the day. In such vaudeville acts, "the core of the humor is the construction of caricature based on familiar ethnic stereotypes and linguistic humor—puns, malapropisms, double entendres, and accent-play, including broad exaggeration and misunderstandings which result from faulty pronunciation" (Mintz 20).

This ethnic humor depended on ethnic stereotypes. Germans like the Gehrigs, for example, were typed as "lazy, stodgily conservative, and of course, also dumb" (21). However, it would be a mistake to read this humor as categorically vicious and xenophobic. Enacted by performers who often belonged to the groups being stereotyped for audiences with a similar ancestral makeup, such ethnic jokes were generally perceived as "harmless fun, light amusement, harmless banter, enjoyed by all" (25). And though ethnic jokes can sometimes be intended or be seen as denigrating towards immigrant groups, scholars have argued that this tendency is "subordinate to their cognitive value, that is, to the ways in which they contribute to cultural awareness, to the process of acculturation" for both the subgroups and the culture at large (25).

Vaudeville's tradition of ethnic humor had many mass-media descendants and heirs: the Marx Brothers' films (Lieberfeld and Sanders 105) and comic strips like *The Yellow Kid* (Meyer) and later *Katzenjammer Kids* (Conolly-Smith 55–56) and *Bringing Up Father* (Soper 269–71), which focused more particularly on recent German and Irish immigrants, respectively, in stereotypical but empathetic ways. It is such texts from the turn of the century through the 1930s that *The Pride of the Yankees* draws on in its formulation of Gehrig's parents and neighborhood. Though biographer Jonathan Eig characterizes the Yorkville neighborhood in upper Manhattan where Gehrig grew up as so heavily German it "had the distinct feel of a bustling Deutschland village" (5), the filmmakers likely opted for a mixed-European feel to evoke more of an idealized "melting pot" ambience and avoid any suggestion of a balkanized ethnic enclave that might characterize the baseball hero as too German and less American.

The tone of gentle mockery common in most vaudeville and vaudeville-derivative acts is carried over in *The Pride of the Yankees,* particularly in the way the filmmakers use Gehrig's parents. In a memorable and often revisited scene depicting Lou's debut with the Yankees, Mr. Gehrig, with his thick German accent, attempts to explain the game of baseball to his wife, who goes so far as asking, as she gestures towards the bases, "Vot do zey do viz de pillows?" The comedy in this scene derives from a presumed familiarity with baseball among the viewership and Mrs. Gehrig's colorfully portrayed naïveté, but the issue of nationality—always present when Gehrig's parents are on screen—complicates the scene somewhat, giving it additional cultural meaning. Here, a presumed basic knowledge of baseball in viewers, and the lack thereof in the ethnic Mrs. Gehrig, are signifiers for "Americanness" and assimilation or the lack thereof. In sharp contrast to his parents, the Gary Cooper–portrayed Gehrig speaks with no trace of a German accent (nor the somewhat nasal New York accent of the real Gehrig) and is obviously well schooled in baseball knowledge, presumably just like the typical American audience in 1942.[14] That the young Gehrig has a collection of baseball cards, can throw the ball, and shows unexpected talent at the plate in the film's opening scene all prove the "Americanness" of this immigrants' son.

This contrast between Gehrig and his parents implies a narrative of assimilation, the cultural dimension of the social uplift central to the American dream. While never expressly putting down Gehrig's parents or the other white ethnic characters in Gehrig's neighborhood, the film continually portrays them as quaint and frequently uses them as comic relief, in contrast to the somewhat idealized, heroic, and thoroughly "American" Gehrig and his wife, Eleanor. Baseball plays a key part in Gehrig's ability to transcend his own marginal ethnic background in the film, not only because it provides the monetary means of social improvement but because, with the longstanding rhetoric of baseball as the quintessential American pastime, it offers the cultural means for climbing the social ladder as well.

The Pride of the Yankees is by no means unique in presenting the game in these ways. The theme of baseball as a tool of assimilation—or, more properly, of "Americanization"—for cultural outsiders has received ample attention in baseball-related texts ranging from academic to popular. Again, the early- to mid-twentieth-century Yankees were as rife with the sons of European immigrants as any Major League team. But it is interesting to note that the film's emphasis on Gehrig's Americanization and lack of stereotypical, perhaps negatively perceived ethnic traits are paralleled in the popular portrayal of the Yankee hero who succeeded Gehrig: Joe DiMaggio. For example, a 1939 *Life* magazine article about DiMaggio addresses his Italian heritage somewhat ambivalently. Author Noel F. Busch is happy to mock Italian Americans generally even as he praises DiMaggio individually. This is evident as he assures readers that DiMaggio speaks with no accent and somewhat condescendingly comments, "instead of olive oil or smelly bear grease, [DiMaggio] keeps his hair slick with water. He never reeks of garlic and prefers chicken chow mein to spaghetti" (69). The author's interest in promoting the ballplayer as "well adapted to most U.S. mores" is clear here. His ethnic heritage is valuable, but only as an obstacle for him to overcome.

This story in *Life*, like *The Pride of the Yankees,* wants to have its cake and eat it too, emphasizing the Euro-ethnic heritage of the baseball hero, likely for the upward-mobility narrative it conjures in American minds, while simultaneously assuring audiences that the boy is thoroughly "all American." In so doing, both texts channel two opposing views on immigrants: that they are noble individuals struggling to live the American dream, or that they are lazy, shiftless, suspect, and culturally, if not genetically, inferior to old-stock Americans. Both texts seem to take something of a middle path. Gehrig and DiMaggio are the "good kind" of immigrant, the kind that proves the validity of the American dream and become "American." In this way, the biographical narrative of these two Yankee heroes articulates the oft-celebrated American dream of upward mobility without making their hero too "un-American." In the case of Gehrig, a son of German immigrants, being portrayed as thoroughly "American" would have been particularly important in the context of World War II.

While this ambivalent, somewhat schizophrenic attitude towards ethnicity is not unique to the way Yankees players were portrayed in mass-media texts, the fact that Gehrig and DiMaggio followed the legacy of Ruth, another former-poor-boy Yankee hero with Euro-ethnic heritage, created in the popular imagination the notion of a legacy of Yankee heroes who stood as a testament to the narrative of European immigrants and the American dream while simultaneously staying firmly in the "all-American" traditional mainstream.

GEHRIG AND THE AMERICAN DREAM: ECONOMIC IMPROVEMENT

The makers of *The Pride of the Yankees* supplement Gehrig's ethnic upward-mobility narrative with numerous references to his changing financial state. While the Gehrig family's social improvement through the cultural assimilation of son Lou is told in a subtler manner, the filmmakers spell out the purely economic side of their upward mobility quite clearly. If the working-class signifiers in the film's opening scene of the boy's pickup game in the sandlot outside their tenement house are not obvious enough, the filmmakers actively impress the Gehrigs' humble economic circumstances upon viewers with Mrs. Gehrig's apology that she will have to pay the rest later when reimbursing the shopkeeper for the window Lou broke. Their lowly socioeconomic status and ambition to rise above it are later conveyed more explicitly when Mrs. Gehrig lectures her son about studying hard and taking advantage of the fabled opportunities of their new homeland. "Look at your papa, look at me. We didn't go to school and what are we? A janitor. A cook," she observes, "I want you to be somebody. . . . In this country you can be anything you want to be." Later, the film even attempts to convey the class-related social stigma Gehrig would have been subject to at Columbia University with a scene that portrays some arrogant fraternity members scoffing at their brother's suggestion that they invite the financially disadvantaged Lou to join their organization. "This fraternity has standards. You just can't ignore his family," one member opines. "Go ahead. Hang a pledge pin on him. Don't expect me to call him brother." Gehrig eventually is allowed into the fraternity but is subjected to a humiliating prank.

Later on, when his mother takes ill and they do not have the money to cover medical treatment, Lou finally opts to go against Mrs. Gehrig's wishes and drop out of the Columbia engineering program to play baseball and take the needed money offered by the Yankees. This detail closely links Lou's baseball career with economic improvement but is careful to do so in a way that highlights Gehrig as noble and self-sacrificing (even if viewers know that Gehrig really preferred baseball all along), and thus, all the more heroic, rather than merely greedy. Once his baseball career has begun, director Wood continues to focus on Gehrig's family, offering plenty of scenes that show Gehrig as breadwinner, first supporting his parents, then courting and providing for his wife, Eleanor.

In brief, Goldwyn and Wood's film shows Gehrig progressing from a humble working-class childhood to an adult role as a stable provider. There is no glitz, glamour, or excess here. Scenes featuring Gehrig and his wife on a date in eveningwear at a local carnival, followed by a dinner of "hot dogs and champagne," during their courtship, or their honeymoon at the ballpark emphasize Gehrig's humility and distances him from any kind of elitism or Jazz Age excess.[15] But Wood seems clearly interested in showing audiences that despite his humble childhood, Gehrig has turned himself into a successful man who ably fulfills the expected role of family provider. Like the issue of ethnicity, this economic uplift is also something the filmmakers wish to portray with some nuance. Gehrig is clearly aligned with the American dream narrative, but this is no rags-to-riches tale, which might give him too much of an air of elitism. This grounding of Gehrig in healthy but relatively modest economic success in the film makes an important impact on Gehrig's status as a hero and, through him, on the Yankees as a cultural icon. Like the ethnic-yet-Americanized treatment of Gehrig's minority background, the moderation projected on his economic uplift gives Gehrig an everyman quality, making him seem not so different or distant from viewers.

This "common man" quality that Gehrig attains through the modest portrayal of his upward mobility helped give the Yankees more of a populist aura. When the film was released, the Yankees had just recently won their fourth World Series in a row at the end of the 1930s and then recaptured the title that fall of '41. While not necessarily pervasive in the broader mainstream culture, this dominance had some baseball fans accusing the organization of elitism or plutocracy. Creamer even suggests that the cry "Break up the Yankees!," a phrase perhaps popularized in a 1939 Coiller's opinion piece with that title by sportswriter Gordon Cobbledick, could occasionally be heard among fans during the 1941 season (*Baseball in '41* 23). Similarly, to many the presence of owner Jacob Ruppert would always "personify the superior quality of the Yankees" (62) and contribute to the aura of wealth and elitism surrounding his club. The portrayal of Gehrig in *The Pride of the Yankees* counters this perception, presenting the Yankees as an organization that, like Gehrig, earned success through hard work and commitment.

THE PRIDE OF THE YANKEES AND POPULISM

This democratic coloring of the Yankees as a cultural icon is highlighted by the very personality and demeanor of Gehrig as portrayed by Gary Cooper. Wes D. Gehring has argued that the actor's portrayal is rooted in the American populist tradition that celebrates its belief in "the common man." Populism draws on a deep American heritage including Jefferson and Jackson, but in early-twentieth-century popular culture, as Gehring suggests, American populism was promoted by the folksy, "cracker-barrel" humorist Will Rogers and the film director Frank Capra, known for such tear-jerking celebrations of the everyman as *It's a Wonderful Life* and *Mr. Smith Goes to Washington*. Gehring views the populist narrative as a genre that typically features "a community of individuals working together for the common good" and is defined by an "optimistic belief in a world still seen as rational" (15) as well as a faith in "families, second chances, . . . traditional American icons like small town pastoral life and baseball," and above all, *"the people"* (20).

The very casting of Gary Cooper in the role of Gehrig helps establish a populist foundation for *The Pride of the Yankees*. Best known for playing the quintessential American male populist hero, the cowboy, Cooper established his rustic everyman charm in *The Virginian* (1929), one of Hollywood's first sound Westerns, and confirmed his status with his roles in *The Texan (1930), The Spoilers* (1930), *The Plainsman* (1936), *The Cowboy and the Lady* (1938), *The Westerner* (1940), and *North West Mounted Police* (1940). These cowboy roles continued after Cooper's 1942 turn in *The Pride of the Yankees* with *Along Came Jones* (1945), *Dallas* (1950), *Garden of Evil* (1954), *Vera Cruz* (1954), *Man of the West* (1958), and his memorable, Academy Award–winning performance in *High Noon* (1952). Supplementing these performances as a rural American icon were starring roles in two populist films directed by Frank Capra himself, *Mr. Deeds Goes to Town* (1936) and *Meet John Doe*

(1941), which helped make Cooper "synonymous with the mythic cinematic image of the inherently good 'aw shucks' American" (Gehring 57).

Though Cooper's baseball skills were limited, many observers commented that his well-established Hollywood persona as the American everyman made him the perfect person to play Gehrig, as "both epitomized what used to be called 'the strong silent American'" (65). As Cooper biographer Larry Swindell has noted, "Gehrig . . . had been sort of a Gary Cooper of baseball, a quiet hero much admired for his character" (238). In addition to his quiet, workmanlike demeanor, Gehrig had acquired a populist public image through his streak of 2,130 consecutive games played.

With the casting of Cooper, this everyman quality of Gehrig's biography was certainly highlighted in *The Pride of the Yankees,* but it doesn't stop there. The celebration of the common man seems to be the particular focus in several scenes of the film, with Cooper's Gehrig consistently embodying the populist theme. The key populist scene does not actually involve Gehrig, however. Relatively early in the first baseman's career with the Yankees, two sportswriters sit on a train debating the value of Gehrig, who at this point was only beginning to prove himself. One reporter, Hank Hanneman, played by Dan Duryea, criticizes Gehrig's already apparent "common man" persona, complaining, "A guy like that is a detriment to any sport. He's a boob with a batting eye. He wakes up, brushes his teeth, hikes out to the ballpark, hits the ball, hikes back to the hotel room, reads the funny papers, gargles, and goes to bed. That's personality, hm?"

The other reporter, Sam Blake—who at this point is not yet Gehrig's close friend but just an admirer—disagrees. Blake calls Gehrig "a real hero" and proceeds to give an impassioned speech that captures the essence of the film's populist theme: "Let me tell you about heroes, Hank. I've covered a lot of 'em, and I'm saying Gehrig is the best of 'em. No front-page scandals, no daffy excitements, no horn-piping in the spotlight . . . but a guy who does his job and nothing else. He lives for his job. He gets a lot of fun out of it. And fifty million other people get a lot of fun out of him, watching him do something better than anybody else ever did it before."

Here Blake not only emphasizes Gehrig's "Average Joe," working-man qualities but lauds them as virtues, despite his colleague's insistence that they make Gehrig bland. Blake then even more overtly asserts Gehrig's status as an everyman when he responds to the other writer's comeback. When Hanneman jokes that Blake might have a point "if all baseball fans were as big boobs as Gehrig," Blake again turns the insult into a virtue, asserting, "They are. The same kind of boobs as Gehrig." Implying that these so-called boobs are really the hard-working, everyday, salt-of-the-earth Americans, Blake's comment forges an important link between Gehrig and the common man. In this scene and others that follow it, the filmmakers present Gehrig as merely an average American male who has been put in the spotlight and portray him as all the better for it.

Sam Blake's thesis statement about Gehrig the everyman is supported in a variety of ways, including the wide array of humble working-class Americans who are shown celebrating while listening to his triumphs on the radio and the natural rapport Gehrig is shown to have with kids. Gehrig's folksy manner of speech serves as another signifier of his everyman quality. When explaining his decision to cut the "apron strings" and deemphasize the role in his life of his sometimes-domineering mother in favor of his then-fiancée, he intones, "You can't run a baseball team with two captains or a household with two bosses. There's only going to be one boss in this house." This sort of corny baseball metaphor is similarly employed later when Gehrig asks the doctor to be forthright with him about his potentially fatal diagnosis. "Go ahead, Doc; I'm a man who likes to know his batting average," he implores. "Give it to me straight . . . is it three strikes, Doc?" While more baseball-centric in *The Pride of the Yankees*, Gehrig's diction in the film recalls Cooper's earlier turns in "common man" roles in Westerns and Capra-directed films, as well as the tradition of folk wisdom found in the likes of *The Adventures of Huckleberry Finn*—such rustic, common-sense truths as, "I don't take no stock in dead people" (Twain 33) or "You can't pray a lie" (202)—and typified in the early twentieth century by Will Rogers. In sum, the filmmakers present Cooper's Gehrig as not just the "pride of the Yankees" but the pride of "the people" as well.

Gehrig's populist image, as emphasized by the film, is particularly important for the impact it had on the perception of the Yankees as a whole. When the film was released in the summer of 1942, in the wake of five Yankee World Series titles in six years, public resentment of the Yankees' "elitism" would have been in ample supply. The film's touting of Gehrig the everyman as "the pride of the Yankees," however, provided a significant counterpoint to this tendency. Though the Yankees certainly were not the only ball club with deep coffers, the reality is that this abundance of funds contributed significantly to the team's success by providing funds for scouting and signing players. No such factors are addressed in *The Pride of the Yankees*. On the contrary, the film implies that the Yankees only achieved their success through the hard work, dedication, and sportsmanship of "Average Joes" like Gehrig. This paradox of populist success replicates the "upward mobility" narrative of the American dream and allows the Yankees' cultural meaning to somehow encompass both elite excellence and the humble everyman.

THE PRIDE OF THE YANKEES AND AMERICAN MASCULINITY

The issue of masculinity is also related to Gehrig's embodiment of the American dream narrative and his status as a populist icon. The way Cooper's Gehrig fills both of these roles coincides significantly with the most prevalent forms of twentieth-century American masculinity, making the film's portrayal of the Yankee hero also an icon of mainstream manhood in some respects. Unlike his embodiment of the American dream and populism, which are more or less complete, however, Gehrig's masculinity as portrayed in *The Pride of the Yankees* deviates in a few significant ways from the mid-twentieth-century norms. These deviations—his shyness, maternal devotion, and emotional sensitivity—are largely rooted in the facts of Gehrig's biography and serve to temper and add nuance to, but not eclipse, the film's portrayal of the slugger as a "self-made man," a man of courage, a successful team leader, and a capable breadwinner and head of family, making him a "model" male in many regards. And through this portrayal, steady manliness is cemented as a quality of the prototypical Yankee hero as well.

Like other scholars of American masculinity, Michael Kimmel has stressed that "manhood is not the manifestation of an inner essence," as is sometimes perceived popularly, but is "socially constructed," something that one performs and attempts (or not) to live up to (*Manhood in America* 81). According to Kimmel, these expectations are largely derived from "participation in the market place . . . based on homosocial competition" with other men, which becomes a key proving ground for American males (82).

Perhaps because of the nation's relatively recent agrarian or frontier past, there exists a need for American men to prove themselves, show that they can be self-sustaining and independent, like a homesteader living on the edge of the wilderness, apart from any supportive community. It is from this tradition that Kentucky senator Henry Clay coined the laudatory informal title of "self-made man" in 1832, a phrase that not only gestures towards the "up-by-his-bootstraps" narrative of the American dream but also describes the gendered social expectations of every American man: he must "make" himself by himself (82).

In this regard, Gehrig as he appears in *The Pride of the Yankees* passes the test of American masculinity with flying colors. The film validates Gehrig's masculinity with Cooper portraying the ballplayer as an unequivocal self-made man. With his baseball paycheck, Gehrig not only lifts himself out of poverty but his parents as well, including paying for his sick mother's medical bills. In this way he succeeds as a specimen of masculinity where his father failed.[16] Later, he takes on the more traditional form of American breadwinner after marrying Eleanor. Gehrig's role as provider is emphasized in one particular sequence of scenes that depicts him leaving home, kissing his wife goodbye, and heading off to the ballpark, to return home later and be asked how his day went. This enactment of the script of a typical day in twentieth-century American domesticity in a baseball setting not only emphasizes Gehrig's competency as a breadwinning husband but also emphasizes the workmanlike mentality he has towards his job.

This quality of dependability and consistency was emphasized in the popular perception of the real Gehrig prior to the film, with his nickname "The Iron Horse" and his renown for setting the record for consecutive games played, something not lost on the filmmakers who devote screen time to both. Again, the financial success Gehrig achieves through his "up-by-his-bootstraps" journey to becoming a self-made man is relatively modest. He proves a dependable provider and even achieves fame, but nothing resembling glamorous wealth. In fact, such things are eschewed, for, while not inconsistent with the social measure of self-made manhood, such trappings of elitism would compromise Gehrig's position as a populist hero. On the baseball field, however, Gehrig's victories, free from any uncomfortable class connotations, can be unrestrained. As both an individual player and leader of the Yankees, Gehrig proves even more successful than he did in baseball's marketplace, a fact the filmmakers emphasize with anecdotes of dramatic home runs as well as a time-lapse scene depicting the accumulation of trophies on the Gehrigs' mantle, polished and added to, appropriately, by a female hand.

Unlike the modern capitalist marketplace, the realm of sport also has the additional bonus of being a *physical* proving ground, thus aligning Gehrig and his compatriots with the frontiersman and cowboys of America's past who also showed themselves to be "self-made men" in more physical ways. Thus, as a self-made man, Gehrig could hardly be portrayed as more successful in *The Pride of the Yankees*. As such, this representation renders him a "true man" by twentieth-century cultural standards and lends a masculine air to the success synonymous with the Yankees.

While Gehrig is certainly presented as adequate as a self-made man, Kimmel's perspective on the homosocial marketplace environment is more than about proving one can be self-sustaining and provide for a family; it also includes successful competition with other men. With regard to the "proving ground" of American manhood, Kimmel notes that "no sooner is masculinity proved than it is again questioned and must be proved again—constant, relentless, unachievable" (*Manhood in America* 82). This constant need to prove oneself makes competition among men—not merely achieving something, but achieving more and achieving it faster than other men—a key quality in American male culture. Thus, another man's success is frequently felt as a threat to one's own manhood. One of the outgrowths of this culture of "homosocial competition" is what Kimmel describes as "the flight from the feminine"—the rejection of the supposedly "feminine" traits of "nurturance, compassion, and tenderness" as a sign of weakness (85). Kimmel cites "the drive to repudiate the mother" as especially important for a young man to declare his masculine autonomy (85). Eventually, demonstrating power over women, such as one's wife, becomes an important cultural sign of "true" manhood ("Masculinity as Homophobia" 90).

On baseball's playing field, both Gehrig and the Yankees were an unqualified success with regard to "homosocial competition." With his two Most Valuable Player awards, seven selections to the All-Star Team, and six World Series championships with the Yankees, Gehrig was, like his team, no stranger to being considered "the best" in the world of baseball. This fact is certainly not omitted in Sam Wood's film, as it features moments designed to show Gehrig's supremacy as a ballplayer, including the memorable scenario with the sick boy in which Gehrig beats teammate Babe Ruth at his own home-run game. Likewise, the accumulating-trophy scene, the newspaper-headline montage, and the film's closing scenes at Yankee Stadium implicitly celebrate the New York club as professional baseball's unequivocal best. With Kimmel's framework in mind, one sees that this success over other players and teams certainly has its "manly" connotations, perhaps particularly in the case of the Yankees and the team's then-recent dominance from 1936 to 1939. This success lends an "alpha male" connotation to the Yankees and all who associate themselves with the organization, including fans.

Other aspects of Gehrig's life and personality as portrayed in *The Pride of the Yankees,* however, challenge his fulfillment of this aggressive and competitive facet of American masculinity. This is especially apparent in scenes taking place off the baseball field, where twice Gehrig is the target of pranks by a group of his male peers, effectively making him the butt of a joke in front of a broader male social group. In addition to the straw-hat hazing episode with the Yankees in his rookie year, in college his fraternity brothers conspire with a co-ed to lead on the wallflower Gehrig so that they can later mock his awkwardness in romance by parroting and parodying his conversation with her. "You're the one that's wonderful . . . ," they mockingly banter with Lou in earshot the morning after, "will you remember me?" While such scenes may enhance Gehrig's underdog quality for viewers, they certainly do not make him appear manlier by most cultural standards in mid-twentieth-century America.

Perhaps even more damaging in this regard is the portrayal of Gehrig's relationship with his somewhat controlling mother. The close connection between the real Gehrig and his mother is well-established. Eig summed things up succinctly: "If there were a Hall of Fame for mama's boys, Gehrig would have been a shoo-in" (12). The filmmakers showed real nerve for portraying this in the movie, especially in scenes depicting Gehrig as obviously bending his own will to his mother's wishes in seeking a career as a college-educated engineer instead of pursuing his true love, baseball. Likewise, as late as college, Mrs. Gehrig remains Lou's "best girl." This "mama's boy" quality is completely abandoned only when Gehrig's fiancée becomes the new woman in his life.

But even after marriage, the film is still somewhat ambivalent about Gehrig's desire and ability to keep power over the women in his life, an impulse Kimmel's discussion of masculinity suggests he should feel. In many ways, Eleanor is portrayed as Gehrig's equal, especially during their courtship, when she engages in playful and flirtatious verbal banter in the style of "screwball" romantic comedies that were Hollywood staples of the period, such as *It Happened One Night* (1934), *Bringing Up Baby* (1938), *The Philadelphia Story* (1940), and *Woman of the Year* (1942). For instance, when a romantically confused Gehrig sheepishly asks Eleanor, "Aren't you my girl?," she teases him coyly, "Why Lou, I don't know what you mean by your girl. Your best girl? Is that what you mean? Why, whatever gave you that idea?" Later in the conversation, as they discuss Gehrig's pending road trip, she extends his misery, sighing, "I wonder if I'm going to miss you." "Can't you find out before I go?" the thoroughly-in-love and defenseless Gehrig responds. "Nope," she says dryly. "Isn't that too bad? Why is it like that?" Without a witty retort, Gehrig cannot play Spencer Tracy or Cary Grant to Eleanor's Hepburn-like barbs. As evidenced in this dialogue, in many ways Eleanor is actually in the driver's seat in their relationship, far from the alpha-male standard of which Kimmel speaks.

After their marriage, however, while her verbal bantering continues to some extent, the former socialite Eleanor conspicuously becomes a devoted housewife whose main occupation is to support her husband emotionally—to be "the greatest fan a man ever had," as Gehrig puts it. After marrying, the former Miss Eleanor Twitchell, it seems, clearly lives for her husband, a fact symbolized by the care she takes as curator of the scrapbook that memorializes Gehrig and the Yankees' achievements and by Gehrig's anniversary gift to her: a bracelet made out of award pins he won as a ballplayer. Thus, while Gehrig may have been something of a mama's boy exuding a sensitive shyness, the film nonetheless shows him as quite capably upholding the gendered domestic role of "head of household" in nearly every sense of the term.

This progression from the stereotypical mama's boy to patriarchal head of family is significant. Paralleling his climb from his impoverished, ethnic origins to financial success and baseball glory, Gehrig's assumption of normative masculine domestic roles after his years deferring to the wishes of his mother can be read as an emphasis on Gehrig's growth as a man. The film depicts similar progress in his experience with the all-male social sphere. Just as Gehrig eventually takes on a more empowered role in his relationships with women, this man who was once shown to be the butt of jokes from his male peers is portrayed as gaining the considerable respect of his Yankee teammates and becoming the team captain to whom the other players defer in the clubhouse. While Gehrig may come off as overly sensitive and lacking in confidence in many areas for the tastes of some mid-twentieth-century viewers, particularly the men, *The Pride of the Yankees* portrays him growing into a full-fledged man by film's end, and he perhaps even gains additional audience respect for the progress he makes.

Furthermore, it should be noted that many of the hallmarks of American male culture that Kimmel identifies, while not inaccurate, have often been considered to be immoral and unethical behavior. While many men's lives may have indeed been shaped by the cultural pressures to succeed, prove one's superiority to other men, eschew "feminine" characteristics, and dominate actual women, the fact remains that all these tendencies have never been universally praised in every sphere of American culture. This is particularly true of mid-twentieth-century Hollywood films intended for a broad, mixed-gender audience. And because *The Pride of the Yankees* is not merely a sports film but one with many elements of a romantic comedy, Cooper's portrayal of Gehrig must not only fill the role of model male specimen but make him a convincing romantic lead as well. As such, Gehrig's "soft heart" was likely viewed by many as a positive quality and his shyness as an endearing trait that he had to overcome to "get the girl." His eventual assumption of the patriarchal role reassures audiences of the stability of midcentury gender norms (regardless of the stability of such gender roles in reality), but many of the sensitive "feminine" qualities remain part of Gehrig's character throughout the film, keeping him a sympathetic romantic lead and perhaps promoting a model of moral behavior. While not necessarily consistent with the competitive ethos of the male realm of homosocial competition, Gehrig's sensitivity and lack of aggression uphold the Judeo-Christian ethical ideals and the broader American public discourse of which these ideals were a significant part at the time.

Finally, the film's true-to-life tragic conclusion provides a unique opportunity for Cooper's Gehrig to reassert his masculinity. Death represents the ultimate challenge for a male individual's life, as it is the one obstacle or foe that cannot be "beaten." It certainly poses an apparently overwhelming threat to the competitive, win-at-all-costs cultural pressure the American male faces. The world of sports itself provides a good example of perhaps the only script for how to deal with unavoidable defeat in a manly way: to face it honestly with no complaining or "effeminate" whining, while keeping any emotions of grief or sadness from being expressed outwardly. The final act of *The Pride of the Yankees* depicts Gehrig as facing his fatal diagnosis in precisely this manner. When Lou and Eleanor meet after his diagnosis, Eleanor is the only one to shed tears. And in the film's signature scene, Gehrig's Yankee Stadium speech, while others lose their composure, Lou fights back his tears and remains ever the image of strength and bravery. Even the text of his famous speech asserts a manly attitude towards death. He refutes the impulse to complain or ask, "why me?," through his famous rebuttal towards those who "say [he's] had a bad break," claiming that he "considers [himself] the luckiest man on the face of the Earth." His courage is then visually symbolized by his resolute walk into the shadows in the Yankee clubhouse.

The courage with which Gehrig faces his tragic death are even compared to that of a quintessential symbol of American manhood, the soldier, in an opening crawl text that sets the stage for the entire film. It reads, "He faced death with that same valor and fortitude that has been displayed by thousands of young Americans on far-flung fields of battle. He left behind him a memory of courage and devotion that will ever be an inspiration to all men." This reference to courage in battle naturally would have held substantial emotional significance for audiences in the summer of 1942, when the U.S. involvement in the Second World War was only about seven months old. Positioned at the very beginning of the film, the comparison of Gehrig with soldiers who fought in American wars provides audiences with the take-home message they should be looking for even before the story starts. Thus, as per the film's own decree, even given the substantial screen time devoted to Gehrig's journey of upward mobility and the elements of screwball romantic comedy that color the film, it is Gehrig's steady courage while facing death that viewers focus on and remember the most, leaving no doubt about the baseball hero's status as a "real man."

THE PRIDE OF THE YANKEES AND NATIONALISM

This direct comparison of Gehrig to American soldiers does more than just bolster his masculine credentials, however. It also metaphorically wraps the Yankee hero in the American flag, nationalizing his life narrative. It puts a distinct "American" stamp on Gehrig and, through him, on the Yankees. While Gehrig's narrative of upward mobility, his populist everyman qualities, and even his ultimately triumphant masculinity all have ties to traditional American institutions and values—namely, democracy and the capitalist economic system—this connection made to the military provides a more tangible, material evocation of the nation state that the mass audience would recognize.

Thus, the opening crawl text makes the vital tie between the "American way of life" that Gehrig embodies and more overt signifiers of the nation and its government. Gehrig as portrayed by Gary Cooper becomes not just a baseball hero but a national hero. The film transforms him into something of a martyr for what was then still a young world war. Gehrig, cut down tragically in the prime of life like so many soldiers, embodies the "American way of life" that those soldiers were celebrated as defending and spreading to other parts of the world. And as Gehrig, the so-called pride of the Yankees, is shown to be the quintessential American hero, or the pride of America, the Yankees, with their traditions of rags-to-riches heroes and sustained excellence on the field, become synonymous with American greatness. In *The Pride of the Yankees*, the team whose name always gestured towards nationalism officially takes on that role in earnest.

Chapter Three
"THINK OF THE GREAT DIMAGGIO"

Joe DiMaggio and the Mythic Dimension
of Yankee Success in the Postwar Era

*I*n the brief period surrounding his ballyhooed 1939 retirement and the release of *The Pride of the Yankees* in 1942, Lou Gehrig enjoyed—largely posthumously—a prominent cultural status that he never had during his more unsung days as a player. But prior to and following this surprise attention the American public gave to Gehrig and his memory, another Yankee hero was the toast of New York. In his 1936 rookie year he was hailed as the man to replace the void left by Ruth. In the year in which Gehrig died, 1941, this player's exploits would inspire a hit pop song. And in the years following World War II, after the public memory of Gary Cooper's saintly Hollywood Lou Gehrig had faded somewhat, American sportswriters would transform the player into a virtual demigod. This Yankee was centerfielder Joe

DiMaggio, the man who would carry the mantle of Yankee heroism into the postwar era and bring it to new mythic heights.

DiMaggio, nicknamed "The Yankee Clipper" for his graceful style of play, first joined the Yankees in 1936 and made an immediate impact, eclipsing the taciturn Gehrig in terms of fan popularity. As biographer Richard Ben Cramer has explained, while Gehrig lacked "color" in the public imagination, DiMaggio, by contrast,

> was aware from the first moment, aware at every moment, of the hero game. He was alive to the power of the camera: he made himself available, he could smile, and he knew when to smile. With writers he was as alert, as poised and pent as he was in center field. . . .
>
> Joe didn't have to say much. Any words from him were like a confidence that he bestowed, not to be misused. . . . He could bring them in—just enough—so they could play the big game together. (110–11)

While the established elder statesman Gehrig and the newcomer DiMaggio both played vital roles in the Yankees' unprecedented string of four World Series victories in a row from 1936 to 1939, prior to Gehrig's diagnosis, death, and Hollywood hagiography, it was DiMaggio's quiet magnetism that truly excited sportswriters and the public.[1] As Cramer puts it, in the year 1941, when Gehrig died and Cooper, Sam Goldwyn, and Sam Wood were creating the lionizing *The Pride of the Yankees*, "at that time, in the real world, the Pride of the Yanks was Joe" (169).

Popularly portrayed in a manner that encompassed both the familiar populist heroism of Gehrig and a new mythic heroism, Joe DiMaggio eventually became a national idol who served to remind America of its own greatness in the wake of World War II. This unique everyman/superman duality of character is evident in the journalistic reporting of his hitting streak in 1941 and his dramatic comeback from injury in 1949. The centerfielder's double-faceted public image is even more apparent, however, in two very different books published in the early postwar period, DiMaggio's youth-oriented autobiography *Lucky to Be a Yankee* (1946) and Ernest Hemingway's novella *The Old Man and the Sea* (1952). Through these texts DiMaggio's public heroism helped transform the Yankees into an icon of America's national success story, particularly in the postwar period of prosperity and world power. The mythic element of DiMaggio's public persona characterized Yankee success as decreed by destiny, emblematic of the more broadly prevailing cultural notions about American prosperity and power as divinely ordained.

DIMAGGIO AS ALL-AMERICAN POPULIST HERO

It took a tragic diagnosis with a mysterious terminal illness and a popular film eulogy to prevent Lou Gehrig from being eclipsed by Joe DiMaggio. And as baseball fans in the year of the film's release, 1942, surveyed the current Ruth-less and Gehrig-less Yankees for the values lauded in Gehrig by the film, it was that very same DiMaggio who stood out as most representative of the Yankee standard of personal excellence. In many respects DiMaggio bore a resemblance to Gehrig. His background as the son of a poor Sicilian fisherman paralleled Gehrig's as an iconic embodiment of the American dream of upward mobility for European immigrants. Like Gehrig, DiMaggio was a quiet individual who preferred to let his performance on the field speak for itself. Similarly, DiMaggio's no-nonsense attitude, willingness to play through injury, and ability to stay out of the scandal sheets were consistent with the workaday populist values praised in *The Pride of the Yankees*.[2]

Furthermore, like Gehrig's famous feat of playing in 2,130 consecutive games, DiMaggio's signature claim to baseball fame also bolsters his status as a populist hero. In 1941 DiMaggio scored at least one base hit in a streak of fifty-six consecutive games, besting the previous record by twelve games. Like Gehrig's feat, this record testifies to DiMaggio's consistency, his insistence on putting forth his maximum effort day in and day out. Compare this to the occasional Ruthian eruption of superhuman strength associated with home-run hitters. With this consistency, DiMaggio seemed to exhibit a workmanlike quality that effectively complemented Gehrig's legacy and gave further evidence to the notion promoted in *The Pride of the Yankees* that the ball club found success through their work ethic. Thus, DiMaggio helped cement the club's status as a symbol of the American dream of upward mobility through hard work and patience. Just as Gehrig and DiMaggio seemed to prove that the Protestant work ethic could bring the sons of immigrants socioeconomic uplift, the Yankee teams they led seemed to prove it could bring unmatched baseball glory.

DIMAGGIO AS MYTHIC HERO

In addition to this populist image, however, DiMaggio's on-field exploits were also viewed as possessing an element of the superhuman. In the words of biographer Jerome Charyn, "Babe Ruth was loved; Ty Cobb was reviled. Joe DiMaggio was revered, looked upon with an almost religious awe. He was the first saint of baseball when baseball itself was a religion" (1). His fifty-six-game hitting streak serves as an illustrative example. The streak essentially consisted of having one minor success every day, a contrast to the more grandiose and often more recognized contributions such as Ruth's trademark home runs. Nevertheless, the fact remains that achieving the minor success of a base hit *every* day is a very difficult thing to do. A popular saying about baseball goes something like this: baseball is the only game in which someone is thought of as doing very well when they fail seven out of ten times, a reference to the long-held standard of excellence, the .300 batting average, or three hits for every ten batting opportunities. Thus, given about four chances to hit every game, to find success every day for fifty-six games in a row is no small feat. Famed evolutionary biologist, Yankee fan, and baseball "statistical maven" Stephen Jay Gould described the streak as "the greatest accomplishment in the history of baseball, if not all modern sport" (175). This element of defying the odds, combined with the workmanlike, day-by-day nature of the record, has caused DiMaggio's streak to carry both populist *and* superhuman connotations.

This everyman/superman tension is a common theme in the public's perception of DiMaggio. He was consistently described as "born to play baseball" as if he had a divine gift. The terms "grace," "beauty," and "perfection" were often employed to describe DiMaggio's play. As journalist David Halberstam put it, "DiMaggio complemented his natural athletic ability with astonishing physical grace. He played the outfield, he ran the bases, and he batted not just effectively but with rare style. He would glide rather than run, it seemed, always smooth, always ending up where he wanted to be just when he wanted to be there" (*Summer of '49* 46).

Rival Ted Williams once said that "DiMaggio even looks good striking out" (qtd. in Halberstam, *Summer of '49* 47). DiMaggio supplemented this "natural" yet otherworldly "grace" with a desire to play through injuries, which resulted in a large number of "miraculous" comebacks and narratives of self-sacrifice surrounding his career.

This mythical dimension to DiMaggio's public persona recalls the work of a scholar who was roughly the Yankee centerfielder's contemporary: Joseph Campbell. Campbell (1908–1987), an American scholar who studied legendary and mythic narratives of disparate world cultures, argued for a common narrative structure in these myths. He described this "same shape-shifting yet marvelously constant story" he perceived as the *monomyth* (*The Hero with a Thousand Faces* 3). Heavily influenced by Carl Jung, a Swiss psychologist and theorist of archetypes and the so-called collective unconscious, Campbell saw this monomyth in pseudo-religious terms, believing it to be "the secret opening through which the inexhaustible energies of the cosmos pour into the human cultural manifestation" (3). In Campbell's most basic description of the narrative pattern he considered timeless and universal, "A Hero ventures forth from the world of common day into a region of supernatural wonder: fabulous forces are there encountered and a decisive victory is won: the hero comes back from this mysterious adventure with the power to bestow boons on his fellow man" (30).

Many recent scholars have been critical of Campbell's "tendency to think in generic terms" and to oversimplify the differences between cultural traditions, as well as his willingness to allow his own personal spiritualism to influence writing presented as academic (Ellwood x–xii). The fact remains, however, that Campbell identifies a basic narrative pattern—centered on a single heroic figure who delivers or saves his or her (but usually *his*) people—that has been prevalent and influential throughout much of Western culture. Such narratives include stories foundational to the Western tradition like those of Gilgamesh, Beowulf, Moses, Hercules, Jesus, and King Arthur. Even the popular narratives about historical American figures such as George Washington and Abraham Lincoln follow Campbell's pattern, as do more contemporary mass-media texts including the cowboy and superhero narrative genres, the Harry Potter books, and the *Star Wars* film series, which creator George Lucas partially based on Campbell's work and which

Campbell himself held up as a quintessential example of his monomyth (*The Power of Myth* 177–79). If nothing else, Campbell's work and the continuity it posits between these ancient and contemporary narratives at least help explain the profound popularity of these latter stories. Whether or not such stories provide a "secret opening" to the "energies of the cosmos," they do represent a narrative pattern that Americans have certainly grown accustomed to consuming.

These more recent, popular narratives that share structural qualities with the pattern Campbell believed to be universal are particularly relevant as they gesture towards the possibility of including the heroes of modern sport in this tradition of Western heroes. Though Campbell himself never wrote about sports figures, he firmly believed in the importance of finding modern examples of such heroic figures to help render "the modern world spiritually significant" (388). With his proven ability to "bestow boons" (including nine World Series championships) on his fellow Yankees and, in a broader sense, on baseball fans in general, with his impressive clutch performances, and with the American public's tendency to view these heroics through a superhuman or supernatural lens, Joe DiMaggio easily fits into Campbell's monomyth tradition of heroism. And perhaps more important, the line Campbell traces between such modern iterations of heroism and the ancient heroic narratives helps illuminate the nature of Americans' fascination with DiMaggio and the influence his career had on the making of a cultural icon.

In his history-cum-memoir about the last Major League Baseball season before World War II, *Baseball in '41*, Robert W. Creamer asserts that DiMaggio's popular persona did not always have this mythic, superhuman dimension, even as far into his career as the beginning of the memorable 1941 season. His comments are revealing about the evolution of DiMaggio's mythic heroism. For Creamer, "the dignity and grace of [DiMaggio] over the forty years since he quit baseball, combined with story after story about his accomplishments on the diamond, have created an indelible image of perfection" (12) that did not exist earlier in his career. More specifically, Creamer mentions two events of particular importance to the formation of DiMaggio's superhuman persona in the American public eye: the 1941 hitting streak and his dramatic comeback from injury in the middle of the 1949 season (12).

Considering the difficulty of the task of hitting safely in fifty-six games in a row, the fascination and outright awe with which Americans closely followed

DiMaggio's streak is somewhat understandable. Indicative of this adulation are the tributes paid to the Yankee Clipper in commemoration of his feat. In the year of the streak (when DiMaggio also won the league's Most Valuable Player award and the Yankees another World Series title), Alan Courtney and Ben Horner composed pop-song lyrics about the Clipper and his streak that bandleader Les Brown and his orchestra brought to life as "Joltin' Joe DiMaggio" (*Baseball Almanac*). While subject to the hyperbole typical of pop songs, "Joltin' Joe" is revealing for the praise it heaps upon the Yankee hero and for the way it describes Americans' fascination with the streak: "He started baseball's famous streak / That's got us all aglow . . . Joe, Joe DiMaggio / We want you on our side . . . From coast to coast that's all you'll hear / Of Joe the one-man show / He's glorified the horsehide sphere / Joltin' Joe DiMaggio." It then prophesies, "He'll live in baseball's Hall of Fame / He got there blow by blow / Our kids will tell their kids his name / Joltin' Joe DiMaggio." One line particularly speaks to the everyman/superhuman paradox DiMaggio embodied. "He's just a man and not a freak," the song insists, asserting the hero's mere humanity while simultaneously acknowledging that it is scarcely believable he is just a man.

Similarly, the September 29, 1941, issue of *Life* magazine featured a color reproduction of an original painting by Edward Laning depicting what the magazine called "the greatest moment in big-league baseball in 1941": DiMaggio tying the previous hit-streak record of forty-four. Laning's painting shows DiMaggio in a follow-through motion of the famous hit, with his characteristic wide stance. DiMaggio is depicted from the point of view of the grandstand, distant but at the painting's focal point. The wild enthusiasm of the earthy, backlit crowd dominates the canvas's foreground, but their collective gaze directs our eyes to DiMaggio, so small he could be anonymous but exuding his fabled godlike confidence and grace with his manly frame and fluid stride. Overhead, Yankee Stadium's iconic decorative frieze complements the crowd in the foreground to form a visual frame around the conquering hero, fusing the man, the Yankee tradition, and the awestruck masses in a moment of triumph.

While the contents of this jazzy pop song and Norman Rockwellesque painting are telling about how the public viewed and utilized DiMaggio's heroism, perhaps even more telling is the very fact that they exist. In these two works, DiMaggio becomes a muse for the inspiration of American artists. With Goldwyn and Wood's populist *The Pride of the Yankees* still one year away, such tokens of adulation had not been offered to a baseball player since Babe Ruth. Furthermore, these DiMaggio-inspired works more firmly established his credentials as a mythic hero. Like Hercules, Arthur, and Jesus before him, DiMaggio was now the subject of "poetry" and "art," or at least their mass-culture equivalents.

MYTHIC HEROISM AND DIMAGGIO'S 1949 COMEBACK

While the 1941 hitting streak is perhaps most instrumental in awakening the American public to the idea that DiMaggio was somehow more than just a baseball player, his dramatic comeback from injury in 1949 secured his status as a modern American mythic hero in the Joseph Campbell vein. During much of the 1948 season, DiMaggio, who had been susceptible to injury throughout his career, struggled with a painful bone spur in his heel, a problem he hoped to clear up in the off-season. After an operation and attention from the best medical experts the United States had to offer, DiMaggio was still in great pain, leading many, including the Clipper himself, to wonder whether his baseball career might be over. But in late June, with the season half over and the DiMaggio-less Yankees in a pennant race with their surging archrivals, the Boston Red Sox, the acute pain in his heel was suddenly all but gone. DiMaggio unexpectedly flew up to Boston's Fenway Park for the Yankees' three-game stand with the Red Sox and proceeded to defeat their rival seemingly singlehandedly with four decisive home runs in three games, including one that cleared Fenway's famed thirty-foot-high "Green Monster" left-field wall and dramatically clanged off the steel post holding the massive stadium light fixture as if it were some kind of omen (Cramer 266–69; Halberstam, *Summer of '49* 162–64).

The nation's sportswriters struggled for words adequate to describe DiMaggio's dramatic comeback. The article from the *New York World-Telegram* on the third successive day of DiMaggio's comeback shows both enthusiasm and awe: "Once more Joe's flaming spirit, his flair for coming through against odds, his penchant for the dramatic achievement and consummate showmanship were stressed as he drove the ball for three runs, and won for the Yankees by 6 to 3" (qtd. in Smith 92). Perhaps even more revealing in this regard is the August 1, 1949, issue of *Life* magazine, which featured a close-up of DiMaggio on its cover with the accompanying headline "My Greatest Comeback."[3] The article inside, titled "It's Great to Be Back," provides a firsthand account of the drama by DiMaggio himself with, biographer Cramer assures us, the assistance of a ghostwriter (270). DiMaggio's account was preceded by a brief introduction that illustrates the impact of this episode on his public profile:

> During the week of June 26th a $100,000-a-year baseball player named Joe DiMaggio—a shy and retiring young man who up to then had been noted chiefly for his easy grace in the outfield and his mechanical efficiency at punching out base hits—suddenly became a national hero. After being out for nearly half the season with a bad heel that threatened at times to end his career, he got back into uniform and—in perfect fairy-tale fashion—began breaking up game after game by hitting the ball out of the park.
>
> It was one of the most heartwarming comebacks in all sports history and from one end of the country to the other it became the summer's prime topic of conversation, even among people who never saw a game in their lives. DiMaggio had always been a great player, and now he took his place in that select circle of athletes, like Babe Ruth and Jack Dempsey, who are not only admired but also beloved. (66)

Life's coronation-like tone here is all the more significant considering the magazine's general-interest focus and its comments about the event registering outside the confines of sports fandom and emotionally influencing Americans in a broader way.

It is important to note the role the Yankees played in this improbable comeback drama.[4] As the entity that DiMaggio saved from defeat and led to miraculous victory, the Yankees played the most obvious role of the "fellow man" in Campbell's structural framework, the community upon which the returning hero "bestows [his] boon." But just as DiMaggio literally brought victory to the Yankees on the baseball diamond, he also brought emotional, psychological, and spiritual victory to not just Yankee fans but potentially all baseball fans (with the probable exception of Red Sox supporters) and all Americans by providing them with a hero figure through his seemingly superhuman achievements that become a "boon" of inspiration and hope in an otherwise humdrum world. As Cramer retrospectively put it, "This wasn't New York news, but world news. It wasn't about what pitch the Clipper hit ... nor even three games.... This wasn't about Boston eight games back—it wasn't about the pennant race. This wasn't just baseball! It was the greatest comeback in the history of sport! This was—this was ... divine" (269–70).

This mythic and religious language used to describe the DiMaggio-led Yankee victories makes it seem like the team was *destined* to win the pennant that year.[5] In this regard, the New York club paralleled the nation itself in 1949, still fresh from victory in World War II and combating communism in their role as a new world power. To many Americans, the United States' destiny of success, like that of DiMaggio and the Yankees, seemed divinely appointed. This parallel contributed to an increasing tendency to view the Yankees as the embodiment of the triumphant American nation itself, as earlier hinted at in the comparison of Gehrig with American soldiers *in The Pride of the Yankees*.

The narrative pattern of overcoming trials and seemingly insurmountable setbacks featured in this DiMaggio-Yankees saga is common to the Western tradition of hero stories. Campbell includes this "succession of trials" as a hallmark of his monomyth hero narrative (97). More particularly, Campbell focuses on a single culminating trial that enables the hero to truly realize his or her superhuman potential or divine calling. Sometimes this takes the form of a symbolic or literal death followed by an empowered rebirth, with the New Testament narrative of the crucifixion and resurrection of Jesus as the most obvious example. Referencing the biblical story of Jonah, Campbell calls this transformative period of trial as "the belly of the whale" (90).

The narrative account DiMaggio and his ghostwriter provided of his experience with injury and return to the Yankees takes on this "belly of the whale" structure of symbolic death and rebirth. It describes DiMaggio's period of injury as follows:

Sitting in my room I sometimes thought, "Why try to be an athlete at all?" I've had a lot of trouble—spurs on both heels, bad knees, an operation that left two scars on my throwing arm, a Charley horse that made my left thigh knot up big as a cantaloupe, even stomach ulcers. . . . When it piles up like that you begin to wonder.

At night I had trouble going to sleep. If my playing career was over, what was I going to do? Lying awake in bed at night, sometimes until 4 or 5 in the morning, I figured out at least a half dozen careers. (68–69)

Here DiMaggio's sleepless nights as he feared the end of his baseball career easily constitute a metaphoric death, which is played for dramatic contrast with his triumphant return. First, the centerfielder's improvement in health is described in miraculous terms: "One morning I stepped out of bed, expecting the pain to shoot through my heel as usual. Nothing happened. I felt the heel with my hand; it was no longer hot. . . . It was cool" (69). While the humble, everyman tone of the piece prevents DiMaggio from reveling too much in his surprise triumph against the Red Sox, he does give a significant account of the public's adoring reaction to the return of this baseball messiah, back from the dead:

Back at Yankee Stadium it was almost embarrassing. The home town fans seemed to want me to get a hit even more than I did myself—and when I flied out they seemed to be more disappointed than I was. The kids started running out on the field for my autograph. I didn't exactly know what to do. . . . One night at least 30 of them ran out, scooting from the left, right and middle trying to get past the guards. . . . In a way fans have been much too generous. . . . Next day everyone was saying that I was a hero for risking my heel on a play like that. . . . Well, that sort of thing makes you feel funny, and sometimes you wonder how you can ever live up to it—but it's nice. (72)

This public outpouring of adulation is counterbalanced by the tone of humility that DiMaggio's narrative takes, striking an equilibrium between the superhuman status the hero has just earned and his everyman roots.

These humble origins by no means diminish his mythic heroism. In fact, Campbell describes an utterly average or even a below-average social background as common to heroes of Western narratives, writing that mythic heroes often begin life as, or spend part of it disguised as, "the despised one, or the handicapped: the abused youngest son or daughter, the orphan, stepchild, ugly duckling, or squire of low degree" (325–26). Such humble origins strengthen the hero's connections with the people he will lead, protect, and/or save, with prominent examples being Jesus, the stable-born carpenter's son; Malory's King Arthur, an unassuming foster son unaware of his royal blood until he removes the enchanted sword from the stone; or even Superman's alter ego, the clumsy and dull Clark Kent. With this in mind, DiMaggio's humble origins as a poor immigrant fisherman's son and his populist qualities—which seem to persist even as the case for his superhuman heroism mounts—do not detract from his mythic heroism but add to it. Thus, the paradox of DiMaggio's tendencies towards both the superhuman and the everyman find ultimate resolution wherein one strengthens the other. DiMaggio can be both a godlike mythic hero and the humble exemplar of the American dream. In fact, for many Americans, the more these two narrative strands intertwine, the more appealing DiMaggio becomes.

A DIALECTIC OF BASEBALL HEROES

DiMaggio's public image as a populist-superhuman hybrid of a hero can be viewed as something of the culmination of a Hegelian dialectic in the realm of popular baseball (or more specifically, Yankee) heroes. If Ruth, the first Yankee hero and baseball's first truly mass-media-catalyzed popular idol, can be thought of as the larger-than-life, demigod *thesis* of baseball heroism, working-class origins notwithstanding, then the workaday, strong-silent-type Gehrig would be its *antithesis*. DiMaggio's public figure becomes something of a perfect *synthesis* of the two previous heroic models as public demand combined with DiMaggio's background, personality, and style of play to yield a popular persona that captured what were deemed the best qualities of both Ruth and Gehrig. Whether conscious or unconscious, the public celebration of the mixture of Ruth and Gehrig's qualities they saw in DiMaggio, the face of the Yankees throughout the 1940s until his retirement in 1951, also had a refining or redefining effect on the Yankees as a cultural icon, adding some mythic resonance to the "all-American" heroic ideals of *The Pride of the Yankees.*

The figure of DiMaggio also added yet another member to the succession of Yankee heroes—or with the concept of DiMaggio as a culminating dialectical synthesis in mind, perhaps one could even say *progression* of Yankee heroes. Roughly between 1920 and baseball's integration in 1947, a period when Major League Baseball enjoyed significant popularity, the Yankees had with Ruth, Gehrig, and DiMaggio three stars who were easily among baseball's most popular and well regarded. In fact, one could even feasibly argue they were the three biggest baseball names of that era. The effect of these stars all playing for the same franchise had a mutual magnifying effect for both the players and the team. Being a Yankee added something to the legacy of the players and the unbroken succession of such high-profile baseball heroes nearly made the Yankees synonymous with baseball heroism itself. During DiMaggio's career, monuments were erected to both Gehrig (1941) and Ruth (1949) in Yankee Stadium's centerfield (joining a monument to manager Miller Huggins that had been erected in 1929); forming what became known as "Monument Park," these memorials became tangible reminders of this heroic legacy.[6] The fact that DiMaggio, who happened to play centerfield in the vicinity of these memorials, seemed to possess a synthesis of both Gehrig-like and Ruthian qualities further underscored the Yankees' heroic heritage.

DIMAGGIO AS POPULIST HERO IN *LUCKY TO BE A YANKEE*

DiMaggio's dual status as both populist everyman and larger-than-life mythic hero is clearly demonstrated in the different presentations of the centerfielder in two books from the postwar era that were both quite popular but very different: DiMaggio's autobiography, *Lucky to be a Yankee,* and Nobel laureate Ernest Hemingway's *The Old Man and the Sea. Lucky to Be a Yankee,* an "autobiography" directed at an audience of adolescent boys, was ghostwritten by Tom Meany (Cramer 216) in 1946, the year of Major League Baseball's celebrated first season after World War II. This popular juvenile book went through a number of editions and does much to bolster the All-American populist facet of DiMaggio's public figure.

DiMaggio as populist idol emerges immediately and clearly in *Lucky to Be a Yankee*'s first chapter, wherein Meany and DiMaggio present a narrative quite consistent with populist ideals in both content and tone. When recounting a crucial game in the 1948 pennant race with the Boston Red Sox in this first chapter of the updated 1949 edition titled "Almost But Not Quite," DiMaggio, who characteristically played much of the season hampered by injury, talks about "[hobbling] off the field on [his] bum gam," and laments, "It's ancient history, now. We did the best we could and we didn't win" (2). Here the DiMaggio voice, as presented by Meany, carves out a "common man" space with his use of contemporary slang ("bum gam"); short, direct sentences; and an endorsement of the populist values of work ethic and modesty. In fact, the narrative voice so reminded Cramer of *The Pride of the Yankees*, he described the book as "just Joe doing his Gary Cooper thing. (Aw, shucks)" (33).

As a tale of populist heroism, *Lucky to be a Yankee* is not unique among baseball biographies for young boys, nor was it novel when first released. As *New York Times* contributor Andrew Santella described it, "DiMaggio's book followed in a tradition that went back at least to Christy Mathewson's 'Pitching in a Pinch,' published in 1912. The general idea was to provide a good example and tell an inspiring story—a true story, if possible, but inspiring in any case. It would be a long time before any baseball memoirist or his ghostwriter would dare to deviate from that tradition." While the format and content of the book was not new,[7] the fact remains that it was DiMaggio's book, and as the most prominent and popular baseball player in an era when the United States was baseball mad, DiMaggio was arguably the most beloved sports figure of his time. Many even saw the star as embodying the nation itself in the years following World War II.

For instance, in a new introduction to the 1948 edition (and all subsequent printings) of *Lucky to Be a Yankee*, former U.S. postmaster general James A. Farley wrapped DiMaggio in the cloak of patriotism and the American dream:

> [It] is a story that could have happened only in America, the story of Joe, the son of immigrant parents, of a boyhood which was far from luxurious, and his rise to national eminence on the strength of his baseball ability.

I believe Joe's story . . . the story of a boy's life. I hope it will prove of interest to many other American boys, for it is really a story of our times. (7–8)

Here, DiMaggio is not only held up as a shining example of the national cultural myth of upward mobility for European immigrant families, but his personal history is celebrated as "the story of our times." This timeliness that Farley observes in DiMaggio's story is particularly revealing of how many Americans saw themselves and their country. For Farley, DiMaggio's "rise" from his humble boyhood to "eminence" captures the zeitgeist of postwar America, a triumphal America that had emerged from the global conflict, not to mention the national trial that was the Great Depression, with new economic and political clout in the world. In the celebratory mood of the postwar United States, many like Farley saw the country as a whole as living out the fabled American dream of upward mobility: through the sacrifice and perseverance of its citizens, the country was able to pull itself up by its bootstraps and, after the trials and conflicts of history, found itself living the "good life" in the postwar economic prosperity. For Farley and possibly many other Americans, perhaps especially the boys who read his introduction to *Lucky to Be a Yankee*, Joe DiMaggio symbolized the rise of this triumphal America.

PORTRAYAL OF THE YANKEES IN *LUCKY TO BE A YANKEE*

The Yankees as a team and organization naturally shared to some degree in this association with victorious postwar America, but *Lucky to Be a Yankee* offers passages that advance this connection between the Bronx Bombers and the nation as a whole. Specifically, the autobiography frequently describes a loyalty to and a respect, admiration, and even reverence for the New York Yankees that evidently needs no explanation or justification. This parallels patriotic usage of the signifier "America" or "American." The book's title itself, *Lucky to Be a Yankee*, obviously exemplifies this tendency. But DiMaggio and Meany further peppered the book with comments like "The Yankees were my ideal . . . the team I wanted to be with most of all" (23–24) from his years in a minor league. That dream was eventually fulfilled with a contract marked by the celebratory statement, "I was with the Yankees at last" (27).[8] And much later, while reflecting on the significant personnel changes between the World Series champion team of 1941 and the '47 champs, the book's narrator reassures himself and readers, "They were still Yankees, however, and I was lucky to be with them" (91). Perhaps most revealing of such reverential language, however, is a statement attributed to manager Joe McCarthy. When clubhouse horseplay would get a little too rough, *Lucky to Be a Yankee* tells us that the disciplinarian McCarthy would settle his players by quietly intoning something like, "You fellows are Yankees, act like Yankees" (28).

Such ambiguous statements imply an understood explanation or justification for the respect and reverence for the Yankees but never quite supply one.[9] The Yankee signifier is presumed to have enough cultural power to justify and explain itself, not dissimilar from the word "America," which is also often expected, in and of itself, to elicit similar respect and reverence without any further argument or elaboration, perhaps particularly during this postwar period of celebratory patriotism. James A. Farley's use of the phrase "only in America" in the introduction to *Lucky to Be a Yankee* itself is a typical example of this type of usage.

Eventually *Lucky to Be a Yankee* does address the reasons readers should understand its reverence for the club. The DiMaggio-Meany narrator writes: "I did a lot of thinking about what it means to be a Yankee. . . . It is only natural that I should regard the Yankees as a great organization. Any minor leaguer would think the same of his first big league club but when that club turned out to be a winner, and a winner by so decisive a margin, it was difficult to be moderate in your opinion and praise of the team" (41–42).

Here the autobiography lays out clearly the major reason for admiring and respecting the Yankee organization precisely as the one many readers would have assumed: success. As winning is the main organizing principle and value in modern team sports, this should come as no surprise. But it is significant that Americans in this postwar period tended to use this same reason, success, to explain the greatness of their country. Not only had the nation's military been instrumental in ending World War I, and especially the recent World War II, but it could also pride itself on surviving the Great Depression and becoming the great economic and political power of the world with perhaps only one rival.

That rival, the communist Soviet Union, as it turned out, actually provided more motivation for using success—particularly the material abundance of economic success—as a reason for American superiority. For example, in his discussion of the infamous 1959 "kitchen debate" between then–vice president Richard Nixon and Soviet premier Nikita Khrushchev, American cultural historian Benjamin Rader notes that Nixon did not use traditional and, perhaps, expected arguments about the American principles of "freedom, democracy, and philanthropy" as being more ethical than the communist political and economic system. Instead, he continually pointed to "the vast array of wonderful consumer goods that he claimed were available to the typical American family" as indicative of the United States' economic success and prosperity and, thus, the superiority of the American way of life (*American Ways* 314).

Though many Americans during this time period, like many before them and since, would have mentioned the democratic system and individual liberty as reasons for supposed American greatness, this victory-and-abundance-based form of postwar American patriotism that Nixon typified was not uncommon and still holds cultural currency. In this train of thought, citizens of the United States could consider themselves "lucky to be Americans" for the same reason DiMaggio's book advertised the slugger as "lucky to be a Yankee." Both could say they contributed to and enjoyed the spoils of superlative success over their rivals. In this way, DiMaggio and the Yankees became emblematic of the triumphant postwar America. For many, the Yankees were the greatest baseball team for the same reason America was the greatest country, and like DiMaggio in his autobiography, they could describe their admiration and respect for both using similar terms and phraseology.

In a subsequent passage in *Lucky to Be a Yankee*, DiMaggio and Meany elaborate further on the meaning of the Yankee organization beyond its on-field success. On the occasion of the disease-related retirement of Gehrig and the death of owner Jacob Ruppert, both occurring in 1939, they write: "Somehow these two men were symbolic of the Yankee legend. Gehrig, the immoveable, brawny slugger who went along day after day for a decade and a half without missing a ballgame, and Ruppert the millionaire owner. Only a fraction of the Colonel's wealth was in baseball but the Yankees meant more to him than all his other interests. He wanted to win every day and he wanted to win in Yankee fashion—clean sweeps and one-sided scores" (52–53).

Here Yankee baseball success and American economic might are further aligned in the person of Colonel Ruppert. Any potential negative elitist or plutocratic connotations associated with Ruppert's status as a millionaire are offset by Gehrig, whose work ethic and dedication, not to mention his well-known past as the son of poor immigrants (thanks to *The Pride of the Yankees*), represent for the authors of the book a crucial facet of this success. In fact, as it is the figures of Ruppert and Gehrig *together* that are "symbolic of the Yankee legend," the link between success and work ethic is presented as the crux of Yankeeness. They win, but they come by it honestly, through the *American* way of prosperity as dictated by the American dream itself: through hard work, not through any kind of aristocratic privilege. This is as vital an amendment to the celebration of Yankee success as it is to the American triumphalism of the postwar period.

DIMAGGIO AS MYTHIC HERO IN *LUCKY TO BE A YANKEE*

While patriotic populism is *Lucky to Be a Yankee*'s most salient feature, DiMaggio's status as a superhuman mythic hero also comes out in the autobiography. This is nowhere more apparent than in the foreword written by seasoned sportswriter Grantland Rice. No stranger to hyperbole, Rice writes: "No matter how many years you look at sporting events, . . . you never grow blasé or apathetic to the thrill of perfection. . . . Joe DiMaggio possesses that magic gift of perfection in his swing at the plate. If ever an athlete was meant for a sport, Joe DiMaggio was meant for baseball" (vi).

Here, Rice's awestruck use of the terms "gift," "magic," and above all, "perfection" distance the "everyman" DiMaggio not only from the common American but from the typical Major League Baseball star. For Rice, DiMaggio was not only the embodiment of perfection, but he was either born that way or destined to become that way, like some sort of baseball demigod. Rice's hyperbole is corroborated by a story told by sportswriter Joe Williams that serves as the book's final chapter. When talking in 1935 with Tommy Laird, an eccentric fellow sportswriter from San Francisco, Williams asks about DiMaggio, who at that point had been making a name for himself with the Pacific Coast League's San Francisco Seals. Laird responded by saying he would not claim DiMaggio to be a "second Babe Ruth," a "second Ty Cobb," or a "second Tris Speaker" but that "he's better than all three put together!" (152). While obviously intended to be humorous, Laird's comments, which portray DiMaggio as surpassing the talents of three men who were then acknowledged to be, respectively, the best power hitter, best hitter for average, and best outfielder in the game's history, betray the occasional messianic lens through which fans observed DiMaggio. As a player he was seen and described as so complete, so lacking in faults, that only terms of perfection and divinity could express their awe.

Though bookended with accounts from others that paint DiMaggio as superhuman, DiMaggio and Meany's own "aw, shucks" narrating voice in *Lucky to Be a Yankee* certainly would not permit any claims to perfection or anything that would be perceived as braggadocio. There are, however, a few moments where the hero does actually claim something like a divine gift: "It always has been a theory of mine that hitting is a God-given gift. . . . I know that I'm a professional ball player today because at the age of 18 I had a natural gift for hitting and for no other reason whatsoever" (15). With this statement, DiMaggio and Meany are able to maintain the centerfielder's everyman appeal by using a tone of humility and gratitude while claiming a "God-given gift." While this passage does not necessarily assert that such gifts are exclusive to DiMaggio, the notion of being born with special gifts represents a softened version of the superhuman baseball demigod featured in the guest-written foreword and conclusion and thus actually lends these hyperbolic statements some credence. Though most readers probably would not believe that a single DiMaggio is more valuable than three baseball legends combined, the slugger's own comments about his "natural gift" may well encourage them to wonder whether he really did leave the womb with a perfect set of baseball skills. So while the bulk of *Lucky to Be a Yankee* features a DiMaggio narrator doing, as Cramer suggests, his best Gary Cooper, all-American populist impression, the book also hints at and fosters the cult of Saint DiMaggio, God's divine gift to baseball.

HEROISM IN *THE OLD MAN AND THE SEA*

DiMaggio the mythic hero looms even larger in what might seem to many an unlikely place: Ernest Hemingway's 1952 novella, *The Old Man and the Sea*.

A Nobel Prize–winning author (1954), Hemingway is often remembered for his concise, pithy prose and for writing lucidly about stoic and scarred men engaging the violent worlds of war, bullfighting, and big-game hunting. The popular and populist world of Major League Baseball might seem to some as beneath such a serious writer. Hemingway's place as a canonical American modernist is potentially deceiving in this regard, however, as both the popular world of professional baseball and the traditional narrative patterns of Western mythic heroes play important roles in the structure and drama of *The Old Man and the Sea*.

In Leverett T. Smith Jr.'s description of central themes in Hemingway's work, a continuity of interest and purpose linking the work of the Hemingway, the pseudo-religious ideas of Joseph Campbell, and the celebrated career of Joe DiMaggio is evident: "[Hemingway's] work, in general, seems a long search for a setting within which human action might seem meaningful. The most important manifestation of this impulse is Hemingway's frequent use of the sporting world in the settings of his novels and stories. . . . In sports, or in activities which have some of the same basic qualities as sport, Hemingway's characters create their own meaningful world within a world essentially meaningless" (51).

For Hemingway, as for Campbell, the modern world offers little in the way of meaning, and the individual must find for him or herself (usually *him*self) a space within existence that walls off much of the clutter and clatter of industrialized, rationalized society, allowing the individual to act independently and, in so doing, find emotional, psychological, and/or spiritual oneness. Scholars commonly call individuals engaged in this work in Hemingway's writing "code heroes," after their individual code of action. For Campbell, this sought-after, meaningful space is the collective mythic hero narrative, "the secret opening" to the "inexhaustible energies of the cosmos" (3) that renders "the modern world spiritually significant" (388).

For Hemingway, this space is an active rather than a narrative one (but, incidentally, he made a career out of narrating this action), usually a realm of vaguely premodern activity (such as hunting, fishing, or bullfighting), which has its own traditional body of skills and wisdom passed down from person to person. Armed with knowledge of such skills, Hemingway's protagonists negotiate these subworlds as independent agents and live an existence that makes its own meaning. In Smith's view, Hemingway's characters find such a space in a variety of activities, including camping and cooking in the short story "Big Two-Hearted River" (57), but it is the world of sport that Hemingway favors the most, usually championing individual, solitary sporting activities such as bullfighting, hunting, fishing, or boxing, pastimes of which he himself was an aficionado. In *The Old Man and the Sea*, however, he makes the popular world of professional baseball, and the career of DiMaggio, in particular, the setting for his code hero ideal. *The Old Man and the Sea* also happens to be the work where Hemingway's code hero world clearly intersects with the traditional mythic hero in the figures of both the Cuban fisherman Santiago and his idol Joe DiMaggio.

While DiMaggio and U.S. Major League Baseball are featured somewhat prominently in *The Old Man and the Sea*, mentioned five separate times in a novella of a little over 120 pages, the book's main focus is the experience of Santiago, an aging deep-sea fisherman of the Gulf Stream. Over his long career Santiago has achieved some renown among the other local fishermen. Of late, he has befriended the young Manolin, with whom he has been fishing and sharing his knowledge of the craft; but a recent lack of success has made the boy's parents think Santiago is past his prime, and Manolin has reluctantly taken up with another boat. Under this pretext, the story begins with the downtrodden Santiago setting off in his boat in hopes of breaking his recent eighty-four-day streak of futility. He hooks not only the biggest marlin of his career but the biggest marlin he has ever seen. The drama of the novella then centers on his effort to keep the great fish on the line, bring it in, and fend off the predatory sharks trying to scavenge his catch.

As mentioned, this novella comes as close to the structure of mythic hero narratives that Joseph Campbell proposed as anything Hemingway ever wrote. The core plot of *The Old Man and the Sea*—a tale of the aging fisherman suddenly unable to catch fish and then just as suddenly thrust into the greatest struggle of his life in an effort to bring in the biggest fish he has known—is a classic "belly of the whale" story. And while he loses virtually all the saleable meat from the fish to the mobs of scavenging sharks, Santiago nevertheless returns to the fishing village with "boons" for his people: the marlin's head to use in fish traps, the fish's nose spear—the biggest anyone had ever seen—as a souvenir for Manolin, and perhaps more important, the gifts of awe and inspiration to all the fishermen and Santiago's young friend and apparent successor, in particular. As reward for persevering and returning with these largely psychological boons, Santiago, regains the devotion of Manolin.

While Hemingway's hero tale ends with a victory that is more personal and internal than many mythic hero tales identified by Campbell, *The Old Man and the Sea* does the same type of work as the ancient narratives of the Western world. Readers are often reminded of this through Hemingway's persistent usage of primeval, elemental imagery: sea, land, sun, moon, cloud, wind, "the old man," and "the boy." Hemingway also includes occasional biblical references that invite comparison to ancient mythic narratives. This is particularly true of the crucifixion imagery of Santiago uttering a cry described as "a noise such as a man might make, involuntarily, feeling the nail go through his hand and into the wood" (107), of shouldering the mast in weakness on the way home (121), and of sleeping "with his arms out straight and the palms of his hands up" (122).

DIMAGGIO AS MYTHIC HERO IN *THE OLD MAN AND THE SEA*

In this narrative, which successfully registers as both an example of a Hemingway code hero in action and as Campbellian mythic hero tale, Hemingway adds numerous allusions to the professional baseball career of Joe DiMaggio. Had the substantial connections between the public's perceptions of DiMaggio and the tradition of mythic heroes not already been established here, this might seem a strange combination. Indeed, in his *New York Times* review of the novel upon its appearance, Robert Gorham Davis deemed the baseball references an aesthetically poor choice. Scholar Sheldon Norman Grebstein later interpreted the author's baseball references as "interludes of comic relief," labeling the allusions to baseball in Santiago's "struggle with insuperable natural forces" an "incongruous juxtaposition" (193). The evidence, however, suggests that Hemingway was quite sincere in his laudatory references to DiMaggio.[10] Hemingway was, in fact, an admirer of the ballplayer and often sought his company in New York. An oft-recited anecdote describes them at a boxing match together. After a fan had finished heaping praise on DiMaggio, he noticed Hemingway and asked him, "You're somebody, too—aren't you?" The author deadpanned, "Yeah, I'm his doctor" (qtd. in Cramer 241).

In *The Old Man and the Sea,* Hemingway translates his admiration of DiMaggio into a near-idolization of the Yankee slugger by protagonist Santiago. The day before leaving on his fishing journey, Santiago and Manolin, both fans of American baseball, discuss the pennant races in the American and National Leagues. C. Harold Hurley has pinpointed the events of the novella as taking place between September 12 and 16 of 1950, when the Yankees were battling the Tigers for first place in the American League pennant race (78–79). When Manolin asks his opinion, Santiago exudes confidence in the Yankees as eventual pennant winners: "The Yankees cannot lose" (17). When Manolin expresses doubt about Santiago's prediction, saying he fears "both the Tigers of Detroit and the Indians of Cleveland," the old fisherman's confidence is unflagging and revealing. "Have faith in the Yankees my son," he reassures Manolin. "Think of the great DiMaggio" (17).

The semireligious language that Santiago uses in relation to the Yankees clearly distinguishes them from the other clubs. The term "faith" implies not only a confidence in the Yankees' ability to win but also a certain goodness or connection with the divine. One does not "have faith" that anticipated harmful or unpleasant events will take place or that nefarious individuals will indeed be able to accomplish their aims. Thus, as the team in which one should have faith, the Yankees become the protagonists of the Major Leagues and, in effect, extensions of the self for Santiago and Manolin and, through them, for readers as well. While American readers who are baseball fans might feel conflicted if they have other rooting interests and have learned to resent the Yankees and their frequent success over any number of other possible favorite teams, the "faith" the humble Santiago professes in the Yankees encourages readers to "suspend disbelief," if nothing else, and be willing to see the Yankees as protagonists in the context of the novella.

The real substance motivating Santiago's "faith" is, of course, "the great DiMaggio." At this point in the novella no elaboration is provided about why Santiago feels DiMaggio's presence is enough to convince Manolin to have faith in the Yankees, but perhaps many readers, thinking of the events of 1941, and especially 1949, will be able to fill in the blanks. For others, the reverential title "the great" that precedes Santiago's use of his name provides some clues. Further baseball conversation adds somewhat to the Yankees' and DiMaggio's image in Hemingway's book:

> "Tell me about the baseball," the boy asked.
> "In the American League, it is the Yankees as I said," the old man said happily.
> "They lost today," the boy told him.
> "That means nothing. The great DiMaggio is himself again."
> "They have other men on the team."
> "Naturally. But he makes the difference. . . ." (21)

Here "the great DiMaggio" is clearly placed in the hero's role as the one who "makes the difference" for the Yankees. Santiago's comment about him "being himself again" more explicitly evokes the idea, previously expressed in other texts, of DiMaggio as superhuman. For DiMaggio, "born" with natural baseball gifts, merely being "himself" is enough to defeat the other teams. In this passage Santiago's view of the relationship between DiMaggio and the Yankees is refined. While he earlier suggested that Manolin have faith in the Yankees, here it becomes clear that the Yankees themselves must have faith in the difference-making DiMaggio to lead them to victory (even if, in reality, they were a well-rounded club with many contributors). Again, as in the sports journalism surrounding DiMaggio's 1949 comeback, the Yankees are presented as occupying the metaphoric role that we as readers would put ourselves in, the mythic hero's community that depends on his gifts, example, and inspiration.

For Santiago, this relationship is played up by his subsequent comment that he "would like to take the great DiMaggio fishing. . . . They say his father was a fisherman. Maybe he was poor as we are and would understand" (22). Here, Santiago attributes to DiMaggio the empowered mythic hero's empathy for the community he protects or saves. With his comments about being poor, he simultaneously places himself in the position of needing this metaphoric protection or salvation, just as the Yankees depend on him to bring them literal victory on the field.

Much more is revealed about Santiago's devotion to DiMaggio as the novella progresses and he ventures out fishing. Out at sea, the lonely Santiago has a nearly unceasing conversation with himself in his head. On several occasions his thoughts return to DiMaggio, particularly as Santiago encounters hardship or must tolerate pain in his effort to keep the mighty marlin on the line. At one point he tells himself, "I must have confidence and I must be worthy of the great DiMaggio who does all things perfectly even with the pain of the bone spur in his heel. . . . Do you believe the great DiMaggio would stay with a fish as long as I will stay with this one? . . . I am sure he would and more since he is young and strong. Also his father was a fisherman" (68). Here Santiago invokes the name of "the great DiMaggio who does all things perfectly" as one might pray to a Catholic saint. As if DiMaggio were the patron saint of "grace under pressure"—perhaps the key quality of the Hemingway hero in the words of the author himself (qtd. in Parker 29)—Santiago uses thoughts of the Yankee Clipper's perseverance through injury to inspire himself to do the same. He turns to DiMaggio not just for inspiration but as an example of how to react in his situation. This implies that Santiago is beginning to compare his own situation to that of DiMaggio, and thus, while the old fisherman may not have thought this himself, he invites readers to consider him in the same heroic role as the Yankee slugger.

This is also the first time that Santiago mentions DiMaggio's bone spurs, the symbols of his perseverance through pain that plagued him later in his career. More specifically, the bone spurs evoke the end of the 1948 season and the first half of the 1949 season, the "belly of the whale" period that prefigured DiMaggio's "miraculous" 1949 comeback. This is particularly fitting, as at this point in the novella, it is becoming clearer that such a life-defining "belly of the whale" trial has thrust itself upon Santiago as well, further contributing to the theme of Santiago as a mythic hero in his own right.

Later on, Santiago's thoughts turn to DiMaggio again in his moment of triumph. After spearing and at last killing the giant marlin, Santiago thinks to himself, "My head is not that clear. But I think the great DiMaggio would be proud of me today. I had no bone spurs but the hands and the back hurt truly" (97). And still later, after successfully defending his catch against a scavenging shark, he thinks, "I wonder how the great DiMaggio would have liked the way I hit [the shark] in the brain? It was no great thing, he thought. Any man could do it. But do you think my hands were as great a handicap as the bone spurs? I cannot know" (103–4). Santiago's thought that DiMaggio would be proud of his actions in both of these passages advances Santiago's case as mythic hero. While he would probably not go so far as to suggest he has achieved DiMaggio's lofty status, it is clear that Santiago takes pride in his actions as a worthy, DiMaggio-like effort. This is further evident in his comparison of his ailments with DiMaggio's bone spurs. However, for Hemingway, the implications of these passages seem to be that the two are roughly equals in heroism, two individuals living out a meaningful existence through their tenacious demonstration of willpower and adherence to their personal code of conduct under difficult circumstances.

Santiago's thoughts turn to DiMaggio one last time in his triumph. "You were born to be a fisherman as the fish was born to be a fish," he tells himself. "San Pedro was a fisherman, as was the father of the great DiMaggio" (105). Here, Santiago once again invokes his connection to DiMaggio through the fact that his father was a fisherman. But this time, considering Santiago's comment to himself that he was "born to be a fisherman"—an interesting echo of the common sportswriter's comment that DiMaggio was "born to play baseball"—they are linked in a relationship closer to equal. Santiago no longer seeks a model to emulate in the heroic DiMaggio but surmises he has earned his admiration. Furthermore, this time the connection between the two is further sanctified by the inclusion of Saint Peter, who connotes divine approval for them both.

By enduring the pain in his back and hands, and by holding the fish on the line for nearly two days, Santiago shows the same heroic form that the novella suggests DiMaggio did in enduring his bone spurs. As each eventually triumphed, passing through the "belly of the whale" while displaying excellence in their craft, grace under pressure, and adherence to a personal code of action, they both not only become successful Hemingway code heroes and Campbellian mythic heroes but a fusion of the two.

By using DiMaggio as superhuman heroic exemplar to a character who achieves heroic status himself, *The Old Man and the Sea* is perhaps the ultimate tribute to the Yankee centerfielder's public persona as a mythic hero. Written during DiMaggio's final 1951 season and published the following year, Hemingway's novella is as much an apotheosis of "the great DiMaggio" as *The Pride of the Yankees* was Lou Gehrig's hagiography. However, while *The Old Man in the Sea* certainly presents unprecedented levels of poetic expression and thematic depth in characterizing DiMaggio as a mythic hero, it would be a mistake to say that Hemingway transformed him into one. In writing about him the way he did, the author was merely giving more eloquent expression to the way many Americans had been thinking of DiMaggio since his celebrated 1949 comeback at the latest. But Hemingway's novella, cited specifically in his award for the Nobel Prize two years later and still frequently taught in American high school and college literature classes, has preserved this mythic DiMaggio in literary form. In part because of it, DiMaggio's name remains closely linked with baseball heroism today, even for those who know relatively little about the history of Major League Baseball.

MASCULINITY IN *THE OLD MAN AND THE SEA*

While the central theme offered to readers of *The Old Man and the Sea* is the fusion of Hemingway's code hero with the type of mythic heroic narrative highlighted by Campbell, the novella, like *The Pride of the Yankees* before it, also offers its audience a model of masculinity. As hinted at previously, the tradition of Western hero narratives favors men, despite female monomyth heroes such as Esther, Joan of Arc, and the growing number of more contemporary pop-culture iterations. With the plethora of mythic hero stories centered on boys or men, the heroic narrative has also long doubled as male life script. The same could be said for Hemingway's literary code hero. For instance, in Leverett Smith's astute analysis of said figures, every example of an individual seeking "a setting within which human action might seem meaningful" from Hemingway's literary oeuvre is male. These observations should be read as less an indictment of a sexist society and more as evidence that both these versions of heroism, which merge in *The Old Man and the Sea,* are particularly relevant to a study of societal expectations of men.

As it draws on the Hemingway and the Campbellian versions of heroic narrative, both heavily male, *The Old Man and the Sea* and Joe DiMaggio's place in it are certainly worth examining as masculine models, particularly concerning how they might shape the cultural meaning of DiMaggio and the Yankees. The novella does not disappoint in this regard, as Santiago's comments continually frame his actions in the context of manhood. And the "manly" quality that seems to be especially emphasized in Santiago's comments is the very thing that is so strongly connected with his memories of DiMaggio: endurance, particularly endurance of pain. At various points in the book when facing sacrifice or pain, he tells Manolin, or more often himself, "It is what a man must do" (26), "I wish I could show [the fish] what kind of man I am" (64), "It is not bad . . . and pain does not matter to a man" (84), and in what could be an encapsulation of one of the novella's main themes, "I will show [the fish] what a man can do and what a man endures" (66). This final comment offers a grand gesture towards the supposed essentials of male experience and true manhood. Positioned in this way, *The Old Man and the Sea* presents Santiago as embodying the "true essence" of manhood, proven through his physical and psychological perseverance as he struggles with the marlin. DiMaggio, the old fisherman's inspiration and model, shares in this masculine embodiment as well. For Santiago, DiMaggio represents something of a patron saint of persevering through pain, and as evidenced in journalistic writing cited here, this was something for which DiMaggio had a reputation.

SELF-SACRIFICE AND MID-TWENTIETH-CENTURY AMERICAN CULTURE

Masculinity scholar David Savran argues that this glorification of male suffering and endurance of physical pain, which he frames as masochism, is a prevalent theme throughout twentieth-century conceptions of masculinity (3–5), but Jacqueline Foertsch has also described this focus on self-sacrifice for a greater good as part of the cultural legacy of World War II, citing not only the sacrifice of the lives of soldiers but also the patriotic attitude with which many American women took up factory jobs and the country participated in rationing and collected scrap iron (169–79). With this in mind, perhaps the quality of enduring pain and sacrificing oneself for a greater good would have been particularly important for men in the World War II generation.

Always willing to play while hurt to help achieve the greater good of a Yankee victory, DiMaggio's public persona was associated with this concept in popular journalism before the publication of Hemingway's novella, but again, his presence in *The Old Man and the Sea* solidifies this notion in poetic fashion. While Gehrig was compared to brave American soldiers in *The Pride of the Yankees,* DiMaggio actually served in the army during World War II, as did many other prominent Major League ballplayers. Though DiMaggio never saw anything close to combat, the fact that he and his fellow ballplayers did leave the game to join the military may well have helped give baseball more national legitimacy and encouraged Americans to see sacrifice on the ball field and on the battlefield as part of a the same seamless whole of American manliness.[11] Frequently playing with pain and yet still somehow able to lead the Yankees to so many victories, DiMaggio was unparalleled in this kind of manliness in the mind of the public in the years following the war, as indicated by the newspaper coverage of his '49 comeback.

And yet, even as *The Old Man and the Sea* seems to endorse certain national cultural trends like the "culture of sacrifice," it should be noted that in other ways, the novel eschews several other American cultural narratives—most specifically, the American dream. Not only does the main story have an international setting and characters, putting it outside the context of an exclusively national discourse, but it also presents a story that denies the American dream of upward mobility.[12] The impoverished Santiago works hard and sacrifices, and for that he gains an important personal victory; but his rewards are the respect of his peers, the admiration of his apprentice, and self-satisfaction. In fact, the novella even evokes the idea of economic reward and then makes a point of taking it away in tragic fashion through the predatory sharks (97, 118–19, 126).

Thus, Michael Kimmel's concept of "marketplace masculinity"—manhood proven through success as a capitalist and breadwinner—is rejected in Hemingway's book for a more intrinsic masculinity proven through adherence to a personal code of action, including endurance through pain and grace under pressure. Even DiMaggio's background as a poor immigrant fisherman's son, which was seen in texts like *Lucky to Be a Yankee* in the context of his upward mobility from that humble starting point, is evoked to bolster his qualities as a mythic hero and connect him more intimately to Santiago. Of course, this makes sense when one considers that Hemingway's aim in *The Old Man and the Sea,* with its Christ imagery and a discussion of "what a man can do and what a man endures," was not to comment on American society or tell an "American" story but a grand, mythic, even a universal one.

SUCCESS AND MID-TWENTIETH-CENTURY AMERICAN CULTURE

Hemingway's downplaying of DiMaggio's economic upward mobility and material success in favor of his intrinsic heroic strength does not change the fact that the Clipper was celebrated for those more tangible successes by others. Just as he was lauded for embodying "the American story" in James Farley's introduction to *Lucky to Be a Yankee,* so could DiMaggio be celebrated as the essence of American manhood, with his self-made, rags-to-riches story, his drive to endure physical pain as he led the Yankees to nine World Series championships, and even his ability to woo and marry the ultimate Hollywood starlet, Marilyn Monroe, in his postretirement life.

As already suggested, the triumphs and spoils that DiMaggio won were consistent with certain American cultural trends in the postwar era. Even as Foertsch cites a culture of sacrifice as influencing the World War II era, she argues equally for the rise of a nearly opposite culture in the postwar period. While not completely forgetting the sacrifices of the Depression and the War, as Americans entered the 1950s, they quickly adopted a culture of consumption (183). Lizabeth Cohen goes even further, arguing for the emergence of what she describes as a "Consumer's Republic, an economy, culture, and politics built around the promises of mass consumption, both in terms of material life and the more idealistic goals of great freedom, democracy and equality" (7). Evidences of a such a postwar consumption-focused culture can be found not only in the economic upswing, as well as the education and housing booms, but also in the increasing number of commercial products, timesaving devices, and technologies available to supplement and adorn the home, yard, or car garage (Foertsch 183–99). Television, not the least of these new products, offered a new forum for advertising these material goods as well.

It is also important to consider how the Cold War political climate, which set the capitalist United States against the communist Soviet Union, served to promote and justify this culture of abundance and prosperity. During the Cold War, purchasing goods and enjoying "the good life" could be viewed through the politicized lenses of "democracy" and "freedom." As Cohen suggests, such Cold War consumption constituted "powerful symbolism as the prosperous American alternative to the material deprivations of communism" (8). Thus, just as many Americans saw it as their patriotic duty to sacrifice during World War II, so also was it perceived as their patriotic duty to buy in the postwar era.

With his career stretching from 1936 to 1951, from the Depression to the Baby Boom, DiMaggio's public persona was perhaps uniquely positioned to absorb some of both the culture of sacrifice and the succeeding culture of plenty and consumption from these periods. As both an all-American populist who pulled himself up by his bootstraps and a mythic hero whose ultimate sacrifice yielded ultimate victory and its spoils, DiMaggio is paradoxically able to capture both cultural trends. This may have been particularly important for any individuals in the postwar period who might have felt a sensation of vertigo or even guilt at the country's and his or her personal, sudden shift from austerity to plenty, from sacrifice to indulgence. For in DiMaggio, the man who endures the pain of bone spurs as he leads the Yankees to the pennant, this sacrificial past was ever before them, even in bounteous victory.

DIMAGGIO'S IMPACT ON THE YANKEES AS CULTURAL ICON

DiMaggio's impact on the Yankee cultural icon is likewise significant. Before DiMaggio's postwar rise to mythic heroism, the Yankees certainly embodied unparalleled excellence and success. Through Lou Gehrig and *The Pride of the Yankees,* they grew as emblems of national narratives: the American dream of upward mobility, populist work ethic, and traditional masculinity. But in the postwar era, watching or reading about a DiMaggio-led Yankee victory took on, more than ever before, the tone of religious devotion, not just for Yankee fans, and—if the 1949 *Life* magazine cover story is any indication—perhaps not even just baseball fans but the nation as a whole.

Building on baseball's longstanding rhetorical connections to a concept of patriotism and American identity, as well as Gehrig's and DiMaggio's status as emblems and exemplars of the American dream, the pseudo-religious connotations that DiMaggio brought to the Yankees transformed the Bronx Bombers in this postwar period to something of an icon of America's civil religion. Religious studies scholar Christopher H. Evans describes the concept of civil religion as the creation of a "collective national identity through bestowing sacred meaning on a variety of secular symbols, rituals, and institutions"

(14). Evans argues that the game of baseball as a whole, and particularly the institution of Major League Baseball, functions as a civil religion, keying in on the rhetoric from baseball's promoters in the late nineteenth century as laying the foundations for baseball's status as a revered symbol of the United States (19–21).

The annual ritual of the president throwing out the first pitch of the season is alone sufficient evidence for Evans's case. Nevertheless, I submit that the DiMaggio-led Yankees in the postwar period constitute a special case in which baseball's role as civil religion was magnified. Robert Bellah, the originator of the term "civil religion," described American civil religion as being especially "concerned that America be a society as perfectly in accord with the will of God as men can make it, and a light to all the nations" (21). With his popular status as an American mythic hero whose victories often seemed predestined, DiMaggio was able to provide the nation reassurance in this regard.[13]

DiMaggio's popular persona of mythic heroism deepened the reverence and connection with the divine felt by the fans, the "practitioners" of this civil religion. With his "miraculous" 1949 comeback as his crowning achievement, DiMaggio garnered more suggestions of godhood than any player since Ruth. But unlike Ruth, who would mystify crowds with his individual feats of herculean power, DiMaggio's power over the public was more tied to his ability to lead the Yankees to dramatic victory. And while many fans of other baseball clubs certainly could bemoan the Yankees' dominance and complain about the organization's deep pockets, DiMaggio's presence helped sanctify the Yankees, in a manner of speaking. Even fans who did not root for the Yankees would have had a hard time escaping the religious-like language used to describe them as a team of destiny—to "have faith in" them, to use Santiago's words—particularly with the media's attention to DiMaggio's long suffering through injury and proclamations of miraculous comebacks. Thus, the Yankees and their narrative of victories became entwined in religious-like feelings and experience for many Americans. DiMaggio's superhuman goodness both brought to pass and justified Yankee success.

The Yankees were not the only ones enjoying success in the 1940s and 1950s, however. As a nation, the United States had, like DiMaggio, suffered and sacrificed but ultimately emerged as triumphant as the Yankees in both the Second World War and economic recovery. DiMaggio's combination of self-sacrifice and destiny not only justified the Yankees' dominance of the Major Leagues but made it seem right and destined. Americans could draw parallel conclusions about the recent triumphs of their country and quite possibly their own personal economic improvement. Through the dramatic lens of DiMaggio's mythic self-sacrifice and triumph, the Yankees in this postwar cultural moment became, in a sense, America, and America became the Yankees.

DiMaggio's role in baseball's civil religion in the late 1940s and early '50s can be read as part of a broader cultural trend regarding nationalism and faith. Rader emphasizes the degree to which "faith and patriotism frequently blended" in the postwar period (*American Ways* 313). This is corroborated by Cold War historian Dianne Kirby, who emphasizes how during the Truman administration (1945–52) the United States' new world role as the anticommunist leader of the West "was presented as part of America's 'manifest destiny' and sustained by the conviction that the American cause was morally right" (77). Cold War cultural historian Tony Shaw further suggests that in that period "religion became discursively associated in Western popular culture with 'liberty', 'democracy' and 'Western civilisation'" (214). In this vein, the popular understanding of recent history attributed a divine destiny to the nation as a whole. The United States won the war and emerged destined to continue to free the world of communism because God's will worked through its collective efforts in the same way that DiMaggio's miraculous feats manifested the Yankees' destiny to win. Thus, the success of the DiMaggio-led Yankees in the national moment following World War II could be described as an especially potent icon of American civil religion, dramatizing and reassuring Americans of the divine rightness of their recent military and economic success and the role the country was assuming on the world stage.

The Yankees' parallels of national success in the postwar period were further strengthened with the introduction of a new logo in 1947. Up to that point the Bronx Bombers had been represented by their interlocking N.Y. cap logo, their navy blue and white team colors, and particularly their famous pinstriped home uniforms. The new official team logo introduced after the war, however, emphasized the nationalistic connotations of the word "Yankee" and featured an Uncle Sam top hat, complete with stars and stripes, perched atop the barrel of a baseball bat. This logo, with only very minor alterations is still in use today (Frommer, *Remembering Yankee Stadium* 70; D. Stout). In it the signifiers of the Yankees ball club are melded with national signifiers, making Yankee excellence one with American excellence. Through it, the Bronx Bombers' prosperity both provides evidence for and exemplifies American prosperity.

The top hat logo visually represents the nationalistic connotations DiMaggio helped bring to the Yankees in the postwar period. Through his populist work ethic and American-dream life story, DiMaggio, like Gehrig before him, embodied many midcentury American values, and during his tenure as the public face of the team, the Yankees continued their cultural association with these values. But with his mythic public persona projected in texts like *Lucky to Be a Yankee*, *The Old Man and the Sea*, and journalistic profiles, DiMaggio brought new facets to the Yankees as a cultural icon. In a post–World War II period when the mythologizing of America's economic prosperity, and military and political success was increasingly common, DiMaggio's mythic presence helped strengthen the team's nationalistic connections. Through his dualistic everyman/superman public persona, Joe DiMaggio justified and sanctified Yankee success and, by the same right, the triumphant postwar United States.

Chapter Four
"WALL STREET BROKERS AND HAUGHTY BUSINESSMEN"
The Yankees and Brooklyn Dodger Fan Identity

*I*n analyzing the Yankees as a cultural icon from what could be described as a mainstream national perspective, I have focused on national voices of public discourse, particularly those emanating from institutions with established cultural clout that focus attention on sport and baseball only occasionally, such as *Life* magazine, Hollywood movies, and serious literature. This focus is intended to show how a broadly conceived, general American public (which would include, but not be limited to, those who consider themselves active baseball fans) perceived and used the New York Yankees as a cultural icon. By and large, up through Joe DiMaggio's retirement in the early 1950s, these national, mass-media texts presented an image of the Yankees as the essence of American values and American greatness, a reflection of an optimistic perspective on the nation victorious in war and entering a period of prosperity. This characterization of the Yankees would remain vital through the middle of the 1960s, with the torch of Yankee heroism being taken up by Mickey Mantle, whose humble working-class roots, propensity for tremendous Ruthian home runs, willingness to play through injury, and boyish charisma helped make him the idol of many an American youth in the Eisenhower and Kennedy years.

However, coexisting with this generally laudatory national voice was a much more negative perspective on the Bronx ball club, a perspective rooted in the experience of fans of other, less-successful teams. While such perspectives surely must have existed as long as Yankee success existed, in the years following World War II, one group of fans, supporters of local rivals the Brooklyn Dodgers, generated a negative characterization of the Yankees that became prominent and persistent enough to gain national attention.

Dodger fans of this era essentially used the Yankees as a successful, aristocratic counterpoint to help them craft a communal identity as working-class underdogs. The Dodgers met and lost to their crosstown rivals, the storied Yankees, five times between 1941 and '53 before finally beating the Bronx Bombers for their first World Series title in 1955. The Yankees represented the powerful establishment that stood in the way of Dodger supporters' deepest desire as fans. Thus, in the collective worldview of these midcentury fans, the Yankees' association with an idealized narrative of the American dream was turned on its head as the rival team became the main impediment to the Dodgers' own narrative of upward mobility. This "haves-versus-have-nots" dynamic to the Yankees-Dodgers rivalry takes on additional social significance when one considers the Dodgers' role as the leaders of the racial integration of baseball with the Major League debut of Jackie Robinson in 1947, while baseball's established crown jewel, the Yankees, dragged their feet in this regard, remaining one of a handful of lilywhite teams until 1955. For the fans of the Brooklyn Dodgers, the Yankees came to embody both a symbolic and a literal power structure, taking on sociocultural categories of class and race as well as on-field dominance.

FANDOM AND IDEOLOGY

Thus far, with my focus on nationalized, mainstream mass-media texts, I have devoted little attention to fan experience—that is, the meaning the Bronx

Bombers had for their community of fans in New York City, as well as the legions of Yankee devotees across the nation or globe. There were likely a few Americans in the middle decades of the twentieth century who chose to root for the Yankees for ideological reasons connected to their national persona—for the way the team embodied an idealized notion of the American dream or American masculinity—if perhaps only subconsciously. And there were likely more who claimed the Yankees as their favorite team exclusively based on their success and the status it brought them through association. (This has certainly been a suspicion or accusation of fans of other ball clubs through the years.) It would be a mistake, however, to apply such a characterization to the entire community of Yankee fans.

The majority of Yankee fans, then and now, likely became fans for the same reasons supporters of other teams have done: geographic proximity or familial precedent. Thus, I would suggest that the experience of a Yankee fan in the mid–twentieth century, aside from the significant detail of the Yankees' consistent winning, was not that different from that of any other baseball fan. Childhood Brooklyn Dodger fan and American historian Doris Kearns Goodwin learned as much in her early years when she associated with many fans of the rival Yankees in her neighborhood on Long Island. In her memoir of Dodger fandom, Goodwin observes that her best friend, Elaine, a Yankee fan, was "as devoted to her team as I was to the Dodgers" (64). Furthermore, while Goodwin remembers a widespread perception that the Yankees were "supported by the rich and successful" (63), she often remarks that many of her acquaintances who supported the Bronx Bombers did not quite "fit the typical image of the Yankee fan" (65).

Thus, it could be said that there was often some discontinuity between the ideologies the Yankees sometimes represented in popular culture and the sociocultural identities of their actual fans. This is clearly evidenced in Joseph Trumino's paper titled "The Political and Cultural Contradictions of the 'Lefty' Yankee Fan." Trumino ponders his fierce loyalty to the Bronx Bombers (which he attributes to both the place and family he was born into) despite his nearly-as-fierce disagreements with the ideologies that the team— "the Bourgeoisie ... the Chase Bank of baseball" (4)—is associated with in the contemporary popular mind. The existence of Trumino's lighthearted, yet earnest presentation suggests that such a discontinuity between a team's ideological connotations and fan identity is as common today as it was in the mid-twentieth century.

These discontinuities between the experience of Yankee fans and the team's cultural meaning does not necessarily mean that an examination of the Yankees in baseball fan culture is completely useless, however. While investigating and analyzing the experience of Yankee fans may not yield additional insights into the club's status as a cultural icon, exploring the role they play in the fan culture of *other* baseball teams, particularly Brooklyn Dodger supporters in the postwar era, does promise to be interesting.

FAN COMMUNITIES AND THE CREATION OF MEANING

Lawrence Grossberg is among the increasing number of cultural scholars devoting attention to fandom in general as a site of identity formation and cultural production. While this growing body of fandom scholarship has been generally focused on fans devoted to aspects of popular culture that are more overtly "textual"—certain genres of music or musicians, television shows, or film series—the theories and concepts of Grossberg's work are particularly applicable to the world of sports fandom as well.

Grossberg's concept of "mattering maps" is especially relevant to Dodger fans' attitude towards and use of the Yankee cultural icon. He argues that fandom helps fans "map," or bring organization and order to their existence, helping them "divide the cultural world into Us and Them" based on his or her perception of and experience with that object of fandom and what it represents, be it a rock band, comic-book character, sci-fi TV show, or sports team (58). In this way, fandom becomes a powerful tool for building a concept of identity: which values, ideologies, or experiences fans identify with and claim, which they do not, and where they, as individuals, fit in the world. Along with identity, fandom creates a shared community, a sense of "Us," as Grossberg puts it, centralized and unified around the object of fandom and the accompanying values it represents. For Dodger fans, the Yankees acted as an important landmark on their "mattering map," an ever-present counterpoint that reinforced their self-characterization as scrappy, striving underdogs by reminding them of what they were not or did not want to be: empowered, established, or socially elite.

"THE SAD, CRAZY SAGA"

Dodger fans' self-perception as underdogs in contrast to the elitist Yankees is grounded in the two teams' histories on the baseball field itself. Historically, it was neither the Yankees nor the Dodgers who captured hearts and headlines of New York City baseball fans but the New York Giants of John McGraw and Christy Mathewson, who found significant success in National League play during the first two and a half decades of the twentieth century, winning ten pennants in this time period. While the Giants were less successful in the World Series, winning only three times in these years, they dominated the triangular intercity rivalry. The Dodgers mustered two pennants, 1916 and 1920, losing both World Series. The Yankees, meanwhile, fared even worse, not winning any pennants before 1921.

All of this changed when Colonel Jacob Ruppert took over the team and began seriously investing his money in Babe Ruth and other talent, and in the cathedral-like Yankee Stadium in the early 1920s. Soon the Yankees were competing with the Giants for New York City and national baseball supremacy and eventually became the most dominant baseball team in either league over the course of the 1920s and '30s. During this Yankee dominance, the Dodgers, who had shown some promise in their two recent pennant-winning years, tumbled from mediocre to laughably bad. While the Yankees competed almost annually for the title of baseball's best team and the Giants did the same on occasion, the city's third club, Brooklyn, became the league's clowns. The Dodgers of the late 1920s and '30s were notorious throughout the Major Leagues as the "Daffiness Boys," known for losing in comical fashion, such as the instance when several base-running errors saw the Dodgers, "those colorful incapables," to use baseball historians Harold and Dorothy Z. Seymour's phrase, ended up with three men on third base (454–56).

In 1938 the Dodgers hired Larry MacPhail as general manager of the club, and their fortunes quickly improved. MacPhail made many moves to improve the club and its park, culminating in the team's first pennant in twenty years in 1941. Perhaps foremost among McPhail's changes was the hiring of the irascible and popular manager Leo Durocher, whose scrappiness brought a new defiance to the underdog club's persona. In the '41 World Series, the Dodgers met and were defeated by an imposing Yankee team. Many then and now cite the fourth game as the series' turning point. With the Yankees leading the series two games to one but the Dodgers leading the game by a run in the ninth inning with two outs, Brooklyn catcher Mickey Owen inexplicably failed to catch what would have been the third strike to Yankee slugger Tommy Henrich.[1] This strike would have ended the game and evened the series, giving the Dodgers the edge in momentum and putting them only two wins away from the club's first World Series title. But Henrich took advantage of the dropped pitch and advanced to first base, keeping the Yankees alive. The Dodgers never recovered from this small but costly mistake, eventually losing the game to the Yanks, who went on to score four runs and win 7–4. Demoralized, Brooklyn dropped the following game and lost the series.

Owen's dropped third strike set the tone for the narrative tradition Dodgers fans would begin to craft around their team through the 1940s and early '50s. Goodwin underscores the importance such a tradition plays in uniting a sports team's fan community, observing that in the postwar New York metropolitan area, "team affiliation was passed on from father to child, with the crucial moments in a team's history repeated like the liturgy of a church service" (61). For Brooklyn Dodger fans, the dropped pitch of the '41 World Series encapsulated the substance of the Dodger narrative: their dream, a World Series victory, and with it a measure of national and local respect, was constantly just out of reach. The team as a whole had made significant strides since their days as clowns, only to be disappointed at season's end—a motif that would become maddeningly familiar to Dodger fans. The feeling remained that they had not come far enough.

In their Dodger-centric memoirs, Goodwin and a fellow childhood Brooklyn fan, journalist Thomas Oliphant, both claim to be receivers of this Dodger narrative tradition, which Oliphant describes as a "sad, crazy saga, with each year's late flop adding to the lore and legend of the previous one" (153). While Oliphant and Goodwin were both born too late to have any memories of the 1941 Series, both recall being told that specific tale as children. Even though Oliphant's father maintained that the '41 dropped strike gained its critical place in Dodger losing lore only in retrospect, after other late-season collapses seemed to enhance the significance of the moment, the author suggests that, for most Brooklyn fans, "the Dodgers' ensuing history of bitter disappointments in high-pressure situations could be said to have begun the moment Mickey Owen's glove failed to follow [pitcher Hugh]

Casey's pitch" (110). Goodwin presents the 1941 World Series narrative as a Dodger fan's rite of passage or initiation, describing the tale as "a story I was to hear many times from many different people, all ritually re-enacting the tragedy which the years had translated into a strange delight" (42–43).

The next decade and a half would bring much of the same, and the narrative tradition within the community of Dodger fans continued with a cyclical plot of renewed hope being annually swallowed up in stinging defeat. After the Major Leagues' unofficial hiatus during World War II, the Dodgers returned to prewar pennant-winning form and ended the 1946 season in a tie for first place in the National League with the St. Louis Cardinals. This prompted the league's first best-two-out-of-three playoff, which the Cardinals won in two straight games, denying the Dodgers a chance in the World Series. Their fortunes would improve to some degree the following year, however. With the immediate impact of the addition of Jackie Robinson, the Dodgers were even better in 1947, winning the National League but losing a dramatic, closely contested World Series that went the full seven games to the Yankees.

After a down year in 1948, the Dodgers returned to the World Series again in 1949. This Dodger team featured two new stars from the Negro Leagues, Hall of Fame catcher Roy Campanella and pitcher Don Newcombe, who joined future Hall of Famers Robinson, centerfielder Duke Snider, and shortstop Pee Wee Reese, as well as all-stars and fan-favorites Gil Hodges, Carl Furillo, Preacher Roe, and Carl Erskine. Most of this core of players would remain with the Dodgers through the 1955 season, enduring the many heartbreaks and near misses along the way. The first of these for this group was the 1949 World Series itself, which the Casey Stengel–led Yankees took in five closely contested games.

The year 1950 brought even more drama, with Brooklyn starting the season slowly, only to rally and come within one game of tying the Philadelphia Phillies and causing a playoff for the pennant and a chance at a rematch with the Yankees. On the last day of the season, after taking what many observed to be an especially wide turn around third base, leftfielder Cal Abrams was thrown out at home plate trying to score the potential game-winning run against the Phillies, who later won the game in extra innings with a home run by Dick Sisler.[2] This turn of events recalled Mickey Owen's error in the 1941 World Series and served to further the club's image as hard-luck losers among Dodger fans themselves, as well as baseball fans in general.

But this last-minute collapse would pale in comparison to the events of the 1951 season. After jumping out to a fast start, the Dodgers were the frontrunners of the National League for nearly the entire season, holding a thirteen-game lead over their fierce intercity rival the Giants, who were now led by former Brooklyn manager Durocher, as late as August 11. In that month, however, the Dodgers began to lose momentum, while the Giants became red hot, ending the regular season in a tie with Brooklyn and prompting a three-game playoff. After splitting the first two games, the teams headed to the Giants' Polo Grounds for a winner-takes-all showdown. In a close game, Brooklyn finally began to break away, taking a three-run lead into the bottom of the ninth inning, only to have disaster strike. First, the tiring Don Newcombe, who had been dominant until then, gave up a run and put two men on base; then, pitching in relief, Ralph Branca gave up a game-winning three-run homer to Bobby Thomson that sent the Giants to the 1951 World Series. For the second year in a row, the Dodgers lost the pennant in the last inning of their last game of the season. Thomson's home run, dubbed "the shot heard round the world" (after Ralph Waldo Emerson' poetic term for the first gunshot of the American Revolution), remains a touchstone for baseball fans of that era—particularly those living in New York City—and would become yet another symbol of frustration for Dodger fans.

In 1952 and '53 Brooklyn broke their pennant jinx and played in two consecutive World Series. But these seasons also ended in disappointment, as they were handed defeat in both contests by the Yankees yet again. At one point in the 1952 series, the Dodgers seemed to have victory in hand, leading three games to two and needing only one victory to at last claim the championship. But the Yankees bested them twice in a row in two close games to deny them the win. The Yankees' 1953 World Series victory in six games represented five championships in a row, improving upon their previous Major League record of four in a row from 1936 to 1939. Three of these five championships came against the Dodgers, who were still seeking their first.

THE YANKEES AS VILLAINS IN THE DODGERS' NARRATIVE

While the St. Louis Cardinals, Philadelphia Phillies, and their local rival, the New York Giants, all played the role of spoilers at various points for Brooklyn fans, the Yankees were clearly the true villain of their "sad, crazy saga." Every time the Dodgers managed to make the World Series, the Yankees were there waiting to defeat them and their aspirations. During this period, in which world championships became almost routine for the Yankees and their fans, the Dodgers, who were filled with undeniable talent and were, in the minds of their fans, certainly deserving, could never quite manage to win a single one.

This villain's role assigned to the Yankees in the minds of Dodger fans comes through clearly in their recollections to oral historians. Brooklyn fan Bill Reddy put things this way to Peter Golenbock: "There was a feeling of frustration, and it grew worse with every World Series loss, because you would say to yourself, 'When . . . are we ever going to beat [the Yankees]? They can't be invincible. . . . Why can't we beat them?' . . . Every year we got beat. It was such a feeling of frustration. It was getting to be galling" (qtd. in *Bums* 325).

Childhood Dodger fan Florence Rubenstein voiced similar feelings: "The Yankees were always winners and they always had this infuriating arrogance about it. I had cried every year after I would get my hopes up for the Dodgers only to see them lose again. I would get in bed, put my head under the pillow and just cry. . . . Each time a World Series would start it would be like here we go again, and how unfair it all is. But I would hang in there. And after all that time and the way we kept coming back, and tried so hard, we should win already" (qtd. in Oliphant 123).

While he attempts to be a bit more analytical and objective about the issue, even Dodger pitcher Carl Erskine recalled similar feelings:

> See, somehow in sports, life, somehow when you get momentum, it seems you can't turn the dumb stuff around. . . . whenever there was a fluke break, bounce, loop, anything, the darn thing always seemed to go [the Yankees'] way in these close Series. . . . That's just the way it was with the Yankees. Those suckers were tough. . . . But that was just the frustration of playing those guys. Darn it, I don't know if psychologically there was a difference, or whether the Yankee tradition played a part, I don't know what it was, but there was a fine line there somehow that in five World Series against them, we only managed to win one. (qtd. in Golenbock, *Bums* 365)

In his memoir, Oliphant offers more overarching narrative themes to the Dodger fans' experience watching their team lose year after year to the mighty Yankees: "The Brooklyn Dodgers were as much a National team as the Yankees were; where the Yankees personified power and success, the Dodgers symbolized struggle" (32). He suggests that for their fans, "the Dodgers were the epitome of deserving underdog-ism, just as the New York Yankees symbolized Roman Empire–like success and intimidating mastery" (4).

DODGERS AS SYMBOLS OF BROOKLYN

This deserving underdog/successful empire contrast that existed in the collective consciousness of Dodger fans, and to some degree American baseball fans in general, took on a smattering of relevant sociocultural issues that were beyond its intrinsic basic "underdog" narrative. One such issue was the borough of Brooklyn's second-class social status in the context of the city of New York. As home to the nation's advertising, fashion, publishing, broadcasting, and banking industries, as well as the country's largest literary, theater, and visual arts communities, the borough of Manhattan dominated local politics and became a capital of culture for both the nation and the world in the twentieth century. For many Manhattanites, the other boroughs seemed parochial and pedestrian in comparison, and because of New York City's cultural preeminence in the national scene, these attitudes were broadcast across the country.

Brooklyn's perceived cultural inferiority was magnified by history. Until 1898 Brooklyn had been an independent city, but in that year it was officially absorbed into Manhattan's New York City, along with the three other boroughs. Historian Neil J. Sullivan argues that among the boroughs, this change was particularly difficult for Brooklyn: "For all the community's economic and cultural achievements, its consolidation into New York had made it a kind of comic foil to Manhattan. The other boroughs may also have smarted as a result of their second-class status, but as the largest borough in the city, Brooklyn's diminished role required the sharpest adjustment" (15).

Creamer remembers that Brooklyn's perceived position of cultural inferiority made it an easy target for jokes in the 1920s and '30s—the early days of radio, film, and an emerging national popular culture. This coincided with and reflected upon the Dodgers comically bad years at the bottom of the league. "The borough of Brooklyn—Manhattan's Sancho Panza—was America's joke city, a larger Peoria, a bigger Podunk," Creamer writes. "The Brooklyn accent seemed hilarious. Danny Kaye took it to boffo extremes in one of his later routines when the character he was playing declared, 'I'm fwrom Bwrooklyn. My whole family's fwrom Bwrooklyn. I was bawn and bwed in Bwrooklyn.' Radio comedians always got a laugh when they mentioned Brooklyn. For all of Brooklyn's hope, the Dodgers were a joke team from a joke town" (*Baseball in '41* 7–8).

Along with the Dodgers' reflection of the borough's lowly status, Sullivan further argues that even though the Yankees technically play in the Bronx, the intercity rivalry between them and the Dodgers reflected and magnified the cultural tension between Manhattan and Brooklyn: "The Yankees became the image of New York glamour, while the Dodgers, along with Brooklyn, became a comic foil" (10). For Sullivan, the Yankees and the borough of Manhattan were made for each other: "In certain respects, the Yankees mirrored the place of Manhattan in New York City government, the first among equals. Manhattan and the Yankees both dominated their respective spheres in a manner that conveyed arrogance and inevitability. The Yankees attracted fans from the entire metropolitan area" (16). In her memoir, Goodwin corroborates Sullivan's insights, recalling that she always associated the Yankees with the "Wall Street brokers and haughty businessmen" of Manhattan (63).

The Brooklyn-Manhattan tensions that became a facet of the Dodgers-Yankees intercity rivalry took on new significance once the Dodgers began to improve in the early 1940s. With their dramatically improved play and their multiple pennants and World Series appearances, the Dodgers, in Sullivan's words, became "so important to Brooklyn because they symbolized the borough's aspiration to escape a humiliating burlesque role" (15). Creamer remembers Brooklyn's enthusiasm for the newly improved Dodgers spilling over into the rest of the nation during the 1941 season: "The rags to riches story seduced America. Everyone was taken by them. It became an in thing to be a fan of the Dodgers" (*Baseball in '41* 8).

Along with the Dodgers, Brooklyn's less-than-glamorous reputation began to take on new connotations for both Brooklynites and Americans in general in the 1940s. This seemed especially apparent during World War

II in Hollywood's depictions of the American military. Beginning with 1942's *Wake Island*, which featured the character Private "Smaksie" Randall (William Bendix, in an Oscar-nominated performance), "just about every war movie had 'a kid from Brooklyn' in it, usually comic and dumb, though sometimes heroically comic and dumb" (Creamer, *Baseball in '41* 8). About this phenomenon, *New York Times* columnist Russell Baker somewhat cynically observed, "If you'd watched Hollywood's World War II movies you may have thought one of the main things they died for was to save baseball, or at least to save the Brooklyn Dodgers. The basic-war-movie formula of the period called for a kid from Brooklyn to chatter away about the Dodgers between bombardments and kamikaze attacks. Confronted with villainous Axis performers like Conrad Veidt and Richard Loo, Hollywood leading men were apt to declare that the Axis could never crush the spirit of a nation that rooted for the Dodgers."

While Baker presents the underdog populism that these characters embodied with a legitimate skepticism, they are significant for the shift they signaled in the popular connotations the nation associated with Brooklyn. Once something of a national laughing stock, Brooklyn became during the Second World War an icon of American populist values. As Oliphant observes, "These characters could be foolish and buffoons. . . . They could be simple-minded and stubborn, but they were also hardworking, warm, and loving people" (14).

The Dodgers played a key role in this shift in the public's cultural perception of Brooklyn. As the former clowns of baseball became the colorful 1941 pennant winners (with much more success to come after the war) they enraptured much of the country and, by association, helped transform Brooklyn from punch line to the epitome of American populism in the mind of the public. The condescending labeling of Brooklynites as "parochial" or "uncultured" were countered by media portrayals emphasizing the flip side of such adjectives. Parochial became "loyal"; uncultured became "humble." The Dodgers, meanwhile, became one of the primary signifiers of Brooklyn's scruffy underdog populism in the public consciousness, perhaps second only to the famed Brooklyn accent. This is certainly true in the World War II films where moviegoers could tell that the oft-featured "kid from Brooklyn" was the genuine article by his thick accent and his tendency to wax poetic about his hometown Dodgers.

The improved Dodgers' struggles with the storied Yankees in the late 1940s and early 1950s added an interesting wrinkle to Brooklyn's collective pursuit of cultural respectability at midcentury. Just as the success of the Dodgers that began in 1941 had a positive effect on the borough's national profile, so also their inability to beat the Yankees had a detracting effect on the community's social standing. Each time the bridesmaid Dodgers "choked" against the Yankees in the World Series seemed to confirm suspicions that the borough was indeed a deficient or inferior part of bustling, cosmopolitan New York City.

This certainly appears to be the paranoid feeling of Dodgers fans themselves, as indicated by pitcher Carl Erskine's comments after the Dodgers finally beat the Yankees in the 1955 World Series: "It had so much significance. There was personal pride. There was a whole city that now could raise its head, look across the river to the Bronx and Manhattan and say, 'We're number one'" (qtd. in Golenbock, *Bums* 405). As Erskine's observations about the local fans imply, the 1955 victory offered some much-needed resolution to Brooklyn's inferiority complex. But until that monumental 1955 victory, the contested cultural status of Brooklyn within the context of New York and the nation was played out dramatically in their nearly annual clashes with the Yankees. The Dodgers' and Brooklyn's initial promise somehow always gave way to defeat at the hands of the baseball symbols of their cultural superiors, leaving the issue seemingly eternally unsettled.

THE DODGERS AS WORKING-CLASS ICONS

It is perhaps already evident that closely allied with Brooklyn's image consciousness is the issue of socioeconomic class. In their narrative played out on the baseball field in the 1940s and '50s, and particularly in their rivalry with the Yankees, the Dodgers took on a distinct working-class persona. As Dodger fans formulated an identity around their team that celebrated a working-class status and value system, they simultaneously demonized the Yankees and their fans as privileged aristocratic snobs.

Carl E. Prince, in his academic study *Brooklyn's Dodgers: The Bums, the Borough, and the Best of Baseball, 1947–1957*, talks about Brooklyn's residents as being not only predominantly of "lower-middle-class origins," (103) but predominantly "ethnic" as well. "While the fashionable Heights, in the shadow of Brooklyn Bridge, remained generally bedrock elite, native, and Protestant," Prince writes, "the rest of Brooklyn was solidly ethnic: mainly Irish, Italian, and Jewish, with smaller groups of Scandinavians, Greeks, and Poles in the mix" (103). Prince further argues for the prevalence of the conflation of class and ethnicity in "the majority native culture," stating, "inasmuch as foreign origin and lower-class assignment . . . went hand-in-hand, Brooklyn was an especially obvious example of this social judgment" (109). Presumed to be both ethnic and lower class by the nation and the rest of New York, those two markers became integral to Brooklyn residents' identity.

It is difficult to disentangle Brooklyn's ethnic-cum-working-class leanings and the borough's cultural inferiority complex. Indeed, the two seem to be mutually influential. Prince argues as much: "Because of Brooklyn's cultural isolation, both within the borough itself and as a distinct part of greater New York, the sense of class inferiority common to most first and second-generation immigrants could only have been enhanced" (103). Brooklyn's lowly cultural status and the borough's class consciousness were brought even closer in the symbol of a local identity the Dodgers provided the borough.

Just as the team's narrative of struggle, near misses, and an unattained goal parallels Brooklyn's lower cultural status, it likewise resonated with the borough's class consciousness. Like many of Brooklyn's working-class, first- and second-generation immigrants who supported them, the postwar Dodgers were still in the struggle to live the baseball equivalent of the American dream. The postwar Dodgers had made great strides since their years as the clowns of the league in the 1920s and '30s, but their ultimate goal remained out of reach. Similarly, many of Brooklyn's baseball fans would have also felt that their hard work had yielded some socioeconomic gains, but they had yet to "make it"—yet to achieve a certain level of stability and respect, yet to feel they had attained the American dream. For such fans, rooting for the Dodgers provided some sense of solidarity and identity, perhaps allowing them to take pride in their struggle and progress despite their low social standing and the fact that they, like their team, had yet to gain their ultimate goal.

Prince even suggests that the Dodgers acted as a unifier of Brooklyn's ethnic subgroups in this regard: "Overt class consciousness seemed to run higher in Brooklyn than elsewhere in the city, and the Dodgers' presence helped maintain an uneasy truce among ethnic groups. . . . The realities of immigrant differences dominated everyday life. . . . The Dodgers, in this tense setting, formed a social force for acculturation, perhaps an example of the larger role baseball has played in shaping American commonality in the twentieth century" (103).

Perhaps any baseball team might have provided some sense of unity; yet it is significant that the Dodgers' team narrative paralleled the personal narrative of so many Brooklynites. Moreover, the Dodgers offered a more abstract version of the narrative, enabling individuals from one ethnic background to recognize that same narrative in the lives of fellow fans from other ethnic backgrounds. The Dodgers could represent them all.

Just as Dodger fans cultivated a working-class identity for themselves and their team, they likewise used the successful Yankees as a wealthy socioeconomic foil. This is quite apparent in the memoirs of both Goodwin and Oliphant. Goodwin writes about the culture of comparative fan loyalty in her Long Island suburb, asserting, "the Yankees were the 'Bronx Bombers,' whose pinstriped uniforms signified their elite status, supported by the rich and successful," while the Dodgers were thought of as "unpretentious clowns, whose fans were seen as scruffy blue-collar workers who spoke with bad diction" (63). While even Goodwin acknowledges this depiction as an "exaggerated caricature" (63), the existence of the caricature itself reveals the importance of class identity to the ideological borders on Dodger fans' conceptual "mattering map" that Grossberg has suggested.

The association of wealth and privilege with the Yankees is even more prevalent in Oliphant's memoir. The author offers several remembered details that clearly link the Bronx Bombers with a reputation as rich, high-class elites. For instance, Oliphant recounts that the private school he attended on a scholarship was "filled with kids from wealthy families who were nearly all Yankee fans" (28). He even recounts an experience of attending a country club with one such well-off classmate in 1953 and becoming acutely aware that he was "a tiny Dodger island in a sea of Yankee fans" while they watched the televised broadcast of a World Series game in the club lounge (202). Similarly, Oliphant specifies that the baseball loyalties in the law office where his mother worked were clearly divided along class lines, with the partners generally supporting the Yankees and his mother and the other secretaries rooting for the Dodgers (24, 93). Upon this clearly drawn social world of baseball fandom from his childhood recollections, Oliphant sprinkles a number of additional class-conscious digs at the Yankees, from his description of Yankee Stadium as "a majestic palace" (11) with box seats filled with "big shots" (223), to his characterization of postwar Yankee owners Del Webb and Dan Topping as "the boss of a real estate development empire" and "a trust fund child with movie star looks and gobs of money from the Anaconda copper fortune," respectively (160).

This very cut-and-dried world Oliphant describes, where baseball rooting interests most often seem to be a direct result of one's salary (or his or her father's), may be a bit of an exaggeration. Writing in 2005, Oliphant could be accused of magnifying fuzzy childhood memories from fifty years ago, shaping them perhaps by his own current sociopolitical biases. Though he may overgeneralize or embellish, the kernel of Oliphant's characterization of the rivalry's class identity divide is corroborated by Sullivan, Goodwin, and others, lending it some credibility.

As another example, even lifelong Yankee fan Peter Golenbock's nostalgia-tinged first book about the Bronx Bombers of the Stengel years backs up the essence of the Yankees' midcentury class connotations so thoroughly embraced by Oliphant's narrative. Notably, Golenbock gives his book *Dynasty: The New York Yankees, 1949–1964* the subtitle, "When rooting for the Yankees was like rooting for U.S. Steel," inspired by a popular early-1950s aphorism.[3] The author expounds upon the decidedly corporate connotations of this subtitle in his memoir-like introduction where he writes,

> When I was growing up in upper-middle-class suburbia, I attended private school, belonged to a country club, all my friends were white, and I rooted for the Yankees. Which only figured. I felt that the Dodgers and Giants were supported by a different kind of person—the blue-collar masses of the Bronx, Queens, and Brooklyn—and that somehow they were different from the Yankees and me. Later I found out that bank presidents rooted for the Dodgers and Bowery derelicts wore Yankee caps. But in many minds the powerful Yankees were seen to be the embodiment of the Establishment—a fantastically successful corporation with everyone from the owners down to the batboys working together for the good of the firm. (ix)

While the term "Establishment" had additional connotations in the wake of Vietnam and the 1960s counterculture—Golenbock published his book in 1975—the author's characterization of his own experience as a young fan is largely based on economic class. Building on the U.S. Steel metaphor, Golenbock echoes Dodger fans in comparing the Yankee organization and its rooters to elite, upper-crust capitalists "working together for the good of the firm." While Golenbock sides with Goodwin over Oliphant in emphasizing that the notion that all Yankee fans were wealthy and all Dodgers fans were working class was mostly a myth, he highlights the significant role this myth played in the formation of the identities of these two clubs and especially their fans.

"DEM BUMS"

Perhaps the most vital evidence for the class characterization of the Dodgers-Yankees rivalry is *New York World Telegram* cartoonist Willard Mullin's personification of the Brooklyn club and its fans in a "bum" caricature and the eventual embrace of this portrayal by those fans and the organization itself. Supposedly inspired during the "Daffiness Boys" era in 1937 by a cab driver who picked up the cartoonist as he left a game at Ebbets Field and asked him, "Well, what'd dem bums do today?" Mullin began drawing a tramp, complete with patched and tattered clothing and a five o'clock shadow, to embody the spirit of the team and its fans (G. Stout 97). Though the image was originally intended to poke fun at both the team and the borough, Dodger fans eventually embraced it, particularly once the team improved in the 1940s; and soon "Dem Bums" became an unofficial nickname for the club.

The "Bums" theme became a common motif at Ebbets Field and in the broader network of Dodger fan culture. It was not unusual for fans to dress up like tramps themselves and this ragamuffin style became the unofficial dress code for the fan-organized "Sym-Phony Band" that punctuated games at Ebbets Field with moments of musical humor. But the fans were not alone in their embrace of the "Bums" image. The organization itself used illustrations of the Brooklyn Bum drawn by Mullin himself for the front covers of their annual "Year Books" in the first half of the 1950s (Fig. 1), and later in 1957 hired renowned circus clown Emmett Kelly to perform before home

118   *"WALL STREET BROKERS AND HAUGHTY BUSINESSMEN"*

FIG. 1. Dodgers 1952 "This Is Next Year."
Courtesy of the Estate of Willard Mullin. Used with permission.

games dressed up as a tramp, "the living personification of the Bum character" (D'Agostino and Crosby 119).

The "Bums" nickname and image soon became well known to the national community of baseball fans at large. This fact is most clearly demonstrated by the oft-cited cartoon that appeared on the front page of the *New York Daily News* on October 5, 1955, the day after the Dodgers at long last beat the Yankees and won their first and only World Series in Brooklyn. Drawn by Leo O'Mealia but based heavily on Mullin's original creation, the *Daily News* cartoon showed a tramp with the telltale beard scruff flashing a toothless but convincingly wide grin. "Who's a Bum!" the accompanying headline read in large letters typically reserved for events like declarations of war or the sinking of the Titanic.

The class connotations of this chosen mascot for the Brooklyn Dodgers require little in the way of explanation, but it is important to emphasize that Dodgers fans usually wore the Bum iconography as a badge of honor. Brooklyn native and *New York Herald Tribune* sportswriter Roger Kahn maintains that the moniker "Bums" was never used as a "local term of affection" (*The Era: 1947–1957* 16). There is ample evidence, such as buttons and pennants with the Bums nickname, to suggest he is wrong, however; and there can be little doubt that Dodger fans, along with the organization itself, embraced the Bums image with all of its connotations of the underclass.

This embrace takes on additional meaning when one considers that many Brooklynites might have sensed what Dodger historian Glenn Stout argued about Mullin's caricature, that it was not so much intended as a metaphor for the on-field fortunes of the down-and-out 1930s Dodgers—though it certainly succeeds on that level—but that Mullin's caricature "focuses on the futility not on the field but off it, on the Depression-afflicted few who still bothered to turn out at Ebbets Field" (97). This notion of the Bum as a caricature of the Dodgers' Brooklyn fan base is underscored by the fact that the Bum could often be seen speaking in a heavy "Brooklynese" accent/dialect. For example, a delirious Bum from a Mullin cartoon in the wake of the 1955 World Series victory exclaims, "We dood it! We beat 'em! We beat them Yankees! We spot 'em th' foist two games . . . an' we beat 'em! That Podres! Woil' Cham-peens! Me!" The cartoon implies that while the Dodgers may have at last won the championship, they remained irrevocably working class and irrevocably Brooklyn.

Why would a group of people who supposedly already had an inferiority complex embrace an icon that emphasizes their economic disadvantage? Prince offers this rationale: "The 'Bum' was never meant to denigrate the lowly. It represented at heart a lingering Depression mentality that exalted the virtue that it wasn't what you had that mattered, but how you looked at things. In this way, it was a Dodger-focused, widely understood symbol of working-class pride; the emphasis is on class here, for one of the Bum's roles was to mock perceived 'upper class' pretensions" (105). As Prince's comments suggest, the self-consciously working-class aura of the Bum mascot can be thought of as a subtle form of protest aimed at the affluent, the elite, and the successful. To use Grossberg's terminology, the Bum stood as a key signpost on the "mattering map" of cultural values for Brooklyn Dodger fans.

The Yankees, of course, acted as an icon against which these fans protested. This is made particularly clear in some of Mullin's less-famous baseball cartoons. While the cartoonist's Brooklyn Bum has achieved some level of national awareness, less well known are his postwar illustrations of New York's two other teams, the Yankees and the Giants. Caricatures personifying all three teams are depicted together in cartoons used for the cover of a baseball season schedule distributed by The Manufacturers Trust Company throughout the New York area. In these cartoons the New York Giant is, as the nickname dictates, the tallest and largest of the three, but his largeness is portrayed as flab rather than muscle, perhaps evoking the relative decline of the franchise that was once one of the most successful in the early decades of the twentieth century. In contrast to this big but harmless oaf and the Dodgers' short, stocky, and quintessentially scruffy Bum, the pinstriped figure representing the Yankees stands tall, neat, and muscled (Fig. 2). The close-up facial portraits on the cover of the 1953 schedule reveals a square-jawed Yankee, perhaps bearing a slight resemblance to the All-American movie star cowboy and icon of midcentury masculinity, John Wayne (Fig. 3).

Here Mullin does not portray the Yankees as an extreme caricature of American wealth the same way he does the Dodgers and poverty, nor does he in the occasional cartoons for the *World-Telegram* in which the team makes an appearance. Instead, the Yankees and their success are coded as a mainstream ideal of masculinity, perhaps especially as venerated in popular military and Western narratives, whether film, pulp fiction, comics, or television. By drawing on the deep connection between success and "true" manhood as described by Kimmel, Mullin effectively portrays the mainstream postwar view of the iconic Yankees as described in the previous chapter: all-American, victorious, battle-hardened, and ideal in their success. But the presence of the Dodgers' Bum in these illustrations alters this perspective. To the sympathetic viewer, the masculine, idealized Yankee looks privileged and bland in comparison to the scruffy but lovable Bum.

FIG. 2. Cover of the 1951 Schedule of Home Games.
Courtesy of the Estate of Willard Mullin. Used with permission.

It might be going too far, however, to presume it was Mullin's intention to undercut the Yankees' status or make them look elitist in his drawings. Far more likely, the cartoonist's goal was to portray the Yankees as he felt America saw them, and in this regard he succeeded, giving an embodied physical form to an idea that already widely existed in the popular consciousness. I would contend, however, that it *was* the aim of Brooklyn Dodger fans, if perhaps

FIG. 3. Cover of the 1953 Schedule of Home Games. Courtesy of the Estate of Willard Mullin. Used with permission.

only unconsciously, to sabotage the Yankees' iconic status, to make them look elitist and privileged through their conscious adoption of the underclass "Bum" imagery. These performances challenge the Yankees' position as "all-American" or representing America in postwar era.

THE DODGERS, THE YANKEES, AND THE POSTWAR AMERICAN DREAM

The prominent presence of the Dodgers and their fans as a challenge to the established Yankees in postwar sporting culture suggest that America could be something other than the triumphalism and near-constant success of the

Bronx Bombers. And one of the more significant things that Dodgers fans implied was that America could be was working class. Such an assertion of a working-class identity is particularly meaningful considering the strong tendency for popular culture in the 1950s to skew increasingly middle class and suburban in its presentation of the nation. After the crucible of economic depression and world war, many celebrated the relatively prosperous 1950s as the arrival of the long-sought "good life." It seemed to many that the nation as a whole had "pulled itself up by its bootstraps" to achieve a life of abundance.

As Rader suggests, the new medium of television was particularly good at broadcasting such an image of the nation and its citizens "[bleaching] out differences" as it "[shifted] toward a world of suburban uniformity" (*American Ways* 316). This was true, whether in domestic, suburban, and middle-class situation comedies such as *The Adventures of Ozzie and Harriet* (radio 1944–50, television 1952–66) and *Father Knows Best* (1954–60), or in the ever-present advertisements and corporate sponsors offering an increasing variety of consumer goods and products.

In this increasingly mass-media-dominated culture focused on domestic, middle-class prosperity and the suburban "good life," the working-class persona of the Dodgers and their fans acted as a subtle form of cultural protest. While many from the working class *were* able to achieve middle-class status with the help of the G.I. Bill and generous home-loan policies in this era, the Dodgers' Bum persona all but declared that not all Americans had the means to buy the split-level ranch house seen on television and in magazine advertisements. The Dodgers served as a reminder that the triumphal postwar America the Yankees embodied was not the only postwar America.

Even today, the working-class identity of midcentury Dodgers fan culture can act as a powerful antidote to the popular overgeneralization that the reality of 1950s America was reflected in the bland domesticity of *Leave It to Beaver* (1957–63). Though the celebration of suburban abundance in such mass-media texts do accurately capture certain cultural trends and were powerful cultural influences themselves, figures like Willard Mullin's Bum or his fellow Brooklynite, the down-and-out bus driver Ralph Kramden from TV's *The Honeymooners* (1951–55), offer evidence that 1950s American culture was far from monolithic.

While the Dodgers' working-class connotations certainly do not challenge or overturn the American dream narrative that is so vividly embodied in the succession of rags-to-riches Yankee heroes, I would argue that they do portray it in a different context and with a different emphasis. Though the Yankees had an unbroken tradition of stars who lived out an Algeresque narrative beginning as young men of little means, the club's long tradition of success looms over these individual stories of upward mobility. With this tradition of sustained Yankee success figuring large in the personal narrative of upward mobility for all these players, the version of the American dream conveyed by the Yankees places a distinct emphasis on the achieved success or "good life" at the end of the rags-to-riches journey. The disadvantaged backstories of heroes like Gehrig and DiMaggio that had received attention in popular media were always viewed through the lens of their eventual success. As such, the Yankees in the postwar era could effectively be described as an icon of the American dream *achieved*.

Though the Dodgers did not have a high-profile star with a rags-to-riches story as widely broadcast as that of Ruth, Gehrig, or DiMaggio (though, Jackie Robinson, who will be discussed later, came close), the collective narrative of the Brooklyn Dodgers as a team essentially dramatizes this same story of upward mobility, precisely in the manner that the postwar Yankees did not. Not only did the Dodgers' history as the league's laughingstock in the 1920s and '30s make them a candidate for the all-American upward-mobility saga, but the fact that they remained perennial bridesmaids from 1941 until their long-awaited World Series win in 1955 even further enhanced their cultural connotations as underdog outsiders.

Since their team histories led to vastly different cultural connotations, the six World Series meetings between the Yankees and the Dodgers between 1941 and 1955 played out as a metaphoric battle between competing perspectives on the American dream. The Dodgers were a reminder that, in the midst of the postwar culture of abundance and plenty, there were still many who had yet to achieve any imagined notion of this dream.

THE BROOKLYN EXODUS AND THE MIDDLE-CLASS DODGER FAN

It has already been acknowledged as truth that, in terms of socioeconomic class, Yankee and Dodger fans did not quite uniformly correspond with the popular personas of their respective teams. However, it is worth further noting that, ironically, even as the Dodgers' struggles with the Yankees in the late '40s and early '50s symbolically brought issues of class and competing perspectives on the American dream to a national stage, in precisely that same time period an increasing many who identified themselves as Dodger fans could begin to claim experience with the Yankee-like perspective on the American dream—the dream *already achieved.* For in the postwar era, many working-class families that had inhabited the borough—children or grandchildren of European immigrants, whether Irish, Italians, or Jews from Poland, Russia, or Germany—came into their own economically and began departing Brooklyn for the relatively open spaces of middle-class neighborhoods in the villages and suburbs of Long Island.

And as Goodwin suggests, these former Brooklynites brought their baseball loyalties with them: "as earlier immigrants brought their ethnic bonds with them to America, the settlers of suburbia had, for the most part, carried their baseball fidelity from their borough of origin" (61). Goodwin herself, raised in Rockville Centre, Long Island, but the daughter of Michael Kearns, a native of the Brooklyn neighborhood of Flatbush, was the product of this tendency, as were her friends from the block, the Rusts, Dodger fans who had carried their loyalties to Rockville Centre from their original home in the Brooklyn neighborhood of Sheepshead Bay (65–66).

Departing the borough for Long Island between the late 1930s and '40s, Goodwin's father and the Rusts constituted an advance guard of a larger exodus from the borough that swelled in the early 1950s, "the first wave of Brooklyn emigrants," as Golenbock describes it, which was followed by a second wave that "grew to tidal force by the end of the 1950s" (*Bums* 428). This emigration from Brooklyn to communities on Long Island is intimately connected with issues of economic class. As social anthropologist Karen Brodkin details, the economic growth of the postwar era enabled many working-class Americans—many of them children or grandchildren of the European immigrants of the nineteenth century that were considered ethnic inferiors prior to World War II—to improve their lot. "It was a time when the old white and the newly white masses became middle class," she writes (44). The educational opportunities made possible to many men by the GI Bill and the generous home loans granted them by the Federal Housing

Administration enabled many from the working class to not only increase their earning power but also relocate from rented apartments or row houses to larger homes they owned themselves in comparatively more affluent neighborhoods (44–45, 47). This was particularly true for working-class Brooklyn, where people like Brodkin's own parents, who moved from Sheepshead Bay to Valley Stream, Long Island, in 1949, could get their own little piece of the dream of economic uplift and home ownership by departing for the greener pastures to the east (42–43).

As relatively comfortable middle-class suburbanites who continued to root for the Dodgers, the club's strong working-class associations took on interesting meanings for these transplanted Brooklynites. In her memoir, Goodwin outlines her father's "up-by-his-bootstraps" narrative quite clearly, describing how a talent with numbers helped him transcend his lack of formal education and get a job as a bank examiner that "carried him from a Brooklyn tenement to a house with a lawn on Southard Avenue in Rockville Centre" (18). After delineating her father's difficult childhood as the son of Irish immigrants who died when he was young (29), Goodwin further suggests that even though the house she grew up in was "modest in size," to her parents it "was the realization of a dream" (55).

Goodwin's association of her father with this narrative of the American dream of upward mobility colors her perspectives on Brooklyn and the Dodgers, both of which are always filtered through her relationship with her father. "My father had literally grown up with Ebbets Field," she writes, "his devotion to the Dodgers so intertwined with his own biography that my sisters and I could no more have conceived of rooting for another team than of rooting against him" (66). For Goodwin, her father *was* the Brooklyn Dodgers. As such, while she would never have identified personally with the "scruffy, blue-collar" caricature of the Dodger fan, the team's working-class persona strongly correlates with her own sense of her family's past: that, like her father's personal history, they had come from that kind of struggle and disadvantage. Thus, for Goodwin, the Dodgers acted as an icon of the working-class ethos she could claim through her recent familial past, even if her family's current economic situation was more consistent with the Yankee-like condition of having already won out in their American dream. That upwardly mobile, transplanted Brooklyn families—like the Rusts from

Goodwin's memoir, or that of Karen Brodkin, or the thousands of others like them—would have had a similar relationship with Brooklyn and the Dodgers is not only feasible but likely. For such families, the Dodgers and their strong working-class persona may have been particularly useful in providing some sense of continuity. In addition to helping them maintain ties to their old home of Brooklyn, their Dodger fandom gave them a continuing claim on some sense of a working-class ethos and loyalty, despite the fact that they were no longer part of the literal working class in economic terms. Acknowledging the relative superficiality of this connection, it constitutes a connection nonetheless.

The decision to continue to support the Dodgers, then, while likely done primarily out of loyalty and familial precedent, nevertheless encouraged, through Grossberg's "mattering map" concept, a value system that emphasized and held up the condition of struggling to achieve one's dream as more important than the actual achieving of it. By embracing the Dodgers and their working-class identity, middle-class fans in Long Island or anywhere else, even if they never had direct connections to Brooklyn itself, could identify themselves with, and perhaps romanticize, a working-class ethos that was no longer, or perhaps never was, part of their actual personal or familial economic experience. In such scenarios, support for the Dodgers' iconic identity and disdain for the Yankees' ceased to be a class-based politics of identity and became more about ideology.

It would be foolish to pretend that most Dodger fans extrapolated their devotion to an underdog team and formed a sociocultural ideology solely on this basis. Nevertheless, the cultural connotations of the Yankees-Dodgers rivalry certainly provided opportunity. Quite clearly, this claiming of personal ideological territory is what the Harvard-educated, Pulitzer Prize–nominated journalist Thomas Oliphant engages in his 2005 memoir, as he caricatures the Yankees and their fans from his youthful memories as the privileged elite, while casting himself and his fellow Dodger fans as scrappy, hopeful strivers. His claim on the Dodgers provides an excellent example of the condition of embracing not a working-class identity but a working-class ethos through their persona. Disregarding any implications about his loyalties in partisan politics or opinions about contemporary economic policy, Oliphant's act of claiming loyalty with the Dodgers of his youth, while simultaneously distancing himself from the successful Yankees of that past, clearly projects a distinct imagining of the nation as mediated through a specific take on the American dream narrative: one that focuses on and romanticizes a heroic struggle of working for the dream that may still be ongoing for many, rather than championing an image of the nation basking in the well-deserved fruits of a harmonious good life it has already earned. For Oliphant, it was the Dodgers' persona that most characterized the nation and the "true" American dream, not that of the triumphant Yankees, as evidenced in his declaration that "for baseball, the New York Yankees ruled the 1950s; in the larger context of the country in the 1950s, the Brooklyn Dodgers were America's Team" (7). That Oliphant uses the narrative of these two teams in the postwar era to make such an ideological statement in 2005 is a testament to the power of both as cultural icons.

THE YANKEES, DODGERS, AND RACE

In the postwar era, African Americans represented a significant number of citizens who had not achieved—nor been given much of a chance to achieve—any kind of mythic "good life" that the triumphant Yankees seemed to imply. Historically, this had been as true in the world of professional baseball as it was in any other American institution. As historian Jules Tygiel argues, however, with the signing of Jackie Robinson in 1946, Major League Baseball helped lead the way in the nation's long journey towards integration, preceding nearly all other key milestones in the history of desegregation (*Baseball's Great Experiment* 9).

The whole of baseball did not embrace integration all at once and without conflict, however; individual clubs integrated one by one and at their own pace. The Dodgers and the Yankees were on the opposite ends of the spectrum with regard to integration. Brooklyn president Branch Rickey put Brooklyn in the lead of desegregation. He initiated integration by signing Robinson to the Dodgers franchise, and the club followed up Robinson's 1947 major-league debut with the addition of Don Newcombe and Roy Campanella in 1949, Joe Black in 1952, Jim Gilliam in 1953, and black Cuban Sandy Amoros in 1954. These acquisitions meant that in 1954, with Newcombe or Black on the pitcher's mound and the potential for four other black players in fielding positions, the Dodgers became the first baseball club to field a team that was a majority black. This first occurred on July 17, 1954 (Tygiel, *Baseball's Great Experiment* 307). Many other clubs followed suit, gradually becoming integrated to a significant degree. The New York Yankees were not one of them. In fact, the Yankees, the acknowledged kings of baseball during the era when integration took place, were among the last to integrate. When Elston Howard made his debut as the first black Yankee in 1955, only the Philadelphia Phillies, Detroit Tigers, and Boston Red Sox remained unintegrated.

A variety of contributing factors have been proposed for the cause of the Yankees' slow acceptance of integration. Certainly, the Yankees' refusal to integrate was symptomatic of the American League in general, whose teams, with a few exceptions, drafted black talent less quickly and frequently when compared to the National League. Yet, David Halberstam suggests that the Yankees front office itself set the tone for this reticence (*October 1964* 54). Halberstam further argues that the Yankees' failure to integrate can largely be attributed to general manager George Weiss's personal views on race, which disseminated down through the ranks of scouts, such as Tom Greenwade, who had helped Branch Rickey in scouting Jackie Robinson but was told by Weiss, "Now, Tom, I don't want you signing any niggers. We don't want them" (55). Roger Kahn corroborates Halberstam's conclusion, describing how, "after three martinis," the "third highest executive" (apparently Weiss) asserted that a black man would never appear in a Yankee uniform, explaining, "We don't want that sort of crowd. It would offend boxholders from Westchester to have to sit with niggers" (*Boys of Summer* 164).

Whatever the reason for the Yankee organization's hesitancy, the Yankees became the "white team" in the context of New York City baseball in the postwar era. While Brooklyn remained the league leader in integration, the Giants organization followed the Dodgers' lead, desegregating quickly and thoroughly. In 1949 Hank Thompson and Monte Irvin debuted to officially integrate the Giants. In 1951 they added Willie Mays and started Major League Baseball's first all-black outfield. Thus, in the decade when, as the subtitle of Roger Kahn's book *The Era, 1947–1957* described it, "the Yankees, the Giants, and the Dodgers Ruled the World," the Yankees effectively became New York's all-white team. The success of these three New York City clubs during this period helped broadcast this nationally.

The combination of being one of the last "lilywhite" teams and being the most dominant team in baseball did much to shape the Yankees' popular image in the postwar period. This contrast was made all the clearer by the fact that they met the Dodgers so many times on baseball's biggest stage in such a short period. In light of the context of race and integration, these World Series battles took on aspects of sociological conflict and historical drama, anticipating and embodying the slow advance of racial integration in the United States.

In this dramatic narrative played out before the American public on the baseball diamond, the Dodgers became a symbol of integration for Americans. Oliphant captures some of this distinct role they came to fill in the national culture: "The Dodgers had a unique glow because they were the team that broke the color line; not only that, they had gone way beyond this to give a still-segregated and essentially racist society one of its few glimpses of equal opportunity itself. In the African-American community Jackie Robinson was beyond hero status; and in a growing part of white America that was embarrassed by overt racism a decade after World War II, Robinson's heroic achievement was a powerful symbol of hope that easily became affection for his integrated team" (43).

But the Dodgers were far more than just a symbol of integration. Tygiel argues that Jackie Robinson and the other black players who followed him into the majors led the way for civil rights on the ground level, providing its advocates with "a model of peaceful transition through militant confrontation, economic pressure, and moral suasion" (*Baseball's Great Experiment* 9). Dodger president Branch Rickey's signing of Robinson to a major league contract in 1946 and Robinson's major league debut the following year preceded and prefigured all the oft-observed hallmarks of the civil rights movement, including the desegregation of the military in 1948, the *Brown v. Board of Education of Topeka* decision in 1954, and the Montgomery bus boycott of 1955.

The Dodgers also came to occupy an important place in the African American community, in particular. Tygiel describes black baseball fans affixing "their loyalty to not only Robinson, but the Dodgers as well" (*Baseball's Great Experiment* 167). This loyalty in the African American community, together with the presence of Robinson and several other black players who followed closely on his heels, effectively made Brooklyn the "black" team in the national consciousness. Though there was certainly some resistance to integration among both Dodgers players of southern birth and white ethnic Brooklyn fans (Kahn, *The Era* 34–36; Golenbock, *Bums* 155–59), the team's association with the nation's racial outsiders generally harmonized with the cultural persona of scrappy, working-class bridesmaid underdogs it had cultivated for itself. And once again, the Yankees were there to act as the perfect foil.

The Yankee-Dodger rivalry's uncanny parallel of the national struggle over integration, the main rising social conflict of the era, is perhaps its most important cultural significance. It would be both naïve and glib to presume that Dodger fans were all integrationists and Yankee fans all segregationists. True, Oliphant seems to imply such a neat and clean liberal/conservative split in his memoir. He characterizes Dodger fans as a coalition of the noble working class and progressive intellectuals, while it seems all Yankee supporters of the author's acquaintance were stodgy, conservative capitalists or spoiled prep-school kids (24, 28, 93, 151). As reductive as such a representation is, it does gesture towards the historic reality: the Yankees' failure to integrate until 1955, their elitist cultural connotations among Brooklyn fans, and their literal and metaphoric role of constant spoiler of Dodger hopes and dreams on the field.

With the Yankees' all-white lineup, their continual defeat of the integrated Dodgers represented a deferral of the dream of civil rights as well. This would have been particularly and painfully true for black baseball fans, many of whom, as Tygiel suggests, had adopted the Dodgers as their team following Robinson's debut. Just as the collective hopes of African Americans for socioeconomic uplift were thwarted by the irrationality of lingering racism, so also were the integrated Dodgers repeatedly, frustratingly, and sometimes inexplicably barred from the success the Bronx Bombers represented.

This is reflected in evidence suggesting that black baseball fans increasingly saw the Yankees as "the white team" in the late 1940s and early '50s. African American author Ernest Gaines suggests as much in retrospect in his 1971 novel, *The Autobiography of Miss Jane Pittman*, in which the title character succinctly explains that "Jackie and the Dodgers was for the colored people. The Yankees was for the white folks" (203). This notion of the Yankees as a white antagonist to black hopes is borne out in early 1950s sports journalism of black newspapers like the *Pittsburgh Courier, Baltimore*

Afro-American, and *Chicago Defender,* where writers such as Wendell Smith and Sam Lacy kept close watch over and cast a suspicious and often critical eye at the organization's integration efforts, or lack thereof (Tygiel, *Baseball's Great Experiment* 294–99). At one point in October 1953, the *Pittsburgh Courier's* Smith, a champion of desegregation and Jackie Robinson, grew so frustrated with what he saw as hypocrisy and double speak in their efforts to recruit black players, he concluded that the lilywhite Yankees were a "ruthless, vindictive lot" (qtd. in Tygiel, *Baseball's Great Experiment* 294).

The role the Yankees played in this metaphoric racial struggle complements Dodger fans' conception of the team as the embodiment of Manhattan snobbery and upper-class elitism. With these connotations of cultural, economic, and racial privilege and empowerment, the Yankees, for Dodgers fans, were the essence of the established, sometimes unjust American power structure at midcentury.

This alternate perspective on the Yankees is a striking contrast to the heroically triumphal, patriotic postwar Yankees of Joe DiMaggio, or the Yankees that projected populist integrity through the martyred Lou Gehrig in the late 1930s and early '40s. That side of the club, so evident in *The Pride of the Yankees* and the mass-media cult surrounding DiMaggio, represented many of the most celebrated American values: democracy, hard work, a belief in the possibility of upward mobility. With Mantle carrying the torch of that legacy through the 1950s and early '60s, those positive connotations still existed. However, the perspective on the Yankees taken by Dodger fans and introduced to the nation at large through their media attention challenged the face-value acceptance of the health of these values in the United States in that moment. With ultimate success always just out of reach and with their cultural connotations as racial and socioeconomic outsiders, the Dodgers' very existence seemed to suggest that the celebrated, bountiful postwar America represented by the Yankees had a hidden dark side. Not only was the postwar American working class sometimes glossed over or ignored by a culture that increasingly celebrated itself as uniformly middle class and suburban, but even more glaringly, racial prejudice prevented many black Americans from having any real chance at entering that middle class. Notably, the government subsidies for education and housing that many lower-income white Americans took advantage of were denied to people of color (Rader, *American Ways* 314).

The racial context of the Yankees-Dodgers rivalry adds an additional dynamic to the contrasting visions of the American dream narrative the two teams represented. These respective versions of the American dream narrative with contrasting emphases that the Yankees and the Dodgers embodied—self-made success already achieved versus continued struggle and effort in the face of defeat—are quite fitting of the racial profile of each club. The Yankees, with their legacy of high-profile heroes who were sons or grandsons of European immigrants—Germans like Ruth, Gehrig, and Henrich, or Italians like DiMaggio, Berra, Rizzuto, and Lazzeri—roughly represent the standard popular telling of the American dream as imagined in the mid-twentieth century. The Yankees' triumphal version of this narrative, with the emphasis placed on success achieved, is particularly fitting in the postwar era.

The crucible of World War II largely minimized the significance of the white ethnic difference of these Yankee heroes. As Hank Greenberg, the Detroit Tigers' Jewish Hall of Fame slugger during the 1930s and '40s, observed, "When you joined the army, you became an American. When I first broke into baseball, every time they wrote about me, it had something to do with my ethnic background. When the war was over, ballplayers were no longer referred to by their religion. . . . It was an amazing change that took place" (*The Life and Times of Hank Greenberg*).

This was as true in other aspects of American society as it was in baseball. As individuals of various European backgrounds worked together in military companies and war-effort assembly lines, all with the goal of defeating an enemy characterized by bigotry, those of European backgrounds who had once been held in suspicion became fully integrated into the American mainstream. Furthermore, the strong U.S. postwar economy combined with generous government policies assisting former GIs and their brides with college educations and buying a first home enabled many sons and grandsons of European immigrants to move from the working class into an expanding middle class. Rader describes these policies as effectively integrating "into the mainstream a whole chunk of society that had been living on the edge" (Rader, *American Ways* 314).

This socioeconomic uplift of European ethnics had a racial dimension as well. As Matthew Frye Jacobson argues in his book *Whiteness of a Different Color*, the boundaries of the American concept of a mainstream white race—"its internal hierarchies, its proper boundaries, and its rightful claimants"—

have changed and shifted over time, "and it has been a fairly untidy affair" (5). For much of the nineteenth century, many ethnic immigrant groups were not necessarily looked upon as "white" and certainly not part of the American mainstream. David Roediger even argues that the current concept of "ethnicity" did not exist in this period, with recent American immigrants from Southern and Eastern Europe (and sometimes Ireland) often identified as being from various "nation-races" separate and distinct from the favored, "white" old-stock Americans from Northern Europe (18–21). The early twentieth century was then a transitional period with regard to European ethnics and whiteness. But again, by the end of World War II, any lingering doubts about the "racial integrity" of European ethnics had all but disappeared and the term "ethnicity" began to be applied to these peoples rather than "race" (Roediger 25). A new racial boundary had been drawn, with those appearing to be of European decent—and therefore "white"—on one side of the line and people of color—those appearing to be of African, Asian, Native American, or Latin American descent—on the other side (Jacobson 91–93).

Not coincidentally, these Americans of color were not only unable to enter into the privileged circle of whiteness, but racial discrimination largely prevented them from taking advantage of many of the socioeconomic opportunities of the postwar era as well. Thus, while the nation was collectively congratulating itself for enduring the Depression and soldiering through World War II to emerge a powerful economic dynamo, and with many able to own their own homes and think of themselves as "middle class" for the first time, such opportunity was still denied to many on the basis of racial categorization. Most prominent among such groups in the national consciousness at the time were African Americans.

With Jackie Robinson and as many as four additional black Dodgers on the team's roster, the Brooklyn club gave baseball representation to these racially and socioeconomically marginalized Americans. Their many head-to-head matchups with the Yankees and their tradition of white ethnic heroes called into question this established midcentury conceptualization of the American dream. This most common perspective, as visibly seen in *The Pride of the Yankees,* for instance, celebrated the idea of socioeconomic upward mobility for European-descended Americans while simultaneously denying Americans of color this same right and ability. In other words, the Dodgers' high profile in the postwar era all but accused a nation of hypocrisy for reveling in the rhetoric of the American dream but still tolerating segregation. And the Yankees were the prime example of this common perspective. The presence of the Dodgers cast the Yankee American dream as an incomplete and exclusionary one.

The subtle cultural protest that the integrated Dodgers implied was magnified by the way Jackie Robinson was placed in the heroic mold established in the mass media by Ruth, Gehrig, and DiMaggio. A quick survey of Jackie Robinson's pop-culture profile in the late 1940s and early '50s reveals a body of cultural products that closely parallels the types of popular texts that featured those Yankee heroes. Not only was Robinson's image used to sell Wheaties breakfast cereal and plastered on the covers of both *Time* and *Life* magazines, but 1950 also saw the release of a Hollywood-produced film, *The Jackie Robinson Story*, which like nearly all of the biographical baseball movies from the period, follows the pattern of *The Pride of the Yankees* closely. Similarly, the same year also saw the publication of a six-issue series of Jackie Robinson comic books, roughly equivalent in intent and tone to DiMaggio's autobiography for young boys, *Lucky to be a Yankee*. Jazz legend Count Basie even wrote a song, "Did You See Jackie Robinson Hit That Ball?," which became a hit by singer Buddy Johnson, a development reminiscent of the time when "Joltin' Joe DiMaggio" lit up the pop charts in 1941.

Such Robinson-based cultural texts not only demonstrate the immense popularity the ballplayer achieved among black Americans as well as many white Americans, but they also show that Robinson was held up in the American popular consciousness in a way quite similar to and probably patterned after the great white ethnic Yankee heroes of previous decades. This is nowhere clearer than in *The Jackie Robinson Story*, in which the opening narration emphasizes a young Robinson as "an *American* boy" with a "dream that is *truly American*" (emphasis added) and the closing narration similarly describes his story as "one each of us shares." As Robinson, easily one of the most prominent African Americans of the postwar era, was placed firmly on the path of the popular rags-to-riches baseball hero most thoroughly and publicly trod by these white ethnic Yankee idols, the public was forced to confront the idea of the American dream in a black racial context. Because Robinson, 1947 Rookie of the Year, '49 MVP, and a six-time All-Star, filled those shoes so ably—even playing himself in *The Jackie Robinson Story*—the justifications for excluding people of color from the mainstream of American society and culture likely did not hold up as well as they did during the days of the so-called color line. The elevation of Robinson to the same status as Ruth, Gehrig, and DiMaggio in the popular imagination supported an argument that the old model of simultaneously celebrating a white American dream while enforcing a separate and inferior sociocultural sphere for black citizens was elitist, unjust, and outdated.

When added to Dodger fans' conception of the Bronx-based club as elitist, the issue of race helps create an alternate perspective on the Yankees as a cultural icon in the postwar period. This alternative side of the Yankees emphasized hypocrisy, arrogance, and the abuse of power. It made the organization a symbol of the American establishment whose past glory loomed over and limited the success of marginalized others. Although the longstanding triumphal image of the Yankees continued to exert its power, it was also losing its grip on the nation's moral conscience. The counter-narrative of an elitist Yankee organization that flourished in the subculture of Brooklyn Dodgers fans would gain wider circulation in the mid-1950s and '60s, taking on less localized forms and becoming more clearly an expression of a louder, rising voice of sociocultural dissent that transcended baseball.

Chapter Five
"THOSE DAMN YANKEES!"

The Popularization of Yankee Hating in the 1950s

While Brooklyn Dodger fans watched the New York Yankees repeatedly deny their team a modest slice of victory, they were not the only ones getting fed up with the Bronx Bombers' dominance of organized baseball. During the decade of the 1950s—particularly in response to the Yankees' five pennants and World Series victories in a row from 1949 to 1953—negative portrayals of the Yankees became increasingly common in cultural texts on a national level. Such texts include Douglass Wallop's novel *The Year the Yankees Lost the Pennant* (1954) and its Broadway adaptation, *Damn Yankees* (1955–57, film version in 1958), Mark Harris's novel *The Southpaw* (1953), and popular magazine articles chronicling and explaining the rising tide of Yankee hating. While their representation of the New York ball club and cultural uses of the team vary considerably, the overall negative portrayals of the Yankees in these texts are affiliated with a questioning of the vision of postwar America the Yankees embodied—one rooted in success and triumph in economic terms at home and military and political power abroad.

THE YANKEES AS ANTAGONIST IN
THE YEAR THE YANKEES LOST THE PENNANT

One of the most prominent examples of this groundswell of critical perspectives on the Yankees is Douglass Wallop's light Faustian baseball fantasy *The Year the Yankees Lost the Pennant*. Not as embroiled in cultural politics as the critical portrayal of the Yankees common in the Brooklyn Dodgers' fan culture, Wallop's novel nevertheless engages issues of American identity and how well the Yankees actually represent the nation. In contrast to the triumphal Yankees of Joe DiMaggio that were often celebrated as the epitome of the postwar American success story, Wallop's novel presents the Bronx club as an oppressive antagonist in the imagination and sporting lives of sympathetic, everyday American characters. In this way, Wallop's novel—and perhaps particularly its reincarnation as a Broadway musical and, later, a movie musical—translated some of the Dodger fans' critical perspective on the Yankees as a cultural icon to a popular mainstream cultural text, helping disseminate and solidify the gospel of Yankee hating nationally.

The Year the Yankees Lost the Pennant tells of a middle-aged Washington, D.C., real estate salesman, Joe Boyd, a devoted fan of the Washington Senators who would love to see his hapless team win the American League pennant almost as much as he would like to see the mighty New York Yankees lose it.[1] So frustrated is Boyd that when he is propositioned by the devil incarnate, who goes by the name of "Mr. Applegate," he agrees to exchange his soul for a chance to be transformed into the idealized baseball hero Joe Hardy to lead his Senators to the pennant.[2] Though largely devoid of any heavy-handed sermonizing, Wallop's lighthearted tale is largely concerned with exploring issues of wish fulfillment versus appreciation for everyday reality. This is expressed most fully through Boyd's ever-present longing for his old life with his wife, Bess, despite his strong desire to win the pennant for long-suffering Washington manager Benny van Buren and ninety-year-old owner Adam Welch. Boyd also must override his empathy for and attraction to the beautiful and kind Lola, another "lost soul" whom Applegate introduces to him to distract Joe in his longing for his old domestic life.

This moral turn notwithstanding, *The Year the Yankees Lost the Pennant* still emphasizes Boyd's dream of the Senators at long last trumping the Yankees as not merely justifiable but desirable, even necessary. Like Joe Boyd, readers wish they could have it both ways: we know that using the escape clause in Applegate's contract allowing Joe to return to Bess and home is the right thing to do, but so is beating those Yankees for van Buren, Welch, and all the long-suffering Senators fans. In the end, this is precisely the conclusion Wallop gives his readers, as with some clever counter-manipulation of Applegate by the self-sacrificing Lola, Boyd is able to help beat the Yankees in the pennant-clinching game on the last day of the season as Joe Hardy *and* to return home to Bess as his old self later that night.

This ending, which essentially enables Boyd and the readers to have their cake and eat it too, is a testament to the negativity surrounding the novel's portrayal of the Yankees. In an exaggerated take on recent baseball history, Wallop imagines a New York Yankees club four years in the future (1958) that has not lost the American League pennant since 1949—nine in a row, four better than the actual Yankees' and the Major League's best record, five in a row (1949–53).[3] This lopsided relationship between the Bronx Bombers and the rest of the league plays such an important role in Wallop's narrative that it is the subject of his opening sentence: "On the hot and humid night of July 21, 1958, when all signs pointed to a tenth consecutive pennant for the New York Yankees, a manhole cover rose slowly from its resting place near the center of a certain intersection in Washington, D.C." (7). This manhole, naturally, provides narrative entry for Applegate, the devil himself, seemingly the only being capable of ending this American League reign of terror.

This exaggerated (if at times only *slightly* exaggerated) portrayal of postwar Yankee dominance continues throughout the novel, with Boyd and other characters almost always describing the team in hyperbolic terms. For instance, when the transformed Joe Boyd first meets the Yankees on the field with his Senator teammates, Wallop writes, "It has been written that when the Yankees took the field in that decade of the 1950s, they must have appeared seven feet tall to the opposing team, and to the opposing pitcher, even taller when they strode to the plate" (82–83). And when Applegate is attempting to convince Boyd to make their Faustian bargain, he casually remarks, "Did it ever occur to you that you may even die before you see [the Senators] win the pennant again? For that matter you may die before any team other than the Yankees wins it. There's something rather tragic about that, something very sad" (18). Later, during an intimate conversation between Joe and the love-struck Lola, she confesses that she admires his dream of defeating the Yankees, even sees it as a "worthy cause" (131), explaining, "you know, it's ridiculous in a way, but everywhere I go there's such a real bitter antagonism against the Yankees. Even in Hong Kong. A little man asked me not long ago, 'When will the Yankees not win the pennant?' I said I did not know, perhaps never" (131). This exaggeration of Yankee invincibility is echoed in a sports page "letter to the editor" Boyd peruses in the novel's opening chapter; it suggests that the Yankees be forced to "circle the bases five times at top speed" after hitting home runs to tire themselves out or "carry weights, like jockeys" to even the playing field for the rest of the American League (9).

This seemingly supernatural power the Yankees have over the other teams extends to include the supporters of these other clubs, namely the novel's protagonist, Joe Boyd. This is most clearly conveyed through a nightmare he has after learning of Applegate's proposal for the first time. Wallop writes, "When finally he closed his eyes . . . he saw a monster with a bloated, insatiable face, across its swollen chest the word yankees. He was striking the face with a baseball bat" (27).

Boyd's animosity towards the Yankees is perhaps only matched by that of the Washington Senators' nonagenarian owner, the-white-haired Adam Welch, about whom Wallop writes, "though [Boyd] knew him only from newspaper references, he felt that he knew him intimately and for years had admired him for his spirit, his hope, his hatred of the Yankees" (63). Welch's rancor is put on full display in a Senators press conference celebrating the momentous debut of the mysterious rookie, Joe Hardy:

> [Mr. Welch] sank back onto his pillow again, but was immediately up as the [New York–based] reporter named Head sniffed and said, "You mean you think you're going to beat the Yankees?"
>
> "Beat the Yankees!" Mr. Welch was shaking a gnarled forefinger at Head. "You can bet your sweet life we'll beat the Yankees. What makes you think we won't beat the Yankees, young man?"

... "If it wasn't for just blind devil's luck those Yankees would have dropped clear out of the League by now. They'd be down—
... down in the Three-Eye League by now, that's where they'd be," he managed, and then began to grope for his collar button, pulling loose his tie from the round stiff collar. Hands grasped his shoulders and pressed him gently back onto his pillow, where he sat, breathing heavily, eyes watering, but still glaring defiantly at Head. (64–66)

After Welch is calmed down, Senators manager Benny van Buren explains to the offending reporter, "Each year he thinks we're going to lick the Yankees and he keeps on thinking it right up until the end of the season.... But the point is, don't ever mention Yankees around him again. It upsets him" (67).

All these examples point to the fact that the Yankees take on a significant role in the structure and narrative design of the novel. These slightly fictionalized Yankees act as a source of drama with the degree of intimidation and hatred they provoke, and perhaps more important, the dream of both Boyd and the heads of the Senators organization depends on deposing them. The Yankees thus become one of the dual antagonists of Wallop's novel—the other, of course, being the demonic Mr. Applegate. While Applegate is the more direct antagonist, the shifty, double-crossing villain that Boyd must out-maneuver, the Yankees perhaps occupy a more important role. In addition to being literal opponents for Boyd and the Senators, the Yankees also act as a more abstract antagonist. As the entity that has always stood in the way of Boyd's dream of seeing the Senators win the pennant—an unrequited longing that seems to embody all his life's frustrations (9–14)—the Yankees become the metaphoric impediment to his life's dreams and sense of fulfillment. The Bronx Bombers' role as this symbolic antagonist is affirmed by the revelation near the novel's end that Applegate is a devoted Yankee supporter and ostensibly uses his power to ensure their success. "You see, Joe, Old Man Welch was right without knowing it," the Mephisthophelean figure casually remarks. "Because my first allegiance really is to the Yankees" (215–14).

Because Wallop's fantasy is rooted in recent baseball history, perhaps particularly the Yankees' five consecutive World Series victories, its negative perspective on the Bronx Bombers has enhanced significance. A Washington, D.C. native and Senator fan, Wallop, though clearly embellishing, writes like someone who has personally known baseball hardship at the hands of the Yankees. These New York Yankees of the projected near future induce such sheer intimidation in the novel's baseball fans that the Yankees as a cultural icon loom large over the design of this novel. And even though it is hyperbolic fantasy, as baseball statistician and cultural pundit Bill James observes, the novel and the portrayal of the Yankees in it are still grounded in the real, the common, and even the historical (1–3). The Yankees in Wallop's novel are the same Yankees that Americans knew in 1954. They are just more so.

Like *The Pride of the Yankees* and the DiMaggio biography *Lucky to Be a Yankee,* the title of Wallop's novel is dependent on some previous cultural knowledge about the New York ball club.[4] All three titles carry cultural connotations of success, but unlike the two older texts from the 1940s, *The Year the Yankees Lost the Pennant* does not necessarily celebrate that success. Though by the novel's end the title ends up being literal, at first encounter in the 1950s context, Wallop's chosen title seems ironic—wryly suggesting that a failure by the Bronx Bombers to win the American League would be something quite out of the ordinary. Indeed, the novel's plot, in which a Senator fan goes to supernatural lengths to defeat the Yankees, confirms Wallop's droll commentary on the state of the American League. Crucially, the title's tone and the perspective of the novel's protagonist and other sympathetic characters make this Yankee success an annoyance (at the very least) rather than something to be celebrated. Thus, while the titles *The Pride of the Yankees* and *Lucky to Be a Yankee* depend on generally positive cultural associations, *The Year the Yankees Lost the Pennant* presumes negative connotations for the signifier "Yankees." It is the first major mainstream cultural text to do so and as such might represent a turning point of sorts in the general American public's perception of the Yankees' cultural meaning.

DAMN YANKEES AND THE POPULARIZATION OF YANKEE HATING

This is not to say that Wallop invented the practice of Yankee hating. The experience of Brooklyn Dodgers fans offers more than enough evidence to correct this misconception. Naturally, similar animosity towards the Bronx Bombers existed in supporters of other clubs throughout the nation. But as a mainstream, mass-media text existing outside the confines of the subculture of Dodger fans, *The Year the Yankees Lost the Pennant* could act as a lightning rod of sorts for Yankee animosity as no single text had before.

This became even more evident after the book was adapted by Wallop, theater veteran George Abbott, and Broadway composers Richard Adler and Jerry Ross into the highly successful Broadway musical *Damn Yankees*. The show opened in May 1955, only a year after the novel's publication and, after transferring to London's West End in May 1957, ran for a transatlantic total of more than a thousand performances by the time it closed in October of that year.[5] It was nominated for nine Tony awards and won seven of them, including "Best Musical" (*"Damn Yankees,"* Internet Broadway Database).[6] The success on Broadway led to a film adaptation released in September 1958, which essentially re-created the Broadway show on film, including the reprisal of lead performances by Ray Walston as Applegate and Gwen Verdon as Lola and all but three musical numbers (Erickson 142–43).[7] The film was comparatively less successful but still expanded the musical's—and through it, the novel's—cultural influence.

This is particularly true of the novel's anti-Yankee sentiments, something notable considering how many of these aspects of the novel are bleached out of the musical and its film adaptation. Many of the passages bemoaning the exaggerated dominance of these slightly fictionalized Yankees do not get translated into the musical or film. In the movie version, the main exceptions are Joe Boyd's opening scene exclamation of "Those damn Yankees!" as he watches his team lose to the Bronx Bombers on TV (which serves as a segue to the title sequence), and a brief conversation during Boyd/Hardy's tryout about the notion of handicapping the Yankees, wherein Applegate, essentially quoting Wallop's novel, quips, "I read somewhere that they're talking about handicapping the Yankees, making them carry extra weight like racehorses." But gone is the crucial revelation of the Yankees' satanic ties through Applegate's fandom, as is Adam Welch's delirious anti-Yankee tirade, and the majority of Wallop's hyperbolic asides about the Yankees' dominance.

Furthermore, while baseball remains at the center of the musical's plot and is visually prominent in the popular musical numbers "Heart" and "Shoeless Joe from Hannibal Mo," much time and attention in the musical itself, and particularly its advertising, is devoted to Gwen Verdon's character, Lola. Though, as in the novel, she is eventually revealed to be a sympathetic character, early on in the musical, Lola is portrayed as a vamping seductress, inconsistent with the character in the novel. This played-up sex appeal is particularly noticeable in Verdon's musical number "What Lola Wants," arguably the song most popularly linked with *Damn Yankees*. A still from this number featuring Verdon with bare legs spread wide served as the dominant image for the poster for both stage and film musical, neither of which feature so much as a bat, ball, glove, cap, or pinstriped uniform.[8]

This toning down of the anti-Yankee sentiments of the novel and de-emphasis of the story's substantial baseball content, however, is somewhat countered by the change in name. As a title, *"Damn Yankees"* offers a much more critical image of the Bronx Bombers than the content of the musical itself does. Playing off the old southern epithet for a northerner, the title *"Damn Yankees,"* like that of the novel from which it was adapted, draws on the cultural prominence of the team. Rather than wryly commenting on the ball club's dominance, however, the musical title cuts right to the chase, implying the demonic connection that its own plot denies. *"Damn Yankees"* would be hard to overestimate in its importance in the public's overall impression of the phenomenon.

As a cultural entity, the title *"Damn Yankees"* can be seen as the answer or antidote to the moniker *"The Pride of the Yankees,"* capable of adoption as a rallying cry by baseball fans wishing to speak of the Yankees using its decidedly negative connotations. This is true whether the speaker imagines the literal, biblical lineage of the word "damn" and its diabolical implications, or merely wishes to link the team's name with profanity. Indeed, the number of books about the New York ball club with the phrase "damn Yankees" in the title testify to the impact of the musical's appropriation of the old Southern phrase for the Yankees as a cultural icon.[9] The phrase offered those who were growing weary of the Yankees' dominance of Major League Baseball something tangible, evidence that they were far from alone in their animosity towards the club and provided a rallying cry for their cause.

CULTURAL CRITIQUE IN
THE YEAR THE YANKEES LOST THE PENNANT

In terms of sheer popular influence, the title of its musical adaptation is probably the biggest contribution *The Year the Yankees Lost the Pennant* makes towards shaping the Yankees' cultural meaning. That said, the novel's negative portrayal of the Yankees is not without broader implications regarding midcentury American culture. Though Wallop's novel does not engage the same sociocultural critique that Dodger fans' use of the Yankees implies, it nevertheless bears the imprint of the Dodgers/Yankees national sports drama that unfolded between 1941 and the book's publication, wherein the two talented New York City teams met in five World Series, each won by the Yankees. This is evident in the revelation near novel's end that not only is the demonic Applegate a loyal Yankees supporter, but he also admits that "it just so happens that I hate the Dodgers more than I love the Yankees, if you see what I mean," adding, "I couldn't stand to see those Dodgers win the World Series. Those Dodgers have never won a World Series" (246). Wallop's inclusion of the Brooklyn Dodgers—and on the opposite side of the double-crossing devil—in this fantasy that focuses primarily on the Senators and Yankees is testament to the national influence of the Dodgers, their underdog story, and their fans on the increasing prevalence of negative perspectives on the Yankees as a cultural icon.

The novel's negative portrayal does not contain the same social critique along lines of class, race, and regional identity contained in Dodger fans' concept of the New York Yankees. (This is despite the fact that, at the time of the novel's publication, the Yankees still had not fielded their first black player.) In addition to being racially white and ostensibly devoid of any marginalizing ethnicity, Joe Boyd is also portrayed as unambiguously middle class. Nevertheless, the Yankees' antagonistic role in Wallop's novel does subtly imply some broader cultural connotations beyond jealousy at the Bronx Bombers' on-field success. In his introduction to the 2004 reprint of *The Year the Yankees Lost the Pennant,* Bill James's observations about the thematic role of the Yankees in the novel perhaps best communicate this significance. Drawing on some of his own personal experience as a baseball fan and as a human being, James writes, "The Yankees are the normal order of the universe. The team of my childhood was not the Washington Senators, it was the Kansas City Athletics ... but six of one, half dozen of the other (4)."[10] He adds, "Joe Boyd learns, in the end, that he is living the life he was meant to live, and he is most grateful to return to it. The devil and the Yankees will always be with us, but there is much to be grateful for in the lives we are meant to lead" (5).

James's equation of the Yankees with "the normal order of the universe" here suggests that Yankee victory is a sad, and perhaps unjust, but unavoidable fact of life. In *The Year the Yankees Lost the Pennant,* they become a symbol of that unfairness in life we all—or presumably, most of us—experience personally. For James, Wallop's novel implies that, like Joe Boyd, who eventually rejects life as the quintessential baseball superstar to return to his humdrum existence, most of us mere mortals are not destined for the glory and success epitomized by the midcentury Yankees. But James makes the case that Wallop's novel celebrates a personal glory to be found in the unsung struggle of day-to-day existence. Perhaps our lofty dreams may go unrealized, but a truer fulfillment can be found in our relationships and dedication to career or craft.

In Wallop's novel, this concept of nobility in the everyday struggle of life is embodied not only through Joe Boyd and his wife but in the dedication and long suffering of owner Adam Welch, of Lola, who voluntarily returns to her old life as a homely and lonely school teacher to free Boyd from Applegate's grasp, and of Senators' manager Benny van Buren, whom Wallop describes as follows: "Mr. van Buren looked . . . to Joe with eyes crinkled at the corners from many long nights of squinting at pop flies against light towers. They were the eyes of a man who had known great suffering, and Joe felt a wave of sympathy. In his playing days, Mr. van Buren had been a hell-for-leather third baseman, the best the team had ever had. Managing a seventh-place team these five years must have been gall" (39). Here Boyd's admiration and empathy for van Buren are tied to the manager's endurance in the face of continual defeat. It is precisely this endurance and willingness to soldier on despite their unrequited aspirations that make these characters endearing. This is most true for the central protagonist himself, who during the course of the novel develops the empathy that puts him in the double bind of wishing to sacrifice his dream of leading the Senators to the pennant over the Yankees in order to return to his wife, Bess, while simultaneously wishing to sacrifice his life with Bess to help fulfill the dreams of Welch, van Buren, Lola, and all Senator fans.

Because Wallop's novel is a fantasy, we can have it both ways, with all of these characters having their lofty dreams realized.[11] But the value the book places on everyday struggles and sacrifices of oft-defeated people suggests that this resolution is whimsical wish fulfillment, or perhaps a metaphor for the reward everyday Americans deserve but—in the real world, anyway—will never actually have. (For, as James suggests, in the "normal order of the universe," the Yankees will always end up on top.) But these characters in *The Year the Yankees Lost the Pennant* do have each other's empathy, support, and companionship as they struggle, sacrifice, and suffer together. If any "moral" can be drawn from Wallop's lighthearted baseball fantasy, that would be it.

With this subtle celebration of the oft-unsung struggles of average Americans, Wallop not only relishes the chance to imagine an alliance between the Bronx Bombers and the devil, and fantasize about their failure, but he also offers an alternate version of America to the one embodied in the Yankees as a cultural icon. While the concepts of the everyday work ethic and self-sacrifice are certainly contained within the cultural connotations of the Yankees, particularly through media portrayals of Gehrig and DiMaggio, these ideas are always linked with eventual triumph. This component of success or victory within the Yankee concept of struggle and sacrifice is emblematic of a more grandiose version of the American dream, which implies that hard work inevitably leads to significant socioeconomic improvement. In the postwar context, this focus on success is likewise representative and reflective of a broader cultural emphasis on triumph and abundance during the period of economic prosperity and recent national military victory.

But this is not the America portrayed in Wallop's novel, which, as James suggests, manages to be both fantastic and simultaneously grounded in reality. In *The Year the Yankees Lost the Pennant*, despite the dedication, hard work, and sacrifice of its sympathetic characters, an other-worldly power is required to bring them any grand Yankee-like triumph. Like the Bum persona of the Brooklyn Dodgers and their fans, Wallop's novel celebrates struggle, not victory. Thus, without engaging directly in any discussion of politics or economics, the book offers a subtle critique of, and counterpoint to, the postwar America of triumph and plenty embodied in the iconic Yankees at midcentury.

YANKEE HATING IN POPULAR JOURNALISM

The Year the Yankees Lost the Pennant and its musical adaptation constitute the most significant text of the 1950s to represent the Yankees in a negative way, but it is hardly a case of a lone voice crying in the wilderness. Rather, they represent a national groundswell of anti-Yankee sentiment that surfaced in American journalism as well. To a degree unmatched in previous eras, the decade of the 1950s spawned articles in both sports and common-interest magazines that reveal a rising tide of animosity towards the New York Yankees. As one of these authors, Milton Gross, asserted in a 1953 article for *Sport*, "never in the history of sports has such intense feeling of animosity arisen so spontaneously among so many people in so wide an area" (10).

The sheer number of articles published with titles like Jim Murray's "I Hate the Yankees" (*Life* 1950) suggest that this national trend of Yankee hating seems to have been on the increase in the 1950s, particularly during and in the wake of the club's five consecutive World Series victories. But it was not the first manifestation of anti-Yankee sentiment expressed in print journalism on a national level. In February 1939, with the Yankees poised to win their fourth World Series in a row, the general-interest magazine *Collier's* published an article by Cleveland sportswriter Gordon Cobbledick titled "Break Up the Yankees!" The connotations of trust busting suggested by the title are echoed in the sub-headline teaser, which speaks of their "World Series monopoly" as "getting pretty monotonous" (19), and then continues throughout the piece, which cites recently deceased owner Jacob Ruppert's "moneybags" (62) as the primary reason for the "mounting power" of the Yankees' "machine" (19).

Whether Cobbledick invented the phrase or merely appropriated it, "Break up the Yankees!" became something of a rallying cry among baseball fans tired of their "World Series monopoly" in the late 1930s and early '40s (Creamer, *Baseball in '41* 23). The accusations of plutocracy that Cobbledick gave voice to here, couched in somewhat anachronistic language from the turn-of-the-century antitrust era that was nevertheless relevant to a nation emerging from the Depression, remain part of the Yankees' cultural meaning to this day, a dark flip side to their celebrated all-American aura as portrayed in texts like *The Pride of the Yankees*.

But just as the cry of "Break up the Yankees!" among certain baseball fans and insiders would be drowned out by that 1942 film's big-budget, Hollywood-produced celebration of Yankeeness as the essence of what makes the nation great, so also was Cobbledick's article answered with an opposing perspective on the Yankees' success. The following month, the magazine followed up Cobbledick's article with Rud Rennie's interview of Colonel Ruppert, in which the Yankees' owner refuted the accusations of plutocracy, insisting that "money alone does not bring success" and suggesting that "enterprise and initiative would die" if attempts were made to even the playing field by instituting an amateur/minor league draft, as proposed by Cobbledick (61, 63). (Indeed, in 1965, this is exactly what happened, and as Jack Mann suggests, it likely contributed to the Yankees' decline [18, 22–26]).

This somewhat heated *Collier's* dialogue is rich not only with discussion about the Yankees and their role in baseball and cultural significance but also with discussion of the tension between economic freedom and economic inequality in a capitalist system. However, after Rudd's article, the debate over the merits of the Yankees in national magazines disappeared until the '50s. Perhaps the onset of World War II and baseball's direct participation in that military conflict diverted attention to other matters. Or perhaps the fact that other teams, notably the St. Louis Cardinals (World Series winners in 1942, '44, and '46), brought an end to the Yankees late-1930s "monopoly" led baseball fans to dismiss theories of Yankee dominance such as Cobbledick's.

Whatever the reason, this public manifestation of Yankee animosity was not reignited until after the Bronx Bombers' return to American League pennant and World Series glory in 1947, and after their dramatic DiMaggio-led comeback to capture the 1949 pennant from the Red Sox, followed by another series victory. But when the tide of Yankee hating did return, it swelled to new heights; no fewer than seven articles about Yankee hating were published between 1950 and 1961 in both widely circulating national sports magazines and general-interest publications such as *Look, Life,* and the *New York Times Magazine.*

While certainly clear enough in their chronicle of growing dislike for the Yankees nationally, this rash of anti-Yankee articles was, as a whole, ambivalent in its portrayal of the Yankees as a cultural icon. A few, like pieces by Murray, Gross, and Charles Einstein, echoed Cobbledick's accusations of plutocracy from a decade earlier, while others pointedly refuted such notions, like Tim Cohane's insistence that "money alone didn't make the Yankees" (60). While some authors, like Gross, denounced what they saw as the "stuffy haughtiness of the self-styled aristocrat" in the Bronx Bombers and their fans (80), others defended the Yankees as the essence of the American spirit. Charles Dexter, for one, admired the club's "tradition of victory" (30), while Cohane held up Yankee outfielder and World War II marine veteran

Hank Bauer as the epitome of American manhood—"willing to make all the sacrifices [victory] demands" and thus, "in a battle or a ball game, a good man to have on your side" (67).[12]

The fact that these articles, taken collectively, found reason to both agree and disagree with the growing number of Yankee-hating baseball fans is reflective of the complicated relationship Americans had—and still have—with the values the team represented. In the postwar context this ambivalence speaks to the overlapping but also occasionally competing values that were all held up as quintessentially "American" after World War II and during the ensuing national prosperity, including anticommunism, populism, the American dream, equality, economic freedom, and democracy. The Yankees postwar success spoke to all of these values or ideologies by either affirming or negating them, depending on one's perspective, and spoke to different people in different ways.

Sometimes the Yankees even spoke to one single person in different ways, as suggested by *The Year the Yankees Lost the Pennant* author Douglass Wallop's entry in this group of articles. Clear in his distaste for the club's dominance in the novel, the author, when describing the swelling ranks of Yankee haters for a *New York Times Magazine* piece in 1956, confides that while "not a Yankee fan" he *was* a bit of "a Yankee admirer" ("How the Yankees Got that Way" 78). From the man responsible for the most prominent Yankee-hating text of the decade, this comes as quite the confession. Wallop does jokingly affirm that "the New York Yankees are exasperating, irritating and, if not downright un-American, certainly disruptive of American institutions" (26), but he does not sustain that tone or perspective. Even as writers of other articles on Yankee hating like Einstein seemed to be channeling the thesis of Wallop's novel in condemning a "philosophy of triumph" that the Yankees supposedly embodied and encouraged (86), the novelist himself moved in the opposite direction, expressing his admiration for the quality of the Yankees' business operation from the lowest to the highest levels and crediting organization and leadership as the keys to their success (76–78). This revealed admiration from the man who perhaps most singlehandedly advanced the cause of Yankee hating in the 1950s may be the ultimate evidence of Americans' ambivalent relationship with the team and their cultural meaning—both then and now. We both love and hate what they represent.

While the articles themselves end up being ambivalent, they nevertheless serve as a barometer suggesting that the national anti-Yankee sentiment was mounting. As these articles mention extreme Yankee-hating baseball fans like Montana cattle baron Albert Kochivar, "who, at the opening of the 1959 season, offered a hunting trip at his ranch to any American League team 'doing the most' to beat the Yankees out of the pennant" (McGowen 49), along with more modest protests like fans aiming pop bottles at Yankee outfielders in St. Louis or bitter editorials in local New England papers (Cohane 57), it seems clear that no matter what their personal ideologies might have been, as the 1950s progressed and the Yankees continued to win, Americans were identifying less and less with the club.[13]

THE YANKEES IN *THE SOUTHPAW*

While the popular journalism chronicling the rising tide of Yankee hating only occasionally made conscious references to broader cultural connotations that the team had acquired, in 1953, the year the Bronx Bombers won their fifth consecutive pennant and World Series, a novel was published that purposefully utilized the Yankees as a cultural icon to embody the postwar nation. In stark contrast to *The Pride of the Yankees,* this novel, *The Southpaw* by Mark Harris, employs the Yankees as a metaphor for everything its author thought was wrong with postwar America. Through Harris's use of the Yankees' iconic cultural meaning, the book portrays postwar America as tainted and compromised by a prevailing conformism, an overemphasis on success, and an obsession with romanticized notions of its own past.

The Southpaw is the first of four Harris novels featuring the protagonist Henry Wiggen, whom literary scholar Norman Lavers describes as a plain-spoken wise-fool who follows "an established literary tradition which dates at least to Huck Finn, of the naïve and semiliterate narrator telling his story in his own language" (37). In this first novel, Wiggen leaves his father's small-town farm in upstate New York, where he pitched in high school, to join the fictional New York Mammoths, a wealthy, successful, tradition-rich, and talent-laden club that acts as a thin disguise for none other than the New York Yankees.

While Harris's Mammoths are not necessarily the real-life Yankees lifted directly from Major League Baseball's history and given a different name, this fictional club occupies the same role of a storied, traditional powerhouse in their fictional professional league that the Yankees filled in the real-life Major Leagues at the time. For instance, early in the novel, Wiggen reminisces about the dominance of the Mammoths of his childhood, ostensibly in the late 1930s or '40s, when there were "several years running when the Mammoths was in the Series" (30), a streak that evokes the Yankees' then-unmatched string of four World Series championships in a row from 1936 to 1939.

While this position of a storied New York franchise that seems to be the league's most dominant stands as the biggest reason the Mammoths would remind readers of the Yankees, there are a host of other details that confirm this strong comparison. Like the Yankees, the Mammoths have strong rivalries with both the Brooklyn and Boston franchises of their fictional world (209).[14] Like the Yankees, the Mammoths play in an "elegant" (189) stadium that on the occasion of big games can accommodate "80,000 [spectators] if need be" (Harris 50; Fromer 34, 43, 55). Like the Yankees, who were famously owned by beer baron Jacob Ruppert, whose deep pockets lifted the club from obscurity to greatness, the Mammoths are owned by an equally wealthy president of Moors Motor Company, Lester T. Moors, Jr. (Harris 66, 99). Despite this wealth, the Mammoths' upper management, like the Yankees' general managers Ed Barrow (1920–45) and George Weiss (1947–60), has a reputation for tightfistedness (Harris 101; Cramer 68–69, 73, 105; Kahn, *The Era* 209). Finally, Harris describes the Mammoths as frequenting a bar and grill owned by real-life Manhattan restaurateur Toots Shor (285), whose establishment was a legendary hang-out for Yankees players in the 1940s and '50s, particularly stars Joe DiMaggio and Mickey Mantle (Cramer 112–13; Leavy 77).[15]

Additionally, while not a precise roman-a-clef, Harris endows the Mammoths with two characters who seem modeled after two of the most famous Yankees. When Wiggen joins the Mammoths, he becomes acquainted with their most famous player, the aging "Sad" Sam Yale, who bears a strong resemblance to Yankee figurehead Babe Ruth, with his struggles to keep his weight down (Harris 85–86) and a tendency to run himself ragged with his drinking and womanizing (118–19)—facts kept out of his bowdlerized image in the press, particularly in his moralistic biography for boys (238). Even the name of the book, *Sam Yale—Mammoth*, though not directly connected to

Ruth, nevertheless evokes the Yankees with its dependence on the signifier "Mammoth" to communicate something about its subject—ostensibly heroism and excellence—just like Joe DiMaggio's famous sanitized biography *Lucky to Be a Yankee*.

Similarly, when Wiggen joins the club he meets the Mammoths' famous manager Dutch Schnell, who alternately exhibits a resolute sternness and a whimsical, folksy, yet wry sense of humor, much like the legendary Yankee manager at the time of writing, Casey Stengel, who was also nicknamed "Dutch" (Kahn, *The Era* 163). Schnell's Stengel-like drollness is evident in narrator Wiggen's descriptions of numerous of the Mammoth manager's pronouncements as "real sarcastic" (171, 244) and his penchant for telling "funny stories" (169).[16] Again, while Harris's novel is not intended as a roman-a-clef, the allusion to these two legendary figures, Ruth and Stengel, then so intertwined with the public's notion of the Yankees' past and present, solidify the likelihood of readers linking the Mammoths with the real-life Yankee organization. The connection between Harris's fictional club and the Yankees is important because it implies a more direct interaction between the novel, its themes, and the existing reality of contemporary professional baseball in America, particularly the Yankees as an institution and American cultural icon.

CHALLENGING THE YANKEE HEROIC LEGACY

With the Mammoths' strong Yankee parallels, it is significant that as Wiggen acclimatizes to life with the club, he becomes disenchanted with the reality of the team he idolized as a boy. This is perhaps most readily embodied in the person of the Ruth-like "Sad" Sam Yale, the Mammoth's left-handed hurler, whose picture hung above the young Henry's bed. Henry's fascination with Yale is fed by the sanitized biography, a fictional parallel of such biographies of real Major Leaguers, perhaps especially the popular *Lucky to Be a Yankee* and early biographies of Ruth. Harris mimics the highly idealized and moralistic content and style of such books, writing,

> My name is Samuel (Sad Sam) Yale. I was born in Houston, Texas, on March 13, 1918. I had the good fortune of becoming a member of the world-famed New York Mammoths five years ago. . . .

> This book is written in the hope that every American boy now playing the great game of baseball in his home town, wherever that may be, will take inspiration from my straightforward story.... His success or failure... depends on him and him alone.
> I have three simple rules which I live by:
> 1. Take the game seriously...
> 2. Live a clean life, shunning tobacco and liquor in all forms.
> 3. Follow the instruction of your high-school coach...
>
> Most important, have faith in yourself, for the road lies before you, and success will be yours. By the grace of God you will succeed. (33)

The young Wiggen's naïve, wholesale acceptance of this platitudinous prose feeds his goals of becoming a Mammoth himself one day and his heroic, idealized concept of baseball life. He narrates, "I studied the words over and over again, and the picture, and I knowed that moment and ever more that some day I would be a Mammoth and all my dreams come true" (33).

While Ruth is the most obvious historical reference point for the character of Sam Yale, Harris's chosen title for his youth-oriented biography, *Sam Yale—Mammoth,* and its evocation of the famous DiMaggio biography, added to the fact that the novel was written and published around the time of his retirement, make the revered "Yankee Clipper" a relevant figure as well. Both cases evoke the Yankee organization. While the Yankees hardly had a monopoly on the sanitized baseball hero, their concept of a continuous, passed-down legacy of such heroes, which the organization itself promoted through practices like the monuments to Ruth, Gehrig, and Manager Miller Huggins, was unique within Major League Baseball. This would have been particularly true at the time of *The Southpaw*'s publication in 1953, when discussions of Mickey Mantle as a potential heir to the Yankee legacy of Ruth, Gehrig, and DiMaggio enhanced the public profile of this legacy of heroism. Harris parallels this concept of what we might call a "heroic brand" today, with the announcement near season's end by Sam Yale's ghostwriter Krazy Kress that "Dutch Schnell will work on a book this winter. Look for it in April. Title: 'Dutch Schnell—Mammoth'" (343).

When Harris's protagonist learns the truth about Sam Yale, it is not just a refutation of the naïve acceptance of romanticized baseball heroes; given the obvious parallels between the Mammoths and the Yankees, it becomes a specific critique of the Yankee hero at the heart of the Bronx Bombers' iconic cultural meaning. This debunking of the (Yankee) baseball hero through the eyes of the narrator is thorough and somewhat embittered. After learning that Yale's heroic persona is a fiction crafted by sports journalists who ignored the wild nightlife of drinking and womanizing of the nation's chosen star, Wiggen comments, "Such corny crap as that is all behind me now. I ain't even interested in Sad Sam Yale no more. You spend a long period with a fellow and he stops being a hero all of a sudden. Sam ain't all he is cracked up to be. But I didn't know it then. I wasn't but a kid" (35).

Wiggen's comment about "a fellow" ceasing to be heroic once one has spent enough time with him is perhaps a more philosophical critique of the concept of heroes in general, but the ramifications of the baseball context and the propagation of deliberate falsehoods in the name of crafting idealized baseball idols for public consumption are presented as particularly worthy of condemnation by Harris. This is further emphasized in a somewhat comedic and nearly postmodern gesture later in the novel in which Wiggen gives Sad Sam Yale a copy of the book the older Mammoth supposedly wrote to read for the first time. Yale roundly mocks its corny naïveté (238). With the Yankee organization as the most prominent name in baseball heroism, this critique is particularly damaging to their status as embodiment of all that is great about the American nation. For Harris, the Mammoths/Yankees are emblematic of both baseball and the nation as a whole, with their blind devotion to their own sanitized and mythologized past.

CONFORMISM, KOREA, AND THE EXISTENTIAL HERO

Harris continues his critique of postwar America through the New York Mammoths and their parallels with the Yankees with an attack on a national tendency towards conformism. Within the context of anticommunism and the ever-growing influence of mass-produced consumer goods and media sources (particularly television), the topic of conformism was much discussed on many levels of American society during the 1950s. Representative of this discourse of "crisis" is David Riesman's *The Lonely Crowd* (1950), a sociologically based text that gained a large popular audience. In it, Riesman speaks of an intrinsically motivated or "inner-directed" character that dominated nineteenth-century America and contrasts that with an increasingly externally motivated or "outer-directed" national character in the middle of the twentieth century. While Riesman "stated on many occasions that he did not favor the dynamic 'inner-direction' associated with nineteenth-century capitalism" over outer-direction, with its associations of postwar mass culture and corporatism, most Americans nevertheless received *The Lonely Crowd* as "a critique of present-day conformity" and a longing for the "self-made, inner-directed man, the entrepreneur, the frontier farmer and the small businessman" of the previous century (Gilbert 35).

While Harris likely would not add his name to the list of Americans pining for the self-made entrepreneur, *The Southpaw* nevertheless shares some of this anxiety over conformism. Again, Harris uses the Yankee-like Mammoths organization to reveal the problems with what he sees as an overly conformist United States of America in the postwar era.

Harris conveys American conformity through the thoroughly corporate portrayal of the Mammoths organization and the pressure put on the players to burnish the image of the club's tradition both through the demand for victory and avoiding behavior that would cause a "crisis for the organization" (343). Wiggen's teammates typically seem more than happy to comply so long as they receive their deserved financial rewards.[17] The novel's narrator and protagonist eventually begins to adopt some of these habits and attitudes himself, a change most conspicuously marked by his decision to go against his previously held standard of play and throw an illegal spitball to get a much needed out (297–98).[18] Wiggen, however, receives his ethical wakeup call in the form of a reprimand from his girlfriend and future wife, Holly Webster, who accuses him of focusing too much on his paycheck, making his father cry by throwing the spitball, and surrendering his independence and personal values to the point of becoming "the property of the New York Mammoths . . . a little island in the Moors empire" (305). Holly's accusation of surrendering individual freedom to the "Moors empire" is echoed in her final plea to her boyfriend (delivered to readers secondhand in the "Wiggen" vernacular): "You are a lefthander, Henry. You always was. And the world needs all the lefthanders it can get, for it is a righthanded world. You are a southpaw in a starboarded atmosphere. Do you understand?" (307). Holly's use of lefthandedness as a symbol for nonconformity lends additional significance to the novel's title and suggests that the theme of throwing off conformism is central to Harris's text.

Holly's encouragement leads Wiggen to reevaluate the direction of his career in baseball and commit to an individualist concept of himself. This becomes manifest in his final rejection of sportswriter and *Sam Yale—Mammoth* ghostwriter Krazy Kress's repeated invitations to join him and Yale on a tour of military bases in Korea to entertain American troops. Wiggen's pacifist leanings had previously led him to shrug off Kress's insistent invitations: "I am behind the boys but I am against the war" (240). But Holly's anti-conformist pep talk motivates him to use the situation as an opportunity for a personal declaration of independence as he resolutely tells Kress, "Leave us forget Korea. . . . I get my head shot off for no man" (335–37).

In the conformist Mammoths organization, Wiggen's actions lead to some serious fallout. First, Kress writes a vindictive editorial labeling Wiggen "Henry the Whiner" (339) and, "on behalf of [himself] and thousands of indignant Americans," demands an apology (342). Hoping to minimize damage to the public perception of the organization, the Mammoths management reprimands Wiggen and presses him for an apology. This sets up a scene that is perhaps the novel's climax, a confrontation between Patricia Moors, Mammoths' executive and daughter of team owner Lester Moors, and Wiggen:

"I have wrote out an apology," [Moors] said, and she gave me a paper with a big long apology typewrote out on it. Half of it said that everything Krazy said was true, and the other half was practically an invitation for a squad of marines to drag me off by dawn and shoot me.
"I will not apologize," said I.
"Then perhaps you will deny it," she said and she hauled out another paper typewrote like the first, saying that everything Krazy said was lies from beginning to end. "This is the kind of a rhubarb that brings on a crisis for the organization," she said.
"I am not too worried about crisises," I said. "I am through with them. . . . No, I will not sign them, neither of them, neither apologizing nor denying."
". . . It is the organization that must be kept pure and free from scandal. You are a part of the organization."
"I am a part of nothing," I said.
"You owe something to the organization," she said.

"And does it not owe something to the other fellow?" I said. "What does it owe to Bub Castetter that give it 10 years and then was cut adrift?" (343)

Wiggen's rejection of conformism in this passage is strong, particularly in his pithy statement, "I am part of nothing." It is echoed in the approval his soon-to-be fiancé Holly gives him at the season's end: "What [the statistics] do not show is that you growed to manhood over the summer. You will throw no more spitballs for the sake of something so stupid as a ball game. You will worship the feet of no more gods name of Sad Sam Yale nor ever be a true follower of Dutch Schnell. And you will know the Krazy Kresses of this world for the liar they are. You will never be an island in the empire of Moors, Henry, and that is the great victory that hardly anybody wins any more" (348).

Here the Mammoths organization or "empire" comes to represent all conformity-demanding institutions, an idea that might have been particularly applicable to the 1950s Yankees as their unrelenting string of success under the tutelage of Casey Stengel and his "platoon" system always subsumed the needs of the individual to the success of the firm (Mann 100–106).[19] Furthermore, the continual desire by both the press and the Yankee organization to cast Mickey Mantle as the heir to the heroic Yankee legacy of Ruth, Gehrig, and DiMaggio can be read along conformist terms for Mantle as an individual. Mantle biographers suggest, in fact, that this was how the switch-hitting slugger received this trend, which brought him discomfort for the length of his career, particularly early on (Leavy 21–25, 297–98).

With its strong condemnation of conformism, Harris's novel shares thematic elements with some prominent contemporaries including J. D. Salinger's *The Catcher in the Rye* (1951), Joseph Heller's *Catch-22* (published in 1961, but begun in 1953, with a chapter published in 1955 [Heller, "Preface to the Special Edition" 12]), and Arthur Miller's *The Crucible* (1953). Henry Wiggen is seemingly cut from the same cloth as nonconformist heroes Holden Caulfield and John Yossarian, and though those three are ostensibly much less serious in temperament than Miller's dour John Proctor, they significantly share with him a refusal to surrender their name and integrity by conforming to the pressure of empowered institutions. This common thread is particularly relevant when one considers that both *Catch-22* and *The Crucible*, like *The Southpaw*, feature a climactic scene in which the protagonist is pressured to surrender his ideals and individuality by making a skin-saving, but morally compromising deal with one of these empowered institutions (Heller 434–39, 451–52; Miller 142–45).

Like the authors of these other literary works, Harris has not just the specific institutions of the Yankees, organized baseball, big business, or even the Cold War U.S. government and military in mind when he critiques conformism. Harris intends Wiggen's struggle to maintain his personal independence within the Mammoths organization as a metaphor for human existence itself. As Lavers asserts, "[Harris's] symbolism is akin to [Robert] Frost's, which is to say closer to synecdoche than symbol. Frost used a fork in the road to symbolize A Fork in the Road. Harris uses a man's life to symbolize A Man's Life. The terms do not change . . . rather, they extend—any man to Everyman" (37).

With this broad, philosophic goal, *The Southpaw* can be viewed as a work of literature influenced by existentialism, and in this way it is like many others in midcentury American letters, including the aforementioned works by Salinger, Heller, and Miller. Existentialism is a philosophy quite relevant to the topic of conformism. As literary critic Michael Rockler explains,

> For existentialists . . . an individual must define his or her own reality. . . . The existential task of a human being is create his or her own meaning, and the central requirement for living a meaningful life is a continual process of self-definition. A person is not defined by what he or she claims to be, but rather by his or her actions. . . .
>
> Existentialists further believe that the defining process encompasses solitude, choice and freedom. In order to create one's self, freedom of action is required. Hence, one must not become so entangled with the lives of others that one's autonomy is diminished.

With the novel's central conflict becoming not so much an issue of whether the Mammoths will win the pennant and World Series but whether Wiggen will become "an island in the empire of Moors," existentialism and its premium on individual autonomy are at the heart of *The Southpaw*. And as he successfully refuses to let his surroundings define himself, Henry Wiggen becomes—like Holden Caulfield, Yossarian, and John Proctor—an existential hero.

This broad, philosophical reading, however, does not preclude *The Southpaw* from having particular cultural, even political relevance in the context of postwar America. This is most powerfully signaled through the specific mention of the contemporary Cold War conflict in Korea (1951–53). By making the key issue of Wiggen's struggle with conformity the Korean War rather than just an issue related to only the Mammoths organization, Harris gives his existentialist-influenced critique of conformity a particular postwar American context. *The Southpaw* suggests a nation held back by its conformity to the patriotic popular consensus that demanded approval of such military action and demonstrations of world power. The threat of McCarthyism in this time period is particularly relevant and likely influenced Harris's writing. This critique of nationalist conformism is further supplemented by free-thinking catcher and Mammoths malcontent Red Traphagen's assessment of fans in the stadium at the conclusion of the ritual playing of the national anthem: "Land of the free and home of the brave. There ain't a 1 of them free, and there ain't 200 of them brave. 25,000 sheep" (203).

The fact that this critique of American conformism is made through a fictional baseball club modeled on the New York Yankees says a great deal about changing perceptions of the Yankees as a cultural icon. When Harris has his narrator declare at the novel's conclusion that "it is the whole history of the Mammoths that they are short dependable southpaws" (350), it seems clear (based on Holly's earlier use of "southpaw" as a metaphor for nonconformism) that the author is using the Mammoths—and through them, the Yankees—as a synecdoche for the entire nation itself. This link between the Yankees and the nation as a whole in a military context echoes *The Pride of the Yankees* from a decade earlier, where the text of the opening crawl links the heroism of arch-Yankee Lou Gehrig with the heroism of soldiers fighting in World War II. But this time the American-Yankees military link is not celebrated along lines of populist values and heroic self-sacrifice; rather, it is portrayed critically for its demand of blind conformity.

QUESTIONING SUCCESS

The Southpaw also offers a critique of what Yankee-hating journalist Charles Einstein described as the "philosophy of triumph" central to the Yankees and the facet of postwar America they represent. Though Wiggen helps lead the

Mammoths to both the pennant and the World Series, their success is represented as hollow in several passages. One such passage is a description of Manager Dutch Schnell:

> Everybody always asks me, "What kind of man is Dutch Schnell?" I never know exactly what to say. I think he is a great manager, and the statistics back me up in this. His first and only aim in life is winning ball games, and more often he wins them than not.... There is nothing Dutch will not do for the sake of the ball game. If he thinks it will help win a ball game by eating you out he will eat you out. If sugar and honey will do the trick out come the sugar and honey bottle. If it is money you need he will give you money. And if he has not further need for you he will sell you or trade you or simply cut you loose and forget you. (330)

Here Wiggen describes Schnell's commitment to winning as if he feels like he should admire it, but his tone and allusions to sacrificing individuals in the pursuit of winning reveal his intimation that something is not quite right with this, namely the devaluation of the well-being and worth of individuals. This is complemented by Wiggen's description of the scene in the clubhouse after the Mammoths have clinched the pennant: "Oh, winning heals many a wound in the flesh! And I could not help thinking, 'what if we lost? What if 6 games between April and September had went the other way? What then? Would Perry and Swanee be drinking together? Would Red and Sam Yale? And suppose I only won 13 games instead of 26? Would I then be the little golden apple in the eye of Lester T. Moors, Jr.?'" (335). Here Wiggen continues his second-guessing of "the philosophy of triumph," wondering what winning the pennant has actually won them, implying that the pursuit of the pennant has promoted false camaraderie, possibly at the expense of more authentic human interaction and friendship.[20]

This questioning of the ethic of success and victory obviously implies a critique of the Yankees as a cultural icon, and by extension the triumphal and prosperous postwar America as well, though the connection here is less explicit than with the issue of conformity. Still, the two themes are perhaps best viewed together. The Yankees/Mammoths organization and certain elements of the mainstream political and cultural climate in the postwar United States seemed to operate on the assumption that success on the baseball diamond, in business, or in maintaining American world influence and preventing the spread of communism all depended on everyone toeing the party line, so to speak. If Harris's novel encourages readers to ponder the costs of the pursuit of many types of success, intolerance towards nonconformity would certainly be one of those costs.

While at the time never achieving the type of public influence that *Damn Yankees* or perhaps even some anti-Yankees articles in popular publications like *Life* magazine, Mark Harris's *The Southpaw* offers the deepest and most culturally engaged of all the critiques of the Yankees in the boom of Yankee-hating texts in the 1950s. He consciously utilizes the team and their accumulated cultural meaning to offer a critique of the facets of postwar American culture they had come to embody. In so doing, Harris paved the way for future uses of the Yankees as a cultural icon in the late 1960s, when all of the author's indictments of postwar America—the naïve romanticization of its past, conformism, and an obsession with success and victory at the expense of other values—would be taken up with greater energy. In so doing, Harris's novel, like the existentialist-influenced works by Salinger, Heller, and Miller, stands as evidence for W. T. Lhamon's argument that the cultural iconoclasm that is so often primarily associated with the 1960s had its origins in the 1950s, a decade too often thought of as one of uniform conformity and cultural conservatism (xxxviii).

While not all of the negative perspectives on the Yankees that flourished in the 1950s are wedded to the same specific political and cultural critique that Harris's is, they all imply at least a partial rejection of the "philosophy of triumph," the idea that success is an intrinsic part of American identity. Like the Brooklyn Dodger fans and the working-class underdog persona they developed as a counterpoint to the ever-triumphant Yankees, other postwar Americans began voicing their dissent with what the Yankees represented. In an age in which rhetoric about national plenty and progress abounded, the growing numbers of Yankee haters suggested that, for many Americans, victory and success were not the only things that mattered.

Chapter Six

"WHERE HAVE YOU GONE, JOE DIMAGGIO?"

Decline, Cultural Change, and the 1960s

After an era of nearly unbroken Yankee triumph that began in the 1920s, the mid-1960s saw dramatic change. During this tumultuous decade of cultural transition, the Yankees stopped winning, and almost simultaneously, popular perspectives on the club shifted overwhelmingly. While the Yankees were once associated with the most celebrated aspects of the nation and its values, texts in the late 1960s continued and built on the trend of *The Southpaw* and *Damn Yankees,* utilizing the Yankees as an embodiment of the American values that were being rejected by the emerging generation. In particular, former Yankee pitcher Jim Bouton's controversial memoir, *Ball Four* (1970), presenting its author as a friend of the growing youth countercultural movement, portrays the Yankees as the essence of the unjust and empowered "Establishment" these young rebels sought to overthrow.

This perspective is complemented by the song "Mrs. Robinson" (1968) by folk-rock duo Simon and Garfunkel and Ron Kovic's Vietnam War memoir, *Born on the Forth of July* (1976), which likewise reference the Yankees as the embodiment of values that were, in that historical moment, perceived to be fading into America's past.

ON-FIELD DECLINE OF THE YANKEES

After four and a half decades of remarkable and sometimes unparalleled success, the New York Yankees finally fell from grace in the mid-1960s. Their dominant string of five World Series in a row from 1949 to 1953 was followed by a period that was only slightly less dominant. Between 1954 and 1964, the Yankees only failed to win the American League Pennant twice. But uncharacteristically, they began losing in the World Series as often as they won, losing the title to their National League opponents in 1955, '57, '60, '63, and '64. But then in 1965, with the team coming off two World Series losses in a row—something no Yankee team had done since the 1921–22 seasons—things began to unravel completely on the field for the Bronx Bombers. They finished in sixth place with a losing record that year, their worst finish since 1925. In the following four years they finished tenth (last), ninth, and fifth twice in a row.[1] After having been the most dominant presence in baseball for around four decades, the New York Yankees were suddenly a second-rate ball club.

There are a number of factors that have been suggested as reasons for this sudden decline. Most prominently, after the 1964 season, longtime owners Del Webb and Dan Topping sold the Yankees to the Columbia Broadcasting System (CBS). Many cite this new ownership's inexperienced and clumsy handling of the club as instrumental to the Yankees' decline (Golenbock, *Dynasty* 380–83). Some suggest that prior to selling the club Webb and Topping ceased to invest earnestly in the future, leaving CBS with few prospects (Bouton, qtd. in Golenbock, *Dynasty* 375).

As soon as 1967, sportswriter Jack Mann offered the most thorough explanation and theory about the collapse of the Bronx Bombers in his book *The Decline and Fall of the New York Yankees*, whose titular evocation of the Roman Empire was made only partially tongue in cheek. Mann cites as a major turning point Major League Baseball's rule change to create a draft of new amateur talent, requiring all the teams to take turns in signing new prospects. This effectively eliminated the advantage the Yankees had enjoyed because of their financial means and core of tenured talent scouts, which together had allowed the Yankees to sign more and better players (18, 22–26).

But even before the arrival of this new rule, which Mann calls "a system of controlled mediocrity" (12), the Yankees' pipeline of new prospects had been drying up. Their policy of selling young prospects on the idea of playing for the Yankees was starting to become less effective, as other clubs began offering larger and larger signing bonuses, a game the Yankee ownership thought beneath them (Mann 12–13;186–88, Halberstam, *October 1964* 230). To use Mann's colorful phrase, the Yankees "disdained the vulgar rat race" (13). Finally, though the Yankees had officially integrated with the addition of catcher/outfielder Elston Howard during the 1955 season, general manager George Weiss's racist policies cast a long shadow on the Yankee organization during the second half of the 1950s and into the early 1960s. While many other clubs loaded team rosters with black talent, the Yankee organization continued by and large to close off that outlet to itself (Mann 180–83; Halberstam, *October 1964* 231–33). This disadvantage was illustrated in 1963 and '64 when the Yankees were beaten in the World Series by the thoroughly integrated Los Angeles Dodgers (relocated from Brooklyn in 1957) and St. Louis Cardinals, respectively. Mann sums things up best with the concise observation that "times had changed, and the Yankees hadn't" (188).

BASEBALL AND THE CULTURAL CHANGES OF THE 1960S

But the fortunes of the Yankees and the business of baseball were not the only things changing during the 1960s. Much has been made of the sociocultural upheaval of this period and not without reason. In particular, the convergence of the civil rights movement, the protests of the Vietnam War, and the growing youth culture centered in the still-new rock-and-roll music and experimentation with consciousness-altering drugs made for a decade of dramatic cultural conflict and transition. This cultural rupture was most keenly felt along generational lines. Many Baby Boomers, the large cohort of the sons and daughters of the generation that grew up during the Great Depression and fought in World War II, adopted an iconoclastic stance towards the society their parents and grandparents had built, particularly with regard to ideas about race, gender roles, drugs, big business, the role of the military, and the role of the United States in the world in general.

The shift in taste and values that took place during the decade had no small effect on the popular perception of organized baseball. Baseball's popularity during the first half of the twentieth century and its close cultural association with many of the values of the World War II generation led to many associating the sport with a conservative resistance to change in this age of iconoclasm. The values celebrated in many baseball cultural texts from the 1940s and '50s, and values for which the New York Yankees were often presented as epitomizing—self-sacrificing and military-oriented patriotism, heroic masculinity, and faith in the capitalist economic system and the American dream of upward mobility through hard work—were being challenged in the 1960s. And by association, baseball may have begun to appear obsolete. The narrative introduction to the episode of Ken Burns's documentary television miniseries *Baseball* that deals with the 1960's captures this sentiment well: "During the 1960s, the Cold War almost became nuclear war. . . . The Beatles invaded the United States. . . . Americans lost a president and a prophet. Americans fought in Vietnam and then went into the streets to stop that fighting. New civil rights were won, but the country seemed to be coming apart. American cities were set ablaze, campuses erupted, generations clashed. . . . For the first time football would seriously challenge baseball as the national pastime.[2] And some began to wonder if the game mattered at all." This voiceover narration attempts to capture the nation in the throes of violent change with baseball as an aging institution struggling to keep up, a notion echoed later with the concise statement that, "The opening day of the 1968 season was postponed after Martin Luther King, Jr. was assassinated. Baseball seemed irrelevant."

In the 1960s baseball was beginning to feel irrelevant to no group more than the young, the Baby Boomers, whose 1950s childhood coincided with one of baseball's golden ages. The Baby Boom generation was growing up during a period when baseball had a considerable cultural profile. Before professional football and basketball had gained much traction with mainstream sports fans (though this was certainly on the horizon), baseball dominated the culture of sports spectatorship and consumption. And it was arguably a great time to follow baseball, as the Major Leagues were freshly energized by the influx of black talent from the Negro Leagues after the fall of the color line, World Series games were first broadcast on television, and the near-annual meetings between the proven and intimidating Yankees and the underdog, faltering Dodgers captivated the nation. It was a period when Robert Frost's suggestion that "some baseball is the fate of us all" was fairly accurate.

But while young Americans were indeed caught up in Mickey Mantle and Roger Maris's attempt to break Babe Ruth's single-season home run record in 1961, many young people found interests that took them away from baseball as the decade wore on. *Baseball* interviewees Doris Kearns Goodwin and Gerald Early both recount such experiences. Says Goodwin: "In the '60s I was in college and in graduate school and baseball didn't have the vitality for me that the civil rights movement did . . . and somehow the events of the world became so important that I didn't feel I had the time to indulge in the luxury of my childhood. . . . I was so busy in marches that there wasn't time to sit in baseball games."

Early recounts a similar experience with his childhood love of baseball during the 1960s: "At this time in the late '60s I was fourteen, fifteen, sixteen years old and I felt that baseball lost some of its resonance for me because these players did not seem to be in touch with what was going on. Everything had become very politicized. And this is particularly true with black players. They saw if you were to stand up and become political that you were going to be made to suffer. But as a youngster myself, becoming politicized, that was the very point."

The comments of childhood baseball fans Goodwin and Early share the common theme of abandoning baseball for what they perceived as more important things, namely social and political activism. Goodwin's use of the term "the luxury of my childhood" to refer to baseball suggests the image of a generation of naïve, molly-coddled Baby Boomers who came to enlightenment later as college students in the mid- to late 1960s and "became politicized," to use Early's phrase, putting away perceived childish things like baseball.

It seems to be mostly a poetic quirk of history that the collapse of the Yankees dynasty would coincide so neatly with the cultural moment when the American values for which the Yanks had served as icons were being challenged so pervasively. If Mann's theories are to be believed, however, the cultural changes of the 1960s did actually play a small role in the Bronx Bombers' decline. The Yankees' failure to embrace integration significantly diminished the pool of up-and-coming players, and once they did desegregate, they continued to have a "lilywhite" reputation among many black prospects who might prefer to sign with another team (Mann 70, 180). Furthermore, the movement towards "evening the playing field" among Major League clubs with rule changes like the amateur draft can be read as part of a broader cultural trend towards more socialistic ideas and government policies that would include Lyndon Johnson's Great Society domestic programs, as well as the iconoclastic youth's critique of the American capitalist ethic. Whatever the case, the decline of the New York Yankees, icons of American success, certainly seemed to parallel the passing away of many of the values that had been held up through World War II and the economic prosperity that followed.

A FORMER YANKEE'S GRUDGE IN *BALL FOUR*

With the change in the Yankees' on-field success and the broader changes of the '60s came new developments in the way the Yankees were utilized as a symbol in American culture. Foremost in this regard is former Yankee pitcher Jim Bouton's controversial memoir of his 1969 season, *Ball Four*, which utilizes the Yankees as an embodiment of the supposedly unjust and crumbling traditional American power structure.

Published in June 1970, *Ball Four* was written from former fastball pitcher Bouton's experiences attempting to make a comeback from a debilitating arm injury as a knuckleball pitcher with the short-lived Major League expansion franchise, the Seattle Pilots.[3] *Ball Four* is likely most remembered for the scandal it caused. It exposed the vulgarities of the clubhouse to many for the first time and portrayed ballplayers in a most decidedly unheroic manner. But the memoir, edited by sportswriter Leonard Shecter, also stands as a revealing document of cultural history, showing the conflict and tension of the societal transition that was taking place in the late 1960s. Bouton paints this tension in dramatic terms, envisioning himself as a forward-thinking friend of the counterculture and consigning his former team, the New York

Yankees, to the symbolic role of the supposedly out-of-date values of the World War II generation.

Bouton begins building these themes from the very beginning, establishing two key ideas in the memoir's introduction: that he is on the side of the iconoclastic youth in the late-1960s cultural debate and that he loathes the Yankees. Bouton wastes no time in establishing his bitterness towards the club, as the memoir's first paragraph begins, "I dream my knuckleball is bouncing around like a ping-pong ball and I'm pitching a two-hit shutout against my old team, the New York Yankees" (xv).

This desire for revenge and disdain of the once-mighty team for which he helped win pennants in the twilight years of their postwar dynasty becomes a running theme in *Ball Four*. Often Bouton will be discussing a seemingly unrelated topic and his narrative suddenly returns to his dream of avenging himself on the Yankees. Examples abound. In one, he writes: "We were sitting around the clubhouse and I asked [Seattle pitching coach] Sal the Barber [Maglie] about the days when he pitched for the Giants against the Dodgers. He said yeah, he'd never forget those days. 'You know, it's a funny thing,' he said, 'when I pitched against the Dodgers I didn't care if it was the last game I ever pitched. I really hated that club. . . .' I'll have that feeling at least a couple of times this year. When I pitch against the Yankees" (34).

And later, when Bouton is suspicious he might be traded, he writes, "Washington lost 6–0, and I wonder if they can use some pitching help. I sure would like to be with a club in the East, because if there's anything I want to do before I'm through it's win a few games in Yankee Stadium, and being with Washington would give me some extra shots at them. If this sounds like a grudge, it's only because it is" (123).

Bouton's tendency to follow one topical thread only to suddenly veer back toward his revenge fantasies against the Yankees might cause him to appear pathological if not for his wry sense of humor about the subject. But these passages do establish the Bronx Bombers as the primary antagonist in Bouton's mental universe.

At times he does flesh out his history with the Yankee organization and the unfairness he perceived in their treatment of him, giving some reason to his wrath: "You can make a lousy pitcher out of anybody by not pitching him. I'll always believe that's what [Yankee manager Ralph] Houk did to me.

Besides, there's no way the Yankees can justify getting rid of a twenty-nine-year-old body [Bouton] for $12,000 [the amount he was sold for], and before the season is over I'm going to remind a lot of people that they did" (32).

These comments about unfair treatment by the Yankee organization are echoed as Bouton considers the prospect of not making the Pilots' roster in spring training: "I know that if I don't make it, or if I don't get to pitch, it'll be because I wasn't good enough. It won't be on my mind that someone is trying to sabotage me the way I felt when I was with the Yankees" (93). In a moment of paranoia, Bouton even wonders if the Yankee organization is somehow trying to ruin his career with the Pilots: "It occurs to me that the Yankees may have prevailed upon [Seattle Pilots general manager Marvin] Milkes, or the Pilot organization, to soft-pedal me so that I won't embarrass them. These two clubs have made quite a few trades and I know it embarrasses the Yankees to have Hegan doing so well here. So maybe they said, 'Do us a favor, don't let Bouton look good'" (186).

Bouton's hatred for his former team is not confined to desire for personal revenge on them, however, as he makes it clear that he also wishes them ill in general. For instance, during a brief demotion to the Pilots' minor league affiliate in Vancouver, Bouton contrasts his feelings for the Seattle organization with those for his old team: "I listened to the Pilots game over the radio and wouldn't you know it, I found myself rooting for them. When the Yankees sent me down all I wanted was for them to get mashed. Even now I hope they finish lower in their division than the Pilots do in theirs. I can't explain it but that's what I feel" (119). Later on, he informs us, "The Yankees have lost thirteen out of fourteen now and I feel so bad about it I walk around laughing," but he does admit to "beginning to feel sorry" for some of his former teammates (157). These revenge fantasies and bitter memories easily make Bouton the biggest Yankee hater in print since fictitious Washington Senators fan Joe Boyd from *The Year the Yankees Lost the Pennant*. While the fictional Boyd and the real-life Bouton look at the Yankees from two different perspectives—Boyd seeing a tyrant whose dethroning is long overdue, and Bouton, a fallen giant that needs to be killed off completely—their disdainful comments complement each other to cast the Yankee as a powerful entity that has abused its power.

BOUTON AND THE COUNTERCULTURE

Just as Bouton establishes his disdain for the Yankees in *Ball Four*'s opening pages, he likewise begins building an image of himself as a counterculture sympathizer in the introduction to his memoir. A reflective Bouton writes,

> I've heard all the arguments against [professional baseball]. That there are better, more important things for a man to do than spend his life trying to throw a ball past other men who are trying to hit it with a stick. There are things like being a doctor or a teacher or working in the Peace Corps. More likely I should be devoting myself full-time to finding a way to end the war. I admit that sometimes I'm troubled by the way I make my living. I would like to change the world....
>
> ... so I'll save the world when I get a little older.... a man is entitled to devote a certain number of years to plain enjoyment and driving for some sort of financial security. You can always be a teacher or social worker when you've reached thirty-five (xvi–xvii).

Here the foundation of his self-image as "progressive" is clearly laid. In addition to giving mention to specific icons of the New Left—the Peace Corps, opposition to the war in Vietnam—Bouton creates an impression of global awareness, of a desire to help the underprivileged, and a conscience about contributing to society rather than just holding down a job and winning bread. Bouton's expressed pacifism as well his stated rejection of the capitalist-oriented ethic of keeping one's head down and enjoying the bounty American society enabled seem tailor-made to endear him to rebellious youth of the era.

While the pitcher makes no claims of being personally involved with the political and cultural movements associated with the so-called "hippie" counterculture of the later 1960s—marching in an antiwar or civil rights protest, experimenting with psychedelics, or attending an acid rock concert—he clearly expresses his sympathy for their political views and values. In fact, in reporting a visit he made to the notoriously radical University of California–Berkeley campus, Bouton states as much directly, professing empathy for the

"Arab kids arguing about the Arab-Israeli war," the "Black Panthers talking about Huey Newton," and other young people with "long hair and sandals and . . . dirty feet," whom he sees as being "genuinely concerned about what's going on around them," including "Vietnam, poor people, black people [who] are trying to change" what they don't like (145–46). His empathy culminates in a desire to tell the whole campus, "Look, I'm with you, baby. I understand. Underneath my haircut I really understand that you're doing the right thing" (146). In addition to the ideological sympathy that Bouton expresses here, this passage further casts him as a friend of the counterculture merely by associating him with the iconic Berkeley campus.

Bouton supplements this story with a liberal sprinkling of references to a few other countercultural icons throughout *Ball Four*. These include visiting San Francisco's famous hippie district, Haight-Ashbury (he is offered LSD, but is "too chicken to try" it [29]), siding with the young protesters in an argument about the 1968 Chicago Democratic Convention riots (75), bringing a copy of the Bay Area radical underground newspaper the *Berkeley Barb* into the clubhouse (147), and commenting about the irony of the ease with which ballplayers acquire amphetamines (or "greenies") compared to the harsh punishment for marijuana possession (171). Bouton's narrative also includes a seemingly earnest use of the word "groovy" (172), the mention of plans to see *Midnight Cowboy* (288), a record of numerous clubhouse complaints about the length of friend and teammate Steve Hovley's hair (319), and a stated preference for the Beatles over the typically ballplayer-favored country music (379).

His prominent reference to these "hippie" icons notwithstanding, Bouton also impresses on readers that he does not want to be seen a namedropper or a dabbler in his countercultural sympathies, continually asserting and reasserting his left-leaning position on the two major political issues of the day, Vietnam and civil rights. In doing so, he frequently contrasts his own views with the much more conservative position he implies is common in baseball.

Bouton first makes hints about his views on race and civil rights through his sociocultural interpretation of an experience he had as a child:

When I was a kid I loved to go to Giants games in the Polo Grounds . . . when I was about ten years old. . . . [A ball was] hit into the stands and a whole bunch of kids ran after it. I spotted it first, under a seat, and grabbed for it. Just as I did, a Negro kid also snatched at it. . . . He grabbed the ball real hard and pulled it right out of my hand. No complaint, he took it fair and square. I thought about it afterward, about what made him able to grab that ball out of my hand. I decided it had to do with the way we were bought up—me in a comfortable suburb, him probably in a ghetto. I decided that while I *wanted* the baseball, he *had to have it*. (25)

To this personal story, Bouton later more directly references the political application of his views on race while recalling an argument about civil rights with a former teammate, catcher Elston Howard, the first black Yankee, Howard's wife, Arlene, and veteran sportswriter Jimmy Cannon, specifying that "Arlene and I were the militants" (88). Bouton further buttresses his status as a racial progressive through several asides during the course of the narrative that casually but frankly report the subtle—and sometimes not so subtle—racism that remained part of Major League Baseball over twenty years after integration (146, 285, 334, 368, 371–72).

Bouton takes a similar approach in portraying his views on Vietnam, recounting a personal connection to the issue and reiterating his views every so often in an aside. He finds occasion to make his feelings about Vietnam known when recalling his fan club, which formed in the early 1960s: "I heard that one of the fan-club members was in Vietnam. It just doesn't seem right that a member of my fan club should be fighting in Vietnam. Or that anybody should be" (119). While perhaps not as personally significant as his story about struggling over the fly ball with the young African-American boy, Bouton's comments about his fan club member–turned–Vietnam draftee still personalize his views and make him seem genuine in his political stance to readers.

In addition to asserting his opposition to the war in Vietnam, Bouton also bemoans the climate of the baseball clubhouse that discouraged any political nonconformity: "you could talk about the war in Vietnam, only you had to say, 'Look at those crazy kids marching in the street. Why don't they take a bath?' . . . If you said these things, no one would accuse you of talking politics, because you were *right*. . . . On the other hand, if you said things like, 'We've got no right to be in Vietnam,' . . . then you shouldn't be talking about things like that, because you were *wrong*." (84). By portraying himself as a relative nonconformist in the often culturally conservative world of baseball, Bouton parallels his own experience with that of more radical countercultural youths in society at large. In essence, Bouton paints himself as baseball's version of a hippie.

Bouton's self-portrayal as a nonconformist in baseball is echoed in his numerous jokes about being branded as "flaky" (341) by his more traditional teammates and coaches. *Ball Four* is liberally sprinkled with anecdotes about the suspicion with which most of the team regarded Bouton and his two semi-intellectual, counterculture-sympathizing teammates: Mike Marshall, nicknamed "Moon Man" (127), and Steve Hovley, christened "Orbit" (127).[4] In perhaps the most telling incident of conflict between the players who thought of themselves as "one of the boys" (303) and Bouton's small, informal network of "kooks" (223) or "weirdos" (303) is the author's account of Hovley getting teased in the clubhouse when Pilots manager Joe Schultz notices his intellectual, literary reading material—Fyodor Dostoyevsky's *The Possessed*:

> Schultz held the book up in the air and said, "Hey, men, look at this! What kind of name is this?"
> By this time there was a group of guys around him looking at the book like a group of monkeys might inspect a bright red rubber ball. Schultz read off the back cover—a sentence anyway—until he got to the word "nihilism." Hey, Hy," Schultz said to Hy Zimmerman, "what the hell does 'nihilism' mean?"
> "That's when you don't believe in nothing," Zimmerman said.
> Whereupon Schultz, shaking his head and laughing, flung the book back at Hovley, hitched up his towel and strode off, amid much laughter. (242)

Here, Bouton narrates with heavy irony, as confounded as his readers at the way the grown men belittle one of their peers who dares to deviate from the jock-culture norm through intellectual pursuit. In a similar anecdote that essentially conveys the same idea more succinctly, manager Schultz teasingly refers to the chess-playing Marshall as "Brains" as he warms up on the mound (238).

With these stories, Bouton paints the image of the world of baseball as a place where those with the power rule irrationally and persecute those who dare to have any actual insight or a novel thought. The parallels with the rebellious '60s youth and their protest of the American government's policies of racial injustice and the war in Vietnam are clear and intentional here. In one of his more clever and humorous moments, the author describes his perception of this baseball world as follows: "Sometimes I think that if people in this little world of baseball don't think you a little odd, a bit weird, you're in trouble. It would be rather like being considered normal in an insane asylum" (234). By using this insane-asylum comparison, Bouton draws on the same metaphor at the heart of both Joseph Heller's *Catch-22* (1961) and Ken Kesey's *One Flew Over the Cuckoo's Nest* (1962), two iconoclastic novels from earlier in the decade in which protagonists with supposedly questionable sanity are proven much more sane than the institution in which they are trapped. Whether consciously chosen or not, it is no accident that Bouton uses a metaphor that is central to two works so embraced by the countercultural youth of the 1960s.[5] All three share the rebellious Baby Boomers' iconoclastic spirit.

SYMBOLS OF "THE ESTABLISHMENT"

Bouton also views his grudge against the Yankees through the lens of his left-leaning cultural and political views. The Yankees become the dramatic foil to his self-portrayal as a counterculture sympathizer, essentially taking up the role described by the catchall term "The Establishment" in the rhetoric of the counterculture.

Often, Bouton will voice a complaint about one of the so-called "Neanderthal" tendencies in baseball and will hold up the Yankees as the prime example of that tendency he believes to be outdated (xvii). For instance, after discussing the Pilots' frosty reception to some of Steve Hovley's nonconformities, Bouton turns back to memories of his time with the Yankees: "When I first came up with the Yankees there was intolerance of anybody who didn't conform right down the line—including haircut and cut of suit" (59). This pattern is repeated when Bouton complains about unwritten clubhouse rule demanding solemnity after a loss:

> After a loss the club house has to be completely quiet, as though losing strikes a baseball player dumb. . . . The rule is that you're not supposed to say anything even if it's a meaningless spring training loss. . . .
> The important thing is to let the manager and coaches know you feel bad about losing. . . . So you go along with the little game. *And they played this game real hard with the Yankees.* (64, emphasis added)

Thus, while the conformism that Bouton decries here actually occurs with the Pilots and it is implied to be common throughout the Major Leagues, he makes a point of claiming things were even worse with the Yankees. In fact, one might get the impression that Bouton is rebelling against his memories of his days with the Yankees even more than against his current situation with the Pilots.

This pattern of using the Yankees as the ultimate model of baseball "Neanderthalism" continues when Bouton addresses issues that are more specifically political. While Bouton often discusses how his left-leaning political views and countercultural sympathies sometimes alienate him from his more traditionally minded teammates, the picture he paints of the Yankee clubhouse is an archconservative bastion. For instance, a road trip to New York City gives him occasion to write, "There is always a flood of memories when I come back to New York. Like all the trouble I used to get into with the Yankees. One time nobody in the bullpen would talk to me for three days because I said I thought Billy Graham was a dangerous character. This was after he had said that Communists were behind the riots in the black ghettoes. . . . My heavens, you'd think I had insulted Ronald Reagan (214).

Similarly, while labeled a "kook" and a "flake" with the Pilots, Bouton relates that with the Yankees he was occasionally referred to as "that Communist" (33), a moniker that resurfaces when a former Yankee teammate is traded to the Pilots and finds opportunity to revisit it (257, 310). While Bouton characterizes the whole of the Major Leagues as politically conservative, he reserves these accusations of McCarthyism for his former team in the Bronx.

Bouton makes similar comments about the Yankees concerning the issue of integration and race relations among players. He uses music in the clubhouse as a springboard to discuss the race issue: "Well, [first baseman Don] Mincher was talking about going to see Johnny Cash and I imagine when he talks about Johnny Cash it's like the Negro players talking about James Brown. Lots of times in the clubhouse you'll have a radio on and every once in a while it gets switched back and forth between a soul-music station and a country-western station. If you're going good you get to hear your kind of music. In the Yankee clubhouse western music dominated" (54). This subtle suggestion that the Yankee clubhouse was dominated by white players—either because there weren't enough black players or because they wielded less power—is more condemning than it may seem, as it revives the public knowledge that the Yankees were late and resistant to integration.

All told, Bouton's political jabs at the Yankees clearly align them with the side of the cultural divide associated with the World War II generation, with Bouton and his Baby Boomer allies on the opposing side. But for Bouton to turn the Yankees into a symbol of "The Establishment" in the structure of his memoir, he needs to do more than just characterize them as politically right-wing. He also must create the idea that they hold substantial power and that they abuse said power.

This Bouton does in a few different ways. As noted, part of the former Yankee's grudge against his old employer is his theory about the front office conspiring against him. Bouton cannot help but imagine the Yankee owners and management as out to ruin his career and possibly even limiting his success in his comeback with the Pilots to prevent their being left with the potential embarrassment of having released him prematurely (32, 93, 186). While one might expect to find this kind of institutional manipulation of an individual's autonomy in a Kafka novel or, perhaps more proximately and appropriately, Heller's *Catch-22*, Bouton's theories strain credibility just a bit. Nevertheless, the fact that the Yankee organization is so powerful, both in Bouton's mind and in many of his readers', that he would be capable of wondering whether they might be able to control his career with another team is revealing. It reminds one of a more extreme version of Mark Harris's portrayal of the overly corporate Yankee stand-ins, the New York Mammoths, and does much to set up the idea of the Yankees as a big, bad, human-crushing institution.

Also reminiscent of the Mammoths/Yankees from *The Southpaw* is Bouton's account of his struggle with the Yankee front office to obtain what he considered a fair contract. In the later 1960s, the famous director of baseball's Players Association, Marvin Miller, was beginning to shift the balance of power from the owners to the players, negotiating the leagues' first collective bargaining agreement in 1968 to get the players' minimum salary raised from $7,000 to $10,000, with much more on the horizon (Korr 1–10). Contracts and the power struggle between players and the front office were on the minds of many in baseball, and Bouton was no exception. Following a familiar pattern, he bemoans what he sees as the manipulative, underhanded, and unjust practices by baseball owners in general but saves his most venomous language for the Yankees.

In the memoir's opening section, Bouton spends about a page and a half describing the negotiation of his contract with the Pilot organization over the past two years, which included some minor disagreement and haggling—much less than the author anticipated.[6] He then devotes six and a half pages to describe in excruciating detail his history of contract negotiations with the Yankees, a Kafkaesque nightmare of institutional deception, doublespeak, subterfuge, and outright lying (4–10). Bouton's experience could perhaps best be summed up with his understatement, that the Yankees "really fight you" (5). But a more important statement might be his observations about ball clubs' unofficial policy of telling players to keep their salaries secret: "You know, players are always told that they're not to discuss salaries with each other. They want to keep us dumb.... They want to keep us ignorant, and it works" (7). Here the Yankees—all major league clubs to one degree or another, but especially the Yankees—are not merely portrayed as an institutional bully but as a hegemonic organization that attempts to control the information and beliefs of its underlings. Not coincidentally, this control of information and ideology is the very accusation countercultural rebels directed at the militaristic, anticommunist U.S. government and the "military-industrial complex."

To round out his portrayal of the Yankees as a corrupt power structure, Bouton paints the club as simultaneously elitist and miserly. Some of Bouton's passing comments suggest an image of success going to the head of the Yankee organization. Yankee haughtiness can be discerned in passages such as his observation that "the clubhouse here [in Seattle] is kind of cramped and the Yankees would probably sneer at it" (15), or his memories that Yankee executive Dan Topping Jr. (son of co-owner Dan Topping) "had a boarding-school accent that always made you feel like your fly was open or something" (4), or Topping's presumptuous reminder during contract negotiations, "Don't forget your World Series share; you can always count on that" (4). *Ball Four* would certainly not be the first time the Yankees were accused of elitism, but combined with Bouton's imagery of a manipulative organization, this haughtiness becomes more sinister.

It is also complemented with accusations of tightfistedness. In addition to Bouton's suggestion that the Yankee organization fought for every cent in contract negotiations, his description of some Yankee clubhouse policies leaves the impression of an organization flush with its own success while somehow still insistent on pinching pennies: "there's a soda fountain [in the Seattle spring training clubhouse]—Coca-Cola, root beer, 7-Up, cold, on tap, freebie. If Pete Previte saw this he'd go crazy. Little Pete's the No. 2 clubhouse man and he had this mark-up sheet. Every time you took a soft drink you were supposed to make a mark next to your name so he'd know how much to charge you. He spent the whole day going around saying, 'Hey mark 'em up. Don't forget to mark 'em up. Hey, Bouton, you're not marking 'em up" (15).

The notion that the fledgling Seattle Pilot organization (which folded after only one year in the league) would treat the players to free soft drinks while the successful and notoriously wealthy Yankees would insist they pay makes the latter organization seem overly parsimonious. This view of their frugality in spite of wealth, combined with Bouton's accusations of manipulating individuals, casts the Yankees as a tyrannical organization indifferent to the needs and well-being of its underlings, seeking only to take advantage of them. In light of Bouton's linkage of the Yankees with conservative politics and the values of the World War II generation, this collective image of an oppressive hegemonic institution creates strong parallels with the projected image of the American power structure the rebels of the counterculture fought against. In essence, *Ball Four* casts the Yankees as baseball's version of that catchall amalgam of the U.S. government, big business, the "military-industrial complex," and anyone over thirty: "The Establishment."

While Bouton sees "Neanderthal aspects," political conservatism, and abuse of power throughout the culture of Major League Baseball, the Yankees are consistently portrayed as the apogee of tendencies. Generally speaking,

Bouton writes about the Yankees the way we might expect any self-respecting Baby Boomer "flower child" to talk about his or her stereotypical clock-punching, gray-flannel-suit-wearing, whiskey-drinking father: as standing in the way of change through his narrow-minded, dogmatic adherence to a value system that the younger generation sees as unjust and out of date.

THE YANKEES AND THE NEW YORK METS IN *BALL FOUR*

Bouton's countercultural sympathies, his disdain for Yankees, and characterization of them as an icon of the "The Establishment" coalesce in a simple observation about the 1969 baseball season that at first reading may seem like only an attempt at humor. In his entry for June 10, Bouton reports, "I'm pleased to note today that the New York Mets are 28–23 and in second place in their division and that the New York Yankees are 28–29 and in fifth place in their division. Perhaps justice is about to triumph" (210). The comment may seem like merely humorous hyperbole, which it certainly is. But considering the context of baseball history, the contemporary cultural milieu, and Bouton's characterization of the Yankees, this wry observation about justice and the relative fates of the Yankees and the Mets speaks volumes about the mindset of the iconoclasts of the late 1960s and about what the Yankees had come to stand for in this period.

The New York Mets were created as an expansion club in the National League in 1962, partly as an effort to replace the vacated Dodgers and Giants, who had moved to California after the 1957 season. Playing first in the Giants' old Polo Grounds and then in the newly erected Shea Stadium in the borough of Queens, the Mets were initially horrible. As ultimate testament to their early futility, the 1962 Mets, with a record of 40–120, lost more games than any team in the twentieth century. But the club nevertheless won the hearts of New Yorkers (including many former Dodger and Giant fans), selling as many tickets as—and sometimes outdrawing— the Yankees through much of the 1960s (Mann 191–92).[7]

Thus, when Bouton speaks of the inversion of the fortunes of the lowly Mets and the once-mighty and immoveable Yankees as being a long-denied fulfillment of "justice," the parallels with the decade's broader struggle of the disempowered to bring down the traditional power structure are clear, be it the iconoclastic efforts of segregated African-Americans, feminists, or those endless battalions of the young, armed with their "new" ideas about peace and love.

That the underdog Mets—as if reincarnated Brooklyn Dodgers—would go on to win the pennant and beat the favored Baltimore Orioles in the 1969 World Series (though, writing on July 10, Bouton likely would have only guessed this in his wildest dreams) while the Yankees languished for the fifth consecutive season in the second division (the bottom half of the standings) is a fitting end to the upheaval of the decade of the 1960s. Along these same lines, the left-leaning Bouton's recognition of this symbolism with his reference to the pending triumph of justice may be the most telling passage in *Ball Four* in terms of the reinterpretation of the Yankees as a cultural icon in the tumultuous 1960s. An embodiment of the triumphal World War II and postwar America, the Yankees were now the tyrannical but corroding "Establishment," whose comeuppance many believed to be at hand.

BALL FOUR'S AFTERMATH AND THE YANKEES

As scathing as Bouton's portrayal of the Yankees in *Ball Four* was, the material within the covers of the memoir constitutes only a starting point for the way it shaped popular perspectives on the Yankee cultural icon. Controversial for its frank—some might say sensationalized—treatment of clubhouse culture, *Ball Four* became a best-seller upon publication. It won Bouton few friends within Major League Baseball, however. As Peter Golenbock colorfully puts it,

> When Bouton's book was published, exposing some of his teammates as human beings who liked to have fun in human ways, some of those teammates regarded Bouton as Judas reincarnate. Part of the athlete's code has always been, "in this clubhouse what you hear here and see here, stays here." Bouton broke the code. He has suffered for it ever since. He has never been invited to a Yankee Old-Timers' Day game. Mickey Mantle and Ellie Howard, men who were close to him when they were teammates, refuse to have anything to do with him, and the baseball establishment has branded him a traitor. (*Dynasty* 372)

Ball Four invoked the wrath of both Baseball Commissioner Bowie Kuhn, who tried to get Bouton to sign a statement declaring the memoir to be a fictional fabrication (Bouton 408), and the Yankees, who shunned him completely until finally relenting and inviting him back for their traditional Old-Timers' Day in 1998 (Frommer, *Remembering Yankee Stadium* 194–95).[8] All of this, of course, played right into Bouton's hands. Or rather, it further bolstered his credentials as an iconoclast and friend of the counterculture, an enterprise in which he seems heavily invested in the pages of *Ball Four*. As with Newton's third law of motion, this fallout had an equal but opposite effect on the Yankee organization, seemingly confirming to the general public all of Bouton's accusations about them as reactionary and tyrannically controlling.

BALL FOUR AND MICKEY MANTLE

Ball Four's publication likewise had a dramatic effect on the public perception of then–recently retired Yankee centerfielder Mickey Mantle. More than just an All-Star, Mantle was the face of the Yankee organization since at least the mid-1950s, and in light of the club's rapid late 1960s decline, was still arguably the name most connected with the Yankees in the public consciousness at the time of the book's publication. Teammates between 1962 and until Bouton was demoted to the minor leagues, Mantle makes several appearances in Bouton's recollections of his days with the Yankees.

Though his portrayal of the popular Yankee hero is in many ways positive,[9] and it seems clear that Bouton liked Mantle personally, *Ball Four* frankly discussed aspects of the superstar's life that were not common public knowledge: his heavy drinking (30), his participation with teammates in peeping-tom voyeurism at hotels and ballparks (38), and his reluctance to sign autographs, which occasionally resulted in cruelty towards young fans (30). Mantle biographer Tony Castro describes Bouton's portrayal of the Hall of Fame centerfielder as, "in retrospect . . . fair" (238–39), but at the time of the book's release many reviews and articles about the scandalous book focused disproportionately on these details about Mantle (Castro 240). In the words of Castro, this constituted a "devastating blow" to Mickey's public image in these early days after his retirement (238). David Falkner, another Mantle biographer, assesses the damage this way: "It was the age of the antihero and

Bouton's irreverence fit the time perfectly.... As far as Mantle was concerned, the uncritically adoring view the public had of him began to fade. In the years following, the public's image of Mantle was as someone who surfaced for a few weeks each spring to stand around for several hours in his old uniform and then to carouse at night" (214).

In many respects, this shift in Mantle's public image and its timeliness, considering the iconoclasm of the era that Falkner describes, has become a significant part of the Yankee slugger's legacy. One need look no further than the titles of his numerous biographies for confirmation, including Castro's *Mickey Mantle: America's Prodigal Son*, Jane Leavy's *The Last Boy: Mickey Mantle and the End of America's Childhood*, and Falkner's own *The Last Hero: The Life of Mickey Mantle*.

Ball Four's impact on Mantle's public persona had perhaps as much influence on the popular perspective on the Yankees as a cultural icon as Bouton's own complaints about his old club within the text. For Mickey Mantle was more than just a Yankee hero in the public consciousness; he was heir to the legacy of *the* Yankee hero, the tradition of Ruth, Gehrig, and DiMaggio that personified the iconic Yankees and their affiliated values of heroic masculinity and the American dream.

This heroic mantle was thrust upon Mickey, the son of a poor Oklahoma zinc miner, from the very beginning of his career with the Yankees. As the ballplayer himself remembers, "When I came up, [manager] Casey [Stengel] told the writers that I was going to be the next Babe Ruth, Lou Gehrig and Joe DiMaggio all rolled up in one" (qtd. in Castro 50). Stengel's thoughts about the new Yankee messiah were echoed in sports magazine cover stories (Leavy 22–24) and quickly spread through sportswriters to baseball fans and the public at large.[10]

But Mantle's biographers seem to agree that the real confirmation that Mantle was heir to the tradition of Yankee heroism came from clubhouse worker Pete Sheehy. Leavy explains, "Pete Sheehy, the clubhouse man and guardian of Yankee succession, assigned the lockers and the uniform numbers.... He was the institutional memory of the club.... He fetched hot dogs and bicarb for The Babe and joe for Joe D.; he informed a historically challenged rookie that George Herman Ruth's number 3 was not available, nor was Henry Louis Gehrig's 4. As for 5 [DiMaggio's number], everyone knew 5 was still working on immortality. Sheehy gave Mantle 6. 'The Law of Mathematical progression,' the Yankees' public relations man Red Patterson called it" (11–12). Regarding the symbolism of this numerical assignment, Castro concurs, "Sheehy recognized an obvious continuity in the Yankees line of succession: Lou Gehrig had assumed the superstar role after Babe Ruth; DiMaggio's debut had come at the end of Gehrig's career; and now Mantle appeared headed to join the Yankees in DiMaggio's last season" (49).

Mantle sometimes struggled to live up to these impossibly lofty expectations. For instance, after being handed uniform number 6 in his rookie season, he underperformed and had to be sent to the minors to recover his confidence. After being called back up after a month and a half he opted for the now-legendary number 7 instead (Leavy 28). Similarly, Mantle had a hard time equaling Gehrig and DiMaggio's squeaky-clean public image, such as in the spring of 1957, when Mantle and some teammates (including future Yankee manager Billy Martin, who would soon be traded to the Kansas City A's, partly because of the incident) were involved in an intoxicated brawl at New York's Copacabana club that the city's tabloids caught wind of and turned into a headline (166–75).

But in most respects, Mantle fit the Yankee hero's role perfectly. Not only did he possess the everyman's humble-origin story, but he also had an easygoing demeanor and boyish handsomeness that helped make him a favorite with young women as well (Levy 172–73). A switch-hitter, Mantle had extraordinary power at the plate and, like Ruth, became well known for his tremendous tape-measure home-run blasts. In 1961, along with teammate Roger Maris (who actually broke the record), Mantle even challenged Ruth's single-season record of sixty home runs, before bowing out to injury and finishing with fifty-four. In 1956 pop singer Teresa Brewer even recorded a "Joltin' Joe DiMaggio"–style song tribute, "I Love Mickey," as if to put a pop-culture stamp of approval on Mantle's Yankee hero candidacy. But most important, like his predecessors, he continued the Yankees' championship legacy, helping them to many American League pennants (1951, '52, '53, '55, '56, '57, '58, '60, '61, '62, '63, and '64) and World Series titles (1951, '52, '53, '56, '58, '61, and '62).

With this link between Mantle and the storied Yankee past established in both the public's mind and the Yankee organization's, *Ball Four*'s revelations, such as they were, made quite an impact on the team's cultural meaning at the end of the 1960s. As bearer of the torch of Yankee heroism, Mantle, like Ruth, Gehrig, and DiMaggio before him, "was proof of America's promise: [that] anyone could grow up to be president or Mickey Mantle—even Mickey Mantle" (Leavy xv). Mantle himself sensed something of what the American public saw in him, admitting, "I guess you could say I'm what this country is all about" (qtd. in Leavy xv).

Though Ruth's wild off-field antics were far too extreme for the American public not to have some intimation of them, Gehrig and DiMaggio were, by and large, still seen as flawless, canonized baseball saints of the great American success story. Thus, Mantle's flaws as revealed in *Ball Four* were viewed as something of a betrayal of the Yankee legacy. Some may have seen Mantle as an unworthy successor. Others would have presumed that if these relatively salacious details about Mantle were true, the same must be true of all baseball heroes, even the great Yankees heroes. In either case, in 1970, the great American icon, the Yankee hero, was taken down a peg or two in the public's estimation and with it those accompanying ideas about the promise and goodness of the American nation itself.

This disillusionment may have been particularly resonant with that generational cohort who worshiped Mantle growing up, the Baby Boomers. Though not technically a Baby Boomer himself, Joe Pepitone, a teammate and friend from late in Mantle's career, confirms this in his interview with Golenbock: "Mantle had been an idol for so many years to people my age [Pepitone was born in 1940] and your age [Golenbock was born in 1946], and they grow up idolizing him" (qtd. in *Dynasty* 361). Leavy goes even further in hypothesizing such a generational connection, writing simply that "Mantle was the face of postwar America" (120). As such a generational icon, Mantle's public fall from grace would have had a particular effect on Baby Boomers who remembered him from their youth. Pepitone says as much, claiming, "Kids grew up with a lot of good images about Mickey Mantle. They felt good just thinking about him and the next thing you know they're depressed because of what Jim [Bouton] wrote" (qtd. in Golenbock, *Dynasty* 361). One thing that Pepitone seems to overlook in his comments is the fact that many of these fans who idolized Mantle as youngsters were no longer quite so young when *Ball Four* came out. In fact, many of them had lost faith in numerous icons of American greatness and were disillusioned with all sorts of American institutions they had been encouraged to respect and revere as children, including Major League Baseball. Thus, the disillusionment of Baby Boomers with Mantle has resonances both of a personal loss of innocence and of a broader generational disenchantment with the values of their parents.

MANTLE AND GENERATIONAL DISILLUSIONMENT IN *BORN ON THE FOURTH OF JULY*

As an illustrating example, the most immediate and obvious parallel here would be that of Henry Wiggin in Harris's *The Southpaw*, as his learning the truth about mythologized Ruth-Gehrig-DiMaggio-style baseball hero and childhood idol Sam Yale is intended to represent a loss of innocence and passing into a more mature and enlightened state of being. But considering the cultural context of the late 1960s, another parallel to consider would be the journey of a young American like Ron Kovic, author of the antiwar memoir *Born on the Fourth of July* (1976).

While Kovic wrote his memoir in 1974 and it was not published until two years after that, the experiences he describes are firmly rooted in the cultural moment of the late 1960s and the generational disenchantment with the values he and his contemporaries inherited and embraced as kids. In *Born on the Fourth of July*, Kovic writes from the perspective of a paraplegic veteran now protesting the very same war in which he had fought. Reflecting on his own history, he emphasizes his personal naïveté as he recounts an idyllic childhood and his decision to enlist in the Marine Corps during the Vietnam conflict as a patriotic eighteen-year-old. Kovic's transition from sunny patriotism in his youth to iconoclastic protest as a young adult parallels the path taken by many of his generation between the 1950s and early '70s.

Interestingly, writing as an adult in 1974, Kovic closely allies his self-described naïve patriotism with his love of Mickey Mantle and the New York Yankees. This close association between Kovic's love of country and love of the Yankees comes through in the theme of heroism, where the author is quick to link his baseball heroes and military heroes. While Mantle is presented as young Kovic's heroic centerpiece—"like a god" to the young boy and his friends, "a huge golden statue standing in centerfield" (58)—the author recalls cinematic military heroes as occupying that same lofty pedestal. "Like Mickey Mantle and the fabulous New York Yankees, John Wayne in *The Sands of Iwo Jima* became one of my heroes," writes Kovic, citing a specific example (65). Kovic further describes how, when at play, he and his friends imagined themselves as their war-movie heroes in the same way they pretended to be their baseball idols in their sandlot games, emphasizing, "just as we dreamed of playing for the Yankees someday, we dreamed of becoming United States Marines and fighting in our first war" (66). That heroes from World War II movies would occupy roughly the same mental space in a young boy as the heir to the tradition of Yankee heroism speaks volumes not only about the type of masculinity associated with the Yankee hero but also about the degree to which Mantle and those Yankees who came before him had acquired nationalistic connotations.

While it could be argued that Kovic's obsession with Mantle and the Yankees and his conflation of baseball fandom with military-focused patriotism were merely contingent on the fact that he grew up on nearby Long Island, the author's particular emphasis on the concept of victory suggests that the role Mantle and the postwar Yankees played in the drama of his cultural-political transition was unique, that they could not be replaced by just any old baseball club. As Kovic himself stresses, "back then," the Yankees were "winning like they would never stop" (58), a close parallel to the unflagging success the young boy linked with the nation. This notion of "winning" as being the distinguishing characteristic of the American nation is particularly evident in young Kovic's reaction when that victorious legacy is threatened, as it seems to be when the United States' attempt to answer the Soviet Union's successful Sputnik satellite launch with the Vanguard rocket launch fails on live TV in 1957. "We were losing, I thought," the author writes in retrospect, "America wasn't first anymore" (69). This connection between the Yankees, America, and "winning" became a template for the boy personally as well, a fact made clear by his inconsolable tears after his first Little League baseball game ends in a loss (57).

In Kovic's writing about his younger self, the aforementioned "philosophy of triumph" seems to make the Yankees and the United States bleed into each other as they act as heroic beacons for the boy and his life ambitions.

But it is this very philosophy of triumph that Kovic eventually loses faith in as he is confronted firsthand with the Vietnam conflict, which, like many of his generation, he eventually perceives as "a crime against humanity" (177). Writing about himself in the third person, Kovic contrasts the ideals of his younger self with his post-Vietnam outlook:

> All his life he'd wanted to be a winner. It was always so important to win, to be the very best. . . . how hard he'd tried to win even in those simple games. . . . But now it all seemed different. All the hopes about being the best marine, winning those medals. They all seemed crushed now. . . . Like the man he had just killed with one shot. . . . It had been so simple when he was back on the block with Richie or running down to the deli to pick up a pack of Topps baseball cards. . . . It seemed like so much nicer a thing than what was happening around him now, all the faces, the torn green fatigues, and just below his foot was a guy's head with a gaping hole through his throat. (183–84)

While Kovic never specifically describes a disenchantment with the Yankees themselves or his old hero, Mantle, it is clear that the lessons they taught him about winning, the philosophy of triumph they embodied for him, feel naïve and hollow to him now. And among his generation, he was certainly not the only one.

Released in the same year as Kovic's antiwar memoir, the Michael Ritchie–directed movie *The Bad News Bears* echoes the marine veteran's disenchantment with the "win-at-all-costs" mentality he learned in his Little League days while idolizing the Yankees. Rather than having the titular gang of ragtag, ne'er-do-well Bears come up with a typical late-inning comeback to win the local Little League championship, Ritchie's film has them coming up short and celebrating them for their existential superiority over the tightly wound and hard-driven (practically to the point of child abuse) team to which they lose. The success-obsessed Little League team's name? The Yankees.

As *The Bad News Bears*'s script-flipping ending suggests, by the time Kovic actually published his experiences in the mid-1970s, the change in perspective and ideological orientation he went through half a decade earlier in the jungles of Vietnam had practically become mainstream. Though his version of the story might be more dramatic and extreme than the norm, Kovic's transition is essentially a microcosm for the entire generation of countercultural Baby Boomers, who were taught to believe in America and its institutions but during young adulthood lost faith and came to embrace what they saw as higher truths.[11]

Just as Baby Boomers may have felt betrayed by the hero of their youth, Mantle, when learning less-than-heroic personal details from *Ball Four*, many Americans began to feel betrayed by America as they began to learn more about Vietnam, racial policies, and later, Watergate. This parallel is fitting, of course, because, as evidenced by how exulting the success and heroism of the Yankees and the U.S. military in the same breath would have felt natural for Kovic and many Baby Boomers like him, the cultural meaning of the Yankees is closely tied to so many of the values of World War II generation. Thus, the changing perspective on the Yankees, and Mantle specifically, as an icon in the late '60s can be read as part and parcel of this broader disenchantment with the values of the nation's recent past. Leavy certainly interprets Mantle in this way, asserting, "The transformation of The Mick over the course of eighteen years in the majors and forty-four years in the public eye parallels the transformation of American culture from willful innocence to knowing cynicism. To tell his story is to tell ours" (Leavy xxiii).

"MRS. ROBINSON" AND THE PASSING GENERATION

While *Ball Four* both contributed to and reflected the changing public attitudes towards the Yankees the late 1960s, it was not alone. Less political than Bouton's memoir but perhaps further reaching as a cultural representation of the ball club is folk-rock duo Simon and Garfunkel's use of the Yankees as a symbol in their 1968 number-one hit "Mrs. Robinson." Though the song is somewhat opaque in terms of narrative and meaning, the famous lines "Where have you gone, Joe DiMaggio? / A nation turns its lonely eyes to you" gained immediate cultural currency[12] and continues to be a seen as both a touchstone from that era and as a pithy comment on DiMaggio's cultural legacy.[13] This Yankee allusion in "Mrs. Robinson" complements the depiction of the Yankees as symbols of the American values of the older generation that were "rapidly fadin'," to borrow a phrase from one of the new generation's spokesmen, Bob Dylan.

Recorded for an album whose major theme is the passage of time, both personal and historical (Fornatale 85, 93), Simon and Garfunkel's song has thematic overtones of generational change (100).[14] Ostensibly about a woman—the titular Mrs. Robinson—who is being admitted to some kind of retirement/nursing home, rehab center, or psychiatric institution and feels "most of all" that she has "got to hide (something) from her kids," a theme of the generational transition and/or schism is apparent despite the song's difficult-to-pin-down narrative. This theme is magnified by the song's association with the film *The Graduate,* featuring a young Baby Boomer protagonist and his complicated, to say the least, relationship with his parents' generation (77).[15] Similarly, as a duo initially involved in the Greenwich Village folk scene and then making music roughly in the "folk-rock" genre since the middle of the decade, Simon and Garfunkel certainly had ties to the counterculture, as evidenced by their performance at the watershed psychedelic music event, the Monterey Pop Festival, as well as by the antiwar themes in their 1969 television special, "Songs of America." With this context in mind, the character of Mrs. Robinson is perhaps best read as a representative for the entire World War II generation. Her sudden crying out for DiMaggio in the song's last verse—first with the aforementioned famous lines and then echoed with the response, "What's that you say, Mrs. Robinson? / Joltin' Joe has left and gone away"—then becomes a symbol of the shift in values and culture taking place nationally at the time.

Like the old fisherman, Santiago in Hemingway's *The Old Man and the Sea,* Mrs. Robinson cries out not for DiMaggio the man but for DiMaggio the icon, for what he represents: self-sacrificing heroism and grace under pressure. But because we presume Mrs. Robinson is American and because she is an older woman in a pop song in 1968, her DiMaggio would also include not just the personal values he represents but all the cultural values associated with the great Yankee hero tradition and the team itself: a belief in the American dream and American prosperity, and in the goodness and rightness of the nation's position and power in the world.

Unlike Bouton, however, Simon and Garfunkel do not seem to have political motives with their use of the Yankee cultural icon. Though certainly not without their countercultural affiliations, the duo typically veered in their music toward the literary rather than the political.[16] This certainly seems to be the case with "Mrs. Robinson," and particularly in the famous line about DiMaggio, which the duo enunciate with an earnestness suggesting that they too longed for the certainty, abundance, and relative simplicity of the triumphant America the DiMaggio-led Yankees represented. Furthermore, the use of the term "the nation" suggests that Mrs. Robinson is not a lone reactionary but part of a national chorus, keenly feeling the loss of the values in which it was once invested.

When Paul Simon, the song's author and an admitted Mickey Mantle fan, was asked by television personality Dick Cavett why he chose to use DiMaggio's name instead of that of his boyhood hero, Mantle, Simon made the excuse that the syllables of Mantle's name did not fit as well as DiMaggio's (Leavy xx). The obvious truth, however, was that Mantle, who retired the same year the song came out, was too entwined with the present—and, perhaps, the less-than-illustrious Yankee present in particular—to work as a symbol of the longed-for American past. In fact, after his fall from public grace initiated by *Ball Four* a few years after "Mrs. Robinson's" release, the line could be read as a commentary on Mantle and the collapse of heroism he represented. Faced with a less-than-ideal image of Mantle, Americans feel nostalgia for the image of the Yankee hero from the days when sports journalism helped build a hero's saintly status, rather than tear it down.

Less caustic than *Ball Four* and less political in its portrayal of the Yankees as a cultural icon, Simon and Garfunkel's "Mrs. Robinson" nevertheless stands as a companion piece to Bouton's memoir. Like *Ball Four,* it strongly associates the iconic Yankees—who by this point could be said to be leading a cultural existence separate and apart from the baseball team actually being fielded in the Bronx—with an American past that was recent and yet suddenly felt quite distant to many, considering the substantial changes to American society taking place in the 1960s. In a period when baseball in general began to lose its cultural hold on Americans, the Yankees, as a heightened, more concentrated symbol of the populist masculine values generally associated with baseball, and one that emphasized success in a way so harmonious with the triumphal America of the late '40s and '50s, suddenly became icons of yesterday.

Chapter Seven

"YOU'D NEVER GUESS THIS WAS... THE YANKEES"

The "Me" Decade and "The Best Team Money Could Buy"

The sudden collapse of the Yankee dynasty in the late 1960s had as big an impact on the Bronx club's position in the popular imagination as the cultural upheavals of that same period had on the nation in general. In both cases, the break with the past that the late '60s represented tended to polarize Americans, with some longing for a restoration of the successes and glories of the midcentury, while others, focusing on what they saw as moral failings of that same WWII-postwar period, rejoiced that some change had finally come. In the popular consciousness, neither the Yankees nor the United States itself would ever be quite the same after the iconoclasm of the late '60s. And in both cases, this point was driven home by what transpired in the following decade, the 1970s.

With the exception of the 1970 season, in which they finished in second place in the American League East but still fifteen games behind the first-place team, Baltimore, the Yankees were stuck in or near the doldrums of the second division between 1966 and 1973, a shell of the franchise's former self. But the sale of the team to a new owner with deep pockets and a willingness to spend in search of success, George Steinbrenner, brought the Yankees back into contention in the second half of the '70s, inviting comparisons to the storied Bronx Bombers of the past. But even though these Steinbrenner-funded teams won American League pennants in 1976, '77, '78, and '81, and consecutive World Series in 1977 and '78, the way they were perceived by the general American public was a far cry from the legendary Yankees teams of those glory years.

With a number of players acquired through the Major Leagues' new system of free agency for multimillion-dollar contracts, the 1970s Yankees were characterized by a clash of competing, squabbling, and whining egos as reported to the public daily in New York tabloids or chronicled in more reflective texts like New York sportswriter Steve Jacobson's retrospective of reporting the '77 Yankees season, *The Best Team Money Could Buy* (1978), relief pitcher Sparky Lyle's journal of his experiences with the 1978 team, *The Bronx Zoo* (1979), or in the satire and caricatures of renowned *New York Daily News* sports cartoonist Bill Gallo. The '70s Yankees were "superstars," but they were not perceived as *heroes* in the grand Yankee tradition, despite the ways in which they trod a similar path of dramatic success. Rather, they were seen as emblematic of their time, the self-focused, so-called "Me" Decade, and powerfully symbolized the notion that the idealistic heroism of triumphant midcentury America was not only gone but irretrievable. The Yankees of the late-1970s—who won like the Bronx Bombers of the past but at the same time behaved nothing like those bastions of steady, manly heroism and team play—seemed to act as proof to the nation that one truly cannot go home again.

STEINBRENNER, FREE AGENCY, AND PLUTOCRACY

In the 1970s two significant influences combined to once again make the Yankees a target of disdain and jealousy for other Major League teams and fans. While the club had certainly been accused of plutocracy and elitism during their most dominant years in times past, those critiques were frequently tempered with a sizeable, if sometimes begrudging, dose of respect. *The Year the Yankees Lost the Pennant* author Douglass Wallop's admitting as much stands as the best evidence for this general claim. But the circumstances that arose in the '70s dramatically altered this balance between contempt and admiration for the Yankee organization, making the image of the team as wealthy plutocrats out to buy victories much more prominent among the general populace.

Contemporary sportswriter Steve Jacobson's account of the 1977 season, *The Best Team Money Could Buy*, is, as its title suggests, particularly helpful in understanding the rise of this plutocratic perception of the Yankees. Jacobson, who covered the team for the entirety of the 1977 season for the Long Island–based tabloid *Newsday*, kept a diary-style chronicle of those tumultuous months and published it prior to the start of the Yankees '78 campaign. Jacobson drew on both his own experiences as well as the sometimes-inflammatory stories printed in the city's other papers. Not nearly as popular with the American masses as the best-selling *The Bronx Zoo*, which came out the following year, Jacobson's tome is nevertheless useful because his long-form medium allows for and invites more reflection on the potential cultural resonances and broader meanings than daily sports journalism. *The Best Team Money Could Buy* sheds light on what the late-1970s Yankees meant to people at the time, including the theme of plutocracy as well as others that will be discussed later. Furthermore, as Jacobson's daily chronicles draw on the major news stories and published quotes that often created rifts or increased clubhouse tension, it is likewise useful as a sort of compendium of that journalistic record as well.

The Yankees' first step toward becoming known as this "Best Team Money Could Buy" was the Steinbrenner purchase. Heir to his father's Cleveland-based shipbuilding empire, George M. Steinbrenner III always had a taste for sports, as evidenced by his time as a decent collegiate hurdler; his experience as an assistant college football coach at Ohio State, Northwestern, and Purdue; his ownership of the short-lived American Basketball League's Cleveland Pipers; and his failed attempt to purchase his hometown team, the Major League's Indians, with a group of business associates in 1971 (Madden 5–7,

34, 37).[1] But Steinbrenner did not find what he saw as his true calling in the world of sport until after his group's deal to acquire the Indians went south. With his appetite for Major League ownership whetted, Steinbrenner and his associates soon learned that the struggling Yankees franchise was being put on the market after eight years of ownership by the television network CBS. Steinbrenner and his associates jumped at the chance, and this time the deal went through.

It was clear from the very outset that Steinbrenner, now majority owner of the once-proud club, would stop at nothing to restore the Yankees' former greatness. Jacobson identified the nostalgia that colored Steinbrenner's goal of restoring the Yankees to greatness, a longing shared by more than a few American baseball fans:

> They were the team of Babe Ruth and Lou Gehrig, Joe DiMaggio and Mickey Mantle. And then nobody. . . .
> . . . Triple-tiered Yankee Stadium with its monuments to greatness, The House That Ruth Built, became a haunted house. . . .
> But for a lot of people over thirty-five, old enough to have grown up when the Yankees won by fulfilling Manifest Destiny, that name was still magic. George Steinbrenner III was old enough. . . .
> What Steinbrenner wanted was to be the owner of the 1927 Yankees. (Jacobson 16)

Fortunately for Steinbrenner, his project to restore the Yankees happened to coincide with the advent of the second great influence that would eventually come to dramatically shape the American public's perception of the Yankees as baseball's tyrannical plutocrats: free agency. Until the mid-1970s, baseball players had been tied to the team that first drafted them by Major League Baseball's so-called "reserve clause," meaning that unless they were traded by that team to another one, they were contractually bound to their club and legally could not play baseball anywhere else. If they were not happy with their current contract, particularly their salary, players could and often did "hold out"—refuse to play as leverage for negotiating a more favorable contract with their club—but they could not offer their services to another ball club of their own accord. Their current club had exclusive rights to them

(Korr 4). After a long legal battle led by the players' union director, Marvin Miller, an arbiter determined that after ballplayers had fulfilled their contracts with their current club, they then became "free agents" and could sign a new contract with whatever club they wished. As baseball owners had feared, this often was the highest-bidding club, and ballplayers' salaries increased dramatically after the event of free agency (Korr 147–55).

This new way of doing baseball business played right into George Steinbrenner's hands. With a thirst for immediate success and a passion for restoring the organization to its former glory, Steinbrenner's Yankees quickly became the most public beneficiaries of this shakeup of baseball's business structure, with a number of splashy and pricey player signings that made for attention-grabbing sports-section headlines.

The first of these actually occurred before free agency became available for all major leaguers. In 1974 Oakland Athletics ace pitcher Jim "Catfish" Hunter was declared a free agent by an arbiter after the penny-pinching, rule-bending A's owner Charlie Finley was found to have violated Hunter's contract. What then occurred was a harbinger of things to come, as twenty-three of the twenty-four existing Major League teams made a bid in the much-publicized Catfish Hunter sweepstakes, with the winning bidder offering a then-unprecedented $3.5 million over five years (the previous season, Hunter had made $100,000).

The identity of the Catfish's chosen ball club, the New York Yankees, was also a harbinger of things to come. Steinbrenner and the rebuilding Yankees truly came into their own with the onset of free agency for the 1977 season, which Jacobson describes as "the dawn of a harsh new era for baseball" (1). This harsh new era was the perfect setting for Steinbrenner to work his magic. Prior to the '77 season, the Yankees pursued both the most coveted free-agent pitcher, Don Gullet, and the biggest free-agent position player, Oakland A's superstar right fielder Reggie Jackson, and eventually signed both. In 1978 their reputation as a deep-pocketed organization willing to spend whatever necessary to "buy the pennant" was solidified by the high-profile acquisition of flame-throwing free agent relief pitcher Rich "Goose" Gossage, despite the fact that Sparky Lyle—the same player who would write *The Bronx Zoo* during that season—had won the American League's Cy Young Award for outstanding pitching as the Yankees' primary reliever the previous season.

For the new Yankees, the use of cash to ensure success was seemingly a work never finished.

Steinbrenner initially stated in 1973 that he would be a hands-off owner, telling the press that he planned "absentee ownership as far as running the Yankees. We're not going to pretend we're something we aren't. I'll stick to building ships" (qtd. In Madden 15). This soon proved to be far from the truth. As his general manager, Gabe Paul, the man who was supposed to be making all the baseball decisions for the Yankees, privately bemoaned, "It didn't take long for him to become an expert" (qtd. in Madden 60). Soon the owner was not only pushing the acquisition of certain players on his manager, the scouts, and his general manager, but he personally handled the courting and negotiations of Reggie Jackson, a process that gained considerable coverage in the New York press (Mahler 62–66). As such, Steinbrenner quickly became the public face of this new incarnation of the New York Yankees and their new method of acquiring championships—by opening up their wallet.

The accusations of plutocracy, or even of "buying the pennant," were not necessarily completely new for the Bronx-based ball club. The cries of "break up the Yankees" had been heard in certain corners of the American baseball subculture since at least the days of the stoic DiMaggio-, Gehrig-, and McCarthy-led teams of the late 1930s, if not before that. But the changing economics of baseball made things considerably different in the 1970s than they were in the first half of the twentieth century. While the Jacob Ruppert–owned Yankees did work fast to acquire players from other clubs in the early 1920s to quickly bolster the club's meager roster—not infrequently in player-for-cash exchanges like the one that brought the mighty Babe Ruth to the Pinstripes—the Yanks of the late 1920s through the end of the dynasty in the mid-1960s largely put their wealth into infrastructure—into quality scouts and farm clubs to find and develop talent, including not only the legendary heroes Gehrig, DiMaggio, and Mantle, but Hall of Famers like Tony Lazzeri, Bill Dickey, Joe Gordon, Lefty Gomez, Phil Rizzuto, Yogi Berra, and Whitey Ford. The classic Yankee lineups of the mid–twentieth century were largely homegrown, while the standouts from their late-1970s series winners, despite the presence of such homegrown talent like Thurman Munson, Ron Guidry, and Ron White, were perceived as purchased.

And notably, while the Yankees of the 1930s through the 1960s were certainly known to have plenty of cash, the club did not necessarily dole out exorbitant salaries freely in those days. General managers Ed Barrow and George Weiss were known to drive a hard bargain even with their stars, and it was said that in recruiting new young players, Yankee scouts typically tried to sell their prospects on Yankee success and glory, rather than Yankee dollars (Harris 101; Cramer 68–69, 73, 105; Kahn, *The Era* 209; Halberstam, *October 1964* 230). In fact, during the mid–twentieth century, it was not the Yankees but their rival, the hard-luck Boston Red Sox, that gained a reputation as a "country club" for owner Tom Yawkey's generous salaries (Halberstam, *Summer of '49* 146, 148; Weintraub, *Victory Season* 17, 121–22; Shaughnessy, *Curse of the Bambino* 48-49, 51). Thus, while many had always bemoaned the Yanks' deep pockets, they also had to admit that the Yankees were an efficient and well-run organization.

But by the '70s, things had certainly changed. The new free-agent marketplace and Steinbrenner's eagerness to play—and win—that game made for Yankee signings for sums of money that outstripped the imaginations of most middle-class baseball fans, which in turn made Yankee wealth much more palpable to the general populace and pushed it to the foreground of the club's public image. Jacobson summed up the change quite effectively in the introduction to *The Best Team Money Could Buy*—a moniker that certainly did not help the Yankees' plutocratic reputation. "While the old Yankees," he writes, "were hated by the rest of the world for their eternal superiority, the new Yankees were hated because they had been assembled not by the traditional trading and development but by the checkbook. They represented everything middle America—and California, too—hated, feared, and coveted in New York. And the world never does get tired of resenting Goliath and rooting for a David" (Jacobson 1–2).

While Jacobson's text is much more nuanced in its assessment of the 1977 Yankees and the role Steinbrenner's money played in their ultimate success—which, according to the book, required much sacrifice, compromise, and team play, not just raw, purchased talent—his title and occasional comments like the one above create a running motif that reflects the portrayal of the club in the tabloids and distinguishes them from the other Major League teams and, perhaps more important, from the Yankees of old.[2] And in case Jacobson's right-to-the-chase title did not communicate clearly enough, the book's cover featured an image of highly priced superstar-slugger Reggie Jackson inside a big dollar sign.

YANKEE-HATING RESURGENCE

Jacobson was not alone in disseminating the image of the Yankees as a club that owed its success to ownership's deep pockets. This was clear as soon as the club signed Jackson prior to the start of the season. As journalist Jonathan Mahler writes in his ambitious book that overlays the history of the 1977 Yankees with the tumultuous story of debt-addled New York City that year, "Yankees-hating, long dormant as the team's fortunes sagged, was finally returning to fashion on the eve of the 1977 season" (95). This resurgence of Yankee hating did not wane after the season began. Jacobson offers proof in his description of the team's first road trip to Kansas City to face the Royals, whom they had beaten, pre–free agency, in the '76 American League Championship Series: "There was a fan in a long black raincoat behind the Yankee dugout at the start of the game. He had lettered the front of the coat 'stein/brenner' and wore big Elton John sunglasses with dollar signs on the lenses. And he tossed around Monopoly money as if it were real" (Jacobson 63–64). As the season played out, baseball fans across the country would turn out in impressive numbers—nearly matching the two million the Yanks drew at home, their best since 1949—to root against their well-heeled foes (Mahler 319).

But baseball fans were not acting alone in this revival of Yankee hating. The front offices of many baseball clubs actively stoked the anti-Yankee passions among their faithful. In September 1977 Jacobson witnessed an "I Hate the Yankees" fan-promotion night in Cleveland, at which all paying customers at the Indians' Cleveland Stadium received a free "I Hate the Yankees" handkerchief with which to blow their noses (222; Mahler 95).

The renaissance of Yankee hating brought on by the confluence of Steinbrenner and free agency was also manifest in the new cultural paradigms of sports journalism not present during earlier manifestations of American disdain for the Bronx team, such as the dissenting cry of "break up the Yankees" in the late 1930s or the *Damn Yankees* coup in the mid-1950s. In those earlier periods, players and managers were largely mum on the issue of the possibility of unfairness in the Yankees dominance, largely because the unwritten rules of the clubhouse dictated that one publicly respect one's opponents and keep any negative thoughts to oneself, or at least out of earshot of the press.[3] Even the postwar Brooklyn Dodgers avoided criticizing the Yankee organization to journalists. It is also likely that, like many of the journalists who voiced the rising tide of Yankee hating in the '50s, the players and managers from that period at the very least held a begrudging respect for the Yankee organization, recognizing that it was not merely superior funding that put them on top year after year.

By the second half of the 1970s, however, both the economics of baseball and the clubhouse paradigms about speaking one's mind to reporters had drastically changed. Not only was enhanced Yankee funding now able to more quickly and directly affect the team on the field with the advent of free agency, but the broader cultural changes of the 1960s and '70s and specific iconoclastic moments, like the publication of Jim Bouton's *Ball Four*, had exploded the old clubhouse reserve with regard to the press. As such, the players and managers who had previously been mum on the issue of Yankee hating began to match, if not surpass, the fans' expressions of disdain towards these perceived plutocrats.

All of this, of course, played into the hands of sportswriters, particularly those for the New York City tabloids that were so eager to give their readers a frothy, daily dose of drama about baseball's most controversial team. Jacobson's book covers the "highlights," such as they are, of the published verbal venom from other Major League players and managers targeted at the Yankees during the tumultuous '77 season. The condemnation from Detroit's idiosyncratic starting pitcher, Mark "The Bird" Fidrych, directed at the man he sarcastically referred to as "Steinburger" is fairly typical. "You can't go out and buy everything in life," said the quirky fan favorite who won the 1976 Rookie of the Year award. "If they finish second, that'll prove it. They'll watch the World Series just like us" (qtd. in Jacobson 167).

Whitey Herzog, manager of the Kansas City Royals, whom the Yankees would defeat in a painful three American League Championship Series in a row (1976, '77, and '78), certainly had reason to hold a grudge against the Bronx club, and like Fidrych, he focused his critique on Steinbrenner's free-spending ways. As he told the press before the start of their '77 playoff clash, "All of baseball wants us to win. Not that they love us . . . they just hate the Yankees and their check writing" (qtd. in Mahler 320). Earlier that season, Herzog colorfully suggested that the Yankee organization was full of excrement, though he did have the generosity to qualify his statement by adding, "I don't mean the secretaries, so don't include them" (qtd. in Jacobson 269).

'70S YANKEE HATING AND THE BOSTON RED SOX

Perhaps the most famous and public iteration of Yankee hating in the late '70s, however, emanated from the Boston Red Sox. While Boston fans' disdain for everything pinstriped has much more history than the ire drawn by the advent of Steinbrenner's free spending in the new free-agency era, the unequal tenor of the longstanding Red Sox–Yankees rivalry is still very much consistent with the more recent characterization of the Bronx club as moneyed tyrants. Not unlike their midcentury relationship with the Brooklyn Dodgers, the Yankees' rivalry with the Red Sox, which reached fever pitch in the 1970s, did much to disseminate an image of the team as the haughty, privileged bullies keeping the little guys under their thumb.

Like most of the longtime members of the American League, the Red Sox and their fans envied and resented the Yankees' success. For instance, fans of the Cleveland Indians, with seven second-place finishes in the American League standings behind the Yankees (1921, '26, '51, '52, '53, '57, and '58), and the Detroit Tigers, with six (1923, '36, '37, '47, '50, and '61), always had plenty of reasons to bear a grudge against the Bronx Bombers. But with the Red Sox, deeper factors were at work. In addition to the fact that the Sox came in second to the Yankees in 1938, '39, '41, '42, and '49, with the 1949 pennant coming down to a two-game series between the clubs, the bad blood between the Red Sox and the Yankees is shaped by a more general cultural rivalry between the two cities the teams represent. Arguably once the cultural capital of the United States in its days as the shipping center of the new American colonies, the political hub of the Revolution, and the birthplace of Transcendentalism and Abolitionism, Boston's national importance was eclipsed by its larger, more commerce-focused cousin down the coast in the second half of the nineteenth century. In light of this history, some, such as the *Boston Globe*'s Dan Shaughnessy, argue that Bostonians harbor an "inferiority complex" directed towards New York City, and this grudge has shaped their animosity towards the Yankees specifically (*Reversing the Curse* 22): "The New York–Boston rivalry is rooted in geography and American history. . . . America's best and brightest go to school in Boston, then go to work and live in New York. The Hub is quaint, cultural, and alive with fresh new ideas. Boston is Apollo. New York is Zeus" (22).

The history of the two rival clubs parallels this history of their cities' preeminence in the nation. The Red Sox, arguably the most successful club in the first two decades of the twentieth century, lost their glory to the Yankees not only with the sale of Babe Ruth before the 1920 season but through a flotilla of their most promising talent embarking for the big city to the south over a period of about three years, usually in exchange for cash to ameliorate new Red Sox owner Harry Frazee's financial woes. Former Red Sox who contributed to the foundation of the Yankee dynasty as it was being erected included catcher Wally Schang; infielders Everett Scott, Mike McNally, and Joe Dugan; and pitchers Carl Mays, Joe Bush, Sam Jones, Waite Hoyt, and Herb Pennock, these last two becoming Hall-of-Famers. Red Sox manager Ed Barrow, partly out of frustration with Frazee's moves, resigned to become the business manager of the Yankees and is now in the Hall of Fame as well, widely regarded as the architect of the Yankee dynasty for his work in the front office through the 1945 season (Frommer, *Baseball's Greatest Rivalry* 71–81).

The Red Sox had won World Series in 1903, '12, '15, '16, and '18; but after the departure of Ruth and the others, they would not even claim the league pennant again until 1946. The Yankees' rise to glory coincided with Boston's fall from grace, and to many knowledgeable Sox fans, this hardly seemed like a coincidence. Thus, the themes of wealth, power, and unjust inequality are present from the very foundation of the Red Sox–Yankees rivalry, motifs that would surface with a vengeance in the '70s and remain an important part of the relationship today, even in years when the Red Sox have had the *second* highest payroll in the Major Leagues.

The rivalry intensified in the late 1930s through the end of the '40s, when both the Yankees and Sox were good teams, featuring the two players regarded as the best in the game at the time: New York's Joe DiMaggio and Boston's Ted Williams. But the Yanks always managed to get the better of their rivals, notably in the 1949 pennant race that broke more than a few hearts in Boston and seemed to usher in a new period of futility for the Sox (Shaughnessy, Reversing the Curse 23–24). Like Brooklyn Dodger fans, Red Sox rooters looked towards the Yankees' unflagging success as a constant reminder of their own penchant for falling just short. After the "Impossible Dream" season in 1967, in which Carl Yastrzemski and Jim Lonborg lifted the Sox from the previous year's ninth-place finish to come up just one game short of a long-sought World Series title against the heavily favored Cardinals, the Boston club became a force to be reckoned with throughout the 1970s.

This Red Sox renaissance became particularly intriguing in the decade's second half, as the revamped Yankees returned to the franchise's former glory. This renewed tension culminated in the same way it always seemed to before, with the Sox, yet again, giving up a late-summer lead in the standings to lose a close pennant race to their rivals in '77. They then frustratingly repeated the same feat in '78, only in more dramatic terms that recalled the postwar Brooklyn Dodgers: by fumbling an enormous fourteen-game lead over the Yankees in July to end the season in a tie and then lose the pennant in a special one-game playoff—a game they led until the seventh inning.

After a comparatively uneventful period in the 1950s and '60s, the Red Sox–Yankees rivalry returned with a vengeance in the 1970s. Often in sports rivalries, it is the fans who carry the true animosity for the other team, but in the case of the 1970s Red Sox and Yankees, many of the players on the opposing sides truly did not like each other. Most crucial in this regard is the rivalry between the teams' respective catchers, Carlton Fisk and Thurman Munson. Mahler suggests that the catchers "personified" the rivalry as a whole, with the "tall, even-tempered, urbane" Fisk and the "stumpy, grumpy, caustic" Munson embodying "Boston versus New York in a nutshell" (114). The two were often flashpoints for the many brouhahas that erupted between the two clubs during the decade (Shaughnessy, *Reversing the Curse* 25; Frommer, *Baseball's Greatest Rivalry* 56–57). Not to be outdone by the animosity on the field, the 1970s fans of both clubs stoked the fire with a newfound enthusiasm for throwing objects at players on the field (Frommer, *Baseball's Greatest Rivalry* 51, 64, 69; Shaughnessy, *Reversing the Curse* 69) and for the adaptable slogan "Yankees/Red Sox/New York/Boston suck(s)," which took the form of homemade signs, chants, T-shirts, and buttons (Frommer, *Baseball's Greatest Rivalry* 3, 54, 66, 69, 142, 144; Shaughnessy *Reversing the Curse* 69; Mahler 114). Though generally not considered nearly as vulgar now as it was back then, this hallowed tradition continues to the present day (Shaughnessy, *Reversing the Curse* 69–70).

But in terms of actual cultural or ideological content, the most significant Yankee critique to arise from the Red Sox rivalry came from Sox pitcher Bill Lee, who was both a lefthander and a leftist. Jim Bouton had attempted to portray himself as a friend of the hippie counterculture while writing *Ball

Four during the 1969 season, but Bill Lee was probably the closest Major League Baseball ever came to the real thing. Nicknamed "The Spaceman," Lee jogged to work, defended Communist China, and kicked against the pricks with his own special brand of off-the-cuff sarcasm and absurdism. With these predilections, he not surprisingly hated the capitalistic George Steinbrenner. Writing about a September 1977 meeting between the Yankees and the Red Sox, Steve Jacobson characterizes Lee's disdain for Steinbrenner and his Yankees as follows: "Bill Lee, Boston's mystic pitcher, saw [Yankee success] as the result of a pact between Steinbrenner and the devil. How else would the Red Sox hit so many balls so hard and get nothing for it? 'Steinbrenner sold his pancreas to the devil,' Lee said. Was Steinbrenner selling the devil one organ a year? 'Yeah,' Lee said, 'but last year he tricked him. He sold him a Wurlitzer'" (290).

Whether he was intentionally alluding to the demonic bargain from *The Year the Yankees Lost the Pennant* and *Damn Yankees* or not, Lee's comments characterize Steinbrenner as a crafty, wheeling-and-dealing businessman able to pull the wool over the eyes of the devil himself. This persona of the devious businessman resonates with the "haves vs. have-nots" tone of the Yankees' rivalry with the Boston club, as well as with the idea of "buying the pennant" vocalized by various players or with the satirical impersonation by the Kansas City fan who threw around Monopoly money. Steinbrenner certainly did not help his own case when he was convicted for making illegal campaign contributions to Richard Nixon's presidential bid. Together, responses from fans, managers, and players alike constituted a pointed critique and broad cultural disapproval, and suggest that, for all the Yankees' cultural legacy as icons of a wholesome American dream and self-sacrificing manly heroism, the cultural connotations of the Yankee brand in the late 1970s were those of corrupt plutocracy.

Such associations flip the team's legacy of success on its head, transforming the achievement of sustained excellence into a tyrannical reign. It is plausible that passionate insiders like Bill Lee or even the Kansas City Royals fan in the dollar-sign sunglasses[4] may well have had this type of imagery in mind as they pronounced their accusations of baseball hegemony upon the Bronx Bombers. But even for those baseball fans less focused on the past, the here and now was enough, as the here and now of the New York Yankees in the late '70s meant exploiting the new baseball economy to essentially outbid the other teams for the pennant, a decidedly undemocratic image to surface in the wake of the country's bicentennial celebration in 1976. After the Yankees defeated the Royals for the '77 pennant, a columnist for the *Kansas City Times* summed up the way many Americans felt about the club that was beginning to represent the unjust power that comes with wealth: "Truth doesn't prevail. There is no justice" (qtd. in Mahler 327).

"NAZIS," GENERAL VON STEINGRABBER, AND THE YANKEE MILITARY MOTIF

In addition to the plutocratic characterization most common to critiques leveled at the late-1970s Yankees, some caricatures of the team by reinvigorated Yankee haters took on a decidedly military theme. This imagery of overzealous militarism bears a lineage of the counterculture-inspired portrayal of the Yankees as the embodiment of the old-guard American "Establishment" in Jim Bouton's *Ball Four* and other late-1960s texts.

But the over-the-top military caricatures from the Steinbrenner era make even the colorful Bouton look subtle. First and foremost in this enterprise is the Red Sox's Bill Lee. His dislike for the rival Yankees was escalated by a famous on-field brawl in 1976, in which Lee sustained a serious shoulder injury, and the pitcher used a Red Sox–Yankees series the following year to creatively let off some steam to the press. Jacobson documents the scene:

> [Lee] was watching on the sidelines in street clothes while events were unfolding—street clothes for him, that is: a flowing white shirt with a Nehru collar and Indian sandals. "I was afraid they might step on my feet," he said.
>
> Lee still has trouble with the shoulder he hurt wrestling with Graig Nettles last May, but he says he has more trouble accepting what he calls the Yankees' "win-at-any-cost-mentality."
>
> "Last year I was assaulted by George Steinbrenner's Nazis, his Brown Shirts," Lee said. "He brainwashes those kids over there, and they're led by Billy Martin—Hermann Goering II. They've got Steinbrenner, a convicted felon running the club. What else do you expect?" (26)

Needless to say, the Yankees were less than excited about such a comparison. According to Sparky Lyle in *The Bronx Zoo*, the Yankee manager Billy Martin took particular offense: "Billy hated Lee for what he said and had a dead mackerel hung in Lee's locker" (217). The sports pages, however, knew good copy when they saw it, and Lee's remarks echoed throughout the league during the season. Jacobson describes one especially prominent reiteration of Lee's comments that occurred during a subsequent Red Sox–Yankees game in Boston, giving particular attention to the post-1960s generational/cultural divide implied in using military imagery as an insult: "The game had a special flavor of Fenway Park, where the young people seem to dig baseball more than any other place in either league, and are the hippest. You can smell the excitement and the pot in the stands before the game begins. The fans remember how Bill Lee referred to the Yankees as 'neo-Nazis.' As Martin walked across the field before the game they must have recalled that the league president had warned Lee about the temper of his remarks. So the fans picked up for Lee, chanting, 'Sieg heil'" (131–32).

Lee's Nazi comparison and the adoption of this caricature by the Red Sox fans, which was likely partially inspired by Steinbrenner's conspicuously German surname, are nevertheless extreme, evoking a military and ideological regime that has been remembered as the most "evil" in recent history. Using a fascist caricature to insult the club resurrects the counter-narrative about the Yankee tradition discussed in earlier chapters: that it represents everything purportedly wrong with America—the "win-at-any-cost-mentality," to use Lee's words, that crushes individuality and human compassion, and unjustly keeps the powers that be entrenched at the top at the expense of the vulnerable. That someone would compare an icon that had traditionally been seen as so unequivocally American to Nazi Germany seems an especially strong message with none-too-subtle implications about the values of certain elements of American society—perhaps big business, the norms of masculinity, or any other traditions or institutions that might be perceived as supporting the mentality that Lee condemns.

Considering their military flavor, Lee's initial comments may have been primarily directed at the immediate unsportsmanlike violence of which he saw himself as the victim. Far more prominent in the popular mind than any supposed excessive use of violence on the part of the Yankees, however, was an excessive use of wealth. Nevertheless, the power Steinbrenner's Yankees attempted to assert through their spending could certainly have been seen to carry a certain military-like aggression. Thus, the vaguely politically left-leaning perspective on the Yankees featured in *Ball Four*, and earlier and more subtly in Harris's *The Southpaw*, gained new traction and a new wrinkle with the advent of free agency and the ability of ball clubs to use money to build winning teams much more directly and publicly. The aggression with which the Yankees pursued talent on the free-agency market may well have made Lee's hyperbolic comments resonate with many baseball fans, for whom the new free-spending Yankees may have seemed like an empire intent on militantly conquering the universe with the power of their wealth. Again, the notion that wealth could be used as a weapon to assert dominance is an affront to the ideals of democracy and suggests that the Yankees embody a corrupt, "un-American" facet of the United States.

The only problem with this vaguely leftist caricature of the Yankees as military tyrants is that it misrepresents the efficiency and unity of the late-1970s Yankees. While Steinbrenner's ball club certainly conquered, winning both the 1977 and '78 World Series titles, they did not exactly accomplish it with military precision or efficiency. For all that George Steinbrenner may have preached about discipline—and according to Sparky Lyle, he certainly did[5]—the Yankees disagreed and bickered far too much and too publicly to be perceived as marching in literal or ideological lockstep. Thus, it is likely that Lee and those who adopted military metaphors for their Yankee critiques may have been influenced by their impressions of the unity and efficiency of the organization from the late 1930s through the early '60s and combined those memories with Steinbrenner's legitimate aggression and passion.

Perhaps a more accurate military caricature of the late-1970s Yankees was put forth by *New York Daily News* sports cartoonist Bill Gallo. Gallo was arguably the most prominent artist working in the niche genre of sports cartooning during his lifetime, taking up the mantle left by Willard Mullin and Leo O'Melia, the latter of whom Gallo replaced at the *Daily News*. With over a decade as the *News*'s sports cartoonist under his belt by the time of the Yankees 1970s resurgence, Gallo seemed to relish nothing more than pricking the inflated egos he perceived on the Bronx ball club.

And no ego was more deserving than George M. Steinbrenner III, whom Gallo transformed into a Prussian army officer, "General Von Steingrabber," complete with shiny boots, black gloves, and spiked helmet. Probably also inspired by the Yankee owner's surname, Gallo's creation seems to have evolved independently of Lee's "Nazi" caricature. While Von Steingrabber was not infrequently portrayed as losing his temper, as his real-life counterpart often did, he was all bluster and no bite, more of a buffoon than a threatening figure. Not only was his appearance in and of itself comical, with Steinbrenner's rotund figure and face (amplified, of course) crammed into a size-too-small uniform and helmet, but he spoke in an exaggerated German accent and was often portrayed in compromising, decidedly nonmilitary scenarios, such as exerting himself while working a too-small bicycle tire pump (Fig. 4). The military theme contrasted with the silly, ineffectual personality of the Von Steingrabber caricature—perhaps reminiscent of the bungling German army officers on the TV sitcom *Hogan's Heroes* (1965–71)—convey both the seriousness with which the Yankee owner pursued restoring Yankee greatness as well as the ridiculousness of the melodramatic squabbling all his efforts to win spawned. General Von Steingrabber was enthusiastically received and remained part of Gallo's repertoire for the length of Steinbrenner's ownership of the Yankees.[6] But in the late 1970s in particular, the caricature was a pithy

FIG. 4. The Inflated Ego by Bill Gallo. Copyright Daily News, L.P. (New York). Used with permission.

reminder that for all the seriousness—indeed, often *too much* seriousness—with which Steinbrenner and his Yankees sought and won victory, they still looked plenty silly doing it.

THE YANKEE "SOAP OPERA"

While much of the anger or disdain directed at the Yankees from players, managers, owners, sportswriters, and fans alike centered on their willingness to aggressively lure so many free agents to the team with high salaries, this plutocratic image did not exclusively dominate the club's profile with the general public in this period. In fact, as already suggested, the Yankees of the second half of the 1970s, particularly the '77 and '78 World-Series–winning teams, were known as much for their seemingly never-ending soap opera of infighting as they were for the supposed practice of buying victory.

While the Yankees of the late 1970s, like any competitive sports team, were a mix of many personalities that all shaped the team chemistry in some way, there were four individuals in particular who exerted significant influence on the tenor and direction of the club. And those four did not exactly see eye to eye. Reggie Jackson came to the Yankees a bona fide (and self-proclaimed) "superstar," with a lucrative contract to prove it. As such, he brought with him expectations of making an impact and exerting influence on the club. The established Yankee leader at the start of the 1977 season, meanwhile, was hard-hitting catcher Thurman Munson, the team captain, and American League MVP in 1976. Managing the team was Billy Martin, the scrappy, combative onetime second baseman whose tenure with the Yankees (1950–57) coincided with their postwar dynasty and who had a reputation for being a clutch performer as a player and competent tactician as manager, but emotionally unstable. And, of course, with his visions of personally restoring the storied Yankees to greatness, George Steinbrenner was far from the hands-off owner he initially promised to be when he purchased the club. These four men each exerted ample influence on the team. And they were almost constantly at each other's throats.

Scruffy, workmanlike, and traditional, Thurman Munson saw Reggie Jackson as a vain, delusional "hot dog" and resented both Jackson and Steinbrenner for how much more the Yankees were paying the outfielder.[7]

Paranoid about Steinbrenner's attempts at exerting direct influence on on-field matters, Martin saw the signing of Jackson as unnecessary and let that fact drive a wedge between himself and both the owner and the highly paid slugger. Jackson, for his part, did little to ingratiate himself with his new teammates and coaches with his tendency to speak freely to the media and let slip off-hand remarks that overestimated his importance or belittled or offended other members of the ball club.

The press's role in this inner turmoil is not to be discounted. It was frequently a comment to a reporter that would get magnified, taken out of context, and writ large in the next day's papers that would sow clubhouse discord, and Jackson was not the only offender in this regard. The New York City news outlets, meanwhile, lapped up the drama with gusto, particularly the tabloids the *Daily News* and the *New York Post*. But airing of the Yankees' dirty laundry was hardly just the affair of the five boroughs, with the Yankee soap opera receiving national attention in news stories during the course of the seasons, including mainstream publications like *Time* magazine and through Jacobson's and Lyle's three-hundred-page retrospectives.

Written with the help of author Peter Golenbock, who was known for his 1975 oral history of the postwar Yankees, *Dynasty,* Lyle's memoir, in particular, helped solidify the dysfunctional reputation of the late-1970s team with the public. Not only did it become a best-seller, but the clever title, *The Bronx Zoo,* was also suggestive enough that one need not even read the book to form an impression of the successful club's inner squabbling. In fact, the term "Bronx Zoo" quickly gained traction as a nickname for the Yankees themselves and is still frequently used to refer to the late-1970s phase of their history.

But prior to Lyle's book, two incidents during the 1977 season in particular ignited the nation's imagination regarding the club's inner turmoil. The first was precipitated by a profile of Reggie Jackson that sportswriter Robert Ward wrote for *Sport* magazine based on interviews conducted during spring training. Published in the June issue (released in late May, months after the interviews), Ward's article contained a few remarks from Jackson about the roles he and teammate Munson would play that were received as inflammatory. "You know, this team . . . it all flows from me," Ward quotes the outfielder. "I'm the straw that stirs the drink. It all comes back to me. Maybe I should say me and Munson . . . but really he doesn't enter into it. . . . there is just nobody who can do for a club what I can do. . . . Munson thinks he can stir the drink, but he can only stir it bad." The daily sports pages reported on the magazine profile, zeroing in on the "straw that stirs the drink" line and Jackson's less-than-flattering comments about Munson and broadcast them nationally. This not only weakened the already tenuous relations in the Yankee clubhouse but also gave the public an impression of discord among the team (Mahler 111–17; Madden 117).

About three weeks later, the fuse lit by the *Sport* profile and fanned by the pride of the big personalities on the team and their refusal to apologize or forgive exploded in front of a national audience. The Yankees were playing the rival Red Sox, who they were then battling for control of the division, at Boston's Fenway Park in a contest televised nationally on NBC's *Game of the Week*. With the Sox leading 7–4 in the sixth inning, Jackson, never known for his fielding skills, badly played a shallow hit towards him in right field, allowing the hitter to turn the likely single into a double. Manager Billy Martin was never truly on board with having Reggie join the team in the first place, both because he disliked him personally and because he resented Steinbrenner's insistence on signing the slugger. His patience challenged by Jackson's error, Martin opted to make an immediate defensive replacement and took Jackson out of the game. Such a mid-inning decision involving a position player is extremely rare in Major League Baseball and insulted the proud Jackson. As NBC's cameras followed Reggie back into the dugout, a shouting match between the slugger and his tempestuous manager quickly materialized. As noted by on-air commentators, Martin's blood boiled until he charged at the much younger, stronger Jackson and had to be restrained by his coaches.

Needless to say, the dissension in the ranks of the 1977 version of the storied Yankees became evident to the entire country. Sports pages across the country carried news of the power struggle among Martin, Jackson, Munson, and Steinbrenner and the bickering that seemed to permeate the clubhouse. As White Sox manager Bob Lemon intoned, "I can't wait to get the papers every day and read what's going on with the Yankees. It's like [the mid-1970s soap-opera parody] *Mary Hartman, Mary Hartman*" (qtd. in Jacobson 138).

Of particular interest were reports that Steinbrenner was going to fire Martin, which he eventually did the following season but not before the Yankees overtook the Red Sox to win the division and go on to defeat the Royals and earn their second consecutive World Series berth.[8] While the seemingly dysfunctional Yankees' ability to win ballgames may have puzzled some, if anything, their success only magnified their reputation for soap-opera-like infighting off the field. The comments of pitcher Tommy John, a lefthander playing for the Yankees' World Series opponent, the Los Angeles Dodgers, indicate how widespread the news of the Yankee melodrama had become. "So the soap opera goes on," John quipped, after losing the third game of the series in Los Angeles. "Will Billy Martin find success and happiness in a continuing shower of champagne?" (qtd. in Jacobson 341). John's familiarity with the "soap opera" joke and readiness to make such a reference while speaking to the media on the nation's opposite coast suggest that the Yankees' reputation preceded them.[9]

Even *Time* magazine was in on the joke, with a profile of the World Series titled "Nice Guys Always Finish . . . ?" This most mainstream of mainstream American magazines' profile of the Bronx club—described as "high-powered and high-salaried . . . as disputatious, selfish and disdainful of each other as they are talented"—paints a scene for anyone who missed the drama during the season. It begins, "It was a September night in the last days of a frantic pennant race and Yankee Manager Billy Martin tossed in his bed, looking for ways to get even with his boss." A predictable accounting of the season's turmoil follows. Much to the bemusement of many, the "disputatious" Yankees nevertheless triumphed over the Dodgers in six games to win the iconic franchise's first series championship in fifteen years.

During the off-season, the national obsession with the Yankee infighting was stoked by news of another splashy free-agent signing, flame-throwing relief pitcher Goose Gossage, as well as by continued media coverage and speculation, including Jacobson's comprehensive and reflective assessment of the unbelievable 1977 season. In fact, the very existence of Jacobson's book indicates the nation's fascination with the highly paid, squabbling Yankees. That a publisher, the Alfred Knopf Jr.–founded Atheneum, not only saw a market for the book but okayed the provocative title and cover imagery says much about the national interest in the 1977 World Champions. Also indicative of the national interest is the approval of Sparky Lyle and Peter Golenbock's proposal to publish a diary of the relief pitcher's experiences during the upcoming 1978 season. If 1978 turned out to be anything like 1977, the publisher, Crown (a subsidiary of Random House), must have reasoned, it might be a good thing to have a man on the inside to report it firsthand. The publisher was not mistaken.

Appetites were whetted for another season of melodramatic infighting, and that is precisely what occurred. While the ultimate success of the 1977 season softened the hard feelings between the major figures with the Yankees, once the season had begun it was clear that there was still bad blood between Martin and series hero Jackson, as well as his boss, Steinbrenner. By July, sensing he was going to be fired, Billy Martin resigned in a tearful press conference, only to be dramatically introduced just weeks later to Yankee fans on "Old-Timers' Day" with the announcement that he would return to his position as manager for the 1980 season.[10] On top of all this, over the last two and a half months of the season, the Yankees overcame a fourteen-game detriment to tie the Red Sox for first place in the division and then beat them in a one-game playoff, followed by another World Series title over the Dodgers. It truly was a season fit for the eventual moniker Lyle and Golenbock would give it, "The Bronx Zoo," and both the sports press's reporting of the season's drama and Lyle's blow-by-blow account only served to cement the new Yankees' "soap opera" image for many Americans.

EGO

Perhaps the most prevalent theme that surfaces in representation and reception of the infighting on the late-1970s Yankees is the notion of "ego." The Yankees were portrayed as self-serving narcissists out to burnish their own personal legacy above all else. Such self-focus, of course, flies in the face of the ideals of cooperation and self-sacrifice for the good of the team that had been hallmarks of the club as a cultural icon beginning with its crystallization in *The Pride of the Yankees*.

One prominent popularizer of the ego theme was the *Daily News*'s Bill Gallo. In addition to his "Von Steingrabber" caricature of Steinbrenner, Gallo found plenty of other narcissistic targets to tease in his drawings. One such cartoon alluded to the World Trade Center towers, with a caption reading, "True or False: The Twin Towers, soaring 1,350 feet over a five acre plaza on Manhattan's Lower West Side are the biggest things in New York. Answer:

FIG. 5. The Boss Is Always Right by Bill Gallo. Copyright Daily News, L.P. (New York). Used with permission.

False. . . . These two are," followed by an arrow gesturing to a sketch of a giant-sized Steinbrenner and Billy Martin sitting around the perimeter of a comparatively dinky Yankee Stadium, their profiled torsos soaring into the air like the double skyscrapers they supposedly eclipsed (Fig. 5). Steinbrenner, who holds a sand pail and shovel, wears the label "Ego No. 1," and Martin wears one reading "Ego No. 1A." Staring down the manager, Steinbrenner's speech bubble reads: "Listen, kid—it *is* my sandbox, you know!" (56). Not only are the two prominent Yankee leaders roasted for their outsized egos, but their power struggle is lampooned as a childish sandbox row.

Steinbrenner and Martin were not the only Yankees Gallo poked fun at, however. In September 1979 he drew a cartoon featuring Reggie Jackson in a psychiatrist's waiting room with two giant duplicates of himself, one labeled "Reggie's Ego" and the other "Reggie's Unhappiness" (59). A speech bubble coming from outside the panel asks, "Who else is out in the waiting room, nurse?" with the reply, "There is Mister Jackson along with his constant companions." Clearly, Gallo's diagnosis for Jackson's oft-voiced dissatisfaction as a Yankee is the same as his blame for Steinbrenner and Martin's inability to cooperate: an oversized and unchecked ego.

But Gallo was far from alone. "Ego" is a theme that also permeates Lyle's *The Bronx Zoo*. For instance, the book gives an estimation of Martin and Steinbrenner similar to Gallo's. While Lyle's narrative implies that he has a certain amount of respect for his manager, Martin, the relief pitcher does not turn a blind eye to Billy's evident psychological issues. But in Steinbrenner, Lyle saw an even more ego-obsessed head case, opining, "As big an ego as Billy has, George has a bigger one, and he deeply resents the fans' love for Billy" (147). But it is the ego of "superstar" Reggie Jackson that serves as the most frequent target for Lyle's own brand of breezy, laid-back needling, as epitomized by this wry observation early in the narrative: "[Reggie] must want to get his name in the paper real bad" (31). As the book progresses, Lyle continues to mock Reggie's desire for attention and implies a gulf between the slugger's perceived importance and Lyle's own less-than-generous take on his actual contribution.

Lyle lays it on so thick, in fact, that readers cannot help but wonder whether the author bears a personal grudge against Jackson. But if Sparky is less than objective in his estimation of Jackson and does take advantage of the pulpit the book provides to give Reggie a bit of a comeuppance, this would only befit the public perception of the Yankees' social dysfunction as a unit in this era. Thus, even as *The Bronx Zoo* attempts to chronicle the late-1970s Yankee soap opera, it is simultaneously an active participant in that drama.

Observing a phenomenon and participating in that trend at the same time is perhaps even truer regarding Lyle's own ego. While Lyle seems to relish pricking the inflated egos of Steinbrenner and Jackson, much of *The Bronx Zoo* centers on Lyle's own sense of self-importance. While he may not seek media attention in the way he accuses Jackson of, time and again Sparky Lyle proves to be not such a team player himself.

If *The Bronx Zoo* has a central conflict—other than the presumed goal of winning the pennant and defending their title as World Champions—it is Lyle's struggle to adjust from the status he earned and enjoyed as the Yankees' premiere relief pitcher during the 1977 season to a new reality for the 1978 season, which included highly touted and highly priced reliever Rich "Goose" Gossage, acquired as a free agent after six years with the White Sox and Pirates. His pride wounded, Lyle has a difficult time accepting a less-lustrous role, and it does not take long for him to fantasize about being traded.

Lyle's displeasure with the signing of Gossage is certainly understandable. After all, Lyle was awarded the American League's Cy Young Award for his relief work in the 1977 season.[11] Similarly, his frequent complaints that Martin was not using him effectively may have had some merit. However, it is quite clear that Lyle's ideas about "effective use," as detailed in the book, are mostly confined to the role of a "closer"—pitching the last one, two, or three innings when the game was on the line. He expresses particular disdain for being used as a "long man," or entering game after the early exit of a starting pitcher and pitching into the late innings, as well as for being asked to "mop up," or enter a game that is already as good as lost. While usually described in typical comedic fashion, Lyle's antics in response to not being used in the way he desires—refusing to "mop up" when called upon (204) or taking himself out and going straight home after pitching two innings (169)—occasionally come off as childish and not all that far from the egotism of which he accuses Jackson.

Particularly notable in this regard is the day Lyle was at the ballpark early, negotiating a new contract with Steinbrenner, and then, out of frustration over the way the talks went with the owner, elected to go back home instead of play in the evening's game. Lyle describes being recognized by a young fan while sitting in traffic on the way home from the park: "this kid yells 'Hey, Spark. Isn't there a game today?' I said, 'Yep, sure is.' The kid didn't know what to say. It made me laugh" (120). Lyle's interaction with this young fan is especially significant for the way it is both reminiscent of and stands as a contrast to the semi-mythical story of Babe Ruth promising to hit a home run for the sick boy, or the completely fabricated version of Gehrig doing the same in *The Pride of the Yankees*. Rather than playing the role of hero and example to a young boy, Lyle confuses and disappoints. While certainly less dramatic and severe, Lyle's interaction with the young fan plays like a blasé, free agency–era version of the popular legend about White Sox outfielder "Shoeless" Joe Jackson's encounter with a heartbroken young boy who implores, "Say it ain't so, Joe!," after having just learned his baseball idol had been banned from baseball for taking money from gamblers to throw the World Series. It does not exactly compete with the Shoeless Joe story in terms of gravity; nevertheless, in this passage of *The Bronx Zoo*, the days of the grand Yankee hero seem to be a thing of the past, indeed.

THE "ME" DECADE

However the actions of Lyle—or for that matter, of Jackson, Martin, or Steinbrenner—are interpreted, they are certainly a contrast to the themes of self-sacrifice central to the popular portrayal of Lou Gehrig and Joe DiMaggio in the World War II and postwar periods. But just as that emphasis on self-sacrifice can be read as part of a broader cultural trend, the theme of self-before-team prevalent in popular perceptions of the late-1970s Yankee can likewise be described as emblematic of the time, a period then identified, and sometimes still referred to as "the 'Me' Decade."

The term "'Me' Decade" was coined in 1976 by journalist, novelist, and cultural critic Tom Wolfe in an article he wrote for *New York* magazine to describe what he saw as the rise of an inward focus among Americans in the wake of the postwar economic prosperity and the loosening of the possibilities of individual freedom and self-expression that came with the mainstreaming of the late-1960s counterculture (Mattson 37). According to Wolfe, "The old alchemical dream was changing base metals into gold. The new alchemical dream is: changing one's personality—remaking, remodeling, elevating, and polishing one's very self... and observing, studying, and doting on it. (Me!)" Wolfe suggests that in the past such attention to the development of one's self "had always been an aristocratic luxury... since only the very wealthiest classes had the free time and the surplus income to dwell upon this sweetest and vainest of pastimes," but the economic abundance of the postwar era had made it available to virtually all Americans in some form or another. Freed from a toil-focused life by the progress of technology and the rising living standard, Wolfe saw Americans as being increasingly able to say, "Let's talk about Me. . . . Let's find the Real Me."

Wolfe describes the "Me" Decade phenomenon as less a formal movement than a trend made manifest in myriad movements and micro-movements: self-improvement workshops, new forms of therapy, feel-good religious and semireligious groups, and even self-help books. He sees the "Me" Decade as underpinning the so-called "sexual liberation" of American society during the decade and, to some degree, even the "women's liberation" movement. Something of a secular spiritual awakening, the "Me" Decade phenomenon purportedly replaced traditional religious institutions and their firm, prescribed morality with a devotion to finding one's own personal form of truth and happiness, often at the expense of traditional morals. As a "Me" Decade disciple might proclaim, "Let's get rid of all the hypocrisies and impediments and false modesties that obscure the Real Me. . . . Ah! At the apex of my soul is a spark of the Divine" (Wolfe). Similarly, while traditional religious institutions would teach of one's obligations to make sacrifices for the greater good of family and community, the "Me" Decade spirituality suggested that one's highest responsibility was to themselves. As the author himself describes it:

> Most people, historically, have not lived their lives as if thinking, "I have only one life to live." Instead they have lived as if they are living their ancestors' lives and their offspring's lives and perhaps their neighbors' lives as well. They have seen themselves as inseparable from the great tide of chromosomes of which they are created and which they pass on. . . . For anyone to renounce the notion of serial immortality, in the West or the East, has been to defy what seems like a law of Nature. Hence the wicked feeling—the excitement!— of "If I've only one life, let me live it as a ———!" Fill in the blank, if you dare.
>
> And now many dare it!

While the accuracy of Wolfe's "Me" Decade label for the '70s is debatable, what is quite clear is that a discourse centered on ego and Americans' supposedly growing self-focus certainly existed by the second half of the decade (Mattson

35–40). In early 1979, for instance, academic cultural historian Christopher Lasch published a National Book Award–winning tome titled *The Culture of Narcissism* that put forth arguments similar to Wolfe's (Mattson 43–46). Later that year, Lasch would be called on to advise Jimmy Carter as the nation's president struggled to diagnose the problem of his ailing country (91, 93–94). Self-centeredness seemed to be on Americans' minds, and for many, the Yankees of that era were exhibit A.

Reggie Jackson may have been a particularly easy target for such a perspective. Known to be an intelligent man and equally known for his tendency to proclaim himself as such, Reggie was given to waxing philosophical with reporters, reflecting on the nature of the unique life he led, rather than just offering his takes on balls and strikes or the team's prospects in tomorrow's game. Journalists who were seeking more colorful, human copy devoted significant space to Jackson and his often entertaining flights of fancy. As a prime example, a 1974 piece by Roy Blount Jr. in *Sports Illustrated* details how in Jackson's "tastefully-decorated" penthouse apartment not only were there "closets full of good clothes" but also a painting of a flying seagull hanging over the slugger's bed. "He sees himself as Jonathan Livingston Seagull," Blount informs readers, "the fictional gull that breaks away from the crowd to transcend itself and then returns to help others toward limitless flying." This fictional bird, Jonathan Livingston Seagull, is the titular character in pop philosophy writer Richard Bach's 1970 book that was a bestseller for much of the first half of the decade. An allegory about transcending the accepted limit of individual human potential, Bach's book is squarely in the individualized, deinstitutionalized spirituality-cum-self-help realm that Wolfe attempted to chronicle and critique in his essay.

Jackson's association with the book seems to have acquired some staying power in the public consciousness. It is mentioned in both Jacobson's 1978 book (58) and Mahler's work of cultural history published in 2005 (87). Combined with descriptions of Jackson's efforts to cultivate sophisticated taste—as the slugger himself put it in the infamous 1977 *Sport* piece, "Being a superstar . . . can make life very difficult, difficult to grow. So I like to visit with my friends, listen to some *fine* music, drink some *good* wine, perhaps take a ride in the country in a *fine* car" (Ward 204)—Jackson's self-identification with the most famous seagull of the decade only served to cement his reputation as a navel-gazing narcissist.

Other than Jackson, the Yankees of this era do not fit the profile of the starry-eyed flower children out to discover their lives' true purpose that Wolfe imagined. However, popular portrayals and representations of the team at the time clearly convey a tendency for those ballplayers to put themselves and their own development as individual players above the success and well-being of the team. From the late 1930s through the early 1960s, one of the things the Yankees had always signified as a cultural icon was team play, or working for the good of the team at the expense of individual glory. Such values seem quite distant amid sports-page headlines or quotes in best-selling tell-all books about Jackson ignoring Martin's signs, or Martin refusing to play Jackson out of spite, or Munson feeling betrayed by Jackson's lofty salary, or Lyle skipping games in the middle of a pennant race out of frustration with Steinbrenner. Some comments from Lyle in *The Bronx Zoo* are particularly illustrative along these lines: "They're always talking loyalty and teamwork. . . . But the loyalty part they can stick . . . I come to the park every day, and whether it was for the Red Sox or now for the Yankees, I try to win. That's my loyalty. Nothing more. They are paying me to pitch, but that is not loyalty on their part, I don't give a damn what George says" (127).

One could certainly argue that Lyle's assessment of the meaninglessness of loyalty in an organization run by Steinbrenner is spot on, but this would be beside the point. Regardless of where blame might lie, Lyle's comments—particularly the remarks that suggest no difference between playing for the Red Sox and the Yankees, which must have been received as blasphemy to certain ears in both camps—nevertheless reveal that playing for the glory of the Yankees was of comparatively little value to the late-1970s teams. Again, this is a marked contrast to the pattern established by the public image of Gehrig, who proclaimed himself to be the "luckiest man on the face of the earth" for his time with the Yankees, or DiMaggio, who similarly described himself as "lucky to be a Yankee." In other words, in the late 1970s, despite the club's return to success, to many it seemed that individual ego had eclipsed the grand Yankee tradition itself.

In many respects, this change in the popular view of the Yankees from the image of self-sacrifice that became part of the club's iconic cultural meaning at midcentury to one of self-interest was inevitable. The type of sports journalism that had made a national saint out of Joe DiMaggio was long gone, replaced by a press that preferred colorful, if flawed "superstars" to "heroes." And in the wake of the broad cultural changes related to the 1960s counterculture, there were many individuals like Reggie Jackson who were happy to oblige. The old type of heroism was regarded by many, including some athletes themselves, as a relic.

Also influential was the advent of free agency, which magnified players' salaries and the public focus on those rapidly escalating salaries. DiMaggio held out for more money in 1938—he was underpaid at $15,000 a year, wanted $40,000, and eventually settled for $25,000—and was booed for much of that season, but this was soon forgotten and became a footnote in his storied tenure as a Yankee hero. Reggie Jackson's years with the Yankees, meanwhile, will always be characterized by his multimillion-dollar acquisition as a free agent. Free agency also suddenly changed a ballplayer's hope or expectation—as well as that of fans—to spend his entire career with one team. Eventually a new paradigm focused on the individual and his personal career arc, which might include several different teams, was established, but as the late 1970s were the first years of free agency in baseball, the American public was not quite used to this level of individualism in its baseball heroes. Baseball was supposed to be a team game. In this context, tabloid-news items like Jackson's comment that he "didn't come to New York to become a star; [he] brought [his] star with [him]" (qtd. in Mahler 65) or Thurman Munson's public pondering about whether he might be happier playing closer to home for the Cleveland Indians seemed all the more shocking.

All that said, the late-1970s Yankees were a unique bunch. There is perhaps no team in the history of American sport to have had such a clash of personalities, to have fought among themselves so frequently and so publicly. And yet they won. They were not just moderately successful, but they won in a way the Yankees were used to doing, with three pennants in a row and back-to-back World Series titles. And yet, even their success as a team could not eclipse the theme of individual ego. Drawing on remarks from Munson, Steve Jacobson perhaps sums this up best:

> [Munson] never did stop battling Steinbrenner and didn't stop believing in himself. "I never doubted I could win," he said. "'We' is a tough word. I don't know what other people were thinking. There's a lot of 'I's' in 'We.'"

Somehow the "I's" come together. It would take a doctoral dissertation to explain why and how. . . . But the egos were temporarily replaced by pride and the desire to win, which may be stronger than ego or may really be the heart of a ballplayer's ego.[12] (Jacobson 344–35)

SUCCESSFUL BUT NOT "REAL YANKEES"

At one point in *The Bronx Zoo,* Sparky Lyle recounts a scene of mere minor discord during the '78 season when the catchers in the bullpen began squabbling over who should warm up the relief pitcher potentially preparing to enter the game, with both catchers wanting to avoid the less-than-strenuous work. Lyle correctly assesses the reader's diminished view of the team as whole as a result of these two players trying to avoid making a comparatively small effort towards the overall good of the team. "You'd never guess this was the big leagues, the Yankees, the World Champions," he writes, "You'd expect something like this in Little League" (72).

Lyle's focus here is likely on expectations for more professional behavior at the highest level of the so-called national pastime, particularly when the previous year's champions were involved. But his use of that phrase "the Yankees" separated by sequential comas from "the big leagues" and "World Champions" is significant, for "the Yankees" remained a loaded term for Americans. Despite the team's connotations of plutocracy and "soap opera" in the late '70s, the Yankees still carried much of the rich, iconic cultural meaning they had amassed at midcentury. For much of the general public, "Yankees" still conjured visions of an all-American organization characterized by class and excellence, and stories of manly, self-sacrificing heroism. Their success notwithstanding, perhaps the most significant theme that surfaces in the way the Yankees of the late '70s were portrayed and received in the popular culture is the idea that they did not feel like the Yankees. In certain respects, George Steinbrenner had indeed achieved his goal and restored the franchise to greatness, but as Americans who may or may not have had memories of DiMaggio, Yogi Berra, or Casey Stengel read headlines on the sports page of the *Daily News* or *New York Post* about the latest kerfuffle between Billy Martin and Steinbrenner, or saw the release of a tell-all bestseller, or watched Martin and Jackson nearly come to blows on national TV, the words "You'd never guess this was . . . the Yankees" may have felt quite appropriate.

It is one thing for Yankee detractors to take a pessimistic view of the club. The voice of the counter-narrative that turned the Yankees' cultural symbolism on its head was a longstanding tradition by the late 1970s, and the renewed success of the team and their conspicuous spending invited a rejuvenation of Yankee hating. With their accusations of plutocracy and their military-themed caricatures, the Americans who loved to hate the Yankees in the late '70s—be they ideologically committed Bill Lees, or more personally focused Bill Gallos—set the tone for the anti-Yankeeism that is still alive and strong today. The theme of plutocracy, in particular, remains a focal point for those who see the Yankees as emblematic of everything wrong with America, and while this was not necessarily an invention of late-1970s Yankee critics, the combined influence of Steinbrenner and free agency elicited an enthusiastic emphasis on that theme that has largely sustained its prominence ever since.

Yes, Yankee haters had been around a long time. But it was quite a new thing for the true believers—either Yankee fans or those ideologically or emotionally invested in the ball club as an icon of midcentury American values—to witness the triumphant return of Yankee success and still feel like they were losing faith. And yet, this is precisely what happened in the late 1970s. Even with expectations reduced by what occurred in the late '60s for both the Yankees and the nation at large, many Americans simply could not ignore how much the current Yankees failed to measure up to the great Yankees of yore.

This contrast with the Yankee past resurfaces again and again in Jacobson's narration of the 1977 season. One need look no further than the opening lines of his book's introduction:

> The New York Yankees won the Eastern Division championship of the American League, the American League playoff, and beat the Dodgers in the World Series. It was just what the great Yankees did in the dynasty years.
>
> But no Yankee season ever played like 1977. There was nothing in history to prepare the baseball world for what went on inside those sanctified pinstripes. (Jacobson 1)

Jacobson tellingly chooses to begin his book by suggesting that the way the squabbling '70s Yankees were able to replicate the on-field success of the storied teams of the past only emphasized the enormous contrast between the present and the past that was manifest in other ways, ways that were to be elucidated in the pages that followed, in the event that his readers had avoided the sports section for the entirety of the 1977 calendar year. It is further worth noting his use of the term "sanctified pinstripes," an icon that had come to represent an icon and one that meant so much it was granted the sporting equivalent of "holy" status. Of course, Jacobson only evokes such reverent language to show how the '77 club had befouled the grand tradition, or, as he puts it in a slightly more positive way, "The old Yankees won with consummate ease, grace, and dignity. These Yankees won with dirt on their faces" (2).

As Jacobson's diary-like day-by-day account of the wild ride that was the '77 season unfolds, the author peppers his prose with references to the grand symbols of past Yankeeness, always implying how ill fitted the contemporary Yanks are to stand next to them: "[Billy] Martin continues to think of the Yankees as the organization he played for twenty years ago. Nothing is the same except the name and the address. The old flannel pinstripes are double-knits now and the ball park is rebuilt, but his emotional tie is unbroken" (210–11). Later, Jacobson recalls legendary manager Casey Stengel but clarifies, "The distinction is that Stengel's Yankees didn't have this kind of bickering" (233). And after Reggie Jackson scores a game-winning hit in June and describes himself as "just lucky, I guess," Jacobson presses him with a reference the slugger may have been aware of, imploring, "Lucky to be a Yankee? 'Mmmmmm,' Reggie Jackson said." The implication is that Jackson is clearly not Joe DiMaggio.

Often, individuals in the clubhouse would assist in Jacobson's motif, as when the nostalgic Martin criticized Jackson by commenting, "This is not the type of team spirit. It's not the Yankee kind of thing to do. A true Yankee wouldn't do that" (qtd. in Jacobson 339). During the World Series, Dodger coach Jim Gilliam, who played infield for both the Brooklyn and Los Angeles incarnations of the club from 1953 to 1966, gave Jacobson occasion to expand his comparison with the Yankee past to include fans as well.[13] "Other things have changed, too," he writes. "Yankee Stadium used to be the model of decorum, decked with the pennants of dynasties past. Tonight fans ran onto the field. One even threw a smokebomb onto the grass when it was clear that the Dodgers would win. 'These fans are getting unruly, aren't they?' Gilliam said, 'They're not like they used to be here'" (Jacobson 338). Collectively, Jacobson's nostalgic asides create the impression that these new Yankees, while successful, somehow ring hollow, going through the proper Yankee motions (that is, winning) but containing too little of the real meaning.

While Sparky Lyle's account of the '78 season doesn't directly participate in such nostalgic mourning for a past that felt too distant, *The Bronx Zoo* nevertheless provides a glimpse or two into such a tendency among Yankee fans. This is especially clear in one particular moment when Lyle describes his fan mail: "I got a fan letter. It says, 'Dear Sparky, I've been a Yankee fan since I was ten years old, and that's when the Yankees were real Yankees. . . . Here you are making $500,000 for three years, and you're unhappy. Try this out. I'm making $10,000 a year. Why don't you shut your mouth . . . ?'" (Lyle 99). Note the disgruntled fan's use of the term "real Yankee" without any explanation of what it precisely it means to be "real" Yankee. This is because the cultural meaning of "Yankee" is already well established. A real Yankee would obviously represent and uphold the values affiliated with the club since the middle of the century: heroic, self-sacrificing masculinity and a commitment to excellence reflected in sustained success. Whether it is the self-effacing Gehrig from *The Pride of the Yankees*, DiMaggio playing through pain to lead the team in 1949, or even the "platooned" players of the Casey Stengel era, real Yankees sacrificed their individual goals and needs for the good of the team. Real Yankees were supposed to be all about pride won through the team's effort, not the individual effort.

While not quite as detectable in Lyle's account of the fan letter, in the references Jacobson makes to the glorious Yankee past, there is often a tone of sad nostalgia, a mourning for the death of a past that will not, cannot return. Indeed, the advent of free agency and rapidly escalating salaries in baseball as well as the broader cultural anxiety about "ego" at the time certainly would corroborate Jacobson's feelings that the self-centeredness and bickering of late-1970s Yankees are not a passing fad but a sign of things to come. They are a glimpse at, to use the language of poet W. B. Yeats—as Joan Didion did in her grim, apprehensive account of the late-1960s counterculture—the "rough beast. . . [slouching] towards Bethlehem to be born."

In some respects, this sense of a lost golden past was emblematic of the nation as a whole. Just as the Yankees' return to success in the late '70s gave occasion for Americans to compare the contemporary team with their storied progenitors, the nation itself celebrated its two hundredth birthday in 1976, inviting assessments of the condition of the country relative to its founding and history. Only one year earlier, President Gerald Ford had regretfully but bluntly stated that "the state of the union is not good," and by the time of the bicentennial and in the years following, the feeling among the general populace did not change much. After the bloodshed abroad and contention at home surrounding Vietnam and the image of corruption and seeds of distrust sown by Watergate, the nation found itself dealing with a struggling economy and an energy crisis. Additionally, some socially and culturally conservative Americans saw many of the changes invited by the iconoclasm of the 1960s and normalized during the course of the '70s—the loosening of traditional sexual norms, the prevalence of recreational drug use, the shifting of traditional gender roles—as signs of the nation's moral decline (Mattson 9–11, 33–35). In 1979 Gerald Ford's successor, President Jimmy Carter, diagnosed the nation as experiencing a "crisis of confidence." Speaking generally, the America at the end of the 1970s was an America that saw its past as brighter than its present.

When Steve Jacobson wrote nostalgically that "the old Yankees won with consummate ease, grace, and dignity. These Yankees won with dirt on their faces," the same could have been said about the nation itself. Only America was not winning. Thus the Yankees of the late '70s, shot through with embarrassing scandal and vicious infighting not unlike the nation itself since the mid-1960s, became emblematic of the notion that what America once was, it no longer is, nor could be.

This was perhaps made most clear by the events that concluded the 1977 World Series. In the sixth game, played at Yankee Stadium, Reggie Jackson hit three home runs in three straight at-bats to lift the Yanks over the Dodgers and clinch the series victory, their first in fifteen years.[14] Fans in the stadium exploded after the third blast and barely contained their energy for the half an inning remaining before the Yankees would be officially crowned World Series champions. At the final out, the crowd swarmed onto the field, some tossing firecrackers or cherry bombs, while the Yankees, and especially

Jackson, tried to make their way off the diamond and into the clubhouse as quickly and safely as possible (Mahler 336). It was a feat that seemed lifted right out of the lore affiliated with Ruth, DiMaggio, or Mantle, and helped earn Jackson the nickname "Mr. October." And to add to the Ruthian quality of the story, in Jackson's very next appearance in Yankee Stadium, the home opener of the 1978 season, Yankee fans entering the stadium each received a free sample of the new "Reggie!" candy bar. After Jackson hit a home run, fans began showering him with their Reggie! Bars.

In some ways these events seem right in keeping with the heroic Yankee heritage of Ruth, Gehrig, DiMaggio, and Mantle. And yet, in others, Reggie Jackson's three home runs and the subsequent Reggie! Bar incident ring a little hollow in comparison with the legends from the past, largely because of the broader changes in American culture. Reggie would always be a "superstar," to use his own words, but he would never really be a hero, mostly because the media outlets covering Major League Baseball were no longer in the hero-making business. Instead, the newspapers and magazines carried intimate profiles of Jackson sprinkled with equal measures of detail of his glamorous off-field life, acknowledgement of his all-too-human weaknesses, and space for his near-ceaseless self-promotion. Tellingly, when Joe DiMaggio published his ghostwritten autobiography in the late '40s, it was titled *Lucky to Be a Yankee*, and was full of "aw shucks" humility; but when Jackson published a diary of his 1974 season, it was titled *Reggie Jackson: A Season with a Superstar*, and its opening line read, "My name is Reggie Jackson and I am the best in baseball."

Even the affair with the candy bar seemed like an orchestrated ego trip to a certain extent. Jackson had practically been campaigning for a candy bar bearing his own name since his days in Oakland. Blount's 1974 piece on Jackson for *Sports Illustrated* contained a description of Reggie in the A's clubhouse holding a Baby Ruth candy bar, supposedly named for the Babe, in one hand and an Oh Henry! bar, often said to be named after the man who eventually broke Ruth's lifetime home-run record, Hank Aaron, in the other.[15] The question to his teammates: *what will they name my candy bar?* Later, while unhappily playing out his contract in Baltimore after being traded by the A's, Jackson hypothesized aloud to the press, "If I played in New York, they'd name a candy bar after me" (qtd. in Young). Jackson's agent was making pitches to candy companies before his first spring training as a Yankee was over (Mahler 86–87). A closer look at the sports-press archives reveals that Jackson's candy-bar obsession dates back to at least his breakout year in Oakland, 1969, when he was quoted in the *New York Times* as mentioning the Baby Ruth candy bar as a signifier of Ruth's greatness. "To me, Ruth is the greatest home-run hitter that ever lived," he said. "There will never be another Babe Ruth. They named a candy bar after him" (qtd. in Vecsey, "Fame to Reggie Jackson"). Whatever the reality, the perception of the Yankee heroes in the past was that such honors were bestowed upon them by an adoring public; they were not sought after and negotiated through one's agent.

Jackson's very conscious, even calculated pursuit of immortality in the form of chocolate and caramel is emblematic of the way both he and George Steinbrenner's late-1970s Yankees were perceived by many. In their dedicated pursuit of the glory of their progenitors, it appeared they had somehow lost the true spirit of those "real Yankees" who embodied the club's iconic cultural meaning. Be it Steinbrenner's highly publicized pursuit of championships through the power of his pocketbook, Reggie Jackson's self-proclaimed "superstar" status, or the seemingly endless string of inflammatory tabloid quotes from players aimed at each other, their manager, or owner, these Yankees, for all their success, did not *feel like* Yankees. As Jacobson ably put it, results-wise "it was just what the great Yankees did in the dynasty years. But no Yankee season ever played like 1977." More savvy observers realized that this may have had as much to do with broader changes in American culture at large as it did with the Yankees themselves, but in some ways that only enhanced the tragedy. In a certain sense, the Yankees were back. But in another sense, it was clear that the Yankees—the "real Yankees," the iconic Yankees who stood for those midcentury values, for manly, self-sacrificing heroism and national strength and greatness—were lost and gone forever.

Chapter Eight

"ALL THAT ONCE WAS GOOD AND COULD BE AGAIN"

Baseball Nostalgia in the 1980s and '90s and the Return of the Yankees

After the Yankees' brief return to success in the late 1970s, George Steinbrenner continued to exert his free-spending influence on the ball club and on Major League Baseball throughout the next decade, doggedly and passionately pursuing more World Series championships by means of acquiring the most prominent players available through trades and free-agency.[1] But despite Steinbrenner's efforts and perhaps because some of them were misguided, the Yankees were not able to sustain the level of success they found in the 1977 and '78 seasons. In fact, after making the 1981 World Series but losing to the Dodgers—which prompted a bizarre public apology to the city of New York from Steinbrenner for his team's performance—almost a decade and a half would pass before the Yankees would so much as make the playoffs.

Each disappointing year seemed to make Steinbrenner successively more upset and more determined, as he often proclaimed that big changes would be made before the next season, usually meaning the signing of a new big-name player and a new manager. Between 1979 and 1995, the Yankees had no fewer than sixteen managerial changes, with Steinbrenner often rehiring someone he had fired only a year or two before.[2] Only after Steinbrenner was banned from the day-to-day operations of the Yankees for a period of two years did the club begin to turn things around, eventually returning to the playoffs in 1995 and the World Series in '96.

This relatively ineffectual and tumultuous period of Yankee history coincided with a period of great nostalgia and renewed fan enthusiasm for the game of baseball nationally. Baby Boomers who had abandoned baseball in their counterculture-influenced teenage or college days began returning to the game of their youth as they got on in years and began having children of their own in the 1980s and '90s. But Yankee lovers during this nostalgic period in baseball fandom were largely left to tend the embers of their memories or earlier team lore and hope for a renaissance in the Bronx. By the early 1990s the discrepancy between the sorry state of the Yankees' present and the legacy of the longed-for past yielded three cultural texts that both satirized the Steinbrenner era and expressed a nostalgic desire for a return of the glorious Yankee past. In these three texts—Sparky Lyle's "baseball fantasy" novel, *The Year I Owned the Yankees* (1990), the comedy film *The Scout* (1994), and the fictionalized caricature of George Steinbrenner on the hit television sitcom *Seinfeld* (1989–98, with "Steinbrenner" debuting in May 1994)—the characters' frustrations with the present day Yankees and the longings for the Bronx Bombers of yesteryear reveal, like the broader baseball-nostalgia craze from the '80s and '90s, a desire among Americans to reassess, revisit, and reclaim a past that had been rejected in the previous decade.

With the Yankees' iconic associations with the values and culture of pre-countercultural America, the desire for a return of the team's old success became a fitting token for the desire felt and expressed in varying degrees by many maturing American Baby Boomers in this period to reconcile the earlier America of their parents' generation with the one they had been creating in opposition to it since their adolescence and early adulthood in the 1960s. Thus, when the Bronx-based ball club actually did return to their winning ways—creating what many have called a new Yankee dynasty by returning to the playoffs in 1995 and winning the World Series in 1996, '98, '99, and 2000—Americans by and large celebrated this renaissance as a second coming that was long overdue. The Yankees of this period were certainly not without their critics, including both fans and sportswriters who once again accused the organization of plutocratic tyranny. Nevertheless, more broadly, Americans used the late-twentieth-century Yankees as a token of reconciliation with our celebrated, traditional past, whether pining for the return of the "real" Yankees during the down years of the 1980s and early '90s, or exulting in the triumphant return of Yankee success in the late '90s.

THE BASEBALL-NOSTALGIA BOOM

Attendance began increasing in Major League ballparks as soon as 1976, when ticket sales surpassed the 30 million mark for the first time in history. A number of factors have been cited as contributing to this return to baseball by the American public, but likely the most significant underlying cause is generational. In Jules Tygiel's astute words:

> Most significantly, the vast postwar generation, raised in the 1950s, the last era in which professional baseball would reign as the nation's undisputed favorite sport, had reached maturity and returned to its roots. Moving into their thirties and settling down with jobs and families, male baby boomers, many of whom had allowed their baseball allegiances to ebb during the tumultuous sixties, once again appeared at games. With the Vietnam War over in 1975 and the countercultural impulse on the wane, many former protesters staged a symbolic homecoming through baseball. The sheer numbers and growing affluence of the postwar cohort fueled baseball's resurgence. (*Past Time* 202)

Even as much of the country was wringing its hands over the idea that the iconoclasm and individualism of the 1960s had spun out of control and given birth to a narcissistic "Me" culture, and perhaps in reaction to that trend, many Baby Boomers began quietly returning to the hobby of their relatively innocent childhoods.

By the 1980s this increased interest in baseball that was palpable in the swelling game attendance and television viewership began to manifest itself in a myriad of other ways in popular culture. Entrepreneurs began collaborating with former Major League players to hold what became known as "baseball fantasy camps," where thirty-something Baby Boomers who had been nostalgically returning to baseball could now, for the right price, take the field and hone baseball skills with the heroes from their youth (Tygiel, *Past Time* 203–7). The 1980s also saw tremendous growth in the market for baseball memorabilia. Signed photos, baseballs, caps, jerseys, baseball cards, and the like from the legends of the past had become big business by the decade's end (Bloom 16–19).

This nostalgia boom was also felt in the literary market, where serious baseball books for adults proliferated, including many that took on what Tygiel has identified as a "romantic" perspective on the game (*Past Time* 218). Published works like W. P. Kinsella's baseball fantasy novel, *Shoeless Joe* (1983), poet Donald Hall's collection of essays, *Fathers Playing Catch with Sons* (1985), political columnist George F. Will's ode to the "craft of baseball," *Men at Work* (1990), or the writings of a former Yale professor of Renaissance literature who also became the commissioner of baseball, A. Bartlett Giamatti ("The Green Fields of the Mind" [1977]; *Take Time for Paradise* [1989]), all extolled the virtues of the game and celebrated it as a most uniquely American institution.

This romantic celebration of America's national pastime was echoed in celluloid. The 1984 film adaptation of Bernard Malamud's novel *The Natural* (1952) altered the ending to transform the narrative from a cautionary tale to a lyrical celebration of the baseball-hero figure. In 1988 the bawdy comedy about life and love (or at least sex) in baseball's minor leagues, *Bull Durham*, featured an only partially tongue-in-cheek monologue about "the church of baseball" and its ability to feed "the soul, day-in, day-out." Meanwhile, the 1989 adaptation of *Shoeless Joe*, retitled *Field of Dreams*, layered the emotional reconciliation between a father and his former-hippie son over the novel's story of a magical baseball field to epitomize the entirety of the '80s baseball-nostalgia boom and its desires to reinvigorate the present with a turn to a once-abandoned American past.[3] A character from the movie eloquently captures the newfound appeal in this nostalgic return to the game, proclaiming, "Baseball has marked the time. This field, this game, is part of our past.... It reminds us of all that was once was good, and could be again."

These three films, along with the critically acclaimed period drama about the 1919 Black Sox scandal, *Eight Men Out* (1988), and the commercially successful underdog comedy *Major League* (1989), helped create a market for baseball films that briefly flourished in the early to mid-1990s. Between 1992 and 1996, the "baseball film" practically became an American movie genre unto itself, as those five years saw no fewer than twelve movies focused on baseball.[4] While a few such films, like *Cobb* (1994) and *The Fan* (1996), plumbed the depth of the uglier aspects of the game and it history, overall these films were optimistic in tone and positive in their portrayal of baseball, essentially updating the populist underdog stories of mid-twentieth-century baseball cinema for a 1990s audience, with more than the occasional dash of nostalgia thrown in for good measure. Along these same lines, in 1994 PBS aired Ken Burns's nine-part documentary miniseries about the history of the game, *Baseball*. While *Baseball* did not ignore or gloss over the darker moments in the game's history, neither did it shy away from the occasional romantic rhapsodizing of the type found in *Field of Dreams* or the writings of Donald Hall or Bart Giamatti.

Tygiel emphasizes this boom in baseball nostalgia and romanticism as having its origins in baseball fan culture, suggesting that "fans not only rediscovered baseball, they attempted to redefine and reclaim it in their own image" (*Past Time* 200). Tygiel is correct not only in the sense that this proliferation of celebratory baseball pop culture originated outside of the organized professional game—while the league certainly benefitted from it economically, it was not a Major League Baseball marketing campaign—but also in the way many of the texts this movement produced tend to focus on and give voice to the fan.[5] While there are a few exceptions, by and large, prior to this turn in the 1980s, baseball-related cultural products had tended to focus on the ballplayers themselves and the experience of *playing* the game.[6] But beginning in the '80s, fandom was increasingly portrayed and discussed as an integral part of the game.

The proliferation of fan-produced and fan-focused baseball nostalgia was certainly not lost on Major League Baseball itself, and by the early 1990s a number of trends emerged to suggest that the organized professional game was attempting to shape itself to fit the nostalgic, romantic image fans had been conjuring and celebrating during the past decade. Some of these moves by Major League Baseball were subtle. For instance, the leagues began cooperating much more conspicuously with the film industry. Following the pattern established by *Major League* and its portrayal of a fictional Cleveland Indians team, many of the baseball films in the '90s would focus on or at least feature an actual Major League team (usually a fictionalized version of them) and make prominent use of their contemporary team logos, their uniforms, and sometimes their ballparks.[7] This prominent cooperation with the film industry acted as an official validation and embrace of the narrative tradition that existed off the field and outside the leagues' jurisdiction. It helped make this fan-produced culture seem more like an official part of the organized professional game. Another subtle gesture in the direction of conforming to the nostalgic fan movement came in the form of uniforms, as teams in the mid-1980s one by one began rejecting the buttonless, brightly colored pullover styles of the '70s and early '80s for more subdued, traditional, white and gray, button-up uniforms resembling the classic uniforms of the '20s through the '60s (Ballard).[8]

Most significantly and conspicuously, however, organized baseball began to embrace the fan's romantic nostalgia through a new style of ballpark architecture: the so-called "retro" ballpark. In 1992 the Baltimore Orioles, whose fortunes had been flagging since the mid-1980s, opened a new home park, "Oriole Park at Camden Yards." Designed specifically to give fans the sensation of tradition and history, Camden Yards, with its red brick, dark green steel, and asymmetrical playing field, intentionally evoked the ballparks of the early twentieth century in several ways (Rosenweig 3–5).[9]

Upon opening, Camden Yard received rave reviews and instantly became the model for other franchises to follow, with six new parks featuring "retro" styling in the exterior, interior, or both opening before the end of the decade, with plans put in motion for the building of many more to open in the new millennium (10). With these ballparks designed not just to facilitate the viewing of the contest on the field but to create an overall experience rooted in a romantic, nostalgic concept of the game of baseball, the Major Leagues seized on an idea that grew out of the revolution in fan culture that took place in the last decades of the twentieth century. Through the nostalgic fans, organized baseball realized they were not just selling the individual games to potential viewers, they were selling the *idea* of the game to people seeking to work out their own place in American culture and history. And for these people baseball could be marketed as a vital touchstone.

THE YANKEES AND THE NOSTALGIA BOOM

One would think the baseball-nostalgia boom would play right into the Yankees' hands. As the most storied and successful of clubs both during the youth of Baby Boomers and their parents, and already having a reputation of honoring their past through institutionalized memorials like Monument Park and the annual "Old Timers' Day," they seem like the club best equipped to capitalize on this nostalgic return to and embrace of baseball during the 1980s and '90s. And in many ways the Yankees did exactly that: the Pinstripes were well represented in both the fantasy camp and the memorabilia industries, with the aging Joe DiMaggio and Mickey Mantle (who died in 1999 and 1995, respectively) being some of the most sought-after autographs and Mantle lending his services to fantasy camps as well (Cramer 450; Tygiel, *Past Time* 205, 207).

While the Yankees had a comparatively low profile in the mid-to-late-1980s baseball film renaissance, they were well-represented in the subsequent '90s baseball movie boom.[10] Nineteen ninety-two's *The Babe*, of course, lent plenty of camera time to the famous pinstripes and even used a montage of sweeping helicopter shots portraying the immensity of Yankee Stadium—"the House that Ruth Built"—and its lustrous green grass, set to the soundtrack of a swelling, romantic orchestral score as its opening credits sequence, evoking the storied Yankee legacy and Ruth's role as its founding figure. Two years later, *The Scout*, which will be examined more closely later, devoted even more space to the Yankee legacy.

On the whole, however, the Yankees' place in the baseball-nostalgia trend was somewhat subdued and hampered by the harsh reality of what was actually taking place on the field in Yankee Stadium every summer. Other legacy franchises that have long and rich histories and enjoy substantial and widespread fan bases, such as the Cardinals and Dodgers, could match the nostalgia emanating from the bleachers and the grandstand with on-field success. Even comparatively less successful, smaller-market-based, or less followed franchises eclipsed the Yankees in this period, with at least one bright moment of triumph. In fact, in this period of remarkable baseball parity between the Yankees' 1981 World Series appearance and their next playoff berth in 1995, which saw twelve different teams claim the series title, it would not be an overstatement to describe the Yankees as the most consistently mediocre, certainly the most underachieving, team in the Major Leagues. They finished in second place (out of seven) in their division three times (1985, '86, and '93), third twice ('83, '84), fourth once ('87), fifth five times ('82, '88, '89, '91, '92), and in dead last once (1990). Only the moribund Cleveland Indians were more successful at *avoiding* success in this period that coincided with baseball's nostalgia boom.

But it was not just the Yankees' uncharacteristic inability to lift themselves up from baseball's ranks of the ho-hum or the postseason drought—at fourteen years (1981–95), it was the longest since Ruth joined the club in 1920—that bothered fans of the Bronx Bombers and baffled American baseball fans in general. It was the way the organization was run. Long a club of considerable means, the Yankees' financial wellbeing was common public knowledge. Steinbrenner's headline-grabbing, multimillion-dollar player signings guaranteed that. But success did not follow and many suspected that this was not despite Steinbrenner's willingness to spend money to sign the big star but because of his dependence on that practice. Former *New York Times* baseball writer Buster Olney describes what he sees as Steinbrenner's misguided handling of the club as follows:

> Steinbrenner's philosophy was to invest in stars and create bold headlines. He signed free agents . . . hired and fired managers repeatedly, filled the notebooks of reporters with incendiary quotes, and became a tabloid favorite. But it wasn't long before his impetuosity began to erode the power he had built.
>
> Steinbrenner traded no-name prospects for big-name players, strip-mining the Yankees' minor league system—a practice that ultimately inflicted serious damage on the organization, leaving the team without the needed influx of young talent. Some of the best free agents began shying away from Steinbrenner's money, reluctant

to step into the Bronx Zoo dysfunction that was the organization's most discernible trait in the 1980s. (27)

The specter of the Yankee legacy was never too far away in the stadium, with the Old Timer's Day tradition and Monument Park's prominent place on the grounds, but Americans' thirst for baseball nostalgia during the 1980s and early '90s made the heroes and success of the Yankee past loom even larger. And this of course made the current, relatively hapless version of the Bronx club seem even more absurd. While Cardinal and Dodger fans rejoiced in recent success and pondered how these new heroes might stack up with the great teams of the past, those invested in the Yankees could not help but feel left out in the cold.

This tension between the romanticized memories of a glorious, longed-for past and gallingly dissatisfying present can be felt in several of the Yankee-focused products that were part of the great proliferation of baseball-related popular culture of this period. In three popular texts specifically, a reverence for the Yankee past, a satirical critique of the Yankee present, and a fantasy of a Yankee resurgence are all present. Together, these three texts—Sparky Lyle's baseball fantasy novel, *The Year I Owned the Yankees*, the comedy film *The Scout*, and the television sitcom *Seinfeld*'s caricature of George Steinbrenner and the Yankee organization—suggest, through their satire of the present and hope for a return of the Yankee greatness of old, an optimistic belief in the viability of the American past and the possibility of reconciling it with a society that had undergone dramatic changes over the past thirty years.

SATIRICAL CRITIQUES OF STEINBRENNER

Having received significant attention for his irreverent, best-selling *The Bronx Zoo*, Sparky Lyle had probably become more famous as an author than as a Cy Young Award–winning relief pitcher. And when the '80s baseball-nostalgia boom opened up markets for baseball-related writing, Lyle the author got a chance to revive his literary career. Collaborating with baseball ghostwriter David Fisher, Lyle now tried his hand at fiction, imagining himself as owner of his old team and christening it "a baseball fantasy." The novel has its handful of devoted admirers; however, *The Year I Owned the Yankees* did not come close to achieving the success of *The Bronx Zoo*. While Lyle's earlier memoir of the tumultuous 1978 Yankee season remains a classic of baseball writing and received a reprint treatment in 2005, *The Year I Owned the Yankees* has gone out of print and is by and large forgotten. It nevertheless provides a snapshot of the state of baseball in the year of its publication, 1990, and more specifically, it gives insight into how the Yankees were perceived and used as a cultural icon by Americans in the midst of the baseball-nostalgia craze.

Taking on a slightly fictionalized persona that closely mimics the version of himself he presented to the public in *The Bronx Zoo*, Lyle begins his first-person narration with the revelation that a holding company has purchased George Steinbrenner's American Shipbuilding Company and all its subsidiaries, including the New York Yankees, and that he has been selected to be the temporary owner of the club for one year. What follows is a comedic romp through a season with Lyle behind the big desk in the Yankees front office that is vaguely reminiscent of *Catch-22* and its playful, absurdist-style humor. Like the illogical military bureaucracy that begets a carnival-like existence for a fictional World War II U.S. air squadron in Heller's famous novel, Lyle portrays organized professional baseball as a silly circus of superstar players with inflated salaries and inflated egos (a group of whom literally identify themselves "hired guns"), cartoonishly greedy and colluding owners, the first female player (brought on as a publicity stunt by desperate Braves owner Ted Turner), and high-five-induced injuries.

But at the wild center of it all are Sparky Lyle's Yankees, whose roller-coaster ride back to the World Series includes a rookie pitcher who throws a fluke perfect game in his very first Major League start, a technologically enhanced Tommy John complete with a surgically installed arm spring, a telepathic Japanese pitcher, a player whose concussion leads him to not only think he is but to somehow actually play like team star Don Mattingly, and the use of an exaggeratedly elaborate computer analysis of statistical player data to determine game strategy.[11]

A prominent motif in this comedic romp through the baseball season is Lyle the owner's obsession with not turning into "the thing [he] feared the most—The Boss," George Steinbrenner (312). But it seems that the harder Lyle tries to avoid this fate (or at least claims as much), the more his ownership tenure resembles that of Steinbrenner himself, with several moments specifically parodying some of the more notorious habits or episodes from Steinbrenner's stewardship of the Yankees. These include Steinbrenner's tendency to second-guess his manager's decisions or simply dictate decisions himself (76, 103, 149, 237), impulsively fire lower-level employees (106–7), stress out over inconsequential spring-training loses (77), trade away young prospects for established stars (94, 254), and ignore the advice of his "baseball people" (the general manager and scouts who have experience evaluating baseball talent) while manipulating them into making the trades and signing the players *he* wants (95, 209). Like "The Boss," Lyle as Yankees owner also uses the idea of a potential move to New Jersey to leverage a sweetheart deal on their Yankee Stadium lease with the city (138–39), manages to acquire three "really dependable veteran left-handed power-hitting first basemen" (166, a scenario that evokes the Yankees' illogical stockpiling of left-handed, slugging outfielders in the late 1970s), and advocates the circuslike public relations stunt of having a relief pitcher ride a motorcycle into the game, reminiscent of Steinbrenner's flair for over-the-top theatrics, perhaps especially the announcement of Billy Martin's return as manager that had the former second baseman running out onto the field as a surprise on Old Timer's Day in 1978.

These moments satirizing Steinbrenner's ownership are typically accompanied by an intentionally blustery excuse from Lyle about how he realizes that his actions look quite similar to the habits of "The Boss," but in this situation there was no other choice—an obviously transparent defense designed to ensure that readers do not miss the irony. As our narrator and main character subtly transforms into Steinbrenner, the increasing layers of silliness leave us to see the real-life events they parody with the same attitude of bemused exasperation. Lyle's parody suggests that the actual Steinbrenner's tenure belongs in an absurdist baseball fantasy novel as well.

This parody of the Steinbrenner Yankee regime is supplemented by more direct references to the excesses and mistakes of his ownership and their negative effect on the wellbeing of the organization. While much of the novel is the lighthearted fantasy that the cover's subtitle implies, lines like "Yankee fans had become alienated over the last decade... they no longer thought of the Yankees as 'their team'" (110) ring true and stand as a serious critique of Steinbrenner's ownership. The plot device of having Lyle suddenly inherit the club, in particular, provides a chance for Lyle to vent his frustration in this regard, as he provides his first outline of Steinbrenner's offences—overeagerness and impatience with players just called up from the minors, condemning a player for a single crucial error, and trading too many young prospects for aging veteran stars (17-18)—in describing how he intends to right the ship.

The event of Lyle's first taking over the team not only provides an opportunity for this relatively serious baseball talk but also gives the author a chance for some of his zaniest satire with a caricature of the reluctantly exiting Steinbrenner. Despite the recent occurrence of "the bloody anti-Steinbrenner riots" and the "Go George Go campaign," events in Lyle's imagined alternate baseball universe that he references casually (3), and despite the jubilant declaration of "V-G Day" ("Victory over George," presumably) and "Yankee Liberation Day" by the local New York City papers and a tickertape parade for Lyle as new owner (7), Steinbrenner simply refuses to relinquish his hold on the Yankee organization. When Lyle arrives at his office with security guards to expel him, The Boss tries to fire them and literally must be dragged out of his former office, leaving deep furrows in the plush carpet and shouting, "I am the boss! I am The Boss!" (12-13).[12] This diabolical caricature of a delusional Steinbrenner combines with the more serious criticisms of his baseball decisions and with the parody of the Steinbrenner era that unfolds during the course of Lyle's season as owner to yield a fairly stinging critique of the Yankee owner, only deceptively softened by the novel's over-the-top humor.

Lyle's outrageous parody of Steinbrenner's tempestuous and often illogical reign as Yankees owner exorcises the pain of the Yankee faithful through humor, a practice mirrored by *The Scout,* a Michael Ritchie–directed movie released four years later that sought to capitalize on the recent baseball-movie box-office success. Something of a financial and critical flop, like Lyle's novel, *The Scout* is still useful for what it reveals about how Americans thought about and used the Yankees in the early '90s. Having directed 1976's *The Bad News Bears,* Ritchie returned to baseball comedy with a movie about a Yankee scout with a damaged reputation, Al Percolo (played by Albert Brooks, also a cowriter), who happens upon the prospect of a lifetime, Steve Nebraska (Brendan Fraser), an expatriate American in the far reaches of rural Mexico, only to learn later that this player, who is a miracle both on the mound and behind the plate, has some debilitating psychological trauma in his past that threatens his potential to become the next great Yankee hero.

The Scout features a multitude of baseball-related celebrity cameos, including players Bret Saberhagen, Keith Hernandez, and Ozzie Smith, broadcasters Bob Costas and Tim McCarver, and frequent ballpark crooner Tony Bennett. But considering the way it pokes fun of his tenure with the Yankees, it is perhaps most significant that *The Scout* also features George Steinbrenner in a small, self-deprecating role as himself. With Steinbrenner demonstrating himself to be a good sport, the movie's satire of both the extremes of his ownership style and the dearth of recent Yankee success are sincere and on target nonetheless. For instance, when the fictional Yankee general manager, Ron Wilson, announces that while the recently signed Steve Nebraska would not be eligible for the regular season, he would be able to take the field in the event the Yankees make the World Series, the press conference erupts into raucous laughter. In this moment, baseball's contemporary reality—and the Yankees' significantly diminished status therein—makes an abrupt intrusion into this baseball fantasy. While the appearances by current or recent Major Leaguers largely register as Hollywood orchestration, this joke at the Yankees' expense would be felt as cold, hard realism for Yankee fans.

Steinbrenner's own portrayal of himself features a number of similar moments, where the self-parody rings true to his actual biography and, by putting it in a new fictional context, reminds viewers of the severity of his frustratingly unique—and, for the past dozen years, largely ineffective—ownership style. Steinbrenner lampoons his own tendency to try to "buy success" by insisting Wilson spend "whatever it takes" to sign Nebraska (an over-the-top $55 million contract, incidentally). His penchant for frothy showmanship and willingness to claim credit for any positive Yankee outcomes are skewered in the scene where the fictionalized Boss not only enthusiastically endorses Percolo's last-ditch attempt to retrieve the panicking Nebraska from the Yankee Stadium roof with a helicopter as a great public-relations stunt ("That's show biz!" he exclaims) but also insists on taking public credit for it. His intimidating personal style is similarly parodied when Percolo, clearly uncomfortable in The Boss's luxury box, perhaps even afraid of making the wrong move and getting fired, is unsure whether Steinbrenner is only kidding when he demands six dollars for the glass of champagne he just poured the scout.

The Scout's Steinbrenner is effective not only because he is played by the man himself but also because the character is written in a way that so closely adheres to a few key nodes of his personality and business practices to feel immediately familiar to baseball fans—perhaps especially Yankee fans—yet exaggerated just enough to call attention to the silliness of what it parodies.

The "Steinbrenner" character featured on the TV show *Seinfeld*, meanwhile, is a bit more of an exaggeration. One of the most iconic and influential programs on television during the 1990s, *Seinfeld* (1989–98) chronicled the daily lives of stand-up comedian "Jerry Seinfeld" (a character that the show's co-creator, the real-life Jerry Seinfeld, who portrayed the fictionalized "Jerry" and was also a stand-up comedian, based heavily on himself) and his three single, thirty-something, Manhattanite friends, Elaine Benes (played by Julia Louis-Dreyfus), George Costanza (Jason Alexander), and Cosmo Kramer (typically just called "Kramer," Michael Richards). As a self-proclaimed "show about nothing" (Armstrong 113), *Seinfeld*, like much of Jerry Seinfeld's stand-up comedy material, focused on "life's little frustrations" (59), the absurdities in the minutia of modern life, and the awkwardness or lack of logic in social conventions—things like unpleasant odors (episodes "The Smelly Car," "The Rye"), airline travel ("The Airport"), or unspoken rules about telephone etiquette ("The Finale"). Not infrequently, a sillier version of Kafka's illogical bureaucracy—often at low levels of authority or administration, like overly demanding or systematized restaurateurs (with the memorable "Soup Nazi" as perhaps the prime example) or overzealous library employees ("The Library")—serves as the source for a given episode's conflict. George Steinbrenner and his tenure over the Yankees, often popularly perceived as overly authoritarian and lacking in both sound baseball and business logic, fit into this narrative framework perfectly.

At the end of the fifth season of *Seinfeld* (1993–94), the character "Steinbrenner," an exaggerated caricature of the Yankee owner, is introduced as George's boss in the latter's new job as the team's assistant traveling secretary ("The Opposite"); but that was not the show's first barb aimed at The Boss, as earlier episodes also lampoon the Steinbrenner-run Yankee Stadium's reputation for petty authoritarianism ("The Letter") and bemoan his penchant for trading away his best young prospects ("The Smelly Car"). This frustration with the Steinbrenner ownership is echoed in the first appearance of the fictionalized caricature of the Boss. Enjoying an out-of-character personal streak of good luck in the season finale by doing exactly the opposite of what his instincts tell him, George lands an interview for his childhood dream job with the once-mighty New York Yankees. When introduced to Steinbrenner himself, the typically nonconfrontational George does "the opposite" and gives the owner (and his potential new boss) a piece of his mind in a way many Yankee fans likely envied, proclaiming: "I must say, with all due respect, I find it very hard to see the logic behind some of the moves you have made with this fine organization. In the past twenty years you have caused myself, and the city of New York, a good deal of distress, as we have watched you take our beloved Yankees and reduce them to a laughingstock, all for the glorification of your massive ego!"

This scene is one of the more memorable of the much-loved series, perhaps largely due to Steinbrenner's surprising response to George's hostile greeting: "Hire this man!" The surprise outcome is in keeping with the episode's running joke that by acting counter to his instincts, the sad-sack George's luck is changing. In fact, it is the culminating expression of that gag. But it is also our introduction to the character of Steinbrenner, or *Seinfeld*'s version of the man, in any case, who would become a series regular during the next three seasons (1994–97), making an appearance in ten episodes.[13] As a commentary on the actual Yankees owner and his tenure with the club, this first encounter, the fictionalized Steinbrenner's surprising and counterintuitive response, affirms and broadcasts the popularly held opinion of the real-life man that had accumulated as melodrama and scandal abounded off the field during the 1980s and early '90s while success on it did not: that as an owner he must be somehow inherently illogical. He either has no idea what he is doing running the club or is just plain nuts. *Seinfeld*, for its part, seemed to side with the latter option.

Seinfeld's caricature of Steinbrenner is considerably more cartoonish than the man's own impression of himself in *The Scout*. Essentially a bumbling, blustery nincompoop who wields his authority over the Yankees like a toddler with a handgun, *Seinfeld*'s Steinbrenner takes many of the actual man's tendencies—his temper, his impulsiveness, his self-obsession, his occasional sudden sentimentality, his aloofness to the experience and needs of his employees—to comedic extremes. Always shot from behind so that only the back of his impeccably coiffed steel-gray hair is seen and voiced by series co-creator Larry David, *Seinfeld*'s Steinbrenner speaks at rambling, breakneck pace and is given to many bizarre, longwinded conversational tangents in between firing directives at his cowering employees.

Perhaps as a gesture towards some of the notoriously ill-advised baseball moves the series itself frequently had evoked, the caricature of Steinbrenner is that of a fairly dimwitted, illogical, and highly suggestible man. Far from a model employee, George is frequently able to pull the wool over his easily duped boss's eyes. For instance, in one episode George leaves his car at the stadium over the course of a few days because he locked his keys in the car, causing Steinbrenner to assume he is coming into work early and burning the midnight oil and thus is immediately worthy of a promotion ("The Caddy"). In another, George is able to get away with sleeping on the job by napping under his desk. The oblivious Steinbrenner, who apparently has nothing better to do, waits in the surreptitiously napping George's office for three and a half hours hoping George will show up and help him identify a song he heard on the radio ("The Nap").[14] In a parody of Steinbrenner's penchant for making extreme, rash decisions, George is also often able to sell him on his unconventional ideas, though the results never turn out the way George planned, such as when Steinbrenner is so swayed by the suggestion to give George's secretary a raise, her salary increase leaves her earning more than George ("The Secretary"). Of the three satires of Steinbrenner in these texts from the early 1990s, *Seinfeld*'s not only made the biggest cultural impact but is likely the most extreme. Even though the Yankees would eventually return to success before the show's run ended, *Seinfeld*'s "Steinbrenner" would cement in the public consciousness the legacy of that grim decade and a half of Yankee history: the image of their owner as a delusional blowhard who was a cancer on the Yankee legacy and the possibility of future success.

Though they take on different tones and colors and did not capture the same popular attention that Seinfeld's caricature did, the satire of Steinbrenner's ownership of the Yankees in *The Year I Owned the Yankees* and *The Scout* essentially suggest the same thing the TV show does: the Yankees have been overseen by an egotistical and bafflingly illogical man. Furthermore, as in *Seinfeld*, their references to recent Yankee futility positioned next to these absurd caricatures of "The Boss" imply the causation with which many baseball fans at the time would have agreed. As Jerry Seinfeld declares in a mock deadpan after learning his nebbishy friend George is being considered for a promotion to assistant general manager for the club, "I can't understand why they haven't won a pennant in fifteen years."

REVERENCE FOR THE YANKEE PAST

While each of these three texts satirize the Steinbrenner era with a certain amount of glee, they exhibit a very different attitude towards the Yankees' storied history. While it may at times require some scrutiny to detect in these often-irreverent comedies, in each of these three Yankee-centric texts from the early '90s, a critique of Steinbrenner is contrasted with a distinct reverence for the glorious Yankee past.

Sparky Lyle's respect for Yankee history comes as a bit of a surprise. In his better-known best-seller, *The Bronx Zoo,* the irreverent Lyle comes across as at best indifferent towards the Yankee tradition, a tendency made abundantly clear in his offhand remark that he really saw no difference between pitching for the Yankees or their archrivals and occasional cultural foils, the Boston Red Sox (127). A little over ten years down the road in *The Year I Owned the Yankees,* however, Lyle not only acknowledges the Yankee legacy but writes about it in a way that, even in the wildly humorous context of the novel, comes across as earnestly respectful. This newfound respect for Yankee history is made clear from the outset, as Lyle intones in the novel's first section: "I'm not really a very sentimental person, but I really did feel something special when I put on the Yankee uniform. I guess it was pride, the feeling that I was good enough to help carry forward the tradition established by some of the greatest players in baseball history: Babe Ruth, Lou Gehrig, Joe DiMaggio, Mickey Mantle, Yogi Berra, Whitey Ford, Roger Maris. And I felt that surge of pride every time I put on that uniform. I think that pretty much all my teammates did, even Reggie Jackson. I know it sounds corny, but it's absolutely true—we felt we were special" (10).

Whether Lyle was just getting sentimental in his old age or was influenced by the swelling culture of baseball nostalgia, his reverence for the Yankees' glory years, complete with the list of the early- and midcentury bearers of the Yankee hero mantle, continues through the course of the book. Lyle peppers his wild spoof of contemporary organized baseball with the occasional rhetorical nods to the Yankee legacy—talk of "pride in the pinstripes" (11), restoring "Yankee tradition"(13), or waxing poetic about the "classic" Yankee uniform (31)—and references to both the legendary Yankee heroes rattled off in his earlier comment, as well as the other men who have contributed to and filled the ranks of the dynasties of the past, such as Casey Stengel (244), Frank Crosetti (109), Phil Rizzuto (190, 291), Moose Skowron (190), Joe Pepitone (71), and Hector Lopez (71). He even references some his "Bronx Zoo" teammates in similar ways in an effort to align that antiheroic era with the traditional iconic Yankees (71, 190, 311).[15] These tributes to the past stand in contrast to the specter of Steinbrenner evoked through both sides of the somewhat schizophrenic fictionalized Lyle: the character's critiques of The Boss's reign on one hand and his own parodic transformation into the thing he hates on the other.

When Lyle is attempting to evict the novel's caricature of Steinbrenner from the Yankee owner's office, the cartoonishly huffy Boss exclaims, "That's impossible.... I am the Yankees; the Yankees are me. Without me, there are no Yankees" (12), but one of the raisons d'être of the novel is to rebuke that proclamation as false. Lyle's many reverent references to the storied Yankee past remind us that the Yankees have been so much more than what Steinbrenner had made them into in that moment at the beginning of the 1990s. They were so much more, and as the novel's fantasy implies, wild and comedic though it may be, perhaps they could be again.

The Scout also supplements its caricature of the Steinbrenner era by paying respects to the Yankee legacy. Much of this reverence for the Yankee past is communicated through the young phenom, Steve Nebraska, who seems to be constantly in awe of the Yankee aura as he interacts with Percolo and other club officials. Like the community-college prospect Percolo scouts in the movie's prelude, Nebraska is immediately impressed when he learns whom the scout represents. "I can't believe it, you're from *the Yankees!?*" he exclaims, "That's so cool!" To which Percolo replies, "They certainly are a legendary team." It seems the idea of playing for the Yankees is what tips the scales for the hesitant Nebraska's decision to leave Mexico and try his luck in the Major Leagues, especially since Percolo emphasizes his affiliation in his formal invitation to the youngster: "Do you want to be a *New York Yankee*?"

The film supplements Nebraska's star-struck, gee-whiz attitude towards the club with a healthy smattering of iconic Yankee references. Not enamored with the current state of the club (particularly his relationship with general manager Ron Wilson), Percolo is still a Yankee through and through, frequently dropping references to legends like Ruth, Mantle, and Whitey Ford. More subtle but perhaps more influential in this regard, however, are *The Scout*'s nonverbal cues to the Yankee legacy—the numerous panoramic shots of Yankee Stadium, including many featuring the sports venue's distinctive and beloved frieze beyond the outfield.[16] These visual cues and their association with the Yankees' storied past are bolstered with verbal references to the stadium's intimidating grandeur. When Nebraska enters it for the first time, for instance, he exclaims, awestruck, *"Yankee Stadium!,"* to himself as he takes the mound and admires his surroundings.

As in *The Year I Owned the Yankees,* the references to the storied Yankee legacy in *The Scout* stand as a contrast to the ineffectiveness and melodrama of the Steinbrenner regime and convey the tension between the past and the present of the once-proud club. In particular, though *The Scout*'s frequent tonal shifts—mixing broad comedy with fairly serious-minded character drama—do not necessarily make for a great film, artistically speaking, they do create a situation in which respect for the Yankee past is allowed to exist in earnest without the wry satire of the Steinbrenner ownership undercutting its sincerity. Both the criticism of the present and the respect for the past are conveyed in full and act as opposing poles or forces that not only create an appropriate backdrop for the narrative question of whether Steve will be able to fulfill his potential as the next Yankee hero but also accurately convey the tension felt by those emotionally invested in the Yankees in this period of both on-field mediocrity and consuming fan nostalgia.

Seinfeld is a bit more complicated in terms of reverence for the Yankee past. With the notable exception of the show's polarizing series finale, *Seinfeld* portrays practically everything with *irreverence*. While *The Scout* balances broad comedy with more serious character drama and *The Year I Owe the Yankees* slips earnest comments about the state of contemporary baseball in between its cheeky parodies, the self-proclaimed "show about nothing" has a subtle irreverence that is all-consuming. Inhabiting a petty, illogical world where, as per the dictates of the show's co-creator and head writer Larry David's mantra "no hugging, no learning" (qtd. in Davis 137), the show's characters neither seek nor find any transcendent meaning in life or in each other. As such, *Seinfeld* can easily be read as absurdism in the most literary sense: narrative in which the meaningless actions of the characters gesture towards the notion of an ultimate meaninglessness to human existence (Baldick 1-2).

While the vast majority of television viewers did and do not have such philosophical considerations on their mind while laughing along with Jerry's wry observations and Kramer's non sequiturs, the experience of watching the show can at times encourage the emotional equivalent of philosophical absurdism. The *Seinfeld* characters exist in a world composed almost exclusively of life's minutia, where higher goals or pursuits are essentially nonexistent and it seems the only motivations are the basest human desires, including survival, comfort, and sensual pleasure—namely sex, good food, and entertainment (which happen to coincide with George's posited ultimate "trifecta" of pleasure: simultaneous intercourse, eating, and television ["The Blood"]). Even the occasional attempt at an act vaguely resembling selflessness is nullified by illogical and random circumstances that end up making the situation worse—often *much* worse (see "The Café" or "The Visa"). In the world of *Seinfeld,* the universe seems to discourage altruism. The end result is a somewhat jaded tone towards the idea of the sacred or the transcendent, the very opposite of reverence.

But if anything is considered sacred in the world of *Seinfeld,* it is baseball. Along with his obsession with and unflinching loyalty to the comic-book character Superman and breakfast cereal, baseball is practically sacrosanct for Jerry. A Mets fan but not a Yankee hater, Jerry eventually becomes disenchanted with his budding friendship with former Mets first baseman Keith Hernandez (played by the ballplayer himself) but remains perpetually in awe of his proximity to someone involved in the Mets' miraculous come-from-behind win in game six of the 1986 World Series ("The Boyfriend, Parts 1 and 2").

Kramer and George display similar attitudes of reverence towards the Yankees, particularly the team as it was during their childhood at the end of their dynasty in the late 1950s and early '60s. In one episode Kramer recounts his experience at a Yankees fantasy camp where he was flabbergasted to find he had punched his idol Mickey Mantle in the mouth during a brouhaha in a game. With the incident "eating [him] up inside," he seeks out Mantle to literally beg (on his knees) for his forgiveness and invites Mickey to hit him back as his penance ("The Visa"). In another episode George reveals to his fiancé his long-held desire to name his firstborn child "Seven," as "a living tribute" to the uniform number worn by Mickey Mantle, who is also *his* idol ("The Seven"). In yet another episode, the characters spot Joe DiMaggio eating (and dunking) donuts at a local coffee shop. While they are initially incredulous that DiMaggio would participate in such mundane human behavior ("The guy slept with Marilyn Monroe. He's in Dinky's Donuts?" scoffs George.), they remain transfixed watching him dunking his donuts in coffee nonetheless ("The Note"). The remarkable thing about all these incidents is the way in which the absurd actions and circumstances surrounding these references to Mantle, DiMaggio, and the golden-age Yankees do not diminish the reverence the characters have for their childhood idols. Like Jerry's willingness and ability to separate Keith Hernandez, the human being, from Keith Hernandez, the New York Met and participant in the Miracle of Game Six, baseball is somehow able to transcend the shallow world they live in, even the ways in which that shallow world touches baseball through the lives of the human players themselves.

This irrational, childlike awe the *Seinfeld* characters exhibit towards baseball is appropriate for the worldview of the show itself and also resonates with the nature of baseball-nostalgia boom more broadly. In an absurd world where traditional pathways to human transcendence—religion, relationships, the pursuit of knowledge—seem rendered inert by the illogical minutia of modern living, it is fitting that these icons from their pre-rational existence as children seem to carry ineffable and inexplicable sacredness and meaning. Since the adult world that presents itself as rational seems to fail at every turn, it makes sense that these characters would seek out tokens of their experiences before entering this irrationally rational adult world for higher meaning. It is not a coincidence that Jerry's other great loves are Superman and breakfast cereal.

And perhaps this describes the appeal of baseball in general during the great nostalgia boom of the 1980s and '90s, as the world of *Seinfeld* is nothing but an exaggerated take on our own. Many Baby Boomers—including Doris Kearns Goodwin and Gerald Early—shed their love of baseball at the same time they began challenging the ideologies of their parents' generation, seeing the game as a token of the out-of-touch American past. But as the idealism of the iconoclastic 1960s collapsed into 1970s malaise—in some respects, a jaded, antiheroic era that could be read as a real-life parallel of *Seinfeld*'s purposeless world of minutia—the appeal of their memories of the stability, innocence, and optimism of their pre-countercultural childhoods suddenly became appealing again. Like Jerry Seinfeld and George Costanza, they looked back to their childhood and found something of real value there.

In *Seinfeld* the tension between the simple, perhaps transcendent, joys of childhood that baseball—and for Kramer and especially George, the golden-age Yankees, in particular—represent and the frustrating irrationality of the "rational," "adult" world is brought to a head through the Steinbrenner character. Even before the introduction of the caricature as a recurring presence on the show, The Boss managed to crush the joy of *Seinfeld*'s Yankee fans on more than one occasion, "ruining [Kramer's] life," as the over-the-top character himself put it, with his habit of trading away all the Yankees' best young talent ("The Smelly Car") and spoiling the friends' dream seats right behind the dugout by having them evicted when Elaine refuses to remove her Orioles cap ("The Letter").[17] This tension is spelled out more clearly when George meets The Boss for the first time in his job interview and unloads the aforementioned frustrated rant that casts Steinbrenner as a buffoonish, egocentric cancer on one of the very few things George reveres.

As Steinbrenner reveals himself to be even sillier and irrational than supposed once George is on the job, the tug-of-war between George's emotional investment in the Yankee legacy and the Steinbrenner regime continues. While George obviously relishes the idea of working for the Yankees—he proudly describes himself as "a Yankee" on more than one occasion ("The Pledge Drive," "The Race," "The Abstinence"), enjoys hobnobbing with players (many actual Yankees made cameos in episodes),[18] and later namedrops them in conversations ("The Opposite," "The Chaperone," "The Pledge Drive")—he finds that actually working in the Yankees office is something of a nightmare. While most of the other employees seem well intentioned, the impulsive, bloviating Steinbrenner often makes the office an absurd, dysfunctional circus where up is down and down is up. As a preposterously illogical businessman, Steinbrenner is the very embodiment of the show's theme of the irrationality of the modern "rational" world. It is telling that after the introduction of the Steinbrenner character, a running gag on the show had other leaders of business and government—namely, Cuban dictator Fidel Castro ("The Race") and the head of the fictional Tyler Chicken corporation ("The Muffin Tops")—portrayed in the same manner as Steinbrenner: shot from behind, sitting at a large desk, and given to long, tangential soliloquies and questionable decision making, as if the man were some kind of disease permeating the modern world.

The juxtaposition of George's belief in the Yankee legacy and Steinbrenner's bumbling theatrics dramatizes the absurdity of rational modern existence intruding on and colonizing the perfect, transcendent icon from his childhood. It also broadcasts, writ large, the experience of many Americans with an emotional investment in the Yankees in the era of baseball nostalgia. (And this may well have included those who weren't necessarily Yankee fans but still chafed at the idea of such an iconic American institution and success story being tarnished so.) Steinbrenner seemed to represent everything wrong with contemporary America; and the Yankee legacy, which The Boss was perceived as holding hostage, embodied the promise of a neglected past, or, to use the words from *Field of Dreams*, "all that was once was good, and could be again."

FANTASIES OF YANKEE RESTORATION

The idea of restoring this past "good" represented by the Yankees is imagined in fairly specific ways in both *The Year I Owned the Yankees* and *The Scout*. Produced after several years of frustrating Yankee futility, both texts present fantasy scenarios of the Yankees returning to the World Series. Significantly, in each case, the Yankees are used as an icon from the American past that eventually proves to still hold meaning and viability in a rapidly changing present.

In *The Year I Owned the Yankees*, Sparky Lyle's fictionalized Yankees increasingly employ an elaborate computer program that analyzes statistical data and suggests hitting and pitching strategies, an exaggerated satire of the then-nascent practice of using computers and advanced statistics to analyze the game. Suggested by a female traveling secretary, Duke Schneider (a play on the name of Brooklyn Dodger centerfielder Duke Snider), whose influence and position with the club steadily rises, Lyle's Yankees go on a winning streak once they commit to following the computer-generated suggestions, even defying expectations and returning to the World Series for the first time in nearly a decade. When squaring off against the Dodgers in the series, however, they suddenly perform poorly, and it is discovered that Schneider, secretly a passionate Dodger fan, has sabotaged the Yankees' game strategies. Schneider and her computer are promptly fired, and the Yankees must face the Dodgers without the assistance of the technology that had helped them all season.

With his Yankees demoralized, owner Lyle rallies his team with a pep talk drawing on the storied Yankee past. He begins: "Look around this room. What do you see? . . . I'll tell you what you see. You see the New York Yankees, the greatest team in the history of baseball. And the Yankees, the real Yankees, have never needed any machines to tell them how to play the game. Did George Herman 'Babe' Ruth need a computer to tell him how to hit 714 home runs?" (310–11).[19] Lyle then proceeds to rattle off the names and iconic accomplishments of legendary Yankee heroes Gehrig, DiMaggio, Mantle, and Maris, animating his team so much that "one by one the players rose and shouted a name, a highlight from the glorious Yankee history" (311). After this audience-participation-infused pep talk, the computer-less but excited Yankees "[storm] out of the locker room" (311) and score a record-setting eleven runs in the first inning, soundly defeating the Dodgers and regaining their place at the top of the Major Leagues.

These details of Lyle's imagined return of Yankee success should be read less as a repudiation of technology—after all, the stat-crunching computer program was no small boon in these fictional Yankees' run through the season—and more as a ringing endorsement of "Yankee pride." In light of Lyle's locker-room speech, the circumstances surrounding the team's World Series triumph imply that, Steinbrenner or no Steinbrenner, what the Yankees mean to baseball and to America is not made irrelevant by the advances of time and technology. Like the iconic accomplishments of Ruth, Gehrig, DiMaggio, and Mantle, *The Year I Owned the Yankees* suggests that the Yankees and the traditional American heroism they came to embody in those glory years still have some currency, even in a world where computers, of all things, are used in baseball.

The Scout couches its fantasy of restored Yankee success in similar terms of reconciling the past and the present. As Al Percolo brings his Mexican discovery and heir-apparent to the Yankee hero tradition, Steve Nebraska, back to the States, it slowly becomes apparent that all is not right with Nebraska, who cries out for Percolo when momentarily separated in a crowded airport and experiences horrific nightmares. The Yankee front office's demand for a complete mental screening reveals what viewers have already suspected, that the flame-throwing pitcher/window-breaking slugger Nebraska has some deeply seated psychological issues, which his therapist, Dr. Aaron (a winking reference to home-run champ Hank Aaron, played by Dianne Wiest), eventually traces back to an abusive father. Although subsequent work with Dr. Aaron is reported to yield positive personal results, Nebraska's desire to play baseball declines, and the doctor speculates that the stress of baseball may be too much for his wounded psyche.

The possibility that Nebraska may have to choose between baseball and psychological health is brought to the fore when the Yankees surprisingly make the World Series, which means that contractually Nebraska is able to pitch. In fact, the organization expects him to. A psychological tug-of-war ensues between Percolo, who insists that he play and cannot understand why he would not, and Nebraska, who in a deep state of panic sheepishly moans, "I don't feel like playing tonight, Al. . . ." This culminates in the bizarre, aforementioned scenario of both men on the roof of Yankee Stadium at the beginning of the World Series with a helicopter hovering overhead. Initially adamant that Nebraska pitch no matter how he "feels"—"You're not some high school kid! You're *a Yankee!*" he insists— Percolo has a change of heart, reasoning that Nebraska's life is his own to live, which is all the phenom really needs to hear. With Nebraska ready to pitch again, this film, which has vacillated between broad comedy and character drama, suddenly switches tone again and becomes an inspiring *Rocky*-like movie as Nebraska takes the mound and performs the unheard-of feat of striking out every single batter on three straight pitches. A celebration ensues with Nebraska being carried off the field in a mass of jubilant men in pinstripes as real-life broadcasters Bob Costas and Tim McCarver wax poetic about his amazing feat.

Viewers are left to extrapolate that the Yankees will follow through and win the entire series, but in any event, the film's conclusion is not subtle:

Nebraska has brought back the long-absent Yankee glory, and he did it while overcoming his own psychological challenges. The particularity of Steve's impediment to success is significant for two reasons. First, it is a relatively new cultural entity. While the field of psychology and its application to specific individuals has obviously been around at least since the turn of the century, in 1994 the mainstream acceptance of its application was still relatively recent, with the inward-focused "Me" Decade, the 1970s, perhaps being the key moment of cultural assimilation.

In any case, the relative newness of psychology is magnified by the second reason such a focus is so remarkable: the hyper-masculine sports setting. Traditionally, particularly in earlier cultural moments before the advent of feminism challenged such gender norms, a player in Nebraska's situation would simply be encouraged to suck it up and get out there and pitch. This notion of masculinity has particular connections to the Yankee cultural icon, with the prominent legacies of the steady, stoic Gehrig who went out to play every day, no matter how he was feeling, or DiMaggio, who gracefully performed in every high-pressure situation. The male stigma towards mental illness is magnified in the masculine world of athletics, and given such a setting, *The Scout* stands out as baseball film that (sometimes) seriously addresses such issues.[20] However, while the movie has its characters pausing to contemplate whether continuing to play baseball is in Nebraska's best interest, it doesn't have them pausing long. In the end, greater sensitivity to mental health and baseball success are shown to be capable of coexisting. Abandoning his potential as the new Yankee hero would essentially be out of the question in the narrative structure of *The Scout*.

The degree to which the movie's conclusion is realistic from a psychological standpoint aside, this compromise between the relatively new paradigm of mental and emotional health and the older paradigm of masculine expectations is particularly significant in *The Scout*'s context of restoring Yankee success. As icons of midcentury American masculinity, the Yankees had always signified buckling down, taking one for the team, or putting one's emotions aside in the pursuit of victory, with Gehrig and DiMaggio being exhibits A and B. In the end, *The Scout* does not necessarily disagree, as Nebraska eventually steels himself and goes into the game to pitch expertly. The film does, however, present a somewhat nuanced portrait of the player as a specimen of masculinity. Most crucially, considerations of mental and emotional health are portrayed as not unimportant, not "sissy stuff," so to speak, even for Yankees. Thus, in this imagined scenario of the return of Yankee glory, the new hero arrives and takes his place in the succession of heroes, but he does so in a way that at least partially embraces changing American mores.

But even as the new is validated, so also is the traditional reasserted. Particularly because the team in question is the Yankees, icons of midcentury America, and not merely an "underdog" club like the California Angels, Cleveland Indians, or Chicago Cubs from other movies of this era, *The Scout*'s ending carries connotations of a reconnection with or return of the past. And since this film also focuses on a tension between contemporary psychology and traditional masculinity, the film's conclusion essentially implies that while new considerations for mental health should certainly not be ignored, the old, masculine, Yankee-hero values of consistency, loyalty, effort, and teamwork still hold meaning in the modern world. We can have our Yankee cake and eat it, too.

By offering a slightly more emotionally in-touch and vulnerable Yankee hero, *The Scout*, like *The Year I Owned the Yankees* and its accommodation of the growing role of technology, imagines a version of the Yankees reconciled with the present and ready for the new millennium. But perhaps more important, in this climate of baseball nostalgia, it suggests that the Yankees and the traditional American heroism affiliated with them, though they perhaps need to be tweaked or tempered at times, are not merely relics of the nation's past.

Though *Seinfeld* does not project a hypothetical scenario positing the Yankees' return to the World Series, it still offers a Yankee restoration fantasy through George's employment with the organization's front office. George's job with the Yankees is clearly outlined as the fulfillment of a childhood daydream from the outset, a crucial detail that builds on previous references to his Yankee fandom and is echoed in his jubilation after landing this dream job. Though George eventually settles into his typical pattern in the Yankee offices—just getting by, with no aspirations—his initial excitement and hope occasionally resurface, and the theme of dream fulfillment returns as he interacts with actual Yankees, played by themselves ("The Chaperone," "The Abstinence"), or not so subtly works in the name of the storied organization or a famous player he rubbed elbows with into a conversation with friends ("The Opposite," "The Chaperone," "The Pledge Drive," "The Mom and Pop Store"), moments that lend a certain "baseball fantasy camp" aura to his job.

In addition to the childhood-dream motif, this fantasy-job scenario is also framed from the very beginning by George's frustrated rant about Steinbrenner turning a once "fine organization" into a "laughingstock" (which ironically wins him the job), a critique that later gains credence through the buffoonish portrayal of Steinbrenner. Together, the dream-job premise and the critique that got him hired cast George's tenure with the club as a "fixing-the-Yankees" fantasy not unlike the one given to the fictionalized Sparky Lyle, or suggested when Al Percolo brings his miracle prospect back to the club.

Too defeatist—certainly with respect to the consummate sad-sack George—to allow this fantasy of Yankee redemption to come to fruition, *Seinfeld* still offers an evocative notion to its viewers through this scenario, particularly those who might share George's disgruntled but hopeful emotional investment in the Yankees.[21] Though it does not invest narrative space to spelling out an imagined scenario of the return of the Yankees, it gestures in that direction in the most personal of ways, by linking it to George's desire to change his own luck. Like the baseball-fantasy-camp trend, George's job with the Yankees connects a reverence for the baseball past to a narrative of personal redemption. In the first Yankees episode in particular, as viewers watch George, who is usually more pitiable than empathetic, somehow land a job with the team he learned to love in his youth, they can't help but identity with his ecstasy. As George joins his friends after his first day of work, dressed in a Yankees jersey and talking about his interaction with Don Mattingly, our inner child leaps in excitement.

The ties between the prospects of renewed Yankee success, George's boyhood love of the team, and his personal redemption created by the employment scenario bring *Seinfeld*'s gesture towards a Yankee-return fantasy into the same territory as *The Year I Owned the Yankees* and *The Scout*: the belief in the past's viability in a more cynical present. Just as the Yankees and all they stand for as icons of midcentury America are shown to retain value in a world where computer technology shapes our decisions and being a man can sometimes mean processing one's daddy issues with the help of a therapist, it is George's simple childhood-born passion for and loyalty to that iconic Bronx-based team that becomes the key to penetrating the irrationality of the "rational," "adult" world and land George his first steady job of the series. In these narratives of imagined Yankee redemption, it is the simplicity of our childhoods and America's past that win out, reasserting their viability to a modern world as the Yanks reassert themselves on the field.

Through their narrative fantasies of a Yankee return, these texts from the early to mid-1990s indicate the investment in the past that is present in the baseball-nostalgia trend as a whole. While acknowledging that the current state of baseball and the Yankees—and perhaps through those national symbols, the nation as a whole—has changed in many ways, these texts imply that a reconciliation with the past is possible and desirable. Notably, the appeals to the Yankee past in these texts are different in tone from the way that past was evoked in the brief period of Yankee resurgence in the late '70s—the "Bronx Zoo" era. In the '70s, the Yankee legacy was primarily used as a way to cast the present in a cynical light. The failure of the dysfunctional but successful clubs—marked by the public feuding of Billy Martin, Reggie Jackson, and Thurman Munson—to behave like "real Yankees" symbolized to many like Steve Jacobson a loss of national innocence that seemed irretrievable. For better or worse, the old all-American heroism that the classic Yankees embodied felt dead.

But in the era of baseball nostalgia, the Yankee past is evoked in much more optimistic ways. Though the present, as embodied in the Steinbrenner ownership, seemed far removed from the past in some ways, that past was not turned to with a sense of loss or cynicism but with reverence and awe. As suggested by the fantasies of a return of Yankee glory found in Lyle's novel, *The Scout*, and to some degree *Seinfeld*, in the new culture of baseball nostalgia, the past was far from irretrievable but was close by, invigorating the present with its eternal promise. These texts utilize the Yankee past in a way that implies not schism but reconciliation, the notion that perhaps the iconic Yankees of the Depression, WWII, and postwar eras—and the kind of heroism and national optimism associated with them—still had relevance, that all that "once was good" perhaps "could be again."

A REAL-LIFE YANKEE RESURGENCE

While optimistic in their faith in the Yankee past, these three texts do not neglect the tension between that rosy nostalgia and the less-than-ideal reality of the Steinbrenner-dominated present. But it was not just Yankee fans who had to deal with such tension during this period of baseball romanticism. As Tygiel observes, "ironically, the new interest in baseball coincided with a controversial transformation of the baseball industry" (*Past Time* 202). This transformation Tygiel cites is the economic change in the game brought on by free agency. Not only did the average Major League salary jump from $45,000 in 1975 to $144,000 in '81 and $891,000 in '91 (Rader, *Baseball* 194), the power struggle between the players and ownership that free agency invited also led to work stoppages in 1981, '85, and '91. Both trends were alienating to fans.

This changing economy helped beget a new paradigm for identity and public persona in American athletes that Michael Weinreb describes as "sports as cult of personality" (282). Increasingly in the 1980s, many athletes picked up where Joe Namath and Reggie Jackson left off, adopting a public persona that bore the stylistic influence of MTV and an emerging hip hop culture and was characterized by aimless, apolitical rebelliousness (perhaps a vestige of the 1960s counterculture) added to egocentric, self-promotional, self-indulgent tendencies (shades of the "Me" Decade) and, at times, a frankly capitalistic impulse (perhaps an influence of the contemporary, financially deregulated, get-rich-quick 1980s). Typified by college football's Brian Bosworth and the NFL's Lawrence Taylor and Jim McMahon, this new way of being was less influential in the more tradition-bound baseball—where the influence of the old heroic model consistent with the Gehrig-DiMaggio Yankee archetype still had considerable influence—than it was in pro or college football and basketball. But it existed on the fringes of baseball, too, perhaps coming to the fore most palpably in the so-called Pittsburgh Drug Trials of 1985 that implicated several players as clients of a cocaine ring.

As such, this youth-centric cultural trend of indulgence and self-promotion in athletes may have been something of a two-edged sword in its effect on baseball nostalgists, both posing a threat as a harbinger of the horrible potential future and acting as evidence for the idea among baseball romanticists that the national pastime was intrinsically special among American sports, particularly for the way it was intertwined with tradition. For many Americans in the 1980s and early '90s, baseball was different. Or at least it *should* be, they thought.

With this in mind, one should perhaps not be surprised that the players' strike of 1994 was received as such a coup by fans. While attendance generally continued to climb and cultural products lauding baseball for its transcendence as an American institution continued to proliferate despite fan disenchantment with the perceived greed of current players throughout the '80s and early '90s, by the time yet another strike that began in August 1994 persisted to the point that the World Series was canceled, fans had had enough. Nostalgia had perhaps facilitated an increase in patience with the game they loved through previous strikes, a drug scandal, and increasing player salaries. But it also fostered a rose-tinted ideal of what baseball should be, and a World Series cancellation brought on by striking millionaire ballplayers clearly violated this ideal for many Americans. The president of the Unites States himself, Bill Clinton, talked about "long-term damage to baseball," and in retrospect baseball historian John Thorn laments that he had "never encountered such bitterness," with friends swearing they "would never watch another baseball game, that they no longer cared about the game" (qtd. in *Baseball: The Tenth Inning*). When the Major Leagues resumed play in April 1995, many fans were reluctant to return.

In a certain sense, the post-strike backlash can be read as perhaps the ultimate expression of the baseball romanticism and nostalgia that had been growing since Baby Boomers began to return to ballparks in the late 1970s. It traumatized the country so much because baseball had come to signify so much. And like a wronged but still-smitten lover, America was anxious to be wooed again (though many swore to the contrary). And much to the delight of longsuffering Yankee fans, the Bronx Bombers would play a significant role in America's great re-enchantment with baseball over the second half of the 1990s.

A number of factors are often pointed to as being instrumental in thawing Americans' frosty feelings towards organized baseball after the strike, including Oriole shortstop Cal Ripken breaking Lou Gehrig's 2,130 consecutive-game streak in September 1995, the emergence of the once-moribund Cleveland Indians as World Series contenders, the opening of several nostalgia-focused "retro" ballparks, and the addition of two new expansion teams in Tampa, Florida, and Phoenix, Arizona, in 1998. But the biggest factor in Americans taking interest in baseball again was a chase for a new single-season home-run record between Mark McGwire of the Cardinals and the Cubs' Sammy Sosa. While this period has now been shadowed by revelations that the parties involved had likely been using banned performance-enhancing drugs, in 1998 America watched with rapt attention as McGwire and Sosa battled to see who could be the first to break Yankee Roger Maris's high-water mark of sixty-one home runs in 1961.

While these factors—most of them catering to fan nostalgia—certainly played a part in wooing Americans back to baseball, the role of the New York Yankees should not be neglected. Baseball's return in 1995 coincided with the Yankees' first playoff berth in fifteen years, and over the next five years, they would claim four World Series titles, earning the right to be called a dynasty once again. The team so many Americans loved and so many other Americans loved to hate was back.

True to precedent, the return of this kind of Yankee dominance eventually invited a backlash, and Yankee haters, their passions lulled into dormancy by a decade and a half of mediocrity, began to reemerge as the championship banners in the Bronx continued to rise. In 1999, for instance, Dean Chadwin published a Marxist-influenced, semi-academic, book-length critique of the Yankees as baseball's hegemonic tyrants. His tome includes an account of a telling incident in Kansas City, where a local radio station sponsored a "Share the Wealth Night" when the Yankees came to town to play the relatively cash-strapped Royals. Campaigning for some form of revenue sharing among Major League teams, Royals fans in the bleachers wore "Share the Wealth" T-shirts, chanted that slogan, and threw dollar bills at Yankee outfielders, and after exiting in the third inning, left skeletons in their seats with signs reading, "Small Markets Are Dying" (Chadwin 253–54). Such actions, reminiscent of similar fan protests during the early days of free agency in the "Bronx Zoo" era, along with talk of plutocracy and economic disparity in baseball, were fairly old-hat for the Yankees and would only increase after the turn of the millennium.

However, by and large, the public response to the return of Yankee success, first in 1996 and then in 1998, when the club set a new American League record by winning 114 games en route to their second World Series win in three years, was overwhelmingly positive. Composed of many homegrown prospects signed in the early 1990s while Steinbrenner's influence over the club was limited due to his eventually rescinded ban from the game, the Yankees of the late 1990s looked and played differently from the Yankee teams of the recent past. With less emphasis on splashy free-agent signings and with the influence of one steady manager, Joe Torre, rather than a revolving door of managers, these Yankees got along and played as a team in a way the "Bronx Zoo" teams of the late '70s or any Yankee club since then never did. Around Yankee Stadium they were received as something of a collective messiah. But even baseball fans who traditionally disliked the Yankees seemed to like this club, people like *Washington Post* baseball writer Thomas Boswell, who "grew up hating the Yankees" but was still willing to state that in the late 1990s, "because of scrappy smart players . . . because of the fact that they showed people how you play team baseball . . . [the Yankees] were a wonderful team to watch" (qtd. in *Baseball: The Tenth Inning*).

What is most striking, however, is how much the rhetoric praising these Yankees is invested in the idea of their being a second coming of the iconic, golden-age Yankees. For instance, a piece in the *New York Observer* after the 1998 World Series win hails manager Torre for his embodiment of the heroic masculine values affiliated with those classic Yankees, gushing, "It is equally easy to appreciate his style, so out of sync with the age of tawdry self-absorption and spinelessness posing as empathy. He has achieved [this victory] without kicking and screaming, without back-page controversies, and, most of all, without calling attention to himself. . . . Mr. Torre has performed the remarkable achievement of putting a new finish on a legacy that had been tarnished by one man's tackiness, that man being George Steinbrenner. . . . Joe Torre is our antidote to the frauds, liars and self-promoters who have defined the decade" (qtd. in Chadwin 12). With references to both the Yankee legacy and a personal style reminiscent of Gehrig and DiMaggio, this piece is clearly interested in casting Torre and his late-1990s Yankees as the spiritual successors to those iconic teams.

An article by the *New York Post*'s George Willis, meanwhile, supplements these appeals to the Yankees as icon of heroic American masculinity by renewing the idea of the team as a national emblem:

> If any team can truly represent the multi-ethnic makeup of New York, it is these Yankees, who are an international blend of cultures that formed one of the greatest teams in the history of baseball.

> ... Together they worked in harmony to win a World Series that most had given them halfway through the season. There were no egos, no prejudices, no bickering. No jealousy, no fights, no backstabbing. Just a team that bonded into one proud unit to wear the pinstripes.
>
> ... The Yankees have always been the world's most famous baseball team, primarily because of the franchise's storied history. But today they represent so much more.
>
> ... Panama. Japan. Australia. Venezuela. Cuba. Puerto Rico, and from Washington to Texas to Florida. The Yankees aren't just New York or America's team. They are the world's team. (qtd. in Chadwin 170)

While the concept of "multiculturalism" that Willis appeals to here may be relatively new, it is filtered through the ideology of the American dream—the idea of a nation composed of immigrants from far-flung places, working hard to create success and coalescing into a unified, if diverse people. The comment about players bonding "into one proud unit to wear the pinstripes," in particular, seems to use the Yankees as a metaphor for the American melting pot. Thus, though Willis mentions the Yankees as being representative of New York on one hand and "the world" on the other, both these comparisons support the one positioned between them: the reinvigoration of the club's traditional role as synecdoche for the American nation. Some of the terms Willis uses or geographic places he mentions may sound new, but the essence of this celebration of the "new" New York Yankees could have been written in 1942.

Inasmuch as the renewed Yankee dynasty of the late 1990s was characterized as a team befitting the legacy of the club's storied past, they acted as a fulfillment of the nostalgic longing expressed earlier in that decade. It was as if Sparky Lyle, Al Percolo, and George Costanza had collectively dreamed them up.

Like the fantasies of Yankee renewal in *The Year I Owned the Yankees* and *The Scout,* the late-1990s Yankees were not a pure throwback but a hybrid of old and new. As indicated by Willis's toast to the club, the Joe Torre–era Yankees, like every other Major League club, were a multicultural entity; one could even describe them as "globalized." This is a contrast to the postwar

Yankees, whose commitment to tradition eventually left them out of step with a major portion of a desegregating country. It is fitting that, in addition to manager Joe Torre, the Yankee heralded as the torchbearer of the club's legacy in the late '90s was Derek Jeter, a biracial, workaday shortstop who was comfortable with the increased media presence in the game. Like DiMaggio, he was known for his clutch play. Like Gehrig, he would eventually set a mark for consistency (first Yankee to collect 3,000 hits). And like Mantle, he was handsome and charming enough to have a devoted following of teenage girls.[22] He seemed to embody things both old and new and thus was a perfect representative for the restored Yankee greatness in the late '90s.

Jeter may also be a good on-field choice to reflect the baseball-nostalgia movement in general. For while they did look towards the past with fondness, generally speaking, the baseball nostalgists were far from luddite archconservatives wishing to turn back the clock as much as possible.

Certainly, baseball nostalgia of the 1980s and '90s constitutes part of a broader cultural shift towards reassessing the break with the past advocated and to varying degrees implemented in American society, politics, and culture during the 1960s and '70s. Politically, the formation of the New Right helped precipitate momentum towards policies that cut against the grain of much of the liberalization and counterculture-inspired movements of the previous two decades, with such relatively conservative trends including the failure of the Equal Rights Amendment, financial deregulation, reduction of federally sponsored social programs, a hardline stance against recreational drug use, the reinvigoration of the Cold War after a period of detente, and welfare reform. President Ronald Reagan, in particular, often used rhetoric and crafted a public persona based on the idea of returning to postwar American confidence. It is no coincidence that the baseball-nostalgia boom was taking place in such a political climate. Both seek to animate the present by turning to the past.

However, it would be a mistake to conflate baseball nostalgia with this rightward political shift of the period or with President Reagan and the cult of personality surrounding him specifically. As Tygiel observes, "The idealization of baseball in the 1980s might easily be interpreted as a reflection of the era of Ronald Reagan, a reassertion of traditional verities and values of a conservative decade. But remnants of the 1960s countercultural thinking ran through much of the fan-based reinvention of baseball" (*Past Time* 219). Rather than interpreting the baseball-nostalgia boom, which was decidedly mixed in terms of political ideology and makeup, as an appendage of Reagan's conservative revolution, perhaps American politics of this era and the baseball-nostalgia boom should be seen as two different manifestations of the same broader cultural change.[23] Following the perspective of Landon Y. Jones, the baseball-nostalgia boom and all the past-focused cultural trends from the end of the 1970s through the '90s might best be considered as originating in and being shaped by the advancing life cycle of the large Baby Boomer generational cohort (Jones 79), who began settling down and raising their own children during this period. As Tygiel suggests, baseball—the obsession of their pre-countercultural youth—served as a lightning rod for many of these Baby Boomers' "symbolic homecoming" to a life of home and family after "sowing their wild oats," so to speak.

As the most visible and successful team during the period of the Baby Boomers' youth, the Yankees figured prominently in this homecoming. And as Yankee nostalgia already examined here suggests—be it the Lyle's computer-assisted Yankees, *The Scout*'s therapy-aided Steve Nebraska, or love poured out for the biracial Derek Jeter and his melting-pot, late-1990s version of the club—the cultural subtext of desires for a Yankee resurgence was never a complete break with the present and return to the past, just as this was not the case for the baseball-nostalgia movement in general. While both a renewed faith in heroes and reinvigorated national pride and optimism seem to be a subtext of both the longing for and celebration of the return of the Yankees, what these cultural voices are really seeking is not a cultural rewind so much as a hybridization, of sorts, of what they saw as the best aspects of pre-1960s America and post-1960s America, a *reconciliation* of the past and present.

This theme of reconciliation is perhaps best expressed by the small but pithy role the Yankees have in what may be the quintessential text of nostalgic baseball romanticism: *Field of Dreams*. In the movie's introductory voiceover narration, main character Ray Kinsella explains that his father, a former minor leaguer with whom he fought about everything, was a Yankee fan, "so of course [Ray] rooted for Brooklyn." But this reference to the midcentury Yankees-Dodgers rivalry does more than just suggest the tendency of this father and son to bicker. As his relationship with his father is intentionally portrayed as the prototypical World War II generation/Baby Boomer schism, Ray effectively represents his entire generation.[24] His father, meanwhile, is a stand-in for the previous one, the generation that lived through the Depression, World War II, and postwar anticommunism—men who witnessed the creation of the great Yankee legacy, might have boyish memories of Ruth, would have worshipped Gehrig and DiMaggio as adolescents and young men, and would have absorbed the cultural values those Yankees came to be an emblem of: heroic masculinity, the promise of the American dream, and a narrative of national success and greatness.

As a Dodger fan and prototypical baby boomer, Ray of course sees his father's team and his father's values as flawed and tyrannical and favors the more progressive, populist baseball symbol. In the baseball loyalties of father and son is coded the great generational conflict of the late-1960s schism that the magical baseball field of the title is meant to heal. While not abandoning certain hippie values, through the field and the ghosts of past Major Leaguers who come to play there, Ray comes to reassess his father and the life he lived, and finds value and goodness where before he only found a reason to rebel and run away.

At the movie's emotional conclusion, the ghost of Ray's father appears as his younger baseball-playing self and the two men play a game of catch. It is no coincidence that he is outfitted in a Yankee uniform, an icon of the pre-1960s American past. The Yankees are Ray's father's team, but in a symbolic, cultural sense, they play the role of the team of every Baby Boomer's father. And the act of playing catch betokens a reconciliation with these fathers, with their values that were present in their childhood before they cast off baseball as a symbol of the out-of-touch American past as Ray Kinsella did.

While perhaps not willing to embrace this past wholesale, in the 1980s and '90s many of Ray's generation began, like him, to reassess the past and their previous desire for a clean break with it as expressed in the '60s counterculture. Specifics certainly vary from case to case, but generally the decades of the '80s and '90s found Americans tempering the headlong plunge into junking the ideologies of the past. Perhaps most commonly, like Ray Kinsella, many Baby Boomers began to find themselves living the kinds of lives they swore they would never live in the days of their iconoclastic youth—the kinds of lives their parents lived, holding down steady, full-time jobs and raising children of their own. It was not exactly the same, necessarily, but still similar enough for them to look back towards the lives of their parents, of the entire World War II generation, and maybe even those who came before them and find value and relevancy there.

Similarly, the return of the Yankees as imagined in *The Year I Owned the Yankees, The Scout,* and *Seinfeld* and the literal return of the team to success in the Joe Torre era both speak to a turn to and reconciliation with the pre-1960s past in the '80s and '90s. In this era the cultural meaning of the Yankees remained the same, but as an icon they were used in a new way, as a symbol of a lost American past that might be worth reclaiming. For an entire generation, they became a symbol of the America of their parents, an America and a past that for the first time in a long while—perhaps since they were children—seemed inviting and valuable once again.

Epilogue
TOWARD A NEW MILLENNIUM

With high school graduation and a year of college under my belt, I was mercifully living out of the country when the Yankees followed their dominant 1998 season with two more World Series wins in 1999 and 2000.[1] Upon my return, however, my older brother once again abetted my Yankee hatred. His relocation to the Boston area rekindled my family's association with the Red Sox, which was a fortunate turn of events. For even though my disdain for the Yankees was as strong as ever, my Dodgers' rivalry with them had been declining since the 1981 World Series. The animosity between the Bronx Bombers and the Red Sox, however, was again rapidly reaching fever pitch, and Christmas of 2002 brought me an exciting gift acquired on my brother's most recent outing to Fenway Park: a "Yankees Suck" T-shirt.

Proudly taking my new shirt back to school with me, I was the envy of a few friends and roommates, and would get the occasional nod and approving comment on campus. However, one day I happened to be wearing that shirt while shopping at the beloved Macey's grocery store in Provo, Utah, and the young woman ringing me up took exception. "I don't like your shirt," she pointedly informed me. "I mean, how could you hate the Yankees? They're cute *and* they're good."

"Well," I thought, "it's hard to reason against that . . ."

| | |

As the sympathetic nods on campus and upset grocery clerk suggest, the return of the Yankee dynasty in the late 1990s and early 2000s has helped guarantee that the team remain as divisive as ever. And while our reasons for loving or hating the pinstriped ball club are still almost always tied to geography, family, or perhaps—ahem—*cuteness,* rather than our political allegiance to conservatism, progressivism, or the Republican or Democratic Parties, the way both Yankee lovers and Yankee haters frame their support or disdain for the team still speaks, like the debates that shape one's political leanings, to the different sides to or perspectives on success, wealth, power, and tradition.

In that sense the more things change, the more they stay the same; and Americans will always have a reason to love or hate the Yankees. And while the ever-shifting cultural milieu will always add new wrinkles to the way the Yankees are used as cultural symbols and the unspoken meanings they carry, the legacy of the key texts and figures from the 1920s through the team's decline in the late 1960s will always be the foundation of the Yankees' iconic cultural meaning.

Just as this period loomed large in the American imagination during the team's brief but uncharacteristic return to success in the late 1970s, and perhaps even more so during the nostalgic period leading up to their renewed glory in the second half of the 1990s, it continues to do so today. In the same way that this period of American history continues to shape our current political debates, the legacy of the midcentury Yankees remains the foundation on which our current concept of the ball club is based, even if many Americans now may be less familiar with past popular perceptions of

Ruth, Gehrig, DiMaggio, and Mantle, or texts like *The Pride of the Yankees, The Old Man and the Sea, Damn Yankees,* or *Ball Four.*

This was clear when displays of local civic pride and patriotism coalesced around the Yankees in the wake of the 9/11 terrorist attacks on New York City, evoking their all-American nationalist associations in texts like *The Pride of the Yankees* and *Lucky to Be a Yankee.* It was clear in the conversations that recently took place surrounding the retirement of contemporary stars Mariano Rivera (Yankee relief pitcher, 1995–2013) and Derek Jeter (retired in 2014), weighing the question of whether they are worthy of the canon of great Yankee heroes. And it was clear in 2003 and 2004, when fans of those longtime Yankee rivals, the Boston Red Sox, took a page from both Brooklyn Dodger fans and Douglass Wallop in rechristening the Yankees "The Evil Empire" and associating them with the villains in the mythic *Star Wars* movie franchise en route to finally beating their nemeses and breaking "the Curse of the Bambino."

Though sometimes overshadowed by the figure of Steinbrenner or slightly reshaped by cultural changes both within baseball and the nation at large, the midcentury development of the Yankees as a cultural icon embodying many of that era's prominent American values, including the American dream, heroic masculinity, and a narrative of national triumph remains a foundational part of the Yankees' ever-shifting and growing cultural meaning. And so does the critical, oppositional perspective on the icon that developed alongside it and what it implied in its disdain for or critique of the Bronx Bombers—that America was, could be, and *should* be things other than what the Yankees represented.

Though baseball may have lost some of its cultural clout to professional and collegiate football and basketball and other sports, the New York Yankees remain as controversial now as they were in the mid-1950s. And in an increasingly globalized world with an increasingly globalized game of baseball, the controversy over the Yankees is no longer confined to the United States of America. As tenured sportswriter George Vecsey observed after noticing a proliferation of Yankee ball caps while traveling abroad in the wake of the Yanks' 1996 World Series win, the team from the Bronx is still "fulfilling the great polar needs of sport. Quite like America itself, the Yankees [are] either classic champions, envied and admired all over the world, or else they [are] haughty oppressors, resented by the downtrodden masses" (*Baseball* 151).

NOTES

INTRODUCTION

1. While studies of the cultural meaning of individual athletes or sporting events have proliferated in recent years, academic analyses of the meaning of sports teams are still too small in number. The few examples include the work of Juffer, Prince, Borer, and Morris.

2. While Barthes himself never used the term "icon" to describe an entity that embodies cultural narratives or ideologies, the word was used in this sense by Charles Sanders Pierce, an American philosopher and language theorist (170). Furthermore, the popular use of the term "icon" perhaps most closely communicates Barthes's theories of cultural symbolism in laymen's terms.

3. As this study seeks to analyze the various representations of the Yankees by a variety of mass-media texts within the context of baseball history as well as a broader American cultural history, it somewhat loosely follows the interdisciplinary methodological approach of Daniel Nathan in his cultural history of another important baseball icon, the 1919 "Black Sox" scandal.

For an academic discussion about the relationship between the institution of Major League Baseball, its history, and baseball-related popular culture and fiction, see David McGimpsey (1–26). McGimpsey astutely insists that baseball fiction is intrinsically linked with the history and present of Major League Baseball (26), but I would argue that it is more useful to think not about a binary of baseball history and historically influenced baseball fiction but of a continuum, a baseball narrative tradition that includes both mutually influential history and fiction as well as the many stories and texts that land somewhere in between those poles.

1. "TO BE YOUNG AND A YANKEE"

1. In reality, Ruppert purchased the Yankees with a partner, Colonel Tillinghast L'Hommedieu Huston, an army engineer captain and veteran of the Spanish-American War. Huston also served in France during World War I and gained the rank of lieutenant colonel. While Colonel Ruppert (whose title was granted based on his service in the National Guard) was the major source of funding, Huston, a military hero, was frequently the public face of the partnership in the early days of their co-ownership (Steinberg and Spatz, *Colonel and Hug* 192). However, Ruppert bought out Huston in the spring of 1923, and the military man retired, leaving the Yankees with only one colonel, whose presence on the business end of the team was a constant throughout the rest of the 1920s and '30s.

2. Ruth received the "Babe" nickname during his first year in the minor leagues. It was intended to imply his youthful naïveté—"young, raw, crude, without sophistication," as biographer Robert W. Creamer puts it (*Babe* 65).

3. In 1904 the World Series was still in its infancy (1903 was the first time it was played) and did not enjoy the stature and authority it now does. McGraw and the Giants decided to boycott the 1904 series, refusing to play the champions of a league they deemed inferior. This is ironic considering McGraw's later struggles to defeat the American League winners: his overall World Series record is three wins to six losses.

4. Eric Rolfe Greenberg's 1983 novel *The Celebrant* provides a fictional account of such immigrant fandom with the story of Jackie Kapinski and his brother Eli, who immigrated with their Jewish family to New York as young boys and became fast devotees of baseball and the New York Giants.

5. A side note: many sportswriters in other American cities bemoaned these consecutive all–New York World Series and used the events as occasion to complain about the preeminent role the Big Apple took for itself in American culture and society in general (Steinberg and Spatz, *Colonel and Hug* 201, 205, 212–13).

6. Such was the Yankees' dominance in the first half of the 1950s that the 1954 Cleveland Indians had to win 111 games, breaking the American League record, to beat a very good Yankee team that won a not record-breaking but still impressive 103 games.

7. Among the speculated reasons for the change were technological improvements in baseball manufacturing, which allowed the woolen string that makes up a baseball to be wound tighter. Also influential was a rule change that hampered pitchers: the banning of "doctoring" the ball with spit (the "spitball") or other substances that caused it to move erratically when thrown. This rule was accompanied by an increase in the rate of replacing game balls to curtail circumvention of the new anti-doctoring rules, a change that also resulted in whiter, cleaner balls that were easier to see and hit.

All these factors considered, however, should not downplay the influence that Ruth's power-focused batting style and talent had on his own high home-run totals as well as on those who followed his approach. For a pithy discussion of these factors, see Steinberg and Spatz's *The Colonel and Hug* (133–34).

8. "Home Run" Baker's well-known nickname is actually somewhat misleading. Earned when he hit two game-tying home runs in the 1911 World Series (each came while facing pitchers now in the Baseball Hall of Fame, Rube Marquard and the legendary Christy Mathewson), Baker's nickname should always be seen in the context of the "dead-ball" era in which he played. While he led the Major Leagues in home runs from 1911 to 1914, he never hit more than twelve home runs in a season, a far cry from the totals Ruth and others would amass in the following decade.

9. In particular, the *New York Daily News,* a popular tabloid founded in 1919 that still enjoys prominent circulation today, benefitted financially from its in-depth, almost daily coverage of Ruth (Steinberg and Spatz, *Colonel and Hug* 214).

10. As if outdoing the old Polo Grounds in terms of size and seating capacity were not enough, after Yankee Stadium's opening-day debut, the *New York Times* commented on the ease of departure from the new park, noting that it "was emptied yesterday . . . in quicker time than the Polo Grounds ever was" (qtd. in Weintraub, *House that Ruth Built* 32).

11. Robert Weintraub credits sportswriter Fred Lieb with inventing the nickname in light of the stadium's short fence in right field and Ruth's left-handed power-hitting ability (*House that Ruth Built* 22).

2. "LET ME TELL YOU ABOUT HEROES"

1. Erickson suggests that such attempts to entice female viewers were common in the first half of the twentieth century, when "'popular elements' referred to those qualities which would entice women moviegoers who—as all males told themselves back then—just hated baseball" (12). But *The Pride of the Yankees* may have been the first time such efforts actually succeeded.

Additionally, the inclusion of a Walt Disney comedic cartoon featurette, "How to Play Baseball," starring the hapless Goofy character in the movie's first theatrical run further points towards the producers' effort to make the film appealing to a broad audience, including young children. Bosley Crowther's contemporary *New York Times* review of the film suggests that this cartoon was made at the special request of Sam Goldwyn himself.

2. The nominations included best picture, Gary Cooper for best actor, Teresa Wright for best actress, art direction, cinematography, special effects, score, sound recording, screenplay, and story (an awards category that no longer exists).

3. In fact, the only other baseball feature film to include a Major League team's name in the title is 1994's *Angels in the Outfield*, about a fictionalized version of the California Angels (now "Los Angeles Angels of Anaheim"). But even in this case, it should be noted that this film is a remake of the identically titled 1950 film that was about a fictional version of the Pittsburgh Pirates who were aided by heavenly beings, to whom the title referred. (The "Angels" nickname still only belonged to Los Angeles's Pacific Coast League franchise at the time.) Thus, even in the 1994 film, the more general use of the word "angel" has greater importance than its more specific meaning as a proper noun in Major League Baseball.

4. The persistence of the New Englander denotation for the word Yankee is, of course, a great irony to the modern baseball fan, as the Yankees have long been fierce rivals of the Boston Red Sox, the team that draws fan support throughout New England.

5. The film version of this speech largely holds true to what Gehrig actually said, with a few variations. In addition to summarizing some passages for the purpose of brevity, including statements about past and present members of the Yankee organization, the movie version places the famous "luckiest man" sentence at the end of the speech, rather than at the beginning, where Gehrig actually pronounced it. This was likely done to enhance the drama, making the "luckiest man" quote the last spoken words in the film.

6. Lazzeri did not actually debut with the Yankees until 1926, and Koenig not until 1925; thus, the two of them were not in fact part of the team during Gehrig's rookie season in 1923. Having these two players present, however, not only allowed the filmmakers to condense and simplify history for a popular audience, but it emphasizes the pressure Lou felt to "measure up" to the established standard of Yankee greatness.

7. For example, when Teresa Wright died in 2005, her name was read along with former Yankees who had also passed on that year at the annual Yankees "Old Timers" game ("Teresa Wright," Internet Movie Database). This close link between the franchise and the film is further evidenced by the way many viewers cite their Yankee fandom (or lack thereof) as influencing their reception of the film, as Internet Movie Database website user "tizzo" asserts, "Being a lifelong Yankee fan, this movie is an all-time favorite." The Rotten Tomatoes film website user "halorocker44," meanwhile, explains, "As much as I dislike the Yankees, Gary Cooper's performance is so good even someone like me can't ignore this film's greatness."

8. The actual sick boy involved in this legendary tale was named Johnny Sylvester. During the 1926 World Series, his father had obtained some baseballs autographed by the Yankees and their opponents the Cardinals, as well as a promise that Ruth would hit a home run to cheer up his sick son (Creamer, *Babe* 327).

9. In addition to the fact that the events related to Gehrig and the sick boy presented in *The Pride of the Yankees* are a complete fabrication, this sequence also mis-

represents Ruth as a man. Despite what would be perceived as his many flaws—notably his insatiable physical appetites for food and sex that Gehrig did not share—many biographers point out that the boisterous Ruth was often quite generous and had a particular soft spot for children, with whom he had great rapport and often savored spending time (Creamer, *Babe* 332–34).

10. In *The Stratton Story* Stewart plays a ballplayer who loses his right leg in an accident, only to make a heroic comeback as a minor-league pitcher. Like *The Pride of the Yankees,* this film also creates dramatic tension with the threat that the baseball hero is cheating on his wife. This time the reassuring revelation is that the protagonist was secretly taking dancing lessons after ballgames as a special gift to his wife.

11. This is ironic because, according to the Yankees' 1920s third baseman Joe Dugan, it was Ruth who once took a bite out of a straw hat. Creamer quotes Dugan, "He was an animal. He ate a hat once. He did. A straw hat. Took a bite out of it and ate it" (*Babe* 330).

12. Bill Dickey would go on to play himself and serve as embodiment of the tradition of Yankee excellence in a cameo in Sam Wood's *The Stratton Story.*

13. DiMaggio's presence is notably missing from the late-1930s Yankees in *The Pride of the Yankees.* Film and baseball historians have not reported on whether he was approached to appear in the film, but it is possible that he was left out of the movie entirely (his name is not even mentioned a single time) out of fear that the presence of "The Yankee Clipper," who had recently enraptured the nation with his fifty-six-game hitting streak in 1941, would eclipse the Hollywood Gehrig as much as he did the real one. In any case, aside from the negative public reaction to DiMaggio's contract battle against the parsimonious general manager Ed Barrow in 1938, the public perception of DiMaggio, as well as his actual clubhouse demeanor, would have fit right in with the focused, no-nonsense portrayal of the late-1930s Yankees in Wood's film (*Baseball in '41* 12–13; Cramer 117–19, 123–27).

14. Lou Gehrig's higher degree of assimilation relative to his parents is far from a Hollywood fabrication. In fact, Eig suggests that Mrs. Gehrig had designs on the Americanization of her son while he was still in infancy. His birth certificate indicates that in the moment of filling it out, Mrs. Gehrig changed her mind and opted to give her son the very American name "Henry" rather than "Heinrich" (7).

15. This could be read as another contrast to Ruth, who spent his money freely and often ostentatiously (Creamer, *Babe* 273, 379).

16. The film makes a single suggestion that the elder Gehrig was employed as a janitor—a generous gesture towards a man whose employment was irregular and infrequent due to poor health, drinking, and an alleged aversion to work (Eig 4–5, 8–9, 21).

3. "REMEMBER THE GREAT DIMAGGIO"

1. Gehrig was an All-Star every year from 1933 to 1938 (and was even voted to the '39 team in the year he was finally sidelined by illness) and won the MVP award in 1936. Nevertheless, some Yankee players agreed with the public in favoring DiMaggio's contributions over Gehrig's on these late-1930s teams. Though Gehrig's statistics from 1936–38 are impressive, George Selkirk summed up the opinion of some in saying, "We needed a leader after Ruth left. Gehrig wasn't a leader. He was just a good old plowhorse" (qtd. in Allen 17).

2. Biographer Richard Ben Cramer suggests that DiMaggio had a taste for showgirls (including his first wife, Dorothy, but it did not stop with her) and occasionally associated with bookies and gangsters, but the press largely prevented this from becoming public knowledge (127–31, 177–78, 242–43).

3. According to Cramer, *Life* paid DiMaggio $6,000 for this cover story, "more than a working man made in a year" (270).

4. Yankee victories in 1949 not only included the three-game sweep of the rival Red Sox but an eventual victory over this same Boston team in a close American League pennant race that came down to the last two games of the season. Though sick with the flu, DiMaggio played and hit a key double in the first game to cut into a 4–0 Red Sox lead and inspire his teammates, who went on to win both games in the series and the pennant (Cramer 270–72). The Yankees then cruised to beat a talented Brooklyn Dodgers club four games to one in the World Series, a welcome win after the previous year's disappointment.

5. In a wry commentary on the mythic language used in reporting and discussing DiMaggio's comeback in late June 1949, Cramer deadpans, "Now that God had a hand in the pennant race it came down to the final two games" (270).

6. It is perhaps fitting that DiMaggio, who would later get his own monument, played centerfield, as did Mickey Mantle, the only other player to have such a monument. Monument Park began with a freestanding block of red granite in deep centerfield to honor the sudden passing of 1920s manager Miller Huggins in 1929 and grew with the deaths of Gehrig in 1941 and Ruth in 1948 (Frommer, *Remembering Yankee Stadium* 53, 78). Thus, until Yankee Stadium was remodeled between 1973 and 1976, which changed the dimensions of the outfield fence and enclosed these memorials in a walled-off "park," the Yankees had monuments to their storied past on their actual field of play. (Commenting in Ken Burns's documentary *Baseball*, both television sports broadcaster Bob Costas and comedian Billy Crystal claimed that when attending games at Yankee Stadium as young boys in the early 1960s, they thought that Ruth, Gehrig, and Huggins were actually buried there beneath the solemn monuments.)

While all Major League Baseball teams seek to celebrate and remember their past in such ways, no team does it with such prominence, solemnity, and grandiosity.

Monument Park has continued to grow, with the erection of plaques and large representations of retired numbers to honor the most successful Yankees. In 1996 and 1999, respectively, granite monuments to Mickey Mantle and Joe DiMaggio were added to those original three. (Like DiMaggio, Manlte also happened to play center field, near the original memorials.) In 2009 all of these were moved to a location just beyond the centerfield wall in the team's new home, *New* Yankee Stadium (Frommer, *Remembering Yankee Stadium* 187, 199).

7. The youth-oriented baseball biography of the *Pitching in a Pinch* and *Lucky to Be a Yankee* tradition also owes much to the Frank Merriwell novels by Gilbert Patten (pen name Burt L. Standish). The Merriwell books (1896–1930) tell of the titular character's boarding-school athletic success, which results from his dedication and upstanding character, bearing the influence of Horatio Alger's tales of upwardly mobile young men (1868–1913) as well as Englishman Thomas Hughes's boarding-school book, *Tom Brown's School Days* (1857).

8. DiMaggio played for his hometown San Francisco Seals of the Pacific Coast League from October 1932 through the 1935 season. While not considered one of the two Major Leagues that could gain a berth in the World Series, the Pacific Coast League operated completely independently from the American and National Leagues and their teams. The PCL clubs were not "farm" teams. Many, including Dennis Snelling, have argued that the PCL was really not a "minor" league at all, rivaling the American and National in quality of play and fan support (2–5). With teams in California, Oregon, and Washington (and briefly, Salt Lake City, Utah, from 1915 to 1925), the PCL served a region far from the cities of the Major Leagues until the Dodgers and Giants moved west in 1958. Incidentally, while playing for the PCL's Seals, DiMaggio hit safely in sixty-one consecutive games in 1935, five games more than his Major League record.

9. DiMaggio supplemented the type of language found in *Lucky to Be a Yankee* with his own public statement on "Joe DiMaggio Day" at Yankee Stadium, the penultimate day of the 1949 regular season. (This was the day before the Yankees clinched their comeback pennant bid over the Red Sox.) DiMaggio stepped up to the microphone and spoke a single sentence: "I'd like to thank the Good Lord for making me a Yankee" (Cramer 272).

10. DiMaggio himself certainly took the mention as sincere praise, as Cramer reports that later in life the retired slugger kept in his car an audio cassette tape of actor Spencer Tracy (who played Santiago in a 1958 film adaptation) reading the novella (427).

11. DiMaggio spent the war playing baseball for the U.S. Army Air Force baseball team and in an army hospital with stomach ulcers (Cramer 208, 211–15).

12. While most of Hemingway's major works are not set in the United States, only *The Old Man and the Sea* does not have an American protagonist.

13. This, of course, is despite the man's many personal flaws, which were largely kept from the public eye, including womanizing (Cramer 127–31, 177–78, 242–43) and connections to mafia figures (140–44). These were certainly inconsistent with most midcentury Americans' concept of being "in accord with the will of God" on an individual level.

4. "WALL STREET BROKERS AND HAUGHTY BUSINESSMEN"

1. Many have suspected that the pitch broke especially sharply because it was an illegal spitball. (Golenbock, *Bums* 74–75)

2. Significant debate took place about who was really to blame in the incident. Phillies outfielder Richie Ashburn was playing shallow, anticipating a bunt, and was thus able to get to the ball quickly, leading some to fault Dodgers third-base coach Milt Stock for signaling for Abrams to attempt to score. Manager Burt Shotton stood by Stock's decision. Soon after the season ended, however, both Stock and Shotton were let go. Abrams stayed with the Dodgers as a reserve for two more seasons (Golenbock, *Bums* 255–60). Dick Sisler's home run, meanwhile, was retroactively "foreshadowed" by Ernest Hemingway in a conversation about the outfielder's power in *The Old Man in the Sea*, which was set during the pennant races in the fall of 1950 but written after they had taken place in 1951 and published the following year (21–22).

3. Roger Kahn, who was then covering the Dodgers for the *New York Herald-Tribune*, described this humorous observation as "the most popular sports comment that autumn" of the 1953 World Series (*The Boys of Summer* 164). The saying is often attributed to comedian Joe E. Lewis (*Baseball Almanac*). Postwar Dodger centerfielder Duke Snider offers—possibly misremembering—a variation on the phrase in an interview for Oliphant's book, recalling, "Somebody said rooting for the Yankees was like rooting for General Motors" (224).

5. "THOSE DAMN YANKEES!"

1. The Senators played in the nation's capital from 1901 to 1960, when they moved to Minnesota's Twin Cities and were renamed the Twins. The Senators were not the most successful of clubs, winning the pennant only three times (1924, '25, and '33) and the World Series once (1924) during their one bright period from the mid-1920s to the mid-1930s. After this era, they returned to their pre-'20s struggles that inspired this popular aphorism: "first in war, first in peace, and last in the American League" (Dryden).

2. For example, Hardy pinch-hits two home runs in the two games of a double header on his first day with the Senators (46). He hits for a .545 average and knocks forty-eight home runs in two months (193).

3. In actuality, the Yankees fittingly failed to win the American League pennant the same year in which Wallop's novel was published, 1954. Despite winning 103 games, their highest total ever under Stengel, the Bronx Bombers finished second to the Cleveland Indians, who set a new Major League record with 111 wins, ostensibly without supernatural assistance. New York would go on, however, to win the pennant in nine out of the next ten years, faltering only in 1959.

4. The fact that the novel is titled *The Year the Yankees Lost the Pennant* and not "The Year the Senators Won the Pennant"—a scenario that in 1954 would have seemed equally unlikely—is a testament to the continued iconic prominence of the Yankees. As with *The Pride of the Yankees*, the word "Yankees" best signified baseball to the American public.

5. When the film was released in Britain, the title was changed to *What Lola Wants*, perhaps either to avoid use of the word "damn" or to avoid confusion on the part of the British audience, for whom the word "Yankees" did not carry such specific sports-related connotations, and may have implied a play insulting all Americans ("Yankees") in general (Erickson 139).

6. Ray Walston also won "Best Performance by a Leading Actor in a Musical" for his performance as Applegate, and Gwen Verdon won in the equivalent female category for her portrayal of Lola. Choreographer Bob Fosse also won the Tony for "Best Choreography" (*"Damn Yankees,"* Internet Broadway Database).

7. Coincidentally, 1958 is also the year in which Wallop's novel was set. Unlike in the novel, the Yankees did not quite achieve the predicted nine pennants in a row, faltering in 1954. They had also lost in the World Series twice since the publication of the novel, in 1955 and 1957.

8. About the *Damn Yankees* movie poster, Erickson quips, "No baseball to speak of, but plenty of 'selling power'" (141).

9. Some titles featuring the moniker from the musical include *Damn Yankee: The Billy Martin Story* (1980), Maury Allen's biography of the irascible second baseman and manager; Dean Chadwin's *Those Damn Yankees: The Secret Life of America's Greatest Franchise* (1999), a semi-academic critique of the late 1990s resurgence of the club; and the collection *Damn Yankees: Twenty-Four Major League Writers on the World's Most Loved (and Hated) Team* (2012), edited by Rob Fleder.

10. The Athletics' short-lived tenure in Kansas City was not a successful one. They moved from Philadelphia in 1955 and, having been purchased by the eccentric and headstrong Charles O. Finley in 1960, departed for Oakland after the 1967 season. While in Kansas City, the A's never finished higher than sixth, and finished in last place

five times in those thirteen years. On top of this disappointing record, baseball historians have suggested that during the second half of the 1950s, as a result of the previously existing business relationship between Athletics owner Arnold Johnson and Yankees owners Topping and Webb, the Kansas City franchise essentially behaved as a Yankee farm team, often participating in lopsided trades with the New York club, giving up such valuable Yankee contributors as Roger Maris, Bobby Shantz, Hector Lopez, Clete Boyer, and Ralph Terry (Katz xiii–xv). With this in mind, Wallop's fantasy notwithstanding, perhaps it could be said that the true devil's bargain involved not the Yankees and the Senators, but the Yankees and the Kansas City Athletics.

11. Not only do the Senators finally beat the Yankees and win the pennant, but Boyd is even able to blackmail Applegate into returning to Lola the physical beauty she gave up as recompense for setting Boyd free.

12. Curiously, but perhaps reflective of the controversy surrounding racial issues, none of these articles focus their criticism of the Yankees on or even mention their failure to field a black player until 1955.

13. The 1959 American League pennant was won by the Chicago White Sox, only the second team to beat the Yankees (who surprisingly finished a distant third) in the AL race during the decade, and the first to do so since 1954. McGowen makes no comment about whether Kochivar made good on his promise.

14. The professional league that Harris's fictional Mammoths play in is an interesting amalgam of the American and National Leagues, with teams in Brooklyn and Pittsburgh (National League cities) and Cleveland and Washington (American League cities), as well as New York, Boston, St. Louis, and Chicago (which, at the time the novel was written, all had a team in both leagues, with the Boston Braves moving to Milwaukee around the same time the novel was published). The Mammoths play Philadelphia (another city then having a team in each league) in the World Series. Excepting the Mammoths, none of the other Major League clubs is ever referred to by a nickname, either fictional or historical. As a child, Wiggen's fascination with baseball leads him to unsuccessfully look for books in his local library with the words "Giants," "Yankee," "Reds," and "'Senators' and such" (31). Thus, it would seem these teams exist in some form in Harris's baseball universe, just as do real-life figures Carl Hubbell (14), John McGraw, Ty Cobb, Shoeless Joe Jackson, Babe Ruth, and Walter Johnson (169).

15. One significant way in which the Mammoths differ from the 1953 Yankees is that they are integrated, beating the real-life Yankees by two years.

16. In one instance, when Schnell is informed in the clubhouse that the team will be paid a visit by Patricia Moors, Mammoths' executive and daughter of team owner Lester Moors, he deadpans, "She will have to wait until I am done pissing" (177). Later, when Wiggen is preparing to visit a teammate in the hospital to deliver the $150 prize of a clubhouse pool, he mentions that "Dutch . . . told me go straight to the hospital

and not get tangled up with any young ladies along the way. This brung another terrific laugh" (333). Such utterances, balancing sarcasm, a certain homespun folksiness, and an occasional modicum of vulgarity, would be right at home with some of Stengel's famous quotes, including what Jack Mann describes as the "Stengel standard" often delivered to sports writers, "You're full of ——, and I'll tell you why" (101), or his observation that "most people my age are dead" (99).

17. Here the World Series bonus is of particular note, for, as mentioned, the Mammoths are portrayed as just as tightfisted with salaries as the real Yankee organization was.

18. While in Harris's novel the practice of throwing a spitball is portrayed as a clearly unethical act and while it has been officially banned in Major League Baseball since 1920, throwing a spitter has not been uniformly perceived as unconscionable throughout baseball, and like many such acts of cheating, it is generally tolerated if one is not caught.

19. While managing the Yankees, Casey Stengel was known to frequently employ a "platoon system"—players sharing playing time at a particular position. Often one would be left-handed and the other right-handed, and would be played on days when the team was facing an opposite-handed pitcher, for favorable statistical batting percentages. Stengel platooned Bobby Brown, Billy Johnson, and Gil McDougald at third base, Joe Collins and Bill "Moose" Skowron at first base, and Hank Bauer and Gene Woodling in left field. Most, if not all, of those players were considered good enough to be everyday starters in their own right.

20. Harris further explores this theme of human friendship and camaraderie in his follow-up to *The Southpaw*, titled *Bang the Drum Slowly* (1956), in which Wiggen returns to the Mammoths the following year but is focused not on winning the pennant but on helping a dying teammate enjoy and feel appreciated in his remaining days of life. The Mammoths win the pennant anyway, but with much greater joy and sense of community than exhibited in *The Southpaw*.

6. "WHERE HAVE YOU GONE, JOE DIMAGGIO?"

1. In the 1969 season, the Major Leagues expanded again and split both American and National Leagues into two divisions. The '69 Yankees finished fifth out of six in the first year of the "American League East."

2. This is an allusion to the eclipse in popularity of baseball by professional football during the late 1960s, a trend punctuated in 1967 when the National and American Football Leagues held their first Super Bowl game. About the sporting year 1967, *Baseball* comments, "It was a great World Series, but that year, more people had watched professional football's first Super Bowl than any Series game. Baseball was now said to

be too leisurely, too serene, too dull to be the national pastime. It was football that was America's true game."

3. A knuckleball, as described by Bouton himself, is a pitch "thrown with the fingertips, and the principle is to release the ball so that it leaves all the fingertips at the same time without any spin on the ball. The air currents and humidity take over and cause the ball to turn erratically and thus move erratically" (20). Unlike most baseball pitches, the knuckleball is actually more effective if not thrown with maximum force; thus, unlike Bouton's old specialty, the fastball, the knuckleball "doesn't take anything out of your arm. It's like having a catch with your sister" (20).

4. Though the practice is largely lost to the changing times and is somewhat forgotten, at the time when *Ball Four* was written, the labels "spacey," "space case," "space cadet," and similar terms (perhaps inspired by the U.S.-Soviet space race) were often applied to individuals perceived as frequently lost in their own thoughts and lacking in "common sense" (233). The connotations of lampooning the counterculture and the "cosmic" worldview they sought should not be neglected here.

5. Both novels were made into movies by filmmakers with countercultural ties—*Catch-22* (1970), directed by Mike Nichols of *The Graduate* (1967) fame, and *One Flew Over the Cuckoo's Nest* (1975), which starred *Easy Rider*'s (1969) Jack Nicholson, directed by Czech New Wave director Milos Forman, who would later make the film adaptation of *Hair* (1979). Also, *Cuckoo's Nest* author Ken Kesey became a leader in the American psychedelic movement, leading his band of "Merry Pranksters" on an LSD-fueled cross-country road trip and then introducing LSD to young people in so-called "Acid Test" event parties up and down the California coast (Torgoff 94–99, 113–30).

6. In 1968 Bouton pitched for the AAA Seattle Angels Pacific Coast League, then affiliated with the California Angels, before transitioning to the Seattle Pilots, a Major League expansion team.

7. The Mets, along with their fellow 1962 expansion team the Houston Colt .45s (later Astros), were founded for a number of reasons. In addition to capitalizing on the market of former Dodger and Giant fans in New York City, there was the threat of the proposed formation of a third Major League, the Continental League, which was going to include a club in the New York area. The National League offered the New York City group an expansion franchise as part of the effort to quash this proposed new league (Tygiel, *Past Time* 186–89). The Mets' Shea Stadium was built on the very plot of land in Flushing Meadows, Queens, that powerful city planner Robert Moses had offered Brooklyn Dodger owner Walter O'Malley when he was looking to replace Ebbets Field. O'Malley refused to accept the land, pointing out that it was in Queens, not Brooklyn, and eventually moved his team to Los Angeles.

8. The bad blood between Bouton and the Yankees continued until their reconciliation in the late 1990s and at least once was made comically public while Bouton

worked as a maverick sports journalist for a New York television station. Writing in 1975, Golenbock recounts the story, which reads like a passage from *Catch-22*, "Last Year Bouton put on a disguise, a beard and moustache, to try out incognito as a 20-year-old-kid pitcher with the Yankees. After his first few pitches, the Yankee scouts recognized his familiar overhand motion. They kept him at the tryout to have the satisfaction of telling him that he had flunked out" (*Dynasty* 372).

9. Bouton, for his part, certainly claims that was his intent, telling Golenbock, "This is the thing that I have felt worse about than anything—Mickey's reaction to the book. Because in many ways I always felt the same way that the other guys felt about Mantle. I loved him. . . . He was winning games for me. He was great around the clubhouse, telling great stories. He was just fun to be around. When I was a rookie he was nice to me. There were so many reasons to love that guy" (*Dynasty* 380).

10. To further foster the notion that Mantle was successor to the great Yankee hero tradition, general manager George Weiss informed him that the official public-relations line was to be that Joe DiMaggio, whom Mantle would replace in centerfield, was his childhood hero, not Stan Musial, Mantle's true preference (Leavy 21).

11. In fact, in an interesting study, Landon Jones proposes that all the cultural tumult of the 1960s is best read as the confusion inherent in the coming-of-age process magnified by the size of the Baby Boomer generational cohort, who went through their teenage years and young adulthood during the 1960s (79).

12. For example, a cartoon from the summer of 1968 by famed *New York Daily News* sports cartoonist Bill Gallo shows then–Yankee manager Ralph Houk sobbing, "Where have you gone, Joe DiMaggio?," with a chart comparing DiMaggio's yearly batting averages from 1936–51 with the '68 Yankees' relatively meager averages (Gallo 304).

13. Biographers continue to refer to the lyric. In fact, Maury Allen's 1975 biography takes the line as its title. Similarly, after DiMaggio's death in 1999, Paul Simon made a special appearance at Yankee Stadium's Joe DiMaggio Day to play the song with the famous lyric (Frommer, *Remembering Yankee Stadium* 199).

14. Songs such as "Bookends Theme," "Old Friends," and "Voices of Old People" (literally just voices of old people Art Garfunkel recorded in retirement homes) speak of personal aging and change, while "America" juxtaposes the past and the present by combining optimistic, turn-of-the-century notions about the American dream with contemporary imagery and angst (Fornatale 88–89).

15. An early version of "Mrs. Robinson" was recorded for the 1967 Mike Nichols film, but it did not yet feature the lyric about DiMaggio.

16. For instance, they recorded a song, "Richard Cory" (1966), which is a retelling of an E. A. Robinson poem. Songs from their album *Parsley, Sage, Rosemary and Thyme* (1966), meanwhile, reference Robert Frost, Emily Dickinson, and Dylan Thomas.

7. "YOU'D NEVER GUESS THIS WAS . . . THE YANKEES"

1. Steinbrenner was a competent hurdler for Williams College but did not come close to the success his father had in the same events at MIT, a fact his hard-driving father never let him forget (Madden 22, 25). The younger Steinbrenner served as a graduate assistant to legendary Ohio State football coach Woody Hayes while studying for a master's degree in physical education there (30).

2. Jacobson actually took the title for his book from Reggie Jackson's comments after they clinched their 1977 World Series championship. The victorious and vindicated Jackson proclaimed, "I just feel grateful, all the stuff that went on. . . . We won, we're the champs. Nobody can say anything anymore. We're the best team money can buy. They can't say Reggie Jackson didn't pay on a winner" (qtd. in Jacobson 326). Even the Yankee players themselves thought of the club in plutocratic terms.

3. See Bouton's *Ball Four* for a description of this old clubhouse paradigm (59). The prominence in collective baseball memory of the few transgressions of this code—such as New York Giants manager Bill Terry's suggestive question about the then-struggling Dodgers, "Is Brooklyn still in the league?"—are, in effect, the exceptions that prove the rule (G. Stout 96).

4. The Royals were an expansion club created and inaugurated in the 1969 season. The team was designed to replace the Athletics, who moved from Philadelphia to Kansas City in 1955 and then departed for Oakland after the 1967 season. Thus it is entirely possible that the Kansas City baseball fan in question had a longer, deeper history of acquaintance with the Yankees' winning ways than the Royals' relatively brief Major League history might suggest.

5. During spring training, according to Lyle, "[George] likes discipline, or, rather, the appearance of it. There's a lot of that . . . in football. It's like being in the Army. Army men shouldn't fool around, and all that crap" (*The Bronx Zoo* 26).

6. Even Steinbrenner himself enjoyed the caricature. He had a friendly relationship with Gallo and supposedly had a Von Steingrabber cartoon hanging on his office wall (Hinckley).

7. Unbeknownst to many, in the spring of 1976, Munson had made an agreement with Steinbrenner that, discounting the highly paid free-agency pioneer Catfish Hunter, he would always be the highest-paid player on the team. When Munson learned what Jackson would be making, he felt betrayed. Steinbrenner tried to justify the discrepancy by saying that much of Reggie's salary would be deferred payment, but the catcher was hardly mollified (Madden 108, 116).

8. When Martin was replaced as manager the following season, it was Bob Lemon, the very same who seemed to revel in the Yankees' dysfunction the previous season, who was, ironically, named to take his place.

9. Like Bob Lemon, Tommy John would also soon become a Yankee. He signed with the Yankees as a free agent for over a half-million dollars per year in 1979.

10. The ball was set in motion for Martin's departure when things boiled over between him and Jackson. Reggie, annoyed at Martin for not playing him in the position—or as often as—he preferred, deliberately ignored a sign from Martin while at bat. Furious, Martin suspended him for five games and made an off-hand comment to a reporter about both Jackson and Steinbrenner: "The two of them deserve each other. One's a born liar and the other's convicted" (qtd. in Madden 144). Unable to tolerate such a reference to his embarrassing Nixon-campaign-contributions scandal, Steinbrenner decided to finally pull the trigger and fire Martin but not before the manager, apparently anticipating the action, retired in an emotional press conference. The announcement of Martin's return—orchestrated by Steinbrenner himself, who apparently had something of a love-hate relationship with the emotional manager and regretted his decision—was milked for all its drama. There was no press release or media conference; instead Martin was introduced at "Old-Timers' Day" as the 1980 manager following the introduction of Yankee legends like Mickey Mantle, Whitey Ford, Yogi Berra, and Joe DiMaggio. Martin ran out onto the field from a hiding place in a Yankee Stadium bathroom so as not to spoil the surprise Steinbrenner sought. The crowd gave Martin an enthusiastic standing ovation (Madden 146–50).

11. As mentioned, many of Steinbrenner's executives questioned the wisdom of acquiring Gossage, but in the end it was likely Lyle's advancing age (thirty-four), combined with Steinbrenner's desire to make a splash every off-season, that won out (Madden 130). Later in life, Lyle said of the situation, "In retrospect, I can understand why he did it. I was getting older and didn't throw 97 miles per hour, and Goose was in his prime. But at the time, I was pretty upset" (qtd. in Madden 131).

12. Tragically, Munson died less than a year after the Yankees' 1978 World Series win, crashing the personal aircraft he was learning to fly in order to visit family more frequently (Madden 169).

13. Sadly, Gilliam suffered a massive brain hemorrhage in September of the following year and died the day after the Dodgers, who would again be the Yankees' opponent in the World Series, clinched the 1978 National League pennant.

14. Since Jackson had hit a home run in his last at-bat of the previous game as well, he actually hit four home runs in consecutive at-bats. (Reggie was intentionally walked his first time at the plate, not counting as an at-bat statistically.) Even more remarkable, each home run in game six came on his first swing, meaning that he hit four home runs on four consecutive swings of his bat. He also hit them off of four different Los Angeles Dodger pitchers.

15. The Baby Ruth candy bar, introduced in 1921, was claimed to be named after President Grover Cleveland's daughter, Ruth. This was twenty-four years after Cleveland's

presidency and seventeen years after his daughter Ruth had actually died, but it was only one year after Babe Ruth nearly doubled his own season home-run record with fifty-four in his first year playing in New York. As such, many suspected the makers of the candy bar were attempting to use Ruth's name to sell candy without having to pay him for an endorsement. The Oh Henry! bar was introduced in 1920, fourteen years before the birth of Hank Aaron, but a popular urban legend held that the candy bar was named after him. Perhaps this rumor started because of the known connection of the Baby Ruth to the Great Bambino and Aaron's eventual succession of the Babe as the Major Leagues' all-time home-run king.

8. "ALL THAT ONCE WAS GOOD AND COULD BE AGAIN"

1. Prominent Steinbrenner acquisitions included All-Stars Tommy John (1979), Dave Winfield (1981), Ken Griffey Sr. (1982), Don Baylor (1983), Rickey Henderson (1985), Steve Sax (1989), and Jesse Barfield (1989).

2. Billy Martin was hired and fired by Steinbrenner a total of five times. Some speculated that had he not passed away in 1989 Steinbrenner would have hired him again. Steinbrenner also hired both Bob Lemon and Lou Piniella to serve second stints as managers within two years of first firing them from the job.

3. In her doctoral dissertation, Susan Gronbeck-Tedesco analyzes all of these films for their treatment of the reconciliation theme.

4. Encouraged by the commercial success of a kid-centric Disney-produced movie about a peewee hockey team, *The Mighty Ducks* (1992)—which borrowed much from the 1976 Little League baseball movie, *The Bad News Bears*—Hollywood studios combined that formula with the nostalgic baseball trend that had yielded earlier box-office successes and produced a string of baseball movies aimed at children, including *The Sandlot* (1993), *Rookie of the Year* (1993), *Little Big League* (1994), and *Angels in the Outfield* (1994). Since baseball had long since been losing ground to football and basketball—to say nothing of the rapidly growing hockey and soccer—in terms of youth interest and participation by this time, perhaps filmmakers were counting on nostalgic Baby Boomer parents to attract families to movie theaters. And indeed, *Rookie of the Year* and especially *The Sandlot* traffic heavily in rose-tinted references to baseball's midcentury golden age.

5. The novels *Shoeless Joe* and Eric Rolfe Greenberg's *The Celebrant* (1983), essays by Donald Hall and Bart Giamatti, and the movies *The Natural*, *Bull Durham*, and *Field of Dreams* all explore what it means to watch baseball, to root for a team or a player, and suggest that fans play an important role in the American tradition and institution of baseball. Many movies from the early to mid-1990s continued this trend, as *The Sandlot* (1993), *Rookie of the Year* (1993), *Angels in the Outfield* (1994), *Little Big League*

(1994), and *The Fan* (1996) all devoted significant energy to exploring the meaning and role of fandom in the game. Similarly, fantasy camps and the memorabilia boom were industries focused on fan participation and the demonstration of their connections to their teams and players.

    6. Some fan-centric exceptions include *The Year the Yankees Lost the Pennant* (1954) and its stage and screen adaptations or Robert Coover's philosophical novel *The Universal Baseball Association, J. Henry Waugh, Prop.* (1968).

    7. Such films include *The Babe* (1992, New York Yankees), *The Sandlot* (1993, Los Angeles Dodgers), *Rookie of the Year* (1993, Chicago Cubs), *Angels in the Outfield* (1994, California Angels), *Little Big League* (1994, Minnesota Twins), *The Scout* (1994, New York Yankees), *Major League II* (1994, Cleveland Indians), and *The Fan* (1996, San Francisco Giants). This trend has continued to some degree beyond this early-to-mid-1990s baseball movie boom, with many subsequent Hollywood films cooperating with the MLB to prominently feature a team and its official contemporary iconography, including *For the Love of the Game* (1999, Detroit Tigers), *Mr. 3000* (2004, Milwaukee Brewers), *Fever Pitch* (2005, Boston Red Sox), *Moneyball* (2011, Oakland Athletics), and *Trouble with the Curve* (2012, Atlanta Braves).

    8. In the early 1970s, following the example of the Oakland A's, the overwhelming majority of Major League teams had switched from the traditional flannel button-up shirts and pants in white (home) or gray (away) to uniforms of brightly-colored polyester double-knit fabric that had no buttons or belts. The tradition-rich Yankees and Dodgers were the only teams to never switch.

    9. In the late 1960s and '70s many ball clubs had moved out of parks built in the first few decades of the century to new, enormous, modern stadiums built of concrete and often used for football as well. Coinciding with the period of baseball's decline in popularity, this architectural style began to be eschewed by baseball romantics who mourned the loss of old, intimate, quirky ballparks like the Brooklyn Dodgers' Ebbets Field (abandoned in 1957 and torn down in 1960); and the Orioles' Camden Yards was designed with this nostalgic fan in mind. Like the parks from the baseball's golden age, it was smaller, built of red brick and dark green steel instead of concrete, and was exclusively used for baseball. It featured architectural quirks, including an asymmetrical playing field designed to evoke such irregularity that developed organically in early-twentieth-century parks as they expanded in piecemeal fashion (Rosenweig 3–5).

    10. In *Major League* the movie's primary antagonist is the fictional conniving Cleveland Indians owner Rachel Phelps, who wants her own team to fail. However, despite the fact that they were at best middling during the mid- to late 1980s, the Yankees fill the role of the literal on-field impediment in the ragtag band of once-lovable losers' journey as heroic underdogs. The Bronx club plays a similar role in 1999's *For the Love of the Game*. Unlike 1976's *The Bad News Bears,* however, the Yankees as an icon keep

a relatively low profile in these two films from the '80s and '90s. They are dwarfed by larger, more nefarious villains and likely do not command much primacy in moviegoers' experience with the films or in their memories of them.

11. Interestingly, Lyle's imagined innovations using computer-analyzed stats soon proved prophetic, with the use of computers to crunch increasingly sophisticated statistical models developing throughout the 1990s and 2000s.

12. If *The Year I Owned the Yankees* were a publication with serious literary pretentions, the deep furrows the exiting Steinbrenner left on the Yankee office carpet could easily be read as symbolizing the scars he left on the once-proud organization. But considering the intended audience for the novel, such analytical scrutiny may indeed be reading too much into it.

Once Steinbrenner is evicted from his office, Lyle cleans out his desk and discovers both a Yankees branding iron and a Nixon-like recording system with tapes from every meeting and conversation of The Boss's ownership (20–21).

13. Steinbrenner is largely absent from the series' ninth and final season (1997–98) because George loses his job with the Yankees at the end of season eight ("The Muffin Tops"). (Actually, in a typically bizarre manner for the show's satire of Steinbrenner, George is "traded" to the Tyler Chicken corporation, which produces chicken-based concessions for Yankee Stadium, including an enigmatic, fermented chicken drink to replace beer.) It is also possible that the return of Yankee success in 1996 made the show's creators and writers feel like that character was losing relevancy. In any case, like many of the show's memorable side characters, Steinbrenner made a cameo appearance in the show's final episode.

14. The song in question, incidentally, is Pat Benatar's "Heartbreaker" (1979).

15. The practice of including the squabbling late-1970s Yankees, who were often not considered "real" Yankees (see *The Bronx Zoo 99*), is perfectly in harmony with the theme of reconciling pre-countercultural America and post-countercultural America that runs throughout these Yankees-focused texts and the baseball-nostalgia movement in general.

16. Often referred to as the "façade," the decorative copper frieze hung from the grandstand roof from 1923 until 1973, when the stadium was remodeled and the iconic frieze was moved to the top of the wall behind the outfield bleachers.

17. True to the nature and tone of the show, even as one of his longest desires is being fulfilled by seats in the Yankee Stadium owner's box, the ever-pessimistic George cannot help but complain that they are in the second row behind the dugout, not the very first.

18. Contemporary Yankees who appeared in episodes of Seinfeld include Danny Tartabull ("The Chaperone," "The Pledge Drive"), Paul O'Neill ("The Wink"), and

Bernie Williams and Derek Jeter ("The Abstinence"). Manager Buck Showalter also appeared in an episode ("The Chaperone")

19. Lyle's use of the term "real Yankees" is ironic considering that he chafed at a fan's notion that he and his teammates did not measure up to the standard of that phrase in *The Bronx Zoo* (99).

20. *The Scout* is not the first baseball film to deal with mental illness, however, as 1957's *Fear Strikes Out* treats the story of real-life Red Sox outfielder Jimmy Piersall, whose overbearing father triggers a nervous breakdown.

21. Ironically, since the Yankees actually did rediscover their past success by winning the 1996 World Series while the show was still running, *Seinfeld* writers were obliged to integrate this event into the eighth season of the series. That they devote relatively little time or space to this significant occurrence is revealing about the show's commitment to its absurd defeatist tone. It is not surprising that the writers have George lose his job less than six months after the Yankees' World Series win.

22. See Olney (209–26) for a nuanced profile of Jeter.

23. Another backwards-looking trend in American culture during this period is movies that paid homage to midcentury narrative genres and structures and featured strong, central hero figures, such as *Star Wars* (1977, sequels in '80 and '83), *Superman* (1978, sequels in '80, '83, and '87), and *Raiders of the Lost Ark* (1981, sequels in '84 and '89).

24. Even though Ray's father, who must have been in his fifties when Ray was born, is a World War I, not WWII, veteran, this is clearly a conceit to allow him to be a Shoeless Joe Jackson fan. The movie's intent for the father-son relationship to represent the deep generational schism between the Baby Boomers and their parents is quite evident.

EPILOGUE

1. Living in Spain's Canary Islands as a missionary for my church between July 1999 and June 2001, I learned a thing or two about Real Madrid and F. C. Barcelona of "La Liga" national soccer league and came to realize that Americans are not the only ones who could turn sports teams into national icons.

WORKS CITED

The Adventures of Babe Ruth. Narr. Steve Martin. NBC Blue Network, 1934. Radio.
Allen, Maury. *Where Have You Gone, Joe DiMaggio?* 1975. New York: New American Library, 1976.
Angels in the Outfield. Dir. Clarence Brown. Perf. Paul Douglas, Janet Leigh. MGM, 1951.
Angels in the Outfield. Dir. William Dear. Perf. Danny Glover, Tony Danza, Christopher Lloyd. Disney, 1994.
Appel, Marty. *Pinstripe Empire: The New York Yankees from Before the Babe to After the Boss.* New York: Bloomsbury, 2012.
Armstrong, Jennifer Keishin. *Seinfeldia: How a Show about Nothing Changed Everything.* New York: Simon & Schuster, 2016.
Babe Comes Home. Dir. Ted Wilde. Perf. Babe Ruth, Anna Q. Nilsson, Louise Fazenda. First National Pictures, 1927.
The Bad News Bears. Dir. Michael Ritchie. Perf. Walter Matthau, Chris Barnes, Tatum O'Neal. Paramount, 1976.
The Babe. Dir. Arthur Hiller. Perf. John Goodman, Kelly McGillis. Universal, 1992.
The Babe Ruth Story. Dir. Roy Del Ruth. Perf. William Bendix, Claire Trevor, William Frawley. Allied Artists Productions, 1948.
Bach, Richard. *Jonathan Livingston Seagull.* New York: Macmillan, 1970.
Baker, Russell. "Maybe Lunkhead Park?" *New York Times,* March 14, 1990.
Baldassaro, Lawrence. Introduction. *The American Game: Baseball and Ethnicity.* Ed. Lawrence Baldassaro and Richard A. Johnson. Carbondale: Southern Illinois UP, 2002.
———. "Before Joe D: Early Italian Americans in the Major Leagues." *The American Game: Baseball and Ethnicity.* Ed. Lawrence Baldassaro and Richard A. Johnson. Carbondale: Southern Illinois UP, 2002.

Baldick, Chris. *The Oxford Dictionary of Literary Terms.* 3rd ed. Oxford: Oxford U P, 2008.

Ballard, Sarah. "Fabric of the Game." *Sports Illustrated,* April 5, 1989. Web. Accessed Aug. 13, 2016.

Barthes, Roland. *Mythologies.* Trans. Annette Lavers. New York: Hill & Wang, 1972.

Baseball. Dir. Ken Burns. Perf. John Chancellor, Bob Costas, Billy Crystal, Doris Kearns Goodwin, Gerald Early. PBS, 1994. Television.

Baseball: The Tenth Inning. Dir. Ken Burns. Perf. Keith David, Thomas Boswell, John Thorn. PBS, 2010. Television.

Bellah, Robert. "American Civil Religion." *Journal of the American Academy of Arts and Sciences* 96 (Winter 1967): 1-21.

Bloom, John. *A House of Cards: Baseball Card Collecting and Popular Culture.* Minneapolis: U of Minnesota P, 1997.

Blount, Roy, Jr. "Everyone Is Helpless and in Awe." *Sports Illustrated,* June 17, 1974. Web. Accessed July 12, 2016.

Borer, Michael Ian. *Faithful to Fenway: Believing in Boston, Baseball, and America's Most Beloved Ballpark.* New York: New York UP, 2008.

Bouton, Jim. *Ball Four.* 1970. New York: Wiley, 1990.

Brewer, Teresa. "I Love Mickey." *Miss Music.* Coral, 1956. LP.

Brodkin, Karen. "How Jews Became White Folks and What That Says about Race in America." *Race, Class and Gender in the United States.* 7th ed. Ed. Paula S. Rothenberg. New York: Worth, 2007.

Broun, Heywood. *The Sun Field.* 1923. Introd. Darryl Brock. Westport, CT: Revive, 2008.

Brown, Les. "Joltin' Joe DiMaggio." Comp. Ben Homer and Alan Courtney. Alan Courtney Music, 1941.

Bull Durham. Dir. Rob Shelton. Perf. Kevin Costner, Susan Sarandon, Tim Robbins. Orion, 1988.

Busch, Noel F. "Joe DiMaggio: Baseball's Newest Star Starts What Should Be his Best Year So Far." *Life,* May 1, 1939, 63–69.

Callahan, John. *The Wonderful World Series.* New York: School Book Fairs, 1979.

Campbell, Joseph. *The Hero with a Thousand Faces.* New York: Pantheon, 1949.

Campbell, Joseph, with Bill Moyers. *The Power of Myth.* 1988. New York: Anchor, 1991.

Castro, Tony. *Mickey Mantle: America's Prodigal Son.* Washington, DC: Brassey's, 2002.

Chadwin, Dean. *Those Damn Yankees: The Secret Life of America's Greatest Franchise.* New York: Verso, 1999.

Charyn, Jerome. *Joe DiMaggio: The Long Vigil.* New Haven, CT: Yale UP, 2011.

Cobb. Dir. Rob Shelton. Perf. Tommy Lee Jones, Robert Wuhl. Warner Bros., 1994.

Cobbledick, Gordon. "Break Up the Yankees." *Collier's,* Feb. 25, 1939, 19+.

Cohane, Tim. "You Can't Beat the Yankees with Pop Bottles." *Look,* June 30, 1953, 57, 59–62, 65.

Cohen, Lizabeth. *A Consumer's Republic: The Politics of Mass Consumption in Postwar America.* 2003. New York: Vintage, 2005.

Conolly-Smith, Peter. "Casting Teutonic Types from the Nineteenth Century to World War I: German Ethnic Stereotypes in Print, on Stage, and Screen." *Columbia Journal of American Studies* 9 (Fall 2009): 48–83.

Coover, Robert. *The Universal Baseball Association, Inc., J. Henry Waugh, Prop.* New York: Random House, 1968.

Cramer, Richard Ben. *Joe DiMaggio: The Hero's Life.* New York: Simon & Schuster, 2000.

Creamer, Robert W. *Baseball in '41: A Celebration of the "Best Baseball Season Ever"—In the Year America Went to War.* New York: Viking, 1991.

———. *Babe: The Legend Comes to Life.* New York: Simon & Schuster, 1992.

———. "Babe Ruth and Lou Gehrig." *The Yankees: The Four Fabulous Eras of Baseball's Most Famous Team.* New York: Random House, 1980.

Crepeau, Richard. *Baseball: America's Diamond Mind, 1919–1941.* Orlando: U of Florida P, 1980.

Crowther, Bosley. Rev. of *The Pride of the Yankees,* dir. Sam Wood. *New York Times,* July 16, 1942.

Cullen, Jim. *The American Dream: A Short History of the Idea that Shaped a Nation.* Oxford, UK: Oxford UP, 2004.

D'Agostino, Dennis, and Bonnie Crosby. *Through a Blue Lens: The Brooklyn Dodgers Photographs of Barney Stein, 1937–1957.* Chicago: Triumph, 2007.

Damn Yankees. Dir. George Abbott and Stanley Donen. Perf. Gwen Verdon, Tab Hunter, Ray Walston. Warner Bros., 1958.

"Damn Yankees." *Internet Broadway Database.* Web. Accessed Feb. 15, 2014.

Davis, Francis. "Recognition Humor." *Atlantic Monthly,* Dec. 1992, 135–38.

Davis, Robert Gorham. "Hemingway's Tragic Fisherman." *New York Times Book Review,* Sept. 7, 1952, 20.

Dexter, Charles. "New Reign of Terror." *Sport,* Feb. 1954, 28–31.

Dickerson, Gary A. *The Cinema of Baseball: Images of America, 1929–1989.* New York: Mecklermedia, 1991.

DiMaggio, Joe. "It's Great to Be Back." *Life,* Aug. 1, 1949: 66–72.

———. *Lucky to Be a Yankee.* 1946. New York: Bantam, 1949.

Dryden, Charles. "Untitled." *Washington Post,* June 27, 1904.

Dylan, Bob. "The Times They Are a-Changin'." *The Times They Are a-Changin'.* Columbia, 1964. LP.

Eig, Jonathan. *Luckiest Man: The Life and Death of Lou Gehrig.* New York: Simon & Schuster, 2006.

WORKS CITED

Eight Men Out. Dir. John Sayles. Perf. John Cusack, Charlie Sheen, Jace Alexander. MGM, 1988.

Einstein, Charles. "Yankees: There Oughta Be a Law." *New York Times Magazine,* Sept. 8, 1957, 96+.

Ellwood, Robert A. *The Politics of Myth: A Study of C. G. Jung, Mircea Eliade, and Joseph Campbell.* Albany: State U of New York P, 1999.

Emerson, Ralph Waldo. "Concord Hymn." 1837. *Emerson's Prose and Poetry.* Ed. Joel Porte and Saundra Morris. New York: Norton, 2001.

Enright, James. "Roaring '20s—Great Time for Waite Hoyt." *Sporting News,* Aug. 7, 1965.

Erickson, Hal. *The Baseball Filmography: 1915 through 2001.* 2nd ed. Jefferson, NC: McFarland, 2002.

Evans, Christopher. "Baseball as Civil Religion: The Genesis of an American Creation Story." *The Faith of 50 Million: Baseball, Religion, and American Culture.* Ed. Christopher Evans and William R. Herzog II. London: Westminster John Knox, 2002.

Falkner, Dave. *The Last Hero: The Life of Mickey Mantle.* New York: Simon & Schuster, 1995.

The Fan. Dir. Tony Scott. Perf. Robert De Niro, Wesley Snipes. Columbia, 1996.

Farley, James A. Introduction. *Lucky to Be a Yankee.* New York: Rudolph Field, 1948.

Fear Strikes Out. Dir. Robert Mulligan. Perf. Anthony Perkins, Karl Malden. Paramount, 1957.

Fever Pitch. Dir. Peter and Bobby Farrelly. Perf. Jimmy Fallon, Drew Barrymore. 20th Century Fox, 2005.

Field of Dreams. Dir. Phil Alden Robinson. Perf. Kevin Costner, Amy Madigan, James Earl Jones, Ray Liotta. Universal, 1989.

Fleder, Rob, ed. *Damn Yankees: Twenty-Four Major League Writers on the World's Most Loved (and Hated) Team.* New York: HarperCollins, 2012.

Foertsch, Jacqueline. *American Culture in the 1940s.* Edinburgh: Edinburgh UP, 2008.

For Love of the Game. Dir. Sam Raimi. Perf. Kevin Costner, Kelly Preston. Universal, 1999.

Fornatale, Pete. *Simon & Garfunkel's Bookends.* New York: Rodale, 2007.

Frommer, Harvey. *Baseball's Greatest Rivalry: The New York Yankees and Boston Red Sox.* New York: Atheneum, 1985.

———. *Five O'Clock Lightning: Babe Ruth, Lou Gehrig, and the Greatest Baseball Team in History, the 1927 New York Yankees.* Lanham, MD: Taylor, 2015.

———. *Remembering Yankee Stadium: An Oral and Narrative History of the House that Ruth Built.* New York: Stewart, Tabori, & Chang, 2008.

Frost, Robert. "A Day of Prowess." *Sports Illustrated,* July 23, 1956. Web. Accessed June 12, 2017.

Gaines, Ernest J. *The Autobiography of Miss Jane Pittman.* New York: Dial, 1971.
Gallo, Bill, with Pete Cornell. *Drawing a Crowd: Bill Gallo's Greatest Moments.* Middle Village, NY: Jonathan David, 2000.
Gehring, Wes D. *Mr. Deeds Goes to Yankees Stadium: Baseball Films in the Capra Tradition.* Jefferson, NC: McFarland, 2004.
Gerlach, Larry R. "German Americans in Major League Baseball: Sport and Acculturation." *The American Game: Baseball and Ethnicity.* Ed. Lawrence Baldassaro and Richard A. Johnson. Carbondale: Southern Illinois UP, 2002.
Giamatti, A. Bartlett. "The Green Fields of the Mind." *Yale Alumni Magazine,* Nov. 1977.
———. *Take Time for Paradise: Americans and Their Games.* New York: Summit, 1989.
Gilbert, James. *Men in the Middle: Searching for Masculinity in the 1950s.* Chicago: U of Chicago P, 2005.
Goodwin, Doris Kearns. *Wait Till Next Year.* New York: Touchstone Book, 1997.
Golenbock, Peter. *Bums: An Oral History of the Brooklyn Dodgers.* New York: Putnam's, 1984.
———. *Dynasty: The New York Yankees, 1949–1964.* Englewood Cliffs, NJ: Prentice-Hall, 1975.
Gould, Stephen Jay. "The Streak of Streaks." *Triumph and Tragedy in Mudville: A Lifelong Passion for Baseball.* New York: Norton, 2004.
Graham, Frank. *The New York Yankees.* New York: Putnam's, 1948.
Grebstein, Sheldon Norman. *Hemingway's Craft.* Carbondale: Southern Illinois UP, 1973.
Greenberg, Eric Rolfe. *The Celebrant.* 1983. Lincoln: U of Nebraska P, 1993.
Gronbeck-Tedesco, Susan L. "Reconciliation in Baseball Movies of the 1980s." Diss. U of Kansas, 1999.
Gross, Milton. "Why They Hate the Yankees." *Sport,* Sept. 1953, 10+.
Grossberg, Lawrence. "Is There a Fan in the House? The Affective Sensibility of Fandom." *The Adoring Audience: Fan Culture and Popular Media.* Ed. L. A. Lewis. London: Routledge, 1992.
Halberstam, David. *October 1964.* New York: Ballantine, 1994.
———. *The Summer of '49.* New York: Perennial, 1989.
Hall, Donald. *Fathers Playing Catch with Sons.* San Francisco: North Point, 1985.
"halorocker44." User rev. of *The Pride of the Yankees. Rotten Tomatoes,* Dec 8, 2007. Web. Accessed Nov. 5, 2014.
Harris, Mark. *The Southpaw.* 1953. Lincoln: U of Nebraska P, 2003.
———. *Bang the Drum Slowly.* 1956. Lincoln, U of Nebraska P, 2003.
Headin' Home. Dir. Lawrence C. Windom. Perf. Babe Ruth, Ruth Taylor, William Sheer. Yankee Photo Corp., 1920.
Heller, Joseph. *Catch-22.* New York: Simon & Schuster, 1961.

———. Preface to the Special Edition of Catch-22. *Catch-22*. New York: Scribner's, 1996.

Hemingway, Ernest. *The Old Man and the Sea*. New York: Scribner's, 1952.

Hinckley, David. "From Daily News' Bill Gallo . . . General Von Steingrabber Chapter 37." *New York Daily News*, Apr. 9, 2002. Web. Accessed July 12, 2016.

Hurley, C. Harold. "The Facts Behind the Fiction: The 1950 American League Pennant Race and *The Old Man and the Sea*." *Hemingway's Debt to Baseball in* The Old Man and the Sea: *A Collection of Critical Readings*. Ed. C. Harold Hurley. Lewiston, NY: Edwin Mellen, 1992.

The Jackie Robinson Story. Dir. Alfred E. Green. Perf. Jackie Robinson, Ruby Dee, Minor Watson. MGM, 1950.

Jacobson, Matthew Frye. *Whiteness of a Different Color: European Immigrants and the Alchemy of Race*. Cambridge, MA: Harvard UP, 1998.

Jacobson, Steve. *The Best Team Money Could Buy: The Turmoil and Triumph of the 1977 New York Yankees*. New York: Atheneum, 1978.

James, Bill. Introduction. *The Year the Yankees Lost the Pennant*. 1954. New York: Norton, 2004.

"Joltin' Joe DiMaggio by Les Brown." *Baseball Almanac*. Web. Accessed Mar. 21, 2014.

Jones, Landon. *Great Expectations: America and the Baby Boom Generation*. New York: Coward McCann, 1980.

Juffer, Jane. "Why We Like to Lose: On Being a Cubs Fan in the Heterotopia of Wrigley Field." *South Atlantic Quarterly* 105.2 (2006): 289–301.

Kahn, Roger. *The Boys of Summer*. 1972. New York: Harper Perennial, 1998.

———. *The Era, 1947–1957: When the Yankees, the Giants, and the Dodgers Ruled the World*. New York: Ticknor & Fields, 1993.

Katz, Jeff. *The Kansas City A's and the Wrong Half of the Yankees: How the Yankees Controlled Two of the Eight American League Franchises During the 1950s*. Hanover, MA: Maple Street Press, 2007.

Kesey, Ken. *One Flew Over the Cuckoo's Nest*. 1962. New York: Signet, 1963.

Kimmel, Michael S. *Manhood in America: A Cultural History*. New York: Free Press, 1996.

———. "Masculinity as Homophobia: Fear, Shame, and Silence in the Construction of Gender Identity." *Race, Class and Gender in the United States*. Ed. Paula S. Rothenburg. New York: Worth, 2007.

Kinsella, W. P. *Shoeless Joe*. Boston: Houghton Mifflin, 1982.

Kirby, Dianne. "Harry Truman's Religious Legacy: The Holy Alliance, Containment, and the Cold War." *Religion and the Cold War*. Ed. Dianne Kirby. New York: Palgrave Macmillan, 2003. Cold War History Series.

Korr, Charles. *The End of Baseball as We Knew It: The Players Union, 1960–1981*. Champaign: U Illinois P, 2002.

Kovic, Ron. *Born on the Fourth of July*. New York: Akashic, 1976.

Laning, Edward. *Untitled.* Painting. *Life,* Sept. 29, 1941, 64.
Lavers, Norman. *Mark Harris.* Boston: Twayne, 1978.
Lasch, Christopher. *The Culture of Narcissism: American Life in the Age of Diminishing Expectations.* New York: Norton, 1979.
A League of Their Own. Dir. Penny Marshal. Perf. Gina Davis, Tom Hanks, Lori Petty, Madonna, Rosie O'Donnell. Columbia, 1992.
Leavy, Jane. *The Last Boy: Mickey Mantle and the End of America's Childhood.* 2010. New York: Harper Perennial, 2011.
Levine, Peter. *Ellis Island to Ebbets Field: Sport and the American Jewish Experience.* Oxford, U.K.: Oxford UP, 1992.
Lhamon, W. T., Jr. *Deliberate Speed: The Origins of a Cultural Style in the American 1950s.* Cambridge, MA: Harvard UP, 2002.
Lieberfeld, Daniel, and Judith Sanders. "Here Under False Pretenses: The Marx Brothers Crash the Gates." *American Scholar* 64.1 (1995): 103–8.
The Life and Times of Hank Greenberg. Dir. Aviva Kempner. 20th Century Fox, 1999.
Little Big League. Dir. Andrew Scheinman. Perf. Luke Evans, Timothy Busfield, Dennis Farina. Columbia, 1994.
Lyle, Sparky, and David Fisher. *The Year I Owned the Yankees: A Baseball Fantasy.* New York: Bantam, 1990.
Lyle, Sparky, and Peter Golenbock. *The Bronx Zoo.* New York: Crown, 1979.
Major League. Dir. David S. Ward. Perf. Tom Berenger, Charlie Sheen, Corbin Bernsen. Paramount, 1989.
Major League II. Dir. David S. Ward. Perf. Tom Berenger, Charlie Sheen, Corbin Bernsen. Paramount, 1994.
Madden, Bill. *Steinbrenner: The Last Lion of Baseball.* New York: Harper, 2010.
Mahler, Jonathan. *Ladies and Gentlemen, the Bronx is Burning: 1977, Baseball, Politics, and the Battle for the Soul of a City.* New York: Picador, 2005.
Malamud, Bernard. *The Natural.* 1952. Alexandria, VA: Time-Life, 1980.
Mann, Jack. *The Decline and Fall of the New York Yankees.* New York: Simon & Schuster, 1967.
Mathewson, Christy. *Pitching in a Pinch, or Baseball from the Inside.* 1912. Lincoln: U of Nebraska P, 1994.
Mattson, Kevin. *"What the Heck Are You Up to, Mr. President?" Jimmy Carter, America's "Malaise," and the Speech That Should Have Changed the Country.* New York: Bloomsbury, 2009.
McGimpsey, David. *Imagining Baseball: America's Pastime and Popular Culture.* Bloomington: Indiana UP, 2000.
McGowen, Roscoe. "Baseball Yes!, Yankees No!" *Street and Smith's 1961 Baseball Yearbook.* Ed. Sam E. Andre. New York: Street & Smith, 1961. 46–51.

McGraw, John J. *My Thirty Years in Baseball*. 1923. Introd. Charles C. Alexander. Lincoln: U of Nebraska P, 1995.

Mercer, Sid. "Whole City Busy with 'Dope.'" *New York Evening Journal*, Oct. 3, 1921.

Meyer, Christina. "Urban America in the Newspaper Comic Strips of the Nineteenth Century: Introducing the Yellow Kid." *ImageTexT: Interdisciplinary Comics Studies* 6.2 (2012): n.p. Dept. of English, University of Florida. Web. Accessed July 6, 2013.

The Mighty Ducks. Dir. Stephen Herek. Perf. Emilio Estevez, Joshua Jackson, Heidi Kling. Disney, 1992.

Miller, Arthur. *The Crucible*. New York: Penguin, 1953.

Mintz, Lawrence E. "Humor and Ethnic Stereotypes in Vaudeville and Burlesque." *Melus* 21.4 (1996): 19–28.

Moneyball. Dir. Bennett Miller. Perf. Brad Pitt, Jonah Hill, Philip Seymour Hoffman, Chris Pratt. Columbia, 2011.

Morris, Tim. "The Friendly Confines of Prose: Chicago Cubs in Fiction." *Northsiders: Essays on the History and Culture of the Chicago Cubs*. Ed. Gerald C. Wood and Andrew Hazucha. Jefferson, NC: McFarland, 2008.

Mr. 3000. Dir. Charles Stone III. Perf. Bernie Mac, Angela Bassett. Touchstone, 2004.

Mullin, Willard. Cover illustration. *1952 Dodgers Year Book*.

———. Cover illustration. *Manufacturers Trust Company 1951 Schedule*.

———. Cover illustration. *Manufacturers Trust Company 1953 Schedule*.

Murray, Jim. "I Hate the Yankees." *Life*, April 17, 1950, 25–36.

Nathan, Daniel A. *Saying It's So: A Cultural History of the Black Sox Scandal*. Urbana: U of Illinois P, 2003.

The Natural. Dir. Barry Levinson. Perf. Robert Redford, Glenn Close, Kim Basinger, Robert Duvall, Wilford Brimley. Tri-Star, 1984.

"New York Yankee Quotations." *Baseball Almanac*. Web. Accessed Sept. 21, 2013.

Oliphant, Thomas. *Praying for Gil Hodges: A Memoir of the 1955 World Series and One Family's Love of the Brooklyn Dodgers*. New York: Thomas Dunne, 2005.

Olney, Buster. *The Last Night of the Yankee Dynasty: The Game, the Team, and the Cost of Greatness*. New York: Ecco-HarperCollins, 2004.

O'Mealia, Leo. "Who's a Bum!" Illustration. *New York Daily News*, Oct. 5, 1955.

Parker, Dorothy. "The Artist's Reward." *New Yorker*, Nov. 30, 1929, 28–31.

Pease, Neal. "Diamonds Out of the Coal Mines: Slavic Americans in Baseball." *The American Game: Baseball and Ethnicity*. Ed. Lawrence Baldassaro and Richard A. Johnson. Carbondale: Southern Illinois UP, 2002.

Peirce, Charles Sanders. *Pragmatism as a Principle and Method of Right Thinking: The 1903 Harvard Lectures on Pragmatism*. Ed. Patricia Ann Turrisi. Albany: State U of New York P, 1997.

Prince, Carl E. *Brooklyn's Dodgers: The Bums, the Borough, and the Best of Baseball, 1948–1957*. Oxford: Oxford UP, 1996.

The Pride of the Yankees. Dir. Sam Wood. Perf. Gary Cooper, Teresa Wright, Babe Ruth. Samuel Goldwyn Productions/RKO, 1942.

Rader, Benjamin G. *American Ways: A History of American Cultures, 1865–Present.* Belmont, CA: Thomson Wadsworth, 2006.

———. *Baseball: A History of America's Game.* Champaign: U of Illinois P, 1992.

Riess, Steven A. *Sport in Industrial America, 1850–1920.* New York: Harlan Davidson, 1995.

———. "Stop Squawking: In Defense of the Yankees." *Collier's,* Mar. 4, 1939, 11+.

Rice, Grantland. Foreword. *Lucky to Be a Yankee.* New York: Bantam, 1949.

Ritter, Lawrence. *The Glory of Their Times: The Story of the Early Days of Baseball Told by the Men Who Played It.* 1966. New York: Harper Perennial, 2010.

Rockler, Michael. "Sam Spade, Existential Hero?" *Philosophy Now* 75 (Sept./Oct. 2009): n.p. Web. Accessed Feb. 13, 2014.

Roediger, David R. *Working toward Whiteness: How America's Immigrants Became White; The Strange Journey from Ellis Island to the Suburbs.* New York: Basic, 2005.

Rookie of the Year. Dir. Daniel Stern. Perf. Thomas Ian Nicholas, Gary Busey. 20th Century Fox, 1993.

Rosenweig, Daniel. *Retro Ball Parks: Instant History, Baseball, and the New American City.* Knoxville: U of Tennessee P, 2005.

The Sandlot. Dir. David M. Evans. Perf. Tom Guiry, Mike Vitar, James Earl Jones, Karen Allen. 20th Century Fox, 1993.

Santella, Andrew. "The Bad Boys of Summer." *New York Times Book Review,* Oct. 1, 2000.

Saussure, Ferdinand de. "From *Course in General Linguistics.*" Trans. Wade Baskins. *Critical Theory since 1965.* Ed. Hazard Adams and Leroy Searle. Tallahassee: Florida State UP, 1986.

Savran, David. *Taking It Like a Man: White Masculinity, Masochism, and Contemporary American Culture.* Princeton, NJ: Princeton UP, 1998.

Schumacher, Harry. "Commissioner Landis Warns Ball Players in Serious Talk in Boston." *New York Globe and Commercial Advertiser,* Jun. 27, 1922.

The Scout. Dir. Michael Ritchie. Perf. Albert Brooks, Brendan Fraser. 20th Century Fox, 1994.

Seinfeld. Created by Jerry Seinfeld and Larry David. Perf. Jerry Seinfeld, Julia Louis-Dreyfus, Jason Alexander, Michael Richards. NBC, 1989–98. Television.

Seymour, Harold, and Dorothy Z. Seymour. *Baseball.* Vol. 2, *The Golden Age.* New York: Oxford UP, 1971.

Shaughnessy, Dan. *The Curse of the Bambino.* 1990. New York: Penguin, 2004.

———. *Reversing the Curse.* Boston: Houghton Mifflin, 2005.

Shaw, Tony. "'Martyrs, Miracles and Martians': Religion and Cold War Cinematic Propaganda in the 1950s." *Religion and the Cold War.* Ed. Dianne Kirby. New York: Palgrave Macmillan, 2003. Cold War History Series.

Sheridan, John B. "Back of Home Plate." *Sporting News,* Apr. 15, 1920.
Shindo, Charles J. *1927 and the Rise of Modern America.* Lawrence, KS: U Kansas P, 2010.
Simon and Garfunkel. "America." *Bookends.* Columbia, 1968. LP.
———. "Bookends Theme." *Bookends.* Columbia, 1968. LP.
———. "Mrs. Robinson." *Bookends.* Columbia, 1968. LP.
———. "Overs." *Bookends.* Columbia, 1968. LP.
———. *Parsley, Sage, Rosemary and Thyme.* Columbia, 1966. LP.
———. "Richard Cory." *Sounds of Silence.* Columbia, 1966. LP.
"Simon and Garfunkel: Songs of America." Dir. Charles Grodin. Perf. Paul Simon, Art Garfunkel. CBS. Nov. 30, 1969. Television.
"Size of Stadium Impresses Crowd." *New York Times,* Apr. 19, 1923.
Smith, Leverett T., Jr. *The American Dream and the National Game.* Bowling Green, OH: Bowling Green U Popular P, 1975.
Snelling, Dennis. *The Greatest Minor League: A History of the Pacific Coast League, 1903–1957.* Jefferson, NC: McFarland, 2011.
Sobol, Ken. *Babe Ruth and the American Dream.* New York: Random House, 1974.
Soper, Kerry. "From Swarthy Ape to Sympathetic Everyman: The Development of Irish Caricature in American Comic Strips between 1890 and 1920." *Journal of American Studies* 39.2 (2005): 257–96.
Speedy. Dir. Ted Wilde. Perf. Harold Lloyd, Ann Christy, Bert Woodruff, Babe Ruth. Paramount, 1928.
Sports Illustrated. *Baseball's 20 Greatest Teams of All Time.* New York: Sports Illustrated, 1991.
Steinberg, Steve, and Lyle Spatz. *1921: The Yankees, the Giants, and the Battle for Baseball Supremacy in New York.* Lincoln: U of Nebraska P, 2010.
———. *The Colonel and Hug: The Partnership that Transformed the New York Yankees.* Lincoln: U of Nebraska P, 2015.
Stout, David. "Henry Alonzo Keller, 87, Artist of the Yankees' Top Hat Logo." Obituary. *New York Times,* June 28, 1995.
Stout, Glenn. *The Dodgers: 120 Years of Dodgers Baseball.* Boston: Houghton Mifflin, 2004.
The Stratton Story. Dir. Sam Wood. Perf. James Stewart, June Allyson. MGM, 1949.
Sullivan, Neil J. *The Dodgers Move West.* New York: Oxford UP, 1987.
Susman, Warren. *Culture as History: The Transformation of American Society in the Twentieth Century.* New York: Pantheon, 1984.
Swindell, Larry. *The Last Hero: A Biography of Gary Cooper.* Garden City, NY: Doubleday, 1980.
"Teresa Wright: Biography." *Internet Movie Database.* Web. Accessed Nov. 5, 2014.
"tizzo." "Best sports biopic . . . ever": User rev. of *The Pride of the Yankees. Internet Movie Database.* Mar. 29, 2006. Web. Accessed Nov. 5, 2014.

Torgoff, Martin. *Can't Find My Way Home: America in the Great Stoned Age, 1945–2000*. New York: Simon & Schuster, 2004.
Trouble with the Curve. Dir. Robert Lorenz. Perf. Clint Eastwood, Amy Adams, Justin Timberlake. Warner Bros., 2012.
Trumino, Joseph. "The Political and Cultural Contradictions of the 'Lefty' Yankee Fan." Presented at 42nd Annual Popular Culture Association National Conference, Boston. Apr. 11, 2012.
Twain, Mark. *The Adventures of Huckleberry Finn: A Case Study in Critical Controversies*. Ed. Gerald Graff and James Phelan. Boston: Bedford/St. Martin's, 1995.
Tygiel, Jules. *Baseball's Great Experiment: Jackie Robinson and His Legacy*. Oxford, UK: Oxford UP, 1983.
———. *Past Time: Baseball as History*. Oxford, UK: Oxford UP, 2000.
Vecsey, George. *Baseball: A History of America's Favorite Game*. New York: Modern Library, 2006.
———. "Fame to Reggie Jackson Just Means a Candy Bar." *New York Times*, July 6, 1969. Web. Accessed July 21, 2016.
Vidmer, Richards. "Gehrig's Three Hits Win for Yanks." *New York Times*, July 17, 1927.
Wake Island. Dir. John Farrow. Perf. Brian Donlevy, Macdonald Carey, Robert Preston, William Bendix. Paramount, 1942.
Wallop, Douglass. "How the Yankees Got That Way." *New York Times Magazine*, Sept. 30, 1956, 26+.
———. *The Year the Yankees Lost the Pennant*. New York: Norton, 1954.
Ward, Robert. "Reggie Jackson in No-Man's Land." *Sport*, June 1977. Web. Accessed July 12, 2016.
Weinreb, Michael. *Bigger than the Game: Bo, Boz, the Punky QB, and How the '80s Created the Modern Athlete*. New York: Gotham, 2010.
Weintraub, Robert. *The House That Ruth Built: A New Stadium, The First Yankee Championship, and the Redemption of 1923*. Boston: Little, Brown, 2011.
———. *The Victory Season: The End of World War II and the Birth of Baseball's Golden Age*. Boston: Little, Brown, 2014.
Will, George F. *Men at Work: The Craft of Baseball*. New York: Macmillan, 1990.
Williams, Raymond. *Keywords: A New Vocabulary of Culture and Society*. Oxford, UK: Oxford UP, 1985.
Wolfe, Tom. "The 'Me' Decade and the Third Great Awakening." *New York*, Aug. 23, 1976. Web. Accessed July 12, 2016.
"Yankee." *National Geographic Education*. National Geographic, n.d. Web. Accessed May 9, 2013.
"Yankee." *Oxford English Dictionary*. Oxford UP, 2013. Web. Accessed May 9, 2013.
"Yankees Win, 6–4; Judge Landis Tells Players What's What." *Boston Globe*, June 27, 1922.
Young, Dick. "Young Ideas." *Sporting News*, Oct. 25, 1975. Web. Accessed July 12, 2017.

INDEX

Aaron, Hank, 228, 255, 287–88n15
Abrams, Cal, 107, 280n2
absurdism, 205, 240–41, 251–53, 291n21; theorizing, 250
Adventures of Babe Ruth, The, 31
Adventures of Huckleberry Finn, The, 58, 151
Adventures of Ozzie and Harriet, The, 123
African Americans, 128–36, 165, 181. *See also* civil rights movement
Alexander, Jason, 244
Alger, Horatio, 124, 279n7
American dream, 25, 37, 48–56, 60, 80–81, 100, 102, 114, 122–28, 277n14; theorizing, 48–49; Yankees and, 5, 37, 50, 52–53, 56, 59, 69–70, 84, 97, 123–24, 133–36, 147, 264
Amoros, Sandy, 128
Anaheim Angels. *See* California Angels
Angels in the Outfield (1950), 276n3
Angels in the Outfield (1994), 276n3, 288n4, 288–89n5, 289n7
Arizona Diamondbacks, 261
Ashburn, Richie, 280n2
Atlanta Braves. *See* Boston Braves
Autobiography of Miss Jane Pittman, 131

Babe, The (film), 289n7; Yankees in 237
Babe Comes Home, 27, 31

Babe Ruth Story, The, 44
Baby Boomers, 7, 97, 175, 177, 180, 266–68, 285n11, 291n24; and baseball, 232, 165–67, 185–90, 232–34, 251–52, 261, 267; and Mantle, 185–89, 237; and Yankees, 266, 267
Bach, Richard. See *Johnathan Livingston Seagull*
Bad News Bears, The, 188, 242, 288n4, 289–90n10
Ball Four, 163, 286n3; controversy, 168, 181; and counterculture, 169, 171–80, 204–5; Mantle in, 181, 182–86, 285n9; Yankee response to, 182, 284–85n8; Yankees in, 168–80, 206
Baker, Frank "Home Run" 20, 275n8
Baltimore Orioles (nineteenth century), 15, 19, 29, 236
Baltimore Orioles (current), 181, 194, 228, 252
Bang the Drum Slowly, 283n20
Barrow, Ed, 12, 152, 199, 203, 277n13
Barthes, Roland, 5–6, 273n2. *See also* semiotics
Baseball (Ken Burns documentary series), 166, 167, 235, 278n6, 283–84n2
baseball: cheating, 823n18; decline in popularity, 166, 185–86, 191, 251–52, 267; fandom, 101–4; in film, 36–38, 234–35, 275n1, 288n3, 288n4, 288–89n5, 289n7; free agency, 196, 222, 260; and immigrants, 49–50, 52–53,

baseball (cont'd)
  114–15; integration of, 3, 128, 165; memorabilia, 234, 237, 288–89n5; and performance enhancing drugs, 262; and World War II 95, 149, 166. See also Baby Boomers; civil religion; nationalism; New York City; nostalgia
Basie, Count, 135
Basketball, 166, 195, 260, 271, 288n4
"Battle of the Sexes," 4
Bauer, Hank, 149–50, 283n19
Beatles, The, 166, 172
Benatar, Pat, 290n14
Bendix, William, 112
Bennett, Tony, 243
Berlin, Irving, 37
Berra, Yogi, 50, 133, 198, 223, 247, 287n10
Best Team Money Could Buy, The, 194–95, 199, 201, 205, 206, 213, 220, 229, 259, 286n2; Yankees in 224–26
bicentennial, American, 206, 227
Black, Joe, 128
Born on the Fourth of July, 164; Mantle in, 186–89; Yankees in, 186–89
Boston, 202
Boston Red Sox, 23, 129; and Babe Ruth, 14, 19, 203, 271; and early-twntieth-century success, 23, 27, 202–3; in film, 289n7, 291n20; as Yankee rivals, 3, 74, 76, 80, 199, 202–8, 212–13, 214, 21, 247, 269, 271, 276n4, 278n4
Boston/Milwaukee/Atlanta Braves, 240, 289n7
Bosworth, Brian, 260
Bouton, Jim, 163, 164, 168, 206, 284n3. See also *Ball Four*
Branca, Ralph, 108
Brennan, Walter, 45
Bringing Up Father, 51
Broadway, 16, 32, 137–38, 143, 281n6
Bronx Zoo, The, 194–95, 197, 207, 208, 210, 213–14, 216–18; Yankees in, 223–24, 226
Brooklyn: accent, 111, 112, 119; as butt of jokes, 110–11; as independent city, 16, 110; as populist icon, 111–13; status compared to Manhattan, 110

Brooklyn/Los Angeles Dodgers, 8, 16, 237, 239, 289n8; and the American dream, 102, 114, 122–28, 133–36; "Bums" nickname, 117; and failure, 105–8, 110, 113, 114, 119, 131, 204; in film, 111–12, 135, 289n7; and Giants, 108, 169, 286n3; move to California, 165, 180, 279n8, 284n7; as national symbol, 110, 112, 128; and racial integration, 3, 128, 165; as symbols of Brooklyn, 110–13; as underdogs, 105–10, 111, 124; and working-class identity, 8, 102, 104, 113–28; as Yankee rivals, 2–3, 8, 102, 105, 108–10, 111, 113, 115–17, 121–22, 145, 167, 200–201, 213–14, 224, 227, 254, 266, 269, 271, 287n13, 287n14; in *The Year the Yankees Lost the Pennant*, 145
Brooks, Albert, 242
Broun, Hayward, 16, 31, 32–33. See also *The Sun Field*
Brown v. Board of Education of Topeka, 130
Bull Durham, 234, 288–89n5
Burns, Ken, 166, 235. See also *Baseball*

California/Anaheim/Los Angeles Angels, 257, 276n3, 284n6, 289n7
Campanella, Roy, 107, 128
Campbell, Joseph, 71–72, 74, 76, 77–78, 86, 87, 88, 92, 93
Capra, Frank, 56, 58
Carnegie, Andrew, 49
Carter, Jimmy, 220, 227
Casey, Hugh, 106–7
Catch-22, 158–59, 162, 175, 177, 240, 284n5, 284–85n8
Catcher in the Rye, The, 158–59, 162
Cavett, Dick, 191
CBS (Columbia Broadcasting System), 164, 196
Celebrant, The, 274n4, 288–89n5
Chicago Cubs, 18, 23, 27, 29, 257, 261, 289n7
Chicago White Sox, 23, 212, 217, 235
civil religion: and baseball, 97–98; theorizing, 97; and Yankees, 97–100
civil rights movement, 128–32, 165, 167, 172–73, 175, 175, 181

Clay, Henry, 49, 60
Cleveland, Grover, 287n15
Cleveland Indians, 19, 38, 89, 195–96, 200, 202, 236, 238, 257, 261, 274n6, 281n3, 289–90n10
Clinton, Bill, 261
Cobb (film), 235
Cobb, Ty, 84, 282n14
Cold War, 6, 76, 83, 96–97, 99, 150, 155, 159–60, 162, 166, 175–76, 187, 265, 267, 284n4
Columbia University, 54
Combs, Earle, 15, 20
comics, 51, 135
conformism, 155–60, 162, 173; theorizing, 155–56; and Yankees, 158, 160, 175–76
Connecticut Yankee in King Arthur's Court, A, 38
consumption/consumerism, 25, 96–97
Cooper, Gary, 40, 42, 52, 56–57, 58, 64, 67, 68, 80, 85, 275n2, 276n7
Costas, Bob, 3, 243, 255, 278n6
counterculture, 163, 165–66, 168, 171–80, 186, 190, 204, 207, 218, 227, 232, 260, 265–67, 284n4, 284n5, 285n11
cowboys. *See* frontier, Western films
Crosetti, Frank, 248
Crucible, The, 158–59, 162
Crystal, Billy, 278n6

Damn Yankees, 32, 137, 142–44, 200, 205, 281n5, 281n6, 281n7, 281n8; See also *The Year the Yankees Lost the Pennant*
David, Larry, 245, 249
Dean, "Dizzy," 38
Dempsey, Jack, 75
Detroit Tigers, 32, 89, 129, 133, 201, 202, 289n7
Dickinson, Emily, 285n16
Dickey, Bill, 31, 42, 46, 198, 277n12
"Did You See Jackie Robinson Hit that Ball?," 135
DiMaggio, Joe, 198, 237, 287n10; and 1949 comeback, 68, 72, 74–78, 89, 91, 93, 95, 98; and American dream, 53, 69, 80–81, 97, 100, 124, 133; and Gehrig, 35–36, 43, 67, 68, 78–79, 83, 277n13, 278n1; and hitting streak, 68, 69, 70, 72–74, 89, 277n13, 279n8; as Italian-American, 53, 69, 133; and Mantle, 152, 183, 184, 191, 285n10; and masculinity, 5, 93–95, 256; in "Mrs. Robinson," 189, 285n12, 285n13, as mythic hero, 8, 68–69, 70–79, 84–85, 87, 88–93, 97–100, 221, 278n5; and nationalism, 68, 80–81, 96–100, 190; and populism/work ethic, 5, 47, 68, 69–70, 73, 77–81, 85, 97, 100; and *Pride of the Yankees*, 68, 69, 277n13; and Ruth, 67, 75, 78–79, 85; in *Seinfeld*, 251; and sportswriters, 68, 100, 221, 278n2, 280n13; as working-class, 69, 78, 89, 95
Disney, 275n1, 288n6
Dostoyevsky, Fyodor, 174
Doyle, Larry, 33
Dugan, Joe, 31, 203, 277n11
Durocher, Leo, 105, 108
Dylan, Bob, 189–90

Early, Gerald, 167, 251
Ebbets Field, 117–18, 119, 126, 289n9
Ederle, Gertrude, 28
ego, 208–9, 216–17, 260 220, 221–22, 228–29, 240, 260, 242, 244, 248; and Yankees, 214–26, 229. *See also* "Me" Decade
Eight Men Out, 235
elitism, Yankees and, 8, 55–56, 58–59, 84, 102–4, 111, 113, 115–17, 120–22, 131, 132, 136, 149, 165, 178–79, 195, 202
Emerson, Ralph Waldo, 108
Erskine, Carl, 107, 109, 113
ethnicity, 14, 15, 23, 49–52, 53, 69, 114, 125–26, 207, 209; theorizing, 133–34; and Yankees, 133
existentialism, 160, 162; theorizing, 159

Fan, The, 235, 288–89n5
fandom, 101–4, 106, 226–8, 235, 241; theorizing, 104
fantasy camps, 234, 237, 250, 258, 288–89n5
Farley, James A., 80–81, 82, 96
Father Knows Best, 123

INDEX

Fear Strikes Out, 291n20
Fenway Park, 74, 207, 269
Fidrych, Mark, 201
Field of Dreams, 234–35, 288–89n5, 291n24; Yankees in, 266–68
Finley, Charlie, 197
Fisk, Carlton, 204
football, 166, 195, 260, 271, 283–84n2, 286n1, 286n5, 288n4, 289n9
For the Love of the Game, 289n7, 289n10
Ford, Gerald, 227
Ford, Whitey, 198, 247, 249, 287n10
Frank Merriwell books, 279n7
Franklin, Benjamin, 49
Fraser, Brendan, 242
Frazee, Harry, 203
frontier, 60–61, 156
Frost, Robert, 159, 167, 285n16
frugality, Yankees and, 152, 179, 198–99, 283n17
Furillo, Carl, 107

Gaines, Ernest. See *The Autobiography of Miss Jane Pittman*
Gallico, Paul, 36
Gallo, Bill 194, 208–10, **209**, **215**, 214–16, 224, 285n12, 286n6
Garfunkel, Art. *See* Simon and Garfunkel
Gehrig, Eleanor, 37, 40, 45, 52, 55, 60, 63, 65
Gehrig, Lou, 198; and American dream, 37, 48–56, 97, 124, 133, 277n14; consecutive game streak, 47, 57, 60, 69, 83, 256, 261; death, 12, 36, 65, 67, 68, 278n1; and DiMaggio, 35–36, 67, 83, 278n1; as German-American, 50–53, 133; and heroism, 45, 48, 55, 57, 66, 218; and home runs/power hitting, 15, 18, 20; "luckiest man" speech, 41, 65, 221, 276n5; and masculinity, 5, 40, 48, 59–66, 256; and populism/work ethic, 8, 37, 43, 44, 47–48, 55, 56, 78, 84; relationship with mother, 58, 62–63; and Ruth, 12, 18, 20, 27, 31, 35, 40–41, 43, 62, 218, 277n15, 278n1; as working class, 50, 54

German Americans, 14, 23, 50–52, 133, 207, 209
Giamatti, Bart, 234, 235, 288–89n5
Gilliam, Jim, 128, 225–26, 287n13
Goldwyn, Sam, 36–37, 68, 275n1
Golenbock, Peter, 109, 113, 116–17, 125, 131, 164, 181, 185, 211, 213–14, 280n1, 280n2, 285n8, 285n9
Gomez, Lefty, 198
Goodwin, Doris Kearns, 103, 106–7, 111, 115–17, 125–27, 167, 251
Gordon, Joe, 198
Gossage, "Goose," 197, 213, 217, 287n11
Gould, Stephen Jay, 70
Graduate, The, 190, 284n5, 285n15
Graham, Billy, 176
Grant, Cary, 63
Great Depression, 5, 7, 47–48, 81, 82, 96, 97, 119, 123, 134, 148, 165, 259, 267
Greek Americans, 114
Greenberg, Hank, 50, 133
Greenwade, Tom, 129
Guidry, Ron, 198

Hall, Donald, 234, 235, 288–89n5
Harris, Mark, 137, 151, 156, 159–60, 177, 283n20. See also *Bang the Drum Slowly* and *The Southpaw*
Harry Potter books, 71
Headin' Home, 27, 31, 38
Heller, Joseph. See *Catch-22*
Hemingway, Ernest, 86, 88–89, 93, 280n12, 280n2; the "code hero," 86–87, 91, 92, 95. See also *The Old Man and the Sea*
Henrich, Tommy, 106, 133
Hepburn, Katharine, 63
Hernandez, Keith, 243, 250, 251
heroism, 45, 48, 55, 57, 66, 153–55, 186; mythic, 8, 14, 18, 34, 44, 68–69, 70–79, 84–93, 97–100, 218, 221, 276n8, 277n11, 278n5; and Yankees, 5, 79, 102, 123–24, 134, 154, 182–85, 196, 221–29, 242, 257, 265, 271, 290n15. *See also* Campbell, Joseph

INDEX   309

Herzog, Whitey, 201
High Noon, 56
hockey, 288n4
Hodges, Gil, 107
Hogan's Heroes, 209
home runs/power hitting, 14, 15, 18, 19–22, 28, 47, 69, 70, 102, 167, 184, 228, 254, 274–75n7; and the 1920s, 20; and Yankees, 13, 14, 15, 18, 19–22
Houk, Ralph, 169, 285n12
Houston Astros/Colt .45s, 284n7
Hovley, Steve, 172, 174, 175
Howard, Elston, 129, 165, 173, 181
Hoyt, Waite, 26, 31, 203
Hubbell, Carl, 18, 282n14
Huggins, Miller, 12, 31–32, 41, 79, 154, 278–9n6
Hughes, Thomas. See *Tom Brown's School Days*
Hunter, Jim "Catfish," 197, 286n7
Huston, Tillinghast L'Hommedieu, 274n1

"I Love Mickey," 184
icons, 6, 273n2. *See also* semiotics
immigration, 14, 15, 16, 23, 49–54, 69–70, 80–81, 84, 114–15, 125–26, 133, 207, 209
"inside game"/"small ball," 19, 21–22
Irish Americans, 15, 50–51, 114, 125–26
Irvin, Monte, 129
Italian Americans, 49–51, 53, 69, 114, 125, 133
It's a Wonderful Life, 56

Jackie Robinson Story, The, 135–36
Jackson, Andrew, 49, 56
Jackson, Reggie, 197–98, 199, 286n2; ego, 216–17, 220, 221–22, 228–29, 260; and Yankee hero tradition, 221–22, 225, 227–29, 247, 287n14; and Yankee infighting, 210–12, 214, 223–24, 259, 287n10
Jackson, "Shoeless" Joe, 218, 282n14
Jacobson, Steve, 194–95, 213. See also *The Best Team Money Could Buy*
James, Bill, 142, 145, 147
Jefferson, Thomas, 56

Jeter, Derek, 265–66, 271, 290–91n18, 291n22
Jewish Americans, 49–50, 114, 125
John, Tommy, 213, 240, 287n9, 288n1
Johnson, Lyndon, 168
Johnson, Walter, 282n14
"Joltin' Joe DiMaggio" (song), 67, 73, 135, 184
Jonathan Livingston Seagull, 220
Jung, Carl, 71

Kafka, Franz, 177–78, 244
Kahn, Roger, 119, 129, 131, 152, 153, 280n3
Kansas City Athletics. *See* Philadelphia Athletics
Kansas City Royals, 200, 201, 205–6, 213, 262, 286n4
Katzenjammer Kids, 51
Kaye, Danny, 111
Keeler, "Wee" Willie, 19
Kelly, Mike "King," 50
Kesey, Ken, 284n5. *See also One Flew Over the Cuckoo's Nest*
King, Billie Jean. *See* "Battle of the Sexes"
Kinsella, W.P. *See Shoeless Joe*
Koenig, Mark, 31, 42, 46, 276n6
Kovic, Ron, 164, 186. See also *Born on the Fourth of July*
Kuhn, Bowie, 182

Lacy, Sam, 132
Landis, Kennesaw Mountain, 24, 31
Laning, Edward, 73
Lasch, Christopher, 220
Lazzeri, Tony, 15, 20, 31, 42, 50, 133, 198, 276n6
Leave It to Beaver, 123
Lee, Bill, 204–9, 224
Lemon, Bob, 212, 286n8, 287n9, 288n2
Lieb, Fred, 16, 20, 22, 275n11
Life (magazine), 53, 73, 75, 97, 101, 135, 148, 149, 162, 278n3
Lincoln, Abraham, 3, 49, 71
Lindberg, Charles, 28, 38
Little Big League, 288n4, 288–9n5, 289n7
Little Orphan Annie, 31

Lloyd, Harold 31, 32
Lonborg, Jim, 203
Lopez, Hector, 248, 282n10
Los Angeles Angels. *See* California Angels
Los Angeles Dodgers. *See* Brooklyn Dodgers
Louis-Dreyfus, Julia, 244
Lucky to Be a Yankee, 68, 221, 225, 228; and mythic heroism, 84–85; and populism, 79–81, 85, 228; in *The Southpaw,* 153–54; Yankees in, 81–84, 273
Lyle, Sparky, 194, 197, 211, 213, 216–18, 221, 226, 239–40, 287n11, 291n19. *See also The Bronx Zoo* and *The Year I Owned the Yankees*

Mack, Connie, 18
MacPhail, Larry, 105
Maglie, Sal, 169
Major League, 38, 235, 236, 289–90n10
Major League II, 289n7
Malamud, Bernard. *See The Natural*
Mantle, Mickey, 198, 237; and Baby Boomers, 185–89, 237; in *Born on the Fourth of July,* 186–89; and DiMaggio, 152, 183, 184, 191, 285n10; and home runs/power hitting, 102, 167, 184; as national symbol, 5, 132, 185, 189; and off-field scandal, 182, 183, 184; and Ruth, 102, 167, 183, 184; in *Seinfeld,* 250–51; shift in public image, 182–83, 189; as working class, 102, 183; and Yankee hero tradition, 43, 102, 132, 154, 158, 182, 191, 247, 285n10, 287n10
Maris, Roger, 167, 184, 247, 254, 262, 282n10
Marshall, Mike, 174
Martin, Billy, 184, 206–7, 210–18, **215**, 221, 223, 225, 241, 259, 281n9, 286n8, 287n10, 288n2
Marx Brothers, 51
Mary Hartman, Mary Hartman, 212
masculinity, 40, 48, 59–66, 93–95, 256; theorizing, 59–60, 61, 93, 94; and Yankees, 5, 59, 61–62, 97, 120, 150, 187, 191, 256–57, 263
Mathewson, Christy, 80, 105, 275n8
Mattingly, Don, 240, 258

Mays, Carl, 31, 203
Mays, Willie, 129
McCarthy, Joe, 40–41, 47, 82, 198
McCarthyism. *See* Cold War
McCarver, Tim, 3, 243, 255
McGraw, John, 14, 17–19, 21–22, 50, 105, 282n14
McGwire, Mark, 262
McMahon, Jim, 260
"Me" Decade, 194, 218–20, 256, 260
Meany, Tom, 79, 81, 85. *See also Lucky to Be a Yankee*
Meet John Doe, 56
Meet Me in St. Louis, 38
Meusel, Bob, 20–21, 42, 46
Midnight Cowboy, 172
Mighty Ducks, The, 288n4
military, Yankees and, 66, 95, 99–100, 149–50, 160, 186–88, 206–10, 224, 286n5
Miller, Arthur. See *The Crucible*
Miller, Marvin, 178, 197
Milwaukee Braves. *See* Boston Braves
Milwaukee Brewers, 289n7
Minnesota Twins, 280n1, 289n7
Monroe, Marylin, 96, 251
Montgomery bus boycott, 130
Monument Park, 79, 154, 196, 237, 239, 278–79n6
Moses, Robert, 284n7
Mr. 3000, 289n7
Mr. Deeds Goes to Town, 56
Mr. Smith Goes to Washington, 56
"Mrs. Robinson," 8, 164, 285n12–13, 285n15; Yankees in, 189–91
Mullin, Willard, 117–23, **118**, **121**, **122**, 208
multiculturalism, 263–64
Munson, Thurman, 198, 204, 210–12, 221–23, 259, 286n7, 287n12
"Murderer's Row," 15, 20–21, 28–29, 41
Musial, Stan, 50, 285n10

Namath, Joe, 260
national symbol, Yankees as, 3–7, 24–25, 33–34, 43, 66, 69, 76, 81–84, 97–100, 101, 110, 122,

128, 138, 151, 155, 162, 168, 179–80, 187, 189–91, 207–8, 227–29, 239, 259, 263–64, 267–68, 271
nationalism, baseball and, 4, 49, 52–53, 95, 97, 114–15, 166, 234, 237, 259, 260–61
Natural, The, 234, 288–89n5
Negro League Baseball, 107, 167
Nettles, Graig, 206
"New Yankee Stadium." *See* Yankee Stadium (2009)
New York City: antagonism towards, 274n5, 23; and baseball, 15–19; and Yankees, 16–17, 199
New York Mets 180–81, 250–51, 284n7
New York Yankees: and 1920s, 25–30, 33–34, 47; 1960s decline, 163–65, 283n1; 1970s infighting, 201, 208–9, 210–14, 222–26, 229, 259; 1980s and early '90s mediocrity, 231–32, 237–38, 246, 253; 1990s resurgence, 233, 262, 291n21; in books, film, music, and TV, *see individual titles*; logo, 5, 27, 99–100; and Manhattan, 111, 132; name, 38–39; as "the new," 13–30, 33; and New York City, 16–17, 199; and off-field scandal, 14, 23, 26, 45, 152, 182, 183, 184, 276–6n9; and other franchises, *see individual cities*; pre-Ruth history, 13–14; as symbol of the past, 164, 170, 175, 180, 189–91, 227–29, 232–33, 253, 257, 259, 267–68. *See also* American dream; Baby Boomers; civil religion; conformism; elitism; ethnicity; fandom; frugality; heroism; home runs/power hitting; masculinity; military; national symbol; nostalgia; populism; power structure/tyrants; race; success; wealth
New York/San Francisco Giants, 23, 27, 105, 289n7, as Dodger rivals, 108, 169, 286n3; and "inside game"/"small ball," 14, 21; and integration, 129; move to California, 180, 279n8, 284n7; and New York City, 15–16, 21; as Yankee rivals, 12–13, 14–15, 16–17, 18–19, 21, 29–30, 33, 105
Newcombe, Don, 107, 108, 128
Nichols, Mike, 284n5, 285n15. See also *The Graduate*

Nixon, Richard, 83, 205, 287n10, 290n12
nostalgia: and baseball, 9, 232–39, 251–52, 259, 260–62, 265–66; and Yankees, 196–7, 223–29, 237–39, 253, 264–68

Oakland Athletics. *See* Philadelphia Athletics
Old Man and the Sea, 8, 32, 68, 279n10, 280n12, 280n2; and masculinity, 93–95; and mythic heroism, 85–93; Yankees in, 89
Oliphant, Thomas, 106, 109, 110, 112, 115–17, 127–28, 130, 131, 280n3
O'Malley, Walter, 284n7
O'Melia, Leo, 119, 208
One Flew Over the Cuckoo's Nest, 175, 284n5
O'Neill, Paul, 290–91n18
Ott, Mel, 18
Owen, Mickey, 106–7

Pacific Coast League, 84, 279n8
Patten, Gilbert. *See* Frank Merriwell books
Paul, Gabe, 198
Pennock, Herb, 31, 203
Pepitone, Joe, 185, 248
performance enhancing drugs, 262
Philadelphia Phillies, 107, 108, 129, 280n2
Philadelphia/Kansas City/Oakland Athletics (A's), 18, 23, 27, 29, 145, 184, 197, 228–29, 281–82n10, 286n4, 289n7, 289n8
Pierce, Charles Sanders, 273n3
Piersall, Jimmy, 291n20
Piniella, Lou, 288n2
pinstripes, 2, 5, 27, 99, 115, 224–25, 237, 247–48
Pittsburgh Pirates, 18, 217, 60
Polo Grounds, 14, 15, 23, 29–30, 108, 275n10
populism, 5, 8, 37, 43, 44, 47–48, 55, 56, 68, 69–70, 73, 78–81, 84–85, 100, 228; theorizing, 56; and Yankees, 58–59, 97, 191
power structure/tyrants, Yankees as, 8, 102, 104, 109, 110, 111, 116–17, 131, 132, 136, 138–42, 148–49, 163, 168, 170, 177, 179, 181–82, 195–201, 205–8, 224, 262, 280n3, 286n2
Pride of St. Louis, 38

Pride of the Yankees, The, 8, 12, 32, 92, 218; and the American dream, 48–56, 84; and DiMaggio, 68, 69, 277n13; and female audiences, 37, 64, 275n1; and masculinity, 40, 59–66; and nationalism, 39, 66, 148, 160, 271; as new precedent in baseball film, 36–37, 135, 275n2, 38; Ruth in, 42, 43–48; title 37–40; Yankees in, 37–43, 46–48

race, 3, 167, 172–73, 175, 175, 181; theorizing, 133–34; and Yankees, 102, 128–36, 145, 165, 168, 176–77, 264–65, 282n12, 282n15

Reagan, Ronald, 176, 265

Reese, "Pee Wee," 107

"retro" ballparks, 236, 261, 289n9

Rice, Grantland, 16, 22, 33, 84

Richards, Michael, 244

Rickey, Branch, 128–30

Riggs, Bobby. *See* "Battle of the Sexes"

Ripken, Cal, 261

Ritchie, Michael. *See The Bad News Bears* and *The Scout*

Rivera, Mariano, 271

Rizzuto, Phil, 50, 133, 198, 248

Robinson, E. A., 285n16

Robinson, Jackie, 4, 107, 124, 128, 130–32, 134; as hero figure, 135–36; in popular culture, 135

Rockwell, Norman, 73

Roe, Preacher, 107

Rogers, Will, 56, 58

romantic comedy films, 63, 64, 65

Rookie of the Year, 288n4, 288–89n5, 289n7

Runyon, Damon, 16

Ruppert, Jacob 12, 14, 16–17, 22–24, 35, 56, 83–84, 105, 148–49, 152, 198, 274n1

Ruth, Babe: and the 1920s, 5, 8, 25; and American dream, 25, 133; and children, 276–77n9; death, 34; and DiMaggio, 67, 75, 78–79, 85; as foundation of Yankee legacy, 34, 237; and Gehrig, 12, 18, 20, 27, 31, 35, 40–41, 43, 62, 218, 277n15, 278n1; and home runs/power hitting, 14, 18, 19–22, 28, 47, 69, 70, 228, 254; and Mantle, 102, 167, 183, 184; and media/advertising, 26–27, 31, 42, 44, 78, 228–29, 287n15, 275n9; as mythic hero, 14, 18, 34, 44, 78, 218, 276n8, 277n11; and off-field scandal, 14, 23, 26, 45, 152, 276–6n9; as overshadowing Yankees, 8, 11, 27, 30–34; in *The Pride of the Yankees*, 42, 43–48; and Red Sox, 14, 19, 203, 271; in *The Southpaw*, 152–54, 282n14; and sportswriters, 14, 44, 152; as working-class, 23, 53, 78

Saberhagen, Bret, 243

Salinger, J.D. *See The Catcher in the Rye*

San Francisco Giants. *See* New York Giants

Sandlot, The, 288n4, 288–89n5, 289n7

Sands of Iwo Jima, The, 187

Saussure, Ferdinand de, 5

Scandinavian Americans, 114

Scout, The, 232, 237, 239, 289n7; masculinity in, 256–57, 266; Steinbrenner in, 243–44, 246–47; Yankees in, 248–49, 255–57, 259, 263

Seattle Mariners, 3

Seattle Pilots, 168, 170, 175, 178, 179, 284n6

Selkirk, George, 278n1

Seinfeld, 232, 239; DiMaggio in, 251; Mantle in, 250–51; Steinbrenner in, 244–47, 252–53, 258, 290n13; Yankees in, 249–53, 257–59, 264, 290n17, 291n21

Seinfeld, Jerry, 244

semiotics, 37–38, 52, 82, 100, 112, 142, 225, 273n3; theorizing, 5–6

Shadow, The, 31

Shoeless Joe, 234, 288–89n5. *See also Field of Dreams*

Shor, Toots, 152

Shotton, Burt, 280n2

Showalter, Buck, 290–91n18

Simon, Paul. *See* Simon and Garfunkel

Simon and Garfunkel, 190–91, 285n13–14, 285n16. *See also* "Mrs. Robinson"

Sisler, Dick, 107, 280n2
Skowron, Moose, 248, 283n19
Slavic Americans, 49–50, 114
"small ball." *See* "inside game"
Smith, Ozzie, 243
Smith, Wendell, 132
Snider, Duke, 107, 253, 280n3
soccer, 288n4, 291n1
Sosa, Sammy, 261
Southpaw, The, 137, 283n20; and conformism, 155–60; and existentialism, 159–60; and heroes, 153–5, 186; *Lucky to Be a Yankee* in, 153–54; Ruth in, 152–54, 282n14; and success, 160–62; Yankees in, 151–55, 158, 160
Soviet Union. *See* Cold War
Speaker, Tris, 85
Speedy, 31, 32
St. Louis Cardinals, 18, 38, 107, 108, 149, 165, 204, 237, 239, 262
Standish, Burt L. *See* Frank Merriwell books
Star Wars, 71–72, 271, 291n23
Steinbrenner, George, **209**, **215**, 217, 286n1, 286n5, 286n6; and ego, 208–9, 214–16, 218, 221, 242, 244, 248; and free spending/wealth, 194–202, 205–6, 208, 210, 229, 231, 238–39, 243, 286n7, 287n11; questionable ownership decisions, 197–98, 232, 238–39, 241–45, 252, 262–63, 287n11, 288n2; in *The Scout*, 243–44, 246–47; in *Seinfeld*, 244–47, 252–53, 258, 290n13; as showman, 197, 231–32, 238–39, 241, 243, 287n10, 287n11; and Yankee infighting, 210–14, 287n10; and Yankee tradition, 196–97, 209, 210, 223, 229, 246, 248; in *The Year I Owned the Yankees*, 240–42, 246–47, 248
Stengel, Casey, 107, 116, 153, 158, 183, 223, 225–26, 248, 281n3, 282–83n16, 283n19
steroids. *See* performance enhancing drugs
Stewart, James, 45, 277n10
Stock, Milt, 280n2
Stratton Story, The, 45, 277n10, 277n12

success, Yankees and, 5, 40–42, 62, 82–84, 96–100, 110, 120, 122–23, 142, 147, 149–50, 160–62, 168, 187, 191, 206, 208
Sun Field, The, 31, 32–33

Tammany Hall, 16
Tampa Bay Rays/Devil Rays, 261
Tartabull, Danny, 290–91n18
Taylor, Lawrence, 260
Terry, Bill 18, 286n3
Thomas, Dylan, 285n16
Thompson, Hank, 129
Thomson, Bobby, 108
Time (magazine), 135, 211, 213
Tom Brown's School Days, 279n7
Topping, Dan, 116, 164, 179, 281–82n10
Torre, Joe, 263–65, 268
Tracy, Spencer, 63, 279n10
Turner, Ted, 240
Twain, Mark. See *The Adventures of Huckleberry Finn* and *A Connecticut Yankee in King Arthur's Court*

Universal Baseball Association, J. Henry Waugh, Prop., The, 289n6

vaudeville, 51–52
Verdon, Gwen, 143–44, 281n6, 281n8
Vietnam War, 117, 164–66, 171–75, 186, 188–89, 227, 233

Wagner, Honus, 50
Wake Island, 112
Wallop, Douglass, 137, 141–42, 150. See also *The Year the Yankees Lost the Pennant*
Walston, Ray, 143, 281n6
Washington, George, 71
Washington Senators, 18, 138–42, 145, 169, 170, 280n1
Watergate, 189, 227
Wayne, John, 120, 187

wealth, Yankees and, 14, 16, 22–25, 33, 55–56, 59, 83–84, 98, 115–17, 148–49, 152, 165, 179, 194–201, 203, 205–6, 208, 224, 229, 262, 280n3
Webb, Del, 116, 164, 281–82n10
Weiss, George, 129, 152, 165, 199, 285n10
Western films, 40, 56, 58, 71, 90
White, E. B., 39
White, Ron, 198
Will, George F., 234
William, Bernie, 290–91n18
Williams, Ted, 71, 203
Wolfe, Tom, 218–20, 221
Wood, Sam, 37, 42, 45, 50, 55, 62, 68
World War I, 20, 24, 33, 82, 291n24
World War II, 5, 7, 33, 47–48, 53, 65–67, 72, 76, 79, 81, 82, 94–96, 99, 101, 107, 111–12, 123, 125, 133–34, 149–50, 165, 168, 187, 240, 259, 267, 291n24
Wright, Teresa, 37, 42, 275n2, 276n7

Yankee Stadium, 3, 5, 15, 22, 24, 29, 32, 42, 62, 73, 79, 105, 116, 152, 196, 215, 225, 239, 241, 244, 249, 275n10–11, 278–89n6, 290n16
Yankee Stadium (2009), 278–89n6
Yastrzemski, Carl, 203
Yawkey, Tom, 199
Year I Owned the Yankees, The, 232, 239; Steinbrenner in, 240–42, 246–47, 248; Yankees in, 247–48, 253–54, 259, 262, 290n15
Year the Yankees Lost the Pennant, The, 137, 205, 289n6; Dodgers in, 145; and suffering, 145–47; title, 142, 144, 281n4; and wish fulfilment, 138–39, 141, 146–47; Yankees in, 139–42, 170, 271. See also *Damn Yankees*
Yeats, W. B., 226
Yellow Kid, The, 51